HURON COUNTY LIBRARY

W9-COJ-178

HURON COUNTY LIBRARY

3 6492 0037 0203

CONSTITUTION, Due

GOVERNMENT,
AND SOCIETY
IN CANADA

' 02233

971
Cai

Cairns, Alan C.
    Constitution, government, and society in Canada :
selected essays / by Alan C. Cairns ; edited by Douglas E.
Williams. -- Toronto : McClelland and Stewart, c1988.
    304 p.

    Bibliography: p. 302-304.
    03314529   ISBN:0771018304 (pbk.) :

    1. Canada - Politics and government. 2. Canada -
Constitutional history. 3. Canada - Constitutional law. I.
Williams, Douglas E., 1949- II. Title

7007   88JUN03   06/wi   1-00433427

WINGHAM BRANCH LIBRARY

HURON COUNTY LIBRARY

CONSTITUTION, GOVERNMENT, AND SOCIETY IN CANADA

SELECTED ESSAYS BY
ALAN C. CAIRNS

edited by Douglas E. Williams

02233

JUL 4 1988

WINGHAM BRANCH LIBRARY

M&S

Copyright © 1988 by Alan C. Cairns and Douglas E. Williams

All rights reserved. The use of any part of this publication reproduced,
transmitted in any form or by any means, electronic, mechanical,
photocopying, recording, or otherwise, or stored in a retrieval system,
without the prior consent of the publisher is an infringement of the
copyright law.

CANADIAN CATALOGUING IN PUBLICATION DATA
Cairns, Alan C.
    Constitution, government, and society

Includes bibliographical references.
ISBN 0-7710-1830-4

1. Canada – Politics and government.   2. Canada – Constitutional
history.   3. Canada – Constitutional law.   I. Williams, Douglas E.,
1949–   . II. Title.

JL31.C35 1988   971   C88-093242-2

Printed and bound in Canada

McClelland and Stewart
The Canadian Publishers
481 University Avenue
Toronto, Ontario

WINGHAM BRANCH LIBRARY

Contents

Editor's Preface / 7

Author's Introduction / 11

Part I: The Constitutional Framework / 25
Chapter 1: The Living Canadian Constitution / 27
Chapter 2: The Judicial Committee and Its Critics / 43

Part II: Electoral Politics / 86
Chapter 3: The Constitutional, Legal, and Historical
Background to the Elections of 1979 and 1980 / 88
Chapter 4: The Electoral System and the Party System in
Canada, 1921-1965 / 111

Part III: The Federal System and the Intergovernmental
Dimension / 139
Chapter 5: The Governments and Societies of Canadian
Federalism / 141
Chapter 6: The Other Crisis of Canadian Federalism / 171

Part IV: Constitutional and Political Change / 192
Chapter 7: The Politics of Constitutional Conservatism / 195
Chapter 8: The Canadian Constitutional Experiment / 229

Acknowledgements / 257

Notes / 258

Selected Bibliography / 302

Editor's Preface

It is an honour to have been asked to edit this volume of the essays of Alan Cairns, one of the most respected Canadian political scientists of his generation. His work has received wide acclaim and has stimulated frequent controversies.

For a number of reasons explored in the author's introduction, written especially for this volume, the essays gathered here are the product of an admittedly "old-fashioned" concept of the discipline. As such, they embody a range of concerns and an intellectual approach that have become increasingly rare as political science has embraced ever more technically sophisticated, frequently quantitative methodologies. The essays that follow thus bear a stronger resemblance to the work of Bagehot, Bryce, Siegfried, Brady, and Corry than they do to that of Easton, Riker, Deutsch, and Eulau.[1]

Throughout the 1950s and 1960s the major trends of analysis in North American political science and sociology tended to view institutional forms and governmental processes as a function of and response to various social and ideological forces. The outlook that prevailed during that time has aptly been characterized by Theda Skocpol in the following terms:

'government' was viewed primarily as an arena within which economic interest groups or normative social movements contended or allied with one another to shape the making of public policy decisions. Those decisions were understood to be *allocations* of benefits among demanding groups. Research centered on the societal 'inputs' to government and on the distributive effects of governmental 'outputs'. Government itself was not taken very

7

seriously as an independent actor, and in comparative research, variations in governmental organizations were deemed less significant than the general 'functions' shared by the political systems of all societies.[2]

In contrast, "old-fashioned" political science insists on the tremendous influence – or "shaping power" as Alan Cairns calls it in his introduction – of institutions, the law, and government in the management and direction of the now unprecedented forces of social, political, and economic change that characterize our times. As he observed in the introductory remarks to his Presidential Address to the Canadian Political Science Association in 1977,

> The impact of society on government is a common theme in the study of democratic polities. Less common is an approach which stresses the impact of government on the political functioning of society. . . . Although I do not doubt that government rides such a tiger of social change that the sweet smile of victory is often on the face of the tiger . . . I am convinced that our approach to the study of Canadian politics pays inadequate attention to the weight of the rider, and to his possession of reins to steer, whips to beat, and various inducements to make the tiger responsive to his demands.[3]

The fact that scholars have very recently acknowledged the need to "bring the state back in" to their analyses after several decades of neglect certainly goes a long way toward disabusing us of the belief that "old-fashioned" habits of thought can be abandoned without significant loss of orientation and self-understanding.

Though "old-fashioned" in comparison with more recent styles of political science, it would be wrong to confuse the type of analysis these essays embody with the sort of occasionally arid, formal-legalistic institutionalism that preceded the triumph of more emphatically "scientific" methodologies in the field. One of their most distinctive characteristics is an abiding concern with "the dialectic between states and peoples," a concern alien to those who approached the study of government as a technical clarification of the division of powers and the strict letter of the law. The principled combination of historical perspective, sociological sensitivity, and institutional analysis that characterizes these essays also explains the unmistakable civics approach they adopt. In the spirit of Tocqueville and contemporary political philosophers like Michael

Oakeshott and the late Hannah Arendt, among others, Cairns has expressed serious misgivings about the "mixture of clinical detachment, sporadic antipathy, and infrequent appreciation" that has come to characterize a good deal of post-war political analysis.[4] More specifically, in discussing a recent Canadian government text, he argued that,

> the replacement of the language of parliamentary government with the language of systems analysis has the effect of distancing [the authors] and their readers from the political system. There is none of the civics approach of sympathetically leading readers to an intimate and positive acquaintance with the political achievements of their forefathers.[5]

Readers will also discern, however, that the concern with civic education and the cultivation of a sense of "constitutional morality" in Cairns's work frequently involve a critical no less than an appreciative attitude toward the political leadership and institutions of our time. Several of the essays thus probe the undeniable difficulties that the growth of big government poses for citizen control and the effective management of intergovernmental relations; another contends that the existing electoral system has balkanized the Canadian party system, thereby exacerbating regionalism and ultimately weakening the national government; still others explore a number of obstacles that frustrate the scholarly and noble task of impartially analysing an evolving constitutional order and system of government.

The years during which these essays originally appeared cover one of the most remarkable periods of constitutional turmoil and political change this country has endured, the hazy repercussions of which have barely begun to be explored. To these profound but uncertain changes in our lives must be added the debates currently underway concerning the merits and weaknesses of the Meech Lake/Langevin Accord, not to mention those entailed by the proposed Free Trade Agreement with the United States. In light of such considerations, there can be little doubt that the publication of these essays – animated throughout by the hope of giving "life and movement" to the Canadian constitution in the most inclusive sense of the term – is especially timely. We will all be better scholars, students, and citizens with the appearance of this collection.

Tough choices and at times stringent criteria have had to be imposed in selecting from among a much larger body of work in compiling this volume. A selected bibliography has been provided for those interested in some of Cairns's work we have been unable to include here. The essays that follow have been organized in terms of four broad areas of concern: the constitutional framework, electoral politics, the federal system and intergovernmental dimension, and constitutional and political change. Cairns's contribution to each of these areas has been controversial, and brief introductions to the four sections that comprise this volume have been provided to orient readers to the context of and some of the more important contributions to these debates.

The volume owes a great deal to the encouragement and support of a number of people. The initial suggestion that I undertake to compile a representative selection of Alan Cairns's work was made by Peter Saunders of Fernwood Books. Shortly thereafter, Michael Harrison, our editor at McClelland and Stewart, began to nurture and sustain the project with great patience and understanding. The publication of this volume obviously would have been impossible without the extremely rich scholarship and support of Alan Cairns. And, finally, it seems only appropriate to thank Professor Donald V. Smiley who wrote in the 1980 Postscript to the Third Edition of his influential text, *Canada in Question: Federalism in the Eighties*, of hoping to nudge Professor Cairns "and some enterprising publisher to gather [his] essays together in one or more volumes of Cairnsiana."[6]

Author's Introduction

In writing this introduction to essays originally published between 1968 and 1984, I am tempted to find a consistency that may not exist, or a timelessness that readers may not discern. Resistance to such temptation seems particularly necessary because their recurring subject matter – the chequered career of the Canadian constitution in the Trudeau era – elicited volatile and erratic reactions from politicians, academics, and other constitution watchers. It was not always easy to keep one's feet on the ground. The imminent demise of the constitution was prematurely announced on several occasions.

On rereading these essays I am struck by the extent of the public involvement they reveal. They suggest that academic generations of political scientists can be defined by the particular issues of contemporary governance that command their attention for a decade and more. The Great Depression directed Canadian social scientists of the 1930s to examine the relationship of a faltering capitalism to the survival prospects of liberal democracy and federalism. More recently, much of the academic agenda for political scientists studying Canada was set by the constitutional agenda. Three essays (Chapters 1, 7, and 8) are direct responses to constitutional concerns. Two others (Chapters 4 and 6) explore the contribution of the electoral system and federalism to centrifugal forces that seemed to be out of control. Two further essays (Chapters 2 and 5) address constitutional concerns only slightly less directly. The first, which examines the logic and coherence of the Canadian criticisms of the Judicial Committee of the Privy Council, was a contribution to constitutional introspection at a time when the Supreme Court, as

11

inheritor of the Judicial Committee's mantle, was under attack. The second, which challenges a sociological perspective on the relations between the governments and societies of Canada, was triggered by the intellectual confusion I sensed at a time when the constitution seemed adrift. Given its context, the remaining essay (Chapter 3), an introduction to a volume dealing with the two federal elections of 1979 and 1980, seems equally likely to be a prisoner of time.

Since I have long been impressed by the wisdom of Dean Inge's statement, "If you marry the Spirit of your generation you will be a widow in the next," and equally by Harold Innis's trenchant criticisms of the politicized social scientists of the thirties, these essays may, at first glance, appear to provide an embarrassment of material for public self-criticism. Possibly they could be defended by an Oscar Wilde-type aphorism that to ignore ephemera is to overlook enduring characteristics of modern life, or they could be labelled as quaintly revealing examples of two decades of constitutional frenzy that future generations may consult to confirm their belief that the past is another country.

My preferred strategy is neither of the preceding, but simply a denial that these essays are only the short-run responses of an agitated citizen/academic to the ten o'clock news. While they were often occasioned by particular events, they share a concern for the long run. They focus on an old constitution with great staying power and on major institutions of government that resist fundamental change. They are discussions of high politics, that is, constitutional politics that deal with the elemental questions of a people's existence.

My view of the constitution, most explicitly argued in "The Living Canadian Constitution," is generous and inclusive rather than technical and limiting. The constitution is not a once-for-all achievement but a continuous creation. A functioning constitution for an historic people such as Canadians is more than an instrumental arrangement of the machinery of government. It is also a set of internalized rules and norms that structures the behaviour of citizens and office holders. It embodies conceptions of community that help mould citizen identities, and it makes a potent contribution to the symbolic order from which Canadians seek recognition and affirmation of their various identities and values.[1]

"The Canadian Constitutional Experiment" explicitly addresses this symbolic, normative component. It portrays the contending governments in the constitutional battles of the 1960s and 1970s as contesting for "possession of our souls."[2] Major constitutional change modifies the pattern of public cues and messages that constantly work on the inner worlds of meanings, identities, and values of the citizenry. Much of the passion pervading constitutional commentary, including the essays reprinted here, is triggered by the intrusive effect of constitutional change on our most intimate conceptions of self. In a politicized world the constitutional order impinges directly and pervasively on the citizenry.

A focus on the constitution raises the perennial questions of Canadian history. Do our constitutional arrangements contribute to our unity or our disunity? Are we a united people divided by our governments, or a divided people whose fragile unity is a product of overarching constitutional arrangements? There are no final answers to these and similar questions, only a never-ending dialogue which, if conducted well, informs discretion with wisdom at moments of constitutional choice.

Fragments of an Intellectual Autobiography

These essays say something of the author, as well as of an academic discipline, and of a country in a period of considerable turmoil. Even the most stringent professional education of a political scientist is filtered through the intellectual autobiographies of individuals. Nevertheless, one of the most difficult challenges for an academic is to bring an authentic, personal voice to the collective disciplinary task of research and writing. Finding and keeping alive the always precarious balance between personal expression and disciplinary constraints is a subtle matter both of judgement and of having something worthwhile to say. Since clones are useless colleagues, the most serious mistake is to sacrifice individuality for disciplinary conformity.

The point of view in these essays reflects a pattern of academic training that departed from what was becoming the norm. My undergraduate training in political science at the University of Toronto (1949-53) was broadly historical, institutional, and philosophical. There was little accommodation to what Bernard Crick later called *The American Science of Politics*,[3] which was then acquiring a very high international profile. My University of Toronto M.A. (1955-57) did little to correct this shortcoming, if such it was, nor did my subsequent doctoral work at Oxford, which had little to do with political science. The unstructured nature of an Oxford D.Phil., with no comprehensives or compulsory course work and a flexible attitude to disciplinary boundaries, was ideal for the rather eclectic social science I employed in my race relations thesis on early British pioneers in pre-imperial east and central Africa.[4]

With this academic background, much of what contemporary political science had become, especially in the United States, passed me by. When I began teaching at the University of British Columbia in 1960, and for several more years, the atypical nature of my academic background was worryingly self-evident to me. The authors, titles, and methodologies that tripped so easily from the lips of colleagues fresh from rigorous American graduate training elicited little spark of recognition in me.

On the other hand, an historical perspective on the dialectic between states and peoples, which was a legacy of my undergraduate days, was reinforced by Oxford. My thesis research stimulated my thoughts about race relations and about the role of imperialism in creating states and nations in an area riven by tribal war and the Arab slave trade in the decades preceding the European takeover.

My first major research after returning to Canada was on the politics and administration of Canadian Indian policy,[5] a classic case of state-sponsored fragmentation of the Canadian community. Indian policy, based on the constitutional allocation of "Indians, and Lands reserved for the Indians" to the federal government, singled out some members of one aboriginal ethnic group for distinctive treatment apart from other Canadians. It then created divisions among aboriginal peoples themselves by the criteria defining status Indians and their rights and disabilities. Additional distinctions developed within the legal-status Indian community between those with and without treaties and, very significant in the contemporary era, between the entitlements of off- and on-reserve Indians. The fragmentation of aboriginal peoples hinders their political unity and works against the development of coherent aboriginal policies by governments.

That research convinced me it was a sociological absurdity to deny the shaping power of law and of a distinctive system of Indian administration on the behaviour and identity of the status Indian population of Canada. It reinforced my inability to believe that institutions, law, and government were somehow inferior, secondary phenomena compared to socio-economic forces or the "real" behaviour of individuals. I have always found incomprehensible any suggestion that a society has an existence distinct from the heritage of political and other institutions, which give it contours and a sense of direction. Without institutions there is no society, only a bunch of strangers milling around on top of the ground sharing propinquity.

My concern for institutions partly explains the old-fashioned nature of the political science in these articles. Except for a few simple tabulations in the electoral system article they are devoid of quantification. They are not based on extensive interviewing of politicians or bureaucrats, nor do they rely on survey research. On the whole, they are products of the study, employ an essayistic style, and are typically driven by a point of view.

Many of the articles attempt to overturn prevalent interpretations of particular institutions or the constitution itself, which may be viewed as the master institution of society. They illustrate the collegial rivalry of academic life, the constant looking for flaws and weaknesses in an argument, the "I'm from Missouri, show me!" syndrome. Unconvinced colleagues have applied the same questioning spirit to several of these articles and have vigorously criticized them.[6] In all cases the debate has been advanced, and on some matters I have modified my position.

The Canadian subject matter of these essays may erroneously suggest that comparative material played no part in their writing. In fact, the literatures and political experiences of other countries explicitly influenced particular essays. The American perspective on the "living American constitution" directly inspired "The Living Canadian Constitution" article. The rich and subtle American scholarship on the American Supreme Court reinforced my frustration with the Canadian literature dealing with the Judicial Committee of the Privy Council. My reading of S.M. Lipset, V.O. Key, Maurice Duverger, and other non-Canadian authors precipitated my questioning of the conventional wisdom about the Canadian electoral system. My receptivity to new ideas in this case may have been stimulated by living in British Columbia, where electoral reform as a form of social engineering to keep the left out of office has been frequently preached and on occasion practised. All of the articles were positively influenced by the cosmopolitan diversity of my political science colleagues at the University of British Columbia and the scholarly eclecticism their presence encouraged.

Scholarship and the Constitution

When I began teaching Canadian government and politics in 1960, the post-war centralist constitutional order, which had previously seemed so stable, was visibly crumbling. The election of the Diefenbaker Conservatives in 1957 ended twenty-two years of Liberal rule and weakened the centralism it had fostered. In 1960 the Union Nationale government in Quebec (1936-39 and 1944-60) was defeated, following the death of Maurice Duplessis in 1959. The new Liberal government of Jean Lesage strongly supported the decentralized federalism that was already emerging in response to "province-building" in English Canada.

The constitutional review process, which followed the 1967 Confederation of Tomorrow Conference convened by Premier Robarts of Ontario, intensified with the Parti Québécois election victory in November, 1976. From then until the Constitution Act of 1982 Canadians inside and outside Quebec "felt the shaking of the earth,"[7] in the prospect that Canada might not survive, an outcome passionately sought and passionately resisted. By the last half of the 1970s, Trudeau's earlier comment that "the whole Constitution is up for grabs"[8] would have had to include Canada itself. Would or could the centre hold, and if so, how, became intensely practical constitutional questions. Were new constitutional arrangements a necessary response to emerging national, provincial, and linguistic identities or to the future demands that domestic and international pressures might generate? Nearly all of the essays reprinted here are informed by this context of constitutional uncertainty and malaise.

English Canadians were ill-prepared to consider these constitutional questions. They had little experience of domestic political tragedy, were complacent in their possession of majority status, and took the constitution for granted in the immediate post-World War II decades. More generally, in spite of various incidents any tolerably educated schoolchild could recite, from the hanging of Riel to the Winnipeg General Strike, Canada in its first century had been a remarkably easy country to govern. Self-indulgent myths to the contrary, sedulously cultivated by Mackenzie King and other parochial devotees of political hypochondria, were properly viewed as ludicrous by anyone with even a fragmentary knowledge of the governments and peoples of the modern world.

The long Canadian history of constitutional continuity and relative domestic tranquility, leavened by comparative affluence, was clearly a blessing. Nevertheless, the relative lack of the stimulus of adversity deprived English Canadians in particular of a rich tradition of constitutional introspection and led to a shallowness of constitutional theorizing when the breakup of the country became a distinct possibility. Constitutional sophistication came more easily to French Canadians, schooled in the understandings that minority status brings.

The quality of constitutional introspection in English Canada was also hindered by the lumberjack myth that conjures up Canadians in plaid shirts standing on the edge of the primeval forest–a new people in the early stages of self-formation. Whatever its validity in other realms, youthfulness is an inappropriate description of the Canadian political and constitutional tradition. Canadians belong to one of the oldest continuing political systems of the world, as a survey of United Nations membership quickly confirms. Canada is now in the second century of its post-Confederation history. The bulk of the country's basic governing arrangements go back to 1867, and many, such as judicial independence, constitutional monarchy, and responsible government, precede Confederation. The failure to recognize the remarkable constitutional longevity of Canada necessarily leads to a failure to understand its sources, a deficiency in political learning likely to produce superficial responses when the constitution is seriously challenged.

Such continuity does not just happen. It is achieved in part by deliberately adjusting a heritage to the myriad unanticipated pressures that all futures bring. A constitutional system must be worked deliberately and tended carefully if it is not to succumb to sclerosis as its environment changes. Such working, as "The Politics of Constitutional Conservatism" suggests, cannot always be equated with the careful cultivation of a gardener. Constitutional change may also come about from the successful employment of threats, skill, and manipulation, as in the making of the 1982 Constitution Act.

Such tending and working, both nuanced and brutal, along with the inevitable encroachments of social forces and changed climates of opinion on constitutional norms and institutional practices, mean that any old constitution is riddled with discrepancies between what the lawyers call the law-in-books and the law-in-action. Such discrepancies are a sign of growth and health when they complement the evolving grain of the system.[9] When they do not, the result is constitutional stagnation or decay.

"The Other Crisis of Canadian Federalism," drafted in the days of pessimism between the 1976 Parti Québécois victory and the referendum, is an almost unrelieved litany of concerns about the contribution of federalism to the growth of big government, and about the latter's incompatibility with either citizen control or any effective management of intergovernmental interdependence. Here, as in "The Governments and Societies of Canadian Federalism," the shaping, leadership role of governments was stressed. However, like the brutal leadership of bulls in china shops, it was viewed in this article as contemptuous of constraints and thus scarcely compatible with the respect and civility a healthy constitutional order requires.

While "The Other Crisis" may have exaggerated the damage competitive big governments were inflicting on the constitution,[10] its central concerns remain valid – the undeniable difficulties that big governments pose for citizen control in liberal democracies, and the necessity for some degree of, in Corry's apt phrase, "constitutional morality"[11] to restrain the excesses of intergovernmental competition.

Unfortunately, no serious study has been undertaken of the reinforcing dialectic between disrespectful attitudes toward a constitution that many thought was headed for the graveyard and the increasing ferocity of intergovernmental hostilities in recent decades. Constitutional morality presupposes a constitution. Particularly in the late seventies and early eighties, numerous domestic equivalents of border incidents threatened to get out of control. Hints of what such a study might uncover are found in several of the following articles. In the same way as the study of war helps us to understand the conditions of peace, a more elaborate study of the constitutional breakdown from which we have emerged would illuminate the contrasting conditions that sustain constitutional civility.

The creation, effective use, and ongoing modifications of the constitution and of major institutions of government are quintessential political acts, for they subtly redefine the people they serve and accord constitutional preference for some values, cleavages, and interests over others. For Riker, institutions are "congealed tastes";[12] for Popper, "*All long-term politics is institutional*";[13] and for Schattschneider political "*organization is the mobilization of bias*. Some issues are organized into politics while others are organized out. . . . the function of institutions is to discriminate among conflicts."[14] Put differently, acts of constitutional and institutional choice are instruments of generational imperialism by which founding generations seek to control their successors. For example, for the federal government the 1982 Charter was not only an instrument to protect rights, but was also part of a grand constitutional design to reshape the identities and allegiances of the Canadian people – to foster a nation-wide rights-bearing consciousness in all Canadians and to keep alive Francophone communities outside of Quebec and an Anglophone community within Quebec.

Eras of constitutional change unleash frantic efforts to harness constitutional support for governmental and private goals. In the making of the Constitution Act of 1982, governments contending ruthlessly for self-interested constitutional change were joined by numerous pressure groups and leaders of social movements, especially of women and aboriginals, who equally sought to buttress their future position by constitutional means.

On the one hand, the potential of constitutional change to fashion and to destroy peoples was the central message of our recent constitutional struggles. The Quebec referendum could have turned out otherwise. On the other hand, the efforts by competing elites to impose their visions on the future were frustrated not only by their contradictory objectives; they were brutally constrained by the imperialism of historic constitutional arrangements. Not only did the inherited constitution dictate the use of almost unworkable procedures for major constitutional reform, but the numerous barnacle-like interests that clung to the constitutional devil-they-knew were barriers to change. The constitution with which Canadians entered their long winter of constitutional introspection emerged largely intact because "in competition with its rivals it alone possesses the supreme advantage of existence. . . ."[15] Shils puts it succinctly: "The existence of tradition is at least as much a consequence of limited power to escape from it as a consequence of a desire to continue and to maintain it."[16]

"Institutions are like fortresses. They must be well designed *and* properly manned."[17] By manning, Popper refers to key officeholders whose discretion may be employed wisely or foolishly. Institutions, however, are also indirectly manned by the external community of commentators who hold no office but whose works justify or delegitimize institutions and strengthen or weaken their relative status in the constitutional framework.

A comprehensive view of those who work the constitution, accordingly, must include those who monitor the performance of institutions, questioning whether they are meeting their mandates and policing the division of labour among institutions. It is often said of judicial decisions that they are the product of judge and company, the latter including not only the lawyers who appear before the bench but the whole intellectual support-structure of law schools, legal periodicals, and the legal commentary and jurisprudence, past and present, produced by generations of scholarly interpreters. Although the phrases seem less natural, it is equally valid and useful to think of constitution and company, federalism and company, or Parliament and company.

A well-functioning institution requires both honourable office-holders and a perpetual dialogue with outside commentators. The task of monitoring basic institutions of government and keeping elites responsible cannot be left to the normal workings of adversarial politics, whose many virtues are weakened by a pervasive partisanship that often sacrifices truth for advantage, by a short-run time horizon hostile to a concern for long-run trends, and consequently, by a generally deficient analytical capacity. The task cannot be left to the bureaucracy, because its members have their own institutional interests to serve and cannot engage in public debate about the policies they administer or the wisdom of the political masters they serve. It cannot be left to the courts because their mandates are too restricted, and they are responsive rather than initiating bodies. Some of the intellectual tending of institutions, and the keeping of them in repair, can only be performed by detached external observers alert to discrepancies between an institution's performance and the purposes it is assumed to serve, and cognizant that changes in the environment in which institutions operate may generate unintended consequences previously absent. Such tending, much of which is undertaken by academics, may lead to an unmasking of an institution's deficiencies or the exposure of other shortcomings in the conventional wisdom that clusters around it.

Unlike practitioners, whose reform suggestions normally emerge from practical difficulties in achieving goals, the contributions of academics typically result from a frustration with an existing literature of explanation or description. For the scholar, reform may be a secondary or non-existent concern compared to the desire to solve a puzzle. Nevertheless, as the Macdonald Commission noted: "The future role of the state, the choice of particular instruments of intervention, and the relative importance of institutions within government will partially reflect the findings of some academic scribbler puzzling over a recalcitrant theorem."[18]

The articles reprinted here have certain characteristics. They have little explicit reform thrust. Often, in defiance of the conventional wisdom, they attribute significant specific consequences, frequently negative, to particular institutions, such as the electoral system, federalism, and the constitution, that structure the activity and shape the identity of Canadians, and to big government, which politicizes our everyday life. The underlying theme is how the constitution and its institutional components shape and structure society; inherent in this theme is an opposition to the assumption that the actions of governments, the functioning of institutions, and political behaviour can be explained almost exclusively by reference to socio-economic forces. My position is probably most emphatically asserted in "The Governments and Societies of Canadian Federalism," an early contribution to the now relatively popular state-centred models of federalism. The hypothesis is that, in an established system, federalism is reproduced by the governments a federal constitution establishes.

The incessant search for better understanding by a sizable brigade of scholars is politically consequential. Institutions viewed through the lens of an obsolete conventional wisdom, or that make real contributions to a functioning system of government an inadequate theory overlooks, are weakened in the never-ending competition among institutions for power and influence. They may be displaced or unwisely "reformed" to the detriment of the overall constitutional system. When the nature, role, strengths, and weaknesses of the constitution itself are misunderstood, the whole system of government suffers. Intellectual confusion and theoretical weakness are most serious at moments of constitutional choice.

Various chapters pick up the theme that the making of effective constitutional policy is hindered by deficiencies in our understanding. Two chapters deal specifically with the relationship between academic analysis and constitutional/institutional change. "The Judicial Committee and its Critics," an historical case study, assesses the quality of the Canadian debate that contributed to the elimination of appeals to the Judicial Committee. The weakening or displacement of a constitutional power centre, such as a final appeal court, is both an intellectual and political task. Intellectually, it requires the demolition of the theories and assumptions that sustain the institution under attack and demands, as well, the making of a case for the anticipated superiority of the successor institution.

The tasks of theory-destroying and theory-building can be well or poorly done. The intertwined political and intellectual rationales employed to mobilize support for the elimination of Judicial Committee appeals were internally contradictory, partly because nationalist and jurisprudential concerns were not always adequately distinguished. The nationalist success in eliminating appeals was purchased at the cost of an incoherent jurisprudence as a guide to the Supreme Court in its new role as a final appeal court. The blending of political and scholarly concerns, of which this is only a mild example, has a tendency to sacrifice the integrity and quality of the latter for the convenience of the former.

"The Electoral System and the Party System" is an early contribution to a contemporary policy debate. The paper attacked the conventional wisdom about the positive contribution of the party system, as influenced by the electoral system, to national integration. It was part of a larger effort to understand how the choice of institutions influences which conflicts and cleavages acquire political salience.[19] It was also driven by the belief that institutions often produce both unintended and unnoticed negative consequences, for the detection of which academics have a major responsibility. The paper concludes that the electoral system balkanized the party system and thus weakened the national government. It ends with a plea for consideration of alternative electoral systems, which, unlike the existing one, would moderate rather than exacerbate a state-threatening regionalism.

The argument that a deficient understanding impedes constitutional functioning is applied in these papers not only to domestic jurisprudence and the electoral system, but also to federalism, to the constitution writ large, and most ambitiously, to the relationships of the governments of Canada to the underlying national and provincial societies. When these separate observations are brought together I am somewhat astounded and slightly perturbed at my own temerity. Fortunately, many others also perform the role of constitutional monitor and critic; there are many voices; and there is no party discipline, although there are schools of thought and fads and fashions. Further, I firmly believe that in the social division of labour such analysis and occasional prescription are among the responsibilities that have been assigned to academics, for the better performance of which they are outside the charmed circle of powerholders.

Various obstacles frustrate the scholarly task of impartially analysing the functioning of the constitution. An old constitution and historic institutions of government are often shrouded in symbolism and viewed as the essence of a people's identity. The resultant reverence or deference can cloud analytical vision or impede the reception of an objective analysis, which may seem sacrilegious to true believers.

Intellectual inertia is an additional impediment to academic understanding. The Depression of the 1930s, along with the successful centralization of World War II and of post-war reconstruction, led a generation of Anglophone observers in the 1940s and 1950s to overlook or underestimate the forces that would once again move Canadian federalism in a centrifugal direction. The tenacity of centralist assumptions was facilitated by the weakness and isolation of the Francophone social science community, whose countervoices on behalf of a Quebec view of federalism were unheard. The Anglophone political science community in that era was also influenced by a pervasive belief that centralization was a necessary response to the forces of industrialism and an unstable capitalism.

A fashionable faddism too responsive to prevalent and shifting climates of opinion often distorts constitutional analysis. Much of the attack on the BNA Act in the 1960s and 1970s was stimulated by various political/intellectual trends – especially the spate of nation-building in the Third World and the counterculture hostility to tradition, with the accompanying belief that the making and unmaking of worlds was an attainable goal for the idealist young. These background assumptions made it too easy to overlook the staying power of institutions, to assume that an ancient constitution was necessarily obsolete and dysfunctional, and to believe that its transformation into an up-to-date instrument of government would not be difficult for contemporary constitutional craftsmen employing pencils and notepads. The social sciences, with their generally ahistorical orientation, made an independent contribution to these profound misunderstandings.

If I did not know that authors are the worst judges of their own imperfections I might have falsely claimed that the following essays are unaffected by these and other biases. Such conceit is the greatest bias of all, to be avoided by all authors who lack the masochistic urge to provide ammunition for their critics.

Conclusion

The tendency to think of constitutions as written statutes is especially misleading for the Canadian constitution, which has shaped the people subject to it for more than a century. In such cases the living constitution is no longer an external arrangement of forms but is part of the intellectual furniture and civic identity of the citizenry. This does not mean a detailed understanding by citizens of obscure constitutional clauses, but rather a basic capacity to feel at home and to function amid the system's complexities.

Albert O. Hirschman recently described how Colombians would explain what he, an outsider, saw as "puzzling situations" by saying with a shy pride, "you must realize that this is a very odd country,"[20] through whose complexities they, of course, could expertly navigate. Something similar is true of Canada, an old, possibly odd, country with historic constitutional arrangements. Both ordinary citizens and leaders have learned the appropriate behaviour to operate a system of great complexity, which reproduces itself by the continuous socialization of new generations to meet its requirements. The latter inherit an evolving pattern of constitutional behaviour in which new elements and traditional practices constantly mingle.

An historic pattern of institutions gathered together in a constitutional framework has a distinctive intellectual existence as a system, or at least arrangement, of ideas about the relations among institutions and between citizens and the state. This intellectual dimension engages the variety of commentators – journalists, academics, creative artists, and involved citizens – an open society generates in profusion. Their constitutional commentary is one of the environments to which, over time, a constitution responds. Some commentators – Eugene Forsey is probably the classic Canadian case[21] – become part of the very constitution they are expounding. Without such commentary, the constitution would have a diminished capacity to adapt and would be excessively subject to the bureaucratic and partisan interpretations of the appointed and elected elites who occupy its key offices. Such a constitution would have only a shallow existence. It would be incapable of meeting the needs of a late twentieth-century liberal democracy. Of the academic disciplines, Law and Political Science are the most frequent contributors to the constitutional introspection that gives life and movement to the constitution. These essays are directed to that end.

PART I

THE CONSTITUTIONAL FRAMEWORK

Editor's Introduction

The essays in this section present two of Cairns's most important contributions to the interpretation of Canadian constitutional government. They share a number of qualities that recur throughout this volume, the most notable being their historical, evolutionary orientation, their stress on the impact and significance of scholarly analysis and interpretation on the performance of our most important political institutions, and their emphasis on the dynamic interdependence of our legal and political systems. In many respects, "The Living Canadian Constitution" is emblematic of Cairns's thought as a whole, a relatively early indication of an enduring range of concerns and style of inquiry. The second piece, "The Judicial Committee and Its Critics," has become a virtually "indispensable background piece for the study of Canadian constitutional law" and recently has become the object of considerable controversy over the role of historical analysis in the assessment of our judicial capacity and the political theory of a representative federal democracy.[1]

The re-publication of these essays at this time should prove to be especially timely inasmuch as the 1982 Charter of Rights and Freedoms gives the Supreme Court significantly enhanced responsibilities in our overall constitutional system. As Cairns recently observed in a review of the first comprehensive history of the Supreme Court,

the Canadian constitutional system can no longer be effectively summed up as a blending of parliamentary government and federalism, for the Charter, and the new responsibilities it gives the courts, changes the significance of both as a byproduct of its enhancement of the status of the citizen as a bearer of rights. The post 1982 role of the Court, accordingly, is based on a significant alteration of the principles on which our constitutional system rests.[2]

These complex relationships between the constitution, citizenship, social change, and political community were the focus of one of the seven main areas of research that Cairns organized in his capacity as research director of the studies of Politics and the Institutions of Government for the Royal Commission on the Economic Union and Development Prospects for Canada (the Macdonald Commission). Introducing a series of interdisciplinary studies of the area, he and his co-coordinator of research in the area, Cynthia Williams, wrote:

. . . a constitution does not just establish the machinery and instruments of government. It also embodies and reflects the values and beliefs of a political community, the terms and conditions on which its members have agreed to live with one another and in relation to the state. While constitutions must adapt to evolving circumstances over time if they are to survive, the notion of a 'living constitution' at best tells only half a story. Over time, constitutions shape and mold a people as much as they are shaped and molded by one. Constitutions embody the highest principles and ideals of a political community, linking the past with the present and future, breathing life into and giving form to the very conception of citizenship.[3]

The remaining essays in this volume probe a number of the more important dimensions of this enormously complex dialectic between the political institutions and citizens of Canada.

Chapter One

The Living Canadian Constitution

The dustbin of recent history is littered with discarded constitutions cast aside after brief and withering exposure to reality. Constitutions capable of responding and adapting to the perils of change have sufficient scarcity value to be treated with the deference appropriate to rare achievements. All the more curious, therefore, has been the detached, unappreciative Canadian attitude to one of the most durable and successful constitutions in the world.

A partial explanation is found in the nature of the British North America Act. It is a document of monumental dullness which enshrines no eternal principles and is devoid of inspirational content. It was not born in a revolutionary, populist context, and it acquired little symbolic aura in its subsequent history. The movement to Confederation was not a rejection of Europe, but was rather a pragmatic response to a series of economic, political, military, and technological considerations. There was no need for the kind of political theorizing that accompanied the American experience of creating a new political entity and exercised a spell on subsequent generations. With the important exception of the federal system, Canada was endowed "with a Constitution similar in Principle to that of the United Kingdom." Constitutional monarchy and responsible government in a parliamentary setting were already part of the Canadian heritage, which was approvingly translated to the larger sphere of action the new Dominion created. No resounding assertions of human rights accompanied the creation of the new polity. The British tradition precluded any approach to their protection premised on comprehensive declarations of principle.

The absence of an overt ideological content in its terms, and the circumstances surrounding its creation, have prevented the BNA Act from being perceived as a repository of values by which Canadianism was to be measured. Further, the first thirty years of its existence were troubled by depression, threats of secession, and constant bickering over its terms. These scarcely constituted the circumstances for the Act to become the symbolic focus for the nascent political system. Consequently, a conscious ideological adherence and loyalty to the BNA Act and the constitution of which it was a part never became overt integral components of the Canadian civic identity.

An additional factor in the Canadian lack of appreciation for the constitution is a confused understanding of the meaning of age and time for institutions. With the passage of time, the intentions of the Fathers of Confederation unavoidably became an increasingly artificial concept with an ever attenuated contact with reality. Their visions were responses to the problems they faced in the light of prevalent conceptions of the role of government. Many of the conditions to which they addressed themselves faded away, to be replaced by conditions they could not predict. In such circumstances deference to their intentions became impossible, for they had none. Nevertheless, the BNA Act, which represents a consolidation of some of their intentions, remains an important constitutional document. This raises the question of how relevant for a contemporary evaluation of the Canadian constitution is the fact that the BNA Act is a century old.

At the most abstract level of institutional analysis, age has a double significance. Positively, a functioning institution of ancient origin acquires the special credibility that derives from its continuing utility for the attainment of one or more specified human goals. In the Darwinian process of institutional competition for survival it has emerged triumphant. Negatively, it is placed on the defensive by the fact that the contemporary circumstances to which it now applies are significantly different from the circumstances to which it was originally a response. Hence, it appears to be tinged with mortality. The graveyard, sooner or later, is its inevitable destination.

To continue the discussion on this level, however, is to grant to the question of age an undeserved importance and a spurious relevance. Institutions do not have a natural life span. They are, when wisely constructed and carefully tended, evolving human arrangements for avoiding the ravages of time by flexibly responding to the demands confronting them. Therefore to discuss the relevance of an institution in terms of its age, defined by the lapse of time since its first beginnings, is to misconceive what an institution is.

Canadian understanding of the constitution would have been much improved had it been consistently viewed in the significant American phrase as a "living constitution."[1] The wise admonition of Holmes reveals a perspective sadly lacking in Canada:

> The provisions of the Constitution are not mathematical formulas having their essence in their form; they are organic living institutions transplanted from English soil. Their significance is vital, not formal; it is to be gathered not simply by taking the words and a dictionary, but by considering their origin and the line of their growth. . . . When we are dealing with words that are also a constituent act, like the Constitution of the United States, we must realize that they have called into life a being the development of which could not have been foreseen completely by the most gifted of its begetters. It was enough for them to realize or to hope that they had created an organism; it has taken a century and has cost their successors much sweat and blood to prove that they created a nation. The case before us must be considered in the light of our whole experience and not merely in that of what was said a hundred years ago.[2]

The virtual absence of this understanding of a living constitution has produced the mistaken belief that the constitution is a century old, that it has already outlived its allotted life span, and that *younger* means *better* and *older* means *worse*. Given this belief it is possible to advocate a new constitution simply because the BNA Act was drafted a century ago. The rather trite conclusion automatically follows that a constitution, or a constitutional document, so heavy with years must be out of date.

In the 1960s there has been a recurrence of the criticism of the constitution as obsolete that was so widespread in the Depression of the thirties. In that troubled decade, the constitution as judicially interpreted was roundly condemned by centralists for the barriers it placed in the way of decisive action by the federal government. The contemporary attack has different roots. One source is the spurt of nation-building and constitution-making that followed the demise of Western imperialism. In much of the Third World, constitution-making became a normal political activity interrupted by secession movements, coups, assassinations, and civil war as the new states struggled to overcome appalling problems and to find a framework for modernization. Whatever the justification for their endemic efforts to resolve their constitutional difficulties, and there are many, only a masochist would find their experience worthy of emulation.

An additional source is the French-Canadian view of recent years that the existing constitution restricts the process of nation-building in Quebec. Hence Marcel Faribault, the late Premier Daniel Johnson, Father Ares, Professor A. Dubuc, and numerous others have issued clarion calls for a new constitution to usher in the new age of emancipation which is part of the rhetoric of the Quebec nationalist intelligentsia. Their search for a new constitution is sustained by English-Canadian writers such as Peter O'Hearn, who finds the "battered hulk of the British North America Act and its train of amendments" unacceptable.[3] Other English-Canadian support is found in politicians who capitalize on any groundswell of opinion, or who naively assume that to be progressive requires a repudiation of the past, at least at the level of oratory. They sympathize with T.C. Douglas, whose own party is more trapped by the shibboleths of the nineteenth century than any other Canadian party, when he states: "The time has come for Canadians to free themselves from the dead hand of the past and forge a constitution that will enable Canada to keep its rendezvous with destiny. . . . I do not think that the dead hand of the past should be allowed to stay the onward march of progress. Human rights are sacred but constitutions are not."[4]

In an age when rapid obsolescence is viewed as the natural and inevitable end for every man-made product, such a thesis quickly finds attentive, receptive hearers. Superficially, it has compelling force, for clearly the conditions of 1867 have passed away. It logically follows that decisions made in the light of those conditions must become increasingly irrelevant with the passage of time.

Crucial to this widespread position is the belief that the constitution is by and large what the Fathers bequeathed to us a century ago. From this perspective the constitution emerged in 1867 in the form of the British North America Act and its accompanying understandings, the product of a small political elite, the Fathers of Confederation, and barring formal amendments, is now what it was then. The confusion is subtle. To view the constitution in terms of what the Fathers intended and immediately achieved fails to see that the constitution is a continuous creation. It accords too much deference to the constitution as it existed in 1867, and too little attention to the contribution of subsequent generations to its evolution.

The Canadian constitution is the body of understandings defining the basic institutions of government and the relationships between them, plus the relationships between governments in the federal system, and between the citizens and those governments. At any given point of time the content of the constitution is a series of living practices worked out by successive generations. It is a product of continuous selection, rejection, and addition. It is always, in a practical sense, contemporary. It is a living instrument of government, wider in scope than the BNA Act, and not restricted to the 1867 intentions of the Fathers. It is an evolving institution that has responded to pressures and flexibly accommodated itself to a variety of needs and changing demands.

The distinction between the constitution as an institution and the key statute that went into its formation is cogently described by Llewellyn in his discussion of the American constitution:

> The discrepancy between theory and fact found in private law is exaggerated in the constitutional field, because under a code of rigid words no easy and gradual rewording of outmoded rules in such manner as to hide the changes made in their content, is possible. The consequence is that with growing age all force in the actual words of a code withers and dies. What is left, and living, is not a code, but an institution. Many of the institution's roots trace back through time into the code. *Many do not.* But the living institution is neither the dead code nor its "interpretation." It is not even by any parthenogenesis descended from its great-grandmother code alone. It is new, it is different, it is growing; and in its blood run so many other streams that resemblance to the code is seldom strong and always confined to single traits.[5]

Evidence on the living nature of the constitution is ubiquitous. The settlement of 1867 was only a beginning. It has been under constant transformation since that time. The major evidence is as follows:

1. The instruments of federal control – disallowance, reservation, and refusal of assent by the Lieutenant-Governor–have fallen into virtual desuetude. If not entirely dead, there is no likelihood

that they will ever again be used in the coercive fashion of the early post-Confederation years.

2. The transformation of Empire into Commonwealth – from "Colony to Nation" – has reduced the ties to Great Britain until all that remains is an increasingly attenuated emotional link, a similarity in the institutions of parliamentary and monarchical government, and an embarrassing leftover in the continuing (entirely formal) role of the British Parliament in the amending procedure.

3. As is well known, the division of powers in the BNA Act was importantly affected by the Judicial Committee of the Privy Council. While its decisions aroused much resentment and may or may not have been appropriate to Canadian needs, it cannot be denied that they made a fundamental contribution to the constitutional evolution Canadians actually experienced.

4. The division of powers was also transformed by the massive engine of the federal spending power and the conditional grants mechanism. Once again the evaluation may be favourable or unfavourable, but it is clear that the result was a marked change in the practical significance of Sections 91 and 92 of the BNA Act. Perhaps the spending power was used indiscriminately. Perhaps its use should have been (or should be) more tightly controlled, but that is not the issue here.

5. The proliferation of federal-provincial meetings of administrators and politicians, culminating in conferences of premiers and prime ministers, has added, as many have pointed out, an important new mechanism of co-ordination for the federal system.

6. Since the onset of World War II the fiscal system has not been the chaos of clashing taxing jurisdictions it was in the Depression. Further, as part of a succession of fiscal agreements, huge equalization grants have been paid to the less well-endowed provinces. The original compulsory federal subsidies have been rendered financially trivial by comparison.

7. The parliamentary system has been transformed by the development of the party system, the institution of party discipline, the emergence of third parties and their recognition, the institution of research staffs for the opposition parties, etc. Recently we have been told that before our very eyes the parliamentary system is being transformed into a presidential system without the requisite checks and balances. The truth of this latter statement is irrelevant for our purposes. What is relevant is that the parliamentary half of

the Canadian wedding of parliamentary government and federalism has not stood still.

8. Even prior to the passage of the Diefenbaker Bill of Rights, the Supreme Court, and particularly Mr. Justice Rand, began to develop a court-supported jurisprudence for the protection of civil liberties. Basing their decisions largely on the flimsy constitutional basis of the preamble to the BNA Act, which stated that Canada was to have "a Constitution similar in Principle to that of the United Kingdom," the court enunciated an important series of civil liberties decisions.

9. Finally, the formal amendments to the Act contributed to its evolution.

Even in the cryptic fashion expressed above, these changes have been of momentous significance in the evolution of the Canadian constitution.

The agents of these changes were largely the politicians and civil servants of both levels of government responding to the demands and opportunities that the possession of office imposed on them. To examine the above list is to have it confirmed that the constitution never has been, and is not now, only what the courts say it is. The evolution of the constitution has been largely guided by successive generations of political leaders and their influential bureaucratic advisers. Admittedly, they did not have a clean slate to work with. Admittedly, the result has been evolution rather than revolution. Admittedly, certain key parts of the constitutional framework remain, in form at least, as they were originally established in 1867. It is also true that a different beginning would have produced a different outcome, but that is true of all human experiments. The point is not that what happened in 1867 did not matter, but that the decisions then made did not constitute a cake of custom that has held subsequent generations of Canadians in unwilling thralldom in a world they never made. The point is that the constitution has worked and grown in response to the shifting conditions thrown up by the passage of time. A constitution which had accommodated for a century the often competing demands of two ethnic groups, which had survived through depression and war, the transformation of a rural society into an urban society, the settlement of the West, and the technological revolution of recent years might have been appreciated in more prosaic times for its real practical virtues, rather than, as was so often the case, being scorned for its absence of symbolic appeal and criticized for a non-existent inflexibility. In the words of Eugene Forsey, "There is no point in change for its own sake, or just for the sake of having the very latest thing in constitutions. (What matters in a constitution is not how new it is but how good it is, how well it works.) The bigger the change, the heavier the onus upon those who propose it to prove that it is necessary, or even useful."[6]

It may be taken for granted that the Canadian constitution, like any other, prejudices some and fosters other public policy outputs. Any constitution, particularly a federal one, will regularly prevent some group of officeholders from attaining some of their policy objectives. To criticize a constitution because it entails this consequence, however, is similar to criticizing the law of gravity. The more precise and relevant question is comparative, whether or not the existing constitution erects more barriers to desired governmental output than would its successor. The answer depends on the nature of the particular new constitution that is advocated. Until that information is available, it is entirely proper to note the flexibility of the existing constitution.

All of the changes noted above are obvious and well known. Why then has so little heed been paid to the message they contain about the flexibility of a living constitution? What explains the constant confusion implicit in the attacks on the constitution because of its age? First, there is sometimes failure to distinguish between the BNA Act and the constitution. Then the relative paucity of formal amendments, especially dealing with the division of powers, has produced a misleading impression of stability belied by our actual experience even in that area. Much of the change that has occurred has not been formally designated as constitutional, and it has not been accompanied by fanfare. It has simply represented the handiwork of busy men attempting to work an ongoing system of government.

A good part of the explanation simply lies in a compartmentalization of the minds of the critics and analysts. While all the changes have been recognized and noted, they have frequently co-existed with the assumption that the constitution is a century old. The absence of the concept of a living constitution has aided in this compartmentalization. The confusion has been deliberately sewn by propagandists who have undertaken partisan attacks on the constitution because it stood in the way of their pet panacea. No century-old document (or constitution), they contend, should be allowed to stand in the way of the people. At the opposite pole, blindness on the part of some constitution-worshippers, who have been reluctant to believe that their god could be affected by anything so mundane as the passage of time, has had some influence.

Finally, the scholarship of historians and lawyers, and to a lesser extent of political scientists, has been obsessed with discovering the true meaning of 1867. Centralists and provincialists, compact theorists and their opponents, have all fought over the BNA Act in an attempt to discover its true meaning, and often to further their partisan objectives. By so doing they have exaggerated the importance of the original agreement of 1867 and have downgraded the changes it underwent in its subsequent expression.

In view of the preceding, two frequent tendencies in the discussion and evaluation of the Canadian constitution have been based on dangerous misunderstandings. It is simply mistaken to attack the existing constitution because of the age of the BNA Act, one of the key documents that went into its making a century ago. Llewellyn describes a working constitution "as being in essence not a document, but a living institution built (historically, genetically) in first instance *around* a particular document."[7] "With every passing decade," stated Carl Brent Swisher, "a constitution written long ago provides less and less guidance for its own interpretation amid patterns of social change and with sheer change in the dictionary meanings of familiar terminology."[8] It is equally fallacious to transform the constitutional settlement of 1867 into a measuring rod against which subsequent deviations can be assessed and their perpetrators chastised. Two American authors describe the "intentions of the framers" as a "filio-pietistic notion that can have little place in the adjudicative process of the latter half of the twentieth century. . . . A nation wholly different from that existing in 1787, facing problems obviously not within the contemplation of the Founding Fathers, can scarcely be governed – except in broadest generality – by the concepts and solutions of yesteryear."[9] The same point was lucidly expressed by Chief Justice Hughes of the United States Supreme Court:

It is no answer to say that this public need was not apprehended a century ago, or to insist that what the provision of the Constitution meant to the vision of that day it must mean to the vision of our time. If by the statement that what the Constitution meant at the time of its adoption it means today, it is intended to say that the great clauses of the Constitution must be confined to the

interpretation which the framers, with the conditions and outlook of their time, would have placed upon them, the statement
carries its own refutation.[10]

To attack the constitution on grounds of age is to fail to see its
living nature. The same failure produces the description of post-
1867 changes as deviations.

This latter approach was very widespread in discussions of judicial review, particularly in criticisms of the Privy Council. Since
lawyers constitute the professional group which has arrogated specialized expertise to itself in this matter, they have an important
responsibility for the misconceptions which heavily influence our
constitutional discussion. I do not forget that one category of legal
criticism of the Judicial Committee was based on the alleged failure
of British judges to treat the BNA Act as a living instrument of government. It is true that to this group Lord Sankey, with his "living
tree" analogy, was the closest thing to a judicial hero that is found
in the law periodicals. However, the other major group of criticisms
was specifically based on the unacceptable conduct of the Judicial
Committee in departing either from the intentions of the Fathers
or the clear meaning of the BNA Act in which those intentions were
presumably embodied. Further, the "living tree" school of Canadian criticism typically also reproached the Privy Council for leading Canada down the provincial path away from the limited,
centralized federalism so wisely chosen in the sixties of the nineteenth century. This was partly because those critics willing
to overtly discuss the constitution in terms of current need were
usually centralists. Consequently, they could not resist appealing
to the Fathers and their original creation as the touchstone of
constitutional wisdom.

In general, the basic language of both constitutional case law and
its Canadian critics stressed fidelity to an ancient document.
O'Connor, the author of the classic fundamentalist statement that
judges should apply the Act in terms of the meanings deliberately
embodied in it by its creators, strongly attacked the Judicial Committee for "most serious and persistent deviation . . . from the
actual text of the Act." He was highly critical of Lord Watson's
"assumption of the guardianship of the autonomy of the provinces.
His proper function was merely that of an interpreter of the meaning of the words of a statute."[11] This position reflected the British
tradition, which instructs judges to apply statutes literally. Thus,

jurisprudence in Canada, both in the language of courts and in that of their critics, has not devised adequate criteria to guide judges in the employment of the discretion they unavoidably possess. This has been unfortunate, for it has meant that much constitutional advocacy has been, literally, meaningless. It has also contributed to the misunderstanding of what a constitution is.

The critics of the Privy Council frequently asserted that its failure rested on an unwillingness to use the variety of historical evidence available to throw light on the intentions of the Fathers, and thus clarify obscurities in the BNA Act. This approach was always fraught with difficulties, but with the passage of time its desirability became increasingly questionable. This was recognized by Professor Strayer in a recent publication. He noted the "very limited" evidence available on the formation of the Act, and, more importantly, questioned its utility in principle. "Conditions have so drastically changed since 1867," he pointed out, "that the particular context in which the Act was passed may have little bearing on the context in which it is now expected to operate."

This position represents a marked change from the obsessive concern with the intentions of the Fathers in the decades prior to the abolition of appeals to the Privy Council. Yet Strayer is still caught in an historical quagmire of his own making. The obligation to appeal to the past is irresistible. His argument continues: "The more crucial question now is: What would the framers have intended had conditions been in 1867 as they are today? Even if the courts could now be induced to make use of external evidence as to the conditions of that time such evidence would be of limited value in answering this hypothetical question."[12]

Unfortunately, we are not told what evidence would be helpful. Given the impossibility of deciding how to undertake this pseudo-historical quest, one wonders why it should be undertaken at all. The assertion of Learned Hand is as valid for Canada as for the United States: "It is impossible to fabricate how the 'Framers' would have answered the problems that arise in a modern society had they been reared in the civilization that has produced those problems. We should indeed have to be sorcerers to conjure up how they would have responded."[13]

In the evolution of a constitution, it is evident that the passage of time does and should reduce the weight to be given to the views and desires of the Fathers or of influential moulders of the constitution at other points of time. As time transforms the conditions to which the constitution must be responsive, the search is not for what was originally intended but for what can be creatively extracted from a constitutional heritage, of which the BNA Act is only a part. The search for the contemporary meaning of the constitution does not consist in minute examination of what was said or intended or achieved a century ago. Such an approach would deny to constitutional unfolding the benefits a century of experience has given us. This generation, its predecessors, and successors partially have and certainly should view the constitution for what it is, a developing responsive tradition neither to be lightly departed from nor to be casually obeyed.

The arrangements of 1867 were never a sacrosanct body of holy writ. Approaches that so regarded them constituted a disservice to the Canadian polity and rested on a misunderstanding of the nature of a constitution. They inhibited change and thus reduced the flexibility essential for survival. Equally important, they blinded their possessors to the changes that did occur. Realistically, all working constitutions are living constitutions springing from, but not bound and gagged by, history. Inadequate recognition of this truth is a significant cause of the constitutional morass in which we now find ourselves. Cryptically, we might say that the constitution has not failed us, so much as we, by our inadequate understanding of its living nature, have failed it. In a living constitution all generations are simultaneously Fathers and Sons, by necessity even if not by choice. King, Bennett, Diefenbaker, and their provincial counterparts were in their own way Fathers as were Macdonald and Cartier. Like Macdonald and Cartier, they were also Sons in that they built on the achievements of their predecessors. There can be no quarrel with the fact that each succeeding generation of Canadians has decided what parts of the constitution they received were viable and worthy of continued life, and which were not. However, we can quarrel with those who, blinded by a deification of the past, resist new departures because the Fathers intended otherwise, or those who propose a new constitution on the mistaken grounds that the existing one, because of its time of origin, is necessarily an inflexible, incompetent instrument for new conditions. The first approach makes us prisoners of the past. The second deprives us of the benefits a rich tradition provides.

To view a constitution as a living constitution has important consequences. It is to recognize that the processes of constitutional change are manifold and unpredictable. The processes of formal amendment and judicial review are neither the only nor the most important vehicles for change. The constitution is constantly interpreted and modified by the men who work it. No new division of powers can prevent the intermingling of the activities of both levels of government in modern conditions. Predictable, clear-cut procedures for change can be obtained in the area of formal amendment, but nowhere else. The Supreme Court can be revamped in various ways, but "the history of judge-made law invites no other view than this: that the parties to the original federal 'bargain' can never be certain that the words in which they have clothed their intentions can ever be more than a rough guide to political activity, or that the range of permissible activity at any time after will bear any exact relation to their intentions."[14]

The terribly difficult problem, frequently overlooked because of obsession with the written text and the more blatant methods of change by amendment and judicial review, is how to devise conventions and understandings by which the other, less obvious methods of change can be brought within a framework of constitutionalism. The main weakness, for example, of the compact theory as a set of criteria for constitutional change did not lie in its hotly contested validity, but in the restricted scope of its intended operation. Even if wholehearted agreement to its terms had existed, this would have represented no more than a control of the amending procedure, one of the least important methods of constitutional change in Canadian history.

This problem is, of course, recognized by influential Quebec spokesmen. The late Premier Daniel Johnson, for example, stated in 1967:

Canada today is faced with a whole series of problems which the Fathers of Confederation . . . could not conceivably have foreseen. . . . Therefore, when a new problem arises in Canada, we are more and more likely to base each government's responsibilities for it, not on constitutional principles, but on considerations of the moment which, in turn, derive from a variety of factors such as relative capacity to act, financial resources or merely the political power wielded by a given area of government. Hence even though there is a written document called the British North America Act from which we may expect some light to be cast on such traditional fields as education and municipal institutions, the allocation of new tasks among governments has not been guided by this document but by decisions mainly based on exigencies of the day. . . . Our present Constitution, perhaps admirable during the age of steam trains, no longer suits Canada's needs in this era of interplanetary rockets.[15]

At the 1966 federal-provincial conference on taxation, Johnson stated:

> Having reached what it considers a turning point in its history, Quebec expects some specific things from the present constitutional system. First, it wants proof that the division of powers written in the constitution is not mere window-dressing and that, accordingly, it can count on the fiscal and financial resources it requires in order to discharge its obligations properly. . . . Quebec also wants assurance that it can exercise, fully and without interference from any quarter, all its powers under the present constitution. It wants the Government of Canada to withdraw from fields which are not federal or in which the provinces have priority.[16]

Essentially the same point was made by Professor Dubuc, who asserted that a century of change had rendered the BNA Act "too far removed from the basic structure and values of . . . [contemporary] . . . society to remain the touchstone for the division of powers," with the consequence that the "most important conflicts are settled on the political level and become confrontations of power; these are the conditions of political chaos."[17]

The general cogency of these critiques can be accepted. The question, however, is what can be done about them. To Johnson and Dubuc the obvious answer is a new constitution whose division of powers reflects the worked-out results of a contemporary agreement, responding to today's conditions, as to what the responsibilities of each level of government should be. Assuming for the moment that agreement could in fact be reached on a new constitution, the contribution this would make to the solution of the problem that troubles Dubuc and Johnson is debatable. Obviously, if Quebec were to be granted greatly enhanced jurisdictional authority, the seriousness of the problem from Quebec's viewpoint would be greatly diminished. The problem would still exist, but its scope would be less extensive. If, however, as seems more likely, a new division of powers did not deviate markedly from the existing division, we would be little better off. It it not entirely clear that an ancient division of powers is more likely to produce "decisions mainly based on exigencies of the day" than is a division freshly minted at a constitutional conference. To some extent the problem arises from the impossibility of devising a comprehensive catalogue of powers into which all proposed legislation can be easily fitted. The operations of modern governments are too complex, the future is too unpredictable, and words are too full of imprecision and ambiguity for such an achievement. Further, the very political processes Johnson and Dubuc decry for the uncertainties they generate can be seen as the instruments to produce the concordance between the division of powers and contemporary requirements they seek. If such processes did not exist, we would really be in a bad way. The difficult problem, as suggested earlier, is to find ways by which they can be brought within a framework of constitutionalism.

The assault on the existing constitution has led to a process of constitutional review out of which a new, or at least a drastically modified, constitution is supposed to emerge. Unfortunately, the justification for this review does not reside in any self-evident likelihood that a new and better constitution can be created. The existing constitution was caught in a barrage of criticism based on its age, which is largely a fraudulent consideration, and a confused battery of French-Canadian demands to break with the past and stake out for themselves a status in Canadian federalism superior to what was apparently possible under the constitution as they perceived it.

From the evidence available, there is little possibility that a new constitution will emerge. Most of the political leaders engaged in constitutional review are dutifully going through the motions with little hope or desire that any major changes will transpire. If their pessimism is correct, Canadians will be left with the existing constitution whose limited sanctity has been further eroded by the criticism to which it has been subjected in the process of review. Its claim to our continued allegiance may come to rest on the flimsy basis that it is the only constitution Canadians have.

The perspective on the constitution adopted in this essay is a reminder that a constitution is not merely a piece of paper. It is a set of relationships between governments and between governments and peoples which has become embedded in the evolving habits and values of successive generations of Canadians. Tinkering with constitutional documents in an era of laissez faire might have left the mass of the citizenry unaffected. However, when governments increasingly involve themselves in the nooks and crannies of our lives, dramatic constitutional change presents a less attractive and less plausible face. It is only necessary to observe the difficulties of successfully introducing major policies, such as medicare or tax reform, to question the feasibility of attempting to change a large part of the constitutional framework from which governments derive their authority and by means of which citizens deal with the government.

A new constitution can be no more than a point of departure. The day after it is proclaimed its evolution away from the agreement just reached will commence. The new settlement will inevitably be subject to the informal processes of change and growth that helped "undermine" the BNA Act. The security and control of the future that can be obtained from a written document are only relative. Further, if a new constitution is created, the short-run result of its implementation inevitably will be an increase in uncertainty and insecurity until the text is fleshed out by the actions of men struggling to make it work. This, of course, is in addition to the uncertainties automatically generated by the simple fact of change from the old constitution to the new. Given these corollaries of a new constitution, we might consider whether constitutions are not like wine – much better when well aged. Perhaps, however, 1867 was not a good year for constitutions.

Chapter Two

The Judicial Committee and Its Critics

The interpretation of the British North America Act by the Judicial Committee of the Privy Council is one of the most contentious aspects of the constitutional evolution of Canada. As an imperial body the Privy Council was unavoidably embroiled in the struggles between imperialism and nationalism that accompanied the transformation of Empire into Commonwealth. As the final judicial authority for constitutional interpretation, its decisions became material for debate in the recurrent Canadian controversy over the future of federalism. The failure of Canadians to agree on a specific formula for constitutional amendment led many critics to place a special responsibility for adjusting the BNA Act on the Privy Council, and then to castigate it for not presiding wisely over the adaptation of Canadian federalism to conditions unforeseen in 1867.

Given the context in which it operated it is not surprising that much of the literature of judicial review, especially since the Depression of the thirties, transformed the Privy Council into a scapegoat for a variety of ills that afflicted the Canadian polity. In language ranging from measured criticism to vehement denunciation, from mild disagreement to bitter sarcasm, a host of critics indicated their fundamental disagreement with the Privy Council's handling of its task. Lords Watson and Haldane have been caricatured as bungling intruders who, through malevolence, stupidity, or inefficiency, channelled Canadian development away from the centralized federal system wisely intended by the Fathers.[1]

This article will survey the controversy over the performance of the Privy Council. Several purposes will be served. One purpose, the provision of a more favourable evaluation of the Privy Council's conduct, will emerge in the following discussion. This, however, is a byproduct of the main purpose of this article: an assessment of the quality of Canadian jurisprudence through an examination of the most significant, continuing constitutional controversy in Canadian history. The performance of the Privy Council raised critical questions concerning the locus, style, and role of a final appeal court. An analysis of the way in which these and related questions were discussed provides important insights into Canadian jurisprudence.[2]

Varieties of Criticism

Criticisms of the Privy Council can be roughly separated into two opposed prescriptions for the judicial role.[3] One camp, called the constitutionalists in this essay, contained those critics who advocated a flexible, pragmatic approach so that judges could help to keep the BNA Act up to date. Another camp, called the fundamentalists, contained those who criticized the courts for not providing a technically correct, logical interpretation of a clearly worded document.

According to the fundamentalists the basic shortcoming of the Privy Council was its elementary misunderstanding of the Act. The devotees of this criticism, who combined a stress on the literal meaning of the Act with a widespread resort to historical materials surrounding Confederation, had four main stages in their argument.[4] Naturally, not all critics employed the full battery of arguments possible.

1. The initial requirement was the provision of documented proof that the Fathers of Confederation intended to create a highly centralized federal system. This was done by ransacking the statements of the Fathers, particularly John A. Macdonald, and of British officials, for proof of centralist intent. Given the known desire of some Fathers for a "legislative union," or the closest approximation possible in 1867, a plethora of proof was readily assembled.

2. The next logical step was to prove that the centralization intended was clearly embodied in the Act.[5] This was done by combing the Act for every indication of the exalted role assigned to Ottawa and the paltry municipal role assigned to the provinces. This task required little skill. Even the least adept could assert, with convincing examples, that the division of powers heavily favoured Ottawa. If additional proof seemed necessary the dominance of the central government could also be illustrated by referring to the pro-

visions of the Act dealing with the disallowance and reservation of provincial legislation, and with the special position of the lieutenant governor as a federal officer.

Once concordance was proved between what the Fathers intended and what they achieved in the Act, the critics could then delve into a vast grab bag of pre-Confederation sources for their arguments. This greatly increased the amount of material at their disposal and strengthened their claim that a prime reason for Privy Council failure was its unwillingness to use similar materials.

3. The third feature of this fundamentalist approach was a definition of the judicial role that required of judges no more and no less than the technically correct interpretation of the Act to bring out the meaning deliberately and clearly embodied in it by the Fathers. Where necessary the judges were to employ the methods of historical research in performing this task. This point was explicitly made by H.A. Smith in his criticism of the English rule against extrinsic evidence in the interpretation of statutes. This, he asserted, was to forbid the courts "to adopt historical methods in solving a historical problem." The consequences were grave:

> . . . an arbitrary and unreasonable rule of interpretation has produced the very serious result of giving Canada a constitution substantially different from that which her founders intended that she should have. A study of the available historical evidence gives us a clear and definite idea of what the fathers of Canadian confederation sought to achieve. By excluding this historical evidence and considering the British North America Act without any regard to its historical setting the courts have recently imposed upon us a constitution which is different, not only in detail but also in principle, from that designed at Charlottetown and Quebec.[6]

In brief, the judge, like Ranke's ideal historian, was to find out "the way it really was," and then apply his historical findings to the cases that came before him.

4. Proof that the Fathers had intended and had created a centralized federal system in the terms of the BNA Act, coupled with the transformation of the judge into an historian, provided conclusive evidence of the failure of the Judicial Committee. This was done by contrasting the centralization intended and statutorily enacted with the actual evolution of the Canadian polity toward a more classical decentralized federalism, an evolution to which the

courts contributed. Since the judges were explicitly directed to apply the Act literally it was obvious that they had bungled their task. As W.P.M. Kennedy phrased it, their "interpretations cannot be supported on any reasonable grounds. They are simply due to inexplicable misreadings of the *terms* of the Act."[7] The same point was made in more polemical fashion by J.T. Thorson in a parliamentary debate on the Privy Council's treatment of the Bennett New Deal legislation:

> . . . they have mutilated the constitution. They have changed it from a centralized federalism, with the residue of legislative power in the dominion parliament, to a decentralized federalism with the residue of legislative power in the provinces – contrary to the Quebec resolutions, contrary to the ideas that were in the minds of the fathers of confederation, contrary to the spirit of confederation itself, and contrary to the earlier decisions of the courts. We have Lord Haldane largely to blame for the damage that has been done to our constitution.[8]

In summary, the fundamentalists simply asserted that the Privy Council had done a bad job in failing to follow the clearly laid out understandings of the Fathers embodied in the BNA Act. O'Connor, the author of the most influential criticism of the Privy Council, viewed their decisions as indefensible interpretations of a lucidly worded constitutional document. He felt that the Act was a marvellous instrument of government, the literal interpretation of which would have been perfectly consonant with the needs of a changing society.[9] The same literal criticism was brandished by a critic of the decision in *Toronto Electric Commissioners* v *Snider* who "arose in his place in the House of Commons and protested against 'a condition which allows the Judicial Committee . . . to shoot holes in our constitution.' "[10] For such critics the failure was technical, a simple case of misinterpretation. All critics who appealed to the intentions of the Fathers or to the clearly expressed meaning of the Act when criticizing the "deviations" of the Judicial Committee fell into this category. Since this gambit was almost universal, this fundamentalist criticism was widespread.[11]

In documenting the emasculation of federal authority, critics concentrated on the opening "peace, order, and good government" clause of Section 91 and on Section 91 (2), dealing with "the regulation of trade and commerce." The former, "the foundation of Macdonald's whole federal system,"[12] was the "favourite whipping-boy of most of the articles and comments on Canadian constitutional law. . . ."[13] According to critics, the peace, order, and good government clause was clearly designed to be the primary grant of federal authority with the enumerated clauses being illustrative, or "for greater certainty but not so as to restrict the generality" as Section 91 declared. The destruction of the utility of the residuary clause, and its subsequent partial revival as a source of emergency power, evoked a series of violent critiques from a host of embittered commentators.[14]

The Privy Council's handling of the trade and commerce power evoked only slightly less indignation. W.P.M. Kennedy, the most influential constitutional analyst of the period from the early twenties to the middle forties, spoke for the bulk of the critics when he protested that it "is reduced to the almost absurd position of being a power which the Canadian Parliament can only call in aid of a power granted elsewhere. . . ." It had been "relegated to a position utterly impossible to defend on the clearest terms of the Act, and one which makes any reliance on it barren and useless."[15]

The decline of peace, order, and good government and the virtual nullification of trade and commerce on the federal side were counterbalanced by the remarkable significance that came to be attached to "property and civil rights" in Section 92.[16] It was this provincial head that H. Carl Goldenberg described as "wide enough to cover nearly all legislation outside of criminal law," including the whole field of social legislation.[17]

In brief, the critics argued, the Privy Council seriously misinterpreted the division of powers in Sections 91 and 92, to the extent that the provinces were left with responsibilities they were neither intended nor competent to handle. Several key decisions raised the status of the provinces,[18] while other decisions enhanced the significance of provincial jurisdiction in Section 92, especially property and civil rights. Conversely, the federal government, originally endowed with potent problem-solving and nation-building capacities, had its powers cribbed and confined to such a degree that the Fathers would not recognize their creation. As a consequence, an explicitly centralized federal system was transformed into its reverse, a decentralized system approximating a league of states.[19]

The previous approach defined the judicial role in terms of the literal, almost technical, task of correctly interpreting a historic document in terms of the intention of its framers. From this perspective the trouble with the Privy Council was that it had got its history wrong, or had misinterpreted the clear phraseology of the BNA Act.

The second stream of criticism rested on contrary assumptions. These critics, the constitutionalists, took their stand with John Marshall's assertion that judges must not forget that they were expounding a constitution.

Critics of this school were hostile to the Privy Council for treating the BNA Act as a statute to be analysed by "the ordinary rules of statutory construction." They asserted that the Judicial Committee should have been an agent for constitutional flexibility, concerned with the policy consequences of their decisions. They flatly rejected the Judicial Committee's own interpretation of its task, to treat "the provisions of the Act in question by the same methods of construction and exposition which they apply to other statutes."[20]

Contrary to the narrow statutory approach officially adopted by the Privy Council, the critics favoured a more generous, flexible, liberal approach that clearly recognized the constitutional significance of judicial review, with its corollary of a policy role for judges. In positive terms these critics spoke variously and vaguely of the need to keep the BNA Act up to date, particularly in its federal aspects. In a variety of ways they believed that a Canadian version of the United States Supreme Court was required. They spoke especially favourably of Lord Sankey, the closest approximation to a hero they could find on the Privy Council, and they delighted in the analogy of the "living tree" he had applied to the BNA Act.[21]

The general tenor of the desired approach is readily apparent from the felicitous phrases used. MacDonald spoke of the need for interpreting the Act "progressively so as to keep it as apt an instrument of government in new conditions as it was in the conditions current at its enactment."[22] Elsewhere he wrote of the necessity for "constant effort to bring and keep the Constitution up-to-date as the source of power adequate to present needs,"[23] and the desirability of "the flexible interpretation that changing circumstances require."[24] Laskin wrote favourably of "those sentiments in existing constitutional doctrine which express principles of growth." He contrasted "the higher level of constitutional interpretation" with the "lower level of statutory interpretation."[25] F.R. Scott, one of the most prolific critics of the Privy Council, praised the "clear recognition" by courts in the United States "that a constitution is primarily intended, not to rivet on posterity the narrow concepts of an earlier age, but to provide a living tree capable of growth and adaptation to new national needs."[26] To A.R.M. Lower, the Act should have been interpreted "as the vehicle for a nation's growth. If the Act is the vehicle of a nation, then the broadest construction must be put on it in order that under it all parts of the nation may have adequate life."[27]

Essentially, these critics were strong on general exhortation and weak on specifics. What they disliked was very clear. Positively, they were concerned with consequences. They recognized the policy role of the judiciary and the dangers of being tied down to the constitutional assumptions of a previous era. The difficulties of formal amendment encouraged them to look to the courts for the injection of flexibility into an ancient document. They also frequently noted the necessity of incorporating a broader range of facts into the judicial decision-making process. From this perspective their orientation was salutary, for the brunt of their message was to make judges more self-conscious than hitherto.

Inevitably the advocates of a living tree, liberal, flexible approach to constitutional interpretation were hostile to *stare decisis*. MacDonald spoke of the "shackles of previous decisions,"[28] Laskin of "the inertia of *stare decisis*," and the "encrustation of *stare decisis*,"[29] and W.P.M. Kennedy of "that uncanny stranglehold with which *stare decisis* seems doomed to rob the law of creative vitality."[30] They were far more concerned with the suitability of the developing constitution to new circumstances than with a narrow fidelity to previous constitutional case law.

Underlying the specific criticisms of the Privy Council was the overriding assumption that a powerful central government endowed with broad-ranging legislative authority and generous financial resources was an essential requirement of modern conditions. "The complications of modern industry and of modern business," asserted W.P.M. Kennedy in 1932, "will sooner or later demand national treatment and national action in the national legislature."[31] In the mid-thirties Vincent MacDonald favourably noted "prevailing political theories which indicate the propriety or necessity of a greater degree of national control over, and governmental intervention in, matters of social welfare and business activity."[32] The general centralist basis of the critics is most clearly found in the writings of the socialist law professor, F.R. Scott, the "unofficial constitutional advisor" of the CCF.[33] On numerous occasions Scott criticized the Privy Council for departing from the centralist federalism established in 1867 and for leaving Canada with a constitution that gravely hampered attempts to solve important public problems. In 1931 he stated:

> Canadian federalism has developed continuously away from the original design. Constitutionally we have grown disunited, in spite of the fact that in other respects, as a result of the increased facility of communication, the rise of our international status, and the general spread of what may be called our national consciousness, we have grown more united. The Dominion Parliament does not play today the full part which the Fathers of Confederation planned for her. . . . Just at the time when the exigencies of the economic situation call for drastic action, for increased international co-operation and for a planned internal social order, we find ourselves with cumbrous legislative machinery and outworn constitutional doctrines.[34]

The same point was made by Laskin in an article shortly after the Second World War. After noting the provincial bias of the Privy Council, he continued: "But has provincial autonomy been secured? In terms of positive ability to meet economic and social problems of interprovincial scope, the answer is no. A destructive negative autonomy exists, however, which has as a corollary that the citizens of a province are citizens of the Dominion for certain limited purposes only."[35]

In the thirties, when the impotence of the provinces was highlighted by the Great Depression, this kind of opinion was greatly strengthened.[36] The interdependence of a modern economy, the growth of national corporations, national unions, and a national public opinion inevitably focused attention on the need for a strong national government. The recently formed CCF with its centralist orientation was inevitably hostile to the decentralizing tenor of Privy Council decisions. The intellectual spokesmen of the left in the League for Social Reconstruction viewed the provinces as reactionary supports of the business community.[37] The Conservatives, who had seen their New Deal program harshly treated by the Privy Council, reacted by raising the issue of abolishing appeals.

In the international arena a different set of factors required strong central governments capable of decisive action by means of treaties that could be negotiated, ratified, and implemented without the inhibitions of a federalist division of powers. In these circumstances Lord Atkins's decision in the Labour Conventions case was viewed as an unmitigated disaster. "While it is true," his judgement stated,

". . . that it was not contemplated in 1867 that the Dominion would possess treaty-making powers, it is impossible to strain the section [132] so as to cover the uncontemplated event."[38]

This particular decision elicited a veritable flood of intemperate, polemical abuse of the Judicial Committee, both at the time and subsequently. The critics found it insulting to Canadian dignity and incompatible with Canadian autonomy that the evolution of Canadian independence from Great Britain should leave the federal government so seriously hampered in its relations with foreign states. F.R. Scott dramatized the choice as between local sovereignty and world peace.[39] W.P.M. Kennedy asserted in 1943 that the treaty situation was fraught with grave consequences for Canadian performance of post-war peace treaties.[40] Vincent MacDonald satirically noted:

> The Dominion's power of treaty implementation is absolute as to types of treaty now obsolete. It is, however, almost non-existent as to many types of treaty called for by modern conditions; for these latter tend in point of subject matter to fall, entirely or largely, within Provincial heads of jurisdiction, as greatly expanded by judicial interpretation. This is a fact of the utmost importance in a day requiring co-operative action of many nations to control international forces of an economic, social or political character.[41]

Thus the critics, particularly the constitutionalists, were convinced that both domestic and foreign policy requirements necessitated the dominance of the central government in the federal system. Their opposition to the Privy Council on grounds of policy was backed by a growing Canadian nationalism. Even some of the early supporters of the Privy Council had recognized that in the fullness of time the elimination of appeals was inevitable. Nationalist arguments had been used by Edward Blake when the Supreme Court was established in 1875.[42] They were later to form a staple part of John S. Ewart's long campaign for Canadian independence in the first three decades of this century. To Ewart the appeal was "one of the few remaining badges of colonialism, of subordination, of lack of self-government."[43] A later generation of critics reiterated Ewart's thesis. In 1947 F.R. Scott stated that the continuation of appeals "perpetuates in Canada that refusal to shoulder responsibility, that willingness to let some one else make our important decisions, which is a mark of immaturity and colonialism."[44] The nationalist argument was incorporated in the official justifications of the Liberal government when appeals were finally abolished in 1949.[45]

The fact that the elimination of appeals occurred simultaneously with the admission of Newfoundland to Canada and a renewed attempt to find a domestic amending procedure was not accidental. On the one hand the meaning and value of the Commonwealth was not what it had been prior to the Second World War. A weakened Britain and an attenuated Commonwealth combined with a stronger and more self-confident Canada to diminish the significance of ties with the mother country, a phrase that had begun to sound quaint and archaic.[46]

The nationalist attack on the Privy Council was fed by the special pride with which many Canadian writers asserted the superiority of Canadian over American federalism. The centralized variant of federalism established north of the "unguarded frontier," in reaction to the destructive effects of a decentralized federalism the American Civil War allegedly displayed, was for many critics part of the political distinctiveness of Canada they prized. In these circumstances, for a British court to reverse the intentions of the far-sighted Fathers was doubly galling. This helps to explain the bitterness with which Canadian writers frequently contrasted the divergent evolutions of the American and Canadian federal systems away from their respective points of origin.

Explanations of the Judicial Committee

Critics of the Privy Council attempted to explain, as well as condemn, the results they deplored. In addition to explanations in terms of incompetence, critics offered specific interpretations of the Privy Council's conduct. One explanation was legal, the assertion that it was natural for judges to attempt to reduce the discretion involved in interpreting vague phrases such as peace, order, and good government. Frank Scott held that the decline of the federal residual power was due to the displeasure of a court of law at the task of having to distinguish between local and general matters. "Rather than commit themselves they have on the whole preferred to support legislation under some specific power, and thus the general residuary power has died of non-use."[47] A legal explanation of the Privy Council's conduct has been given recent support by Professor Browne's attempted justification of the claim that the BNA Act was in fact properly interpreted in the light of its evident meaning.[48]

Occasionally, critics suggested that Privy Council decisions were influenced by political considerations inappropriate to a court. While the nature of these considerations was seldom made clear, the most frequent accusation was that imperial interests were best served by a weak central government.[49] This explanation was consistent with the political bias most frequently attributed to the court, the protection and enhancement of the position of the provinces in Canadian federalism.[50] Proof of this was found in cases favouring the provinces, or restricting federal legislation, and in the provincialist statements these cases frequently contained. Critics also pointed to the several occasions on which the Privy Council referred to the BNA Act as a compact or a treaty.[51] Further proof could be found in the speeches by Lord Haldane explicitly noting a protective attitude to the provinces, especially by his predecessor, Lord Watson.[52] Haldane's candid admissions are of special significance because of the propensity of Canadian critics to single out these two judges for particularly hostile treatment.[53] Haldane stated of Watson:

> . . . as the result of a long series of decisions, Lord Watson put clothing upon the bones of the Constitution, and so covered them over with living flesh that the Constitution of Canada took a new form. The provinces were recognized as of equal authority coordinate with the Dominion, and a long series of decisions were given by him which solved many problems and produced a new contentment in Canada with the Constitution they had got in 1867. It is difficult to say what the extent of the debt was that Canada owes to Lord Watson. . . .[54]

Haldane was also explicit that a judge on the Privy Council had "to be a statesman as well as a jurist to fill in the gaps which Parliament has deliberately left in the skeleton constitutions and laws that it has provided for the British colonies."[55] In view of these overt indications of a policy role favouring the provinces there can be no doubt that Watson and Haldane consciously fostered the provinces in Canadian federalism, and by so doing helped to transform the highly centralist structure originally created in 1867.

An alternative policy explanation deserves more extensive commentary. This was to identify the court with more or less subtlety as defenders of free enterprise against government encroachments. Spokesmen for the Canadian left, such as Woodsworth and Coldwell, were convinced that "reactionary interests have sought to shelter and to hide" behind the BNA Act.[56] F.R. Scott asserted that the "large economic interests" opposed to regulation sided with the provinces, which would be less capable of their effective regulation than would the federal government.[57] The courts, as both Scott and Professor Mallory noted, responded favourably to the protection from control that business sought.[58]

Mallory's description is apt: "The force that starts our interpretative machinery in motion is the reaction of a free economy against regulation. . . . In short the plea of *ultra vires* has been the defence impartially applied to both legislatures by a system of free enterprise concerned with preventing the government from regulating it in the public interest."[59] Business was opposed by labour, which has fought consistently for "greater Dominion jurisdiction, based on the facts of every day life as they must be met today by the Canadian working class population, looking to broader Dominion powers in questions touching the welfare of the wage earners."[60] The tactics of business and labour were pragmatic reflections of self-interest. A necessary consequence of a federal system is that each organized interest will seek to transform the most sympathetic level of government into the main decision-maker in matters which concern it. The evaluation to be put on these tactics, and the responses of the courts to them, however, is another matter. Regardless of the groups that align themselves with different levels of government at different times, it is far from clear that support for provincial authority is necessarily reactionary and support for federal authority necessarily progressive.

There is considerable evidence that influential groups in Canada, including prominent lawyers, opposed the growing regulatory role of the modern state. Sir James Aikins, founder and first president of the Canadian Bar Association, frequently spoke in satirical and hostile terms of modern legislation and the politicians who inspired it. Unlike former times, when harsh and antiquated law was softened by judicial fictions, "changes are dangerously empirical by reason of the easiness with which legislation can be secured, and the lack of comprehension in the legislator of the general principles of the law."[61] He deprecated the fact that experiments in social control had been transferred from courts to legislatures, which produce "an impromptu statute and try . . . [it] . . . out on a resigned public, amending or repealing according to the pained outcry." Legislatures, he felt, had an ephemeral membership, unlike courts or "organized law bodies." Their members were not experts in the law, "only amateurs, and their acts, too often crude and inartistic, run the gauntlet of interpretation and construction by courts and law-yers before they are put right, usually at the expense of some unfor-tunate litigant."[62] Aikins's antipathy to collectivism was shared by many. The report of the Committee on Noteworthy Changes in Statute Law in 1939 to the Canadian Bar Association expressed strong hostility to the growing role of government in the closing years of the Depression. It reported ominously on the extent of socialism in Canada and stated the belief that "private property is the pillar on which our whole civilization rests."[63] Critics of collec-tivism were disturbed by the "new despotism" of government by order-in-council and the developing authority of proliferating tri-bunals, which handled business felt to be the prerogative of the courts.[64]

In brief, collectivism, in Canada as elsewhere, had to be fought out in a variety of arenas, before mass electorates,[65] in parliaments, and in courts.[66] In each arena there were supporters and opponents of the emerging transformation in the role of public authority. The real question is not whether courts were embroiled in the contro-versy, or whether some judges sided with "reactionary" forces. It would be astonishing if such were not the case.

The important questions are more difficult and/or more precise. Were the courts more or less receptive than other elite groups to collectivism? Where did they stand in the general trend to the wel-fare, regulatory state?[67] What were the links between judges and courts and the various influential groups that appeared before them? How did the Privy Council compare with other final appeal courts, or with lower Canadian courts, in its response to collectiv-ism? Research on these questions would be extremely informative in pinning down the role of courts in the transition from the night-watchman state to the era of big government.

Supporters of the Judicial Committee

Depression criticism, followed in the next decade by the elimination of appeals, had the effect that the period in which the Privy Council was under strongest attack has probably had the greatest effect on contemporary attitudes to it. Some of the most influential academic literature dealing with judicial review comes from that period and its passions.[68] As a consequence the Privy Council has typically received a very bad press in numerous influential writings by his-torians, political scientists, and lawyers in the past forty years.

In these circumstances, it is salutary to remember that if its critics reviled it, and turned Watson and Haldane into almost stock figures of fun, the Privy Council nevertheless did have a very broad body of support. Many highly qualified and well-informed analysts gave it almost unstinting praise. Indeed, if its critics reviled it too bitterly, its supporters praised it too generously. Often they wrote in fulsome terms, replete with awe and reverence for this most distinguished court.[69]

It was described as "this splendid body of experts,"[70] as "one of the most unique tribunals in the world,"[71] as a body of judges that "possesses a weight and efficiency as a supreme Judicial tribunal unequalled in the history of judicial institutions . . . a tribunal supremely equipped for the task – equipped for it in unexampled degree."[72] In 1914 Sir Charles Fitzpatrick, the Chief Justice of Canada, claimed that "amongst lawyers and Judges competent to speak on the subject, there is but one voice, that where constitutional questions are concerned, an appeal to the Judicial Committee must be retained."[73] In 1921 the Hon. A.C. Galt, Justice of the Court of King's Bench, Manitoba, replied to the objection that the Privy Council derogated from the dignity of Canadians with the assertion that it was always sensible to employ experts. "Now it so happens that the Privy Council possesses all the advantages, as experts, to deal with legal ailments which the Mayo Brothers possess in dealing with physical ones."[74] Howard Ferguson, Premier of Ontario, ended a eulogy of the Privy Council in 1930 with special praise for Haldane, who protected "the Constitution of this country . . . giving it sane and sound interpretation. . . . In this country of ours we will ever revere the memory of that great man."[75] Another writer observed that it was neither necessary nor "in good taste" for counsel to cite authorities before the Privy Council, "as owing to the great learning and vast experience of the members of the Board, they are usually familiar with such as have a bearing on the matters in question."[76] Supporters referred in an almost bemused way to the diversity of jurisdiction, extent of territory, and range of cases it handled. "Imagination without actual experience," stated Justice Duff, "is hardly adequate to realize the infinite variety of it all. . . ."[77]

The defenders and supporters of the Judicial Committee typically intermingled judicial and imperial arguments. The alleged contribution of the board to uniformity of law between Britain and her colonies and dominions straddled both arguments,[78] while the general assertion that the court was a link of empire was explicitly imperial.[79] It was also from this vantage point – that of a British citizen across the seas – that appeals were viewed and defended as a birthright, and much sentiment was employed over the right to carry one's appeals to the foot of the throne.[80]

A reading of the eulogies of the Privy Council prior to 1930 makes it clear that its most important source of Canadian support was imperial, and only secondarily judicial. The bulk of its supporters regarded it as an instrument of Empire. Rather than viewing its dominant position in the judicial structure as a symbol of Canadian inferiority, they derived pride and dignity from the Empire of which it was a part. They were British subjects first, and Canadians second, although from their perspective there was no conflict between these two definitions. The sentiments that inspired them are well presented in a statement of Justice Riddell in 1910 in which he spoke of

. . . the idea of fundamental union in all British communities – made manifest in concrete form in one great Court of Appeal for all the lands beyond the seas . . . to me there is no more inspiring spectacle than that body of gentlemen in the dingy old room on Downing street, Westminster, sitting to decide cases from every quarter of the globe, administering justice to all under the redcross flag and symbolizing the mighty unity of an Imperial people. . . . One name we bear, one flag covers us, to one throne we are loyal; and that Court is a token of our unity.[81]

The immediately preceding set of arguments was essentially imperial. One important set of arguments, however, was jurisprudential. This was the frequently reiterated thesis that the great virtue of the Privy Council was its impartiality, a product of its distance from the scene of the controversies it adjudicated, and, unlike the Supreme Court, its absence of any direct link with either level of the governments whose interests clashed in the courtroom. In the quaint phraseology of the time, the committee was without those local prepossessions, so the argument went, which inevitably influence the decisions of local courts and thus prejudice the impartiality necessary in the judicial role.[82]

In his presidential address to the Canadian Bar Association in 1927 Sir James Aikins spoke critically of the role of the American Supreme Court in augmenting national power, a court "appointed and paid by that central government, resident in the same place and within the influence and atmosphere of Congress and the Executive, consequently removed from any contact with the capitals or governments of the several states." He went on to mention that largely similar conditions prevailed in Canada, and similar results might be expected should the Supreme Court become the final appeal court. He concluded with the rhetorical question: "will it not be in the best interests of all to have constitutional interpretation made by an Empire Court which is not appointed or paid by or in the immediate environment of one of the parties interested?"[83]

To the critics of the Privy Council, impartiality, or absence of local prepossessions, simply meant ignorance. Nevertheless, the argument is of some importance if only because of its durability. It is prominent in the contemporary debate over the Supreme Court. In recent years English Canadians have defended the Supreme Court on grounds of its impartiality, while French Canadians have criticized it on grounds of its insensitivity to their distinctive culture and special position in Canadian federalism. Further, this particular image of a good court is a reflection of one of the enduring visions of the judicial role – the blind eye of justice. It is also very close to the ideals behind the principle of judicial independence, and it is integrally related to the positivist conception of the judicial role, to the concept of the impartial third party as chairman, and to the concept of neutrality. This image, in brief, includes one of the ubiquitous central values that inevitably and properly intrudes into discussions of the role of public officials in general and judges in particular.

Sociological Justification of the Judicial Committee
The defence of the Privy Council on grounds of its impartiality and neutrality is, however, difficult to sustain in view of the general provincial bias that ran through their decisions from the 1880s. This was the most consistent basis of criticism the Judicial Committee encountered. A defence, therefore, must find some support for the general provincialist trend of its decisions.

It is impossible to believe that a few elderly men in London deciding two or three constitutional cases a year precipitated, sustained, and caused the development of Canada in a federalist direction the country would otherwise not have taken. It is evident that on occasion the provinces found an ally in the Privy Council, and that on balance they were aided in their struggles with the federal government. To attribute more than this to the Privy Council strains credulity. Courts are not self-starting institutions. They are called into play by groups and individuals seeking objectives that can be furthered by judicial support. A comprehensive explanation of judicial decisions, therefore, must include the actors who employed the courts for their own purposes.[84]

The most elementary justification of the Privy Council rests on the broad sociological ground that the provincial bias pervading so many of its decisions was in fundamental harmony with the regional pluralism of Canada. The successful assertion of this argument requires a rebuttal of the claim of many writers that the Privy Council caused the evolution of Canadian federalism away from the centralization of 1867.[85]

From the vantage point of a century of constitutional evolution the centralist emphasis of the Confederation settlement appears increasingly unrealistic. In 1867 it seemed desirable and necessary to many of the leading Fathers. "The colonial life had been petty and bitter and frictional, and, outside, the civil war seemed to point to the need of binding up, as closely as it was at all possible, the political aspirations of the colonies."[86] Further, it can be argued that what appeared as overcentralization in the light of regional pluralism was necessary to establish the new polity and to allow the central government to undertake those nation-building tasks that constituted the prime reasons for union.

It is, however, far too easily overlooked, because of the idolatry with which the Fathers and their creation are often treated, that in the long run centralization was inappropriate for the regional diversities of a land of vast extent and a large, geographically concentrated, minority culture. The political leaders of Quebec, employing varying strategies, have consistently fought for provincial autonomy. The existence of Quebec alone has been sufficient to prevent Canada from following the centralist route of some other federal systems. In retrospect, it is evident that only a peculiar conjuncture of circumstances, many of them to prove ephemeral, allowed the degree of central government dominance temporarily attained in 1867.[87]

In the old provinces of Canada and the Maritimes provincial loyalties preceded the creation of the new political system. Nova Scotia and New Brunswick were reluctant entrants into Confederation, while Lower Canada sought to obtain as much decentralization as possible. A striking series of successes for the new Dominion might have generated the national loyalty necessary to support the central government in struggles with the provinces.

Instead, the economic hopes on which so much had been placed in the movement to Confederation proved illusory and contributed to the undermining of federal prestige. Intermittent depression for most of the first thirty years of the new polity seriously eroded the flimsy supports for centralization on which Macdonald and some of his colleagues depended. The military dangers, an important original justification for a strong central government, rapidly passed away. The thrusting ambitions of provincial politicians, bent on increasing the power and resources of their jurisdictions, wrested numerous concessions from the federal government by a variety of methods, of which resort to the courts was only one. Their conduct was sustained by the almost inevitable rivalry between politicians of the two levels of government, especially when belonging to opposed political parties.[88]

The provinces, which had initially been endowed with functions of lesser significance, found that their control of natural resources gave them important sources of wealth and power, and extensive managerial responsibilities. By the decade of the twenties, highways, hydroelectric power, a host of welfare functions, and mushrooming educational responsibilities gave them tasks and burdens far beyond those anticipated in 1867. By this time the centralizing effect of the building of the railways and the settlement of the West was ended by the virtual completion of these great national purposes.

As the newer provinces west of the Great Lakes entered the union, or were created by federal legislation, they quickly developed their own identities and distinct public purposes: their populations grew; their economies expanded; their separate histories lengthened; their governmental functions proliferated; and their administrative and political competence developed. They quickly acquired feelings of individuality and a sense of power that contributed to the attenuation of federal dominance in the political system.

Only in special, unique, and temporary circumstances – typically of an emergency nature – has the federal system been oriented in a centralist direction.[89] The focus of so many Canadian academic nationalists on the central government reflected their primary concern with winning autonomy from the United Kingdom. An additional and less visible process was also taking place. Canadian political evolution has been characterized not only by nation-building but by province-building.[90] Further, it is too readily overlooked that with the passing of time Canada became more federal. In 1867 there were only four provinces in a geographically much more compact area than the nine provinces which had emerged by 1905, and the ten by 1949. If a province is regarded as an institutionalized particularism the historical development of Canada has been characterized by expansion, which has made the country more heterogeneous than hitherto.

In response to this increasingly federal society the various centralizing features of the BNA Act fell into disuse, not because their meaning was distorted by the courts, but because they were incompatible with developments in the country as a whole. In numerous areas, decentralizing developments occurred entirely on Canadian initiative, with no intervention by the Judicial Committee. The powers of reservation and disallowance were not eroded by the stupidity or malevolence of British judges but by concrete Canadian political facts. The failure to employ Section 94 of the BNA Act to render uniform the laws relating to property and civil rights in the common law provinces was not due to the prejudice of Lords Watson and Haldane but to the utopian nature of the assumptions that inspired it and the consequent failure of Canadians to exploit its centralizing possibilities.

The preceding analysis of Canadian federalism makes it evident that the provincial bias of the Privy Council was generally harmonious with Canadian developments. A more detailed investigation provides added support for this thesis.

At the time when Privy Council decisions commenced to undermine the centralism of Macdonald there was a strong growth of regional feeling. During the long premiership of Oliver Mowat, 1872-96, Ontario was involved in almost constant struggle with Ottawa. The status of the Lieutenant-Governor, the boundary dispute with Manitoba and the central government, and bitter controversies over the federal use of the power of disallowance constituted recurrent points of friction between Ottawa and Ontario. Friction was intensified by the fact that, with the exception of the brief Liberal interlude from 1873 to 1878, the governing parties at the two levels were of opposed partisan complexion, and by the fact that Mowat and Macdonald were personally hostile to each other.[91] The interprovincial conference of 1887, at which Mowat played a prominent part, indicated the general reassertion of provincialism. The "strength and diversity of provincial interests shown by the conference," in the words of the *Rowell-Sirois*

Report, "indicated that, under the conditions of the late nineteenth century, the working constitution of the Dominion must provide for a large sphere of provincial freedom."[92] Nationalism had become a strong political force in Quebec in reaction to the hanging of Riel and the failure of the newly opened West to develop along bicultural and bilingual lines. Nova Scotia was agitated by a secession movement. The Maritime provinces generally were hostile to the tariff aspects of the National Policy. Manitoba was struggling against federal railway policies. British Columbia was only slowly being drawn into the national party system after the belated completion of the CPR in 1885. It was entering a long period of struggle with the Dominion over Oriental immigration. In addition, the late eighties and early nineties constituted one of the lowest points of national self-confidence in Canadian history.[93] It was a period in which the very survival of Canada was questioned. By the late 1890s, when economic conditions had markedly improved, a new Liberal government, with provincial sympathies, was in office. The year of the much criticized Local Prohibition decision was the same year in which Laurier assumed power and commenced to wield federal authority with much looser reins than had his Conservative predecessors. "The only means of maintaining Confederation," he had declared in 1889, "is to recognize that, within its sphere assigned to it by the constitution, each province is as independent of control by the federal Parliament as the latter is from control by the provincial legislatures."[94]

The Privy Council clearly responded to these trends in a series of landmark decisions in the eighties and nineties.[95] Unfortunately, it is not possible to provide detailed information on whether or not their decisions were supported or opposed by a majority or minority of the Canadian people. What can be asserted is that provincial political elites vigorously used the courts to attain their objectives of a more decentralized federal system. Further, they apparently received widespread popular support for their judicial struggles with Ottawa.[96] Premier Mowat of Ontario, who used to go personally to London for the appeals,[97] was received as a hero on his return from his engagements with the federal government.[98] It can thus be safely asserted that the Privy Council was not acting in isolation of deeply rooted, popularly supported trends in Canada. For critics of the Judicial Committee to appeal to the centralist wishes of the Fathers is an act of perversity that denies these provincialist trends their proper weight and influence.

It would be tedious and unnecessary to provide detailed documentation of the relative appropriateness of the decisions of the Judicial Committee to subsequent centrifugal and centripetal trends in Canadian society. It can be generally said that their decisions were harmonious with those trends. Their great contribution, the injection of a decentralizing impulse into a constitutional structure too centralist for the diversity it had to contain and the placating of Quebec that was a consequence, was a positive influence in the evolution of Canadian federalism.[99] Had the Privy Council not leaned in that direction, argued P.E. Trudeau, "Quebec separatism might not be a threat today: it might be an accomplished fact."[100] The courts not only responded to provincialism. The discovery and amplification of an emergency power in Section 91 may have done an injustice to the intentions of Macdonald for the residuary power, but it did allow Canada to conduct herself virtually as a unitary state in the two world wars in which centralized government authority was both required and supported.

The general congruence of Privy Council decisions with the cyclical trends in Canadian federalism not only provides a qualified sociological defence of the committee but also makes it clear that the accusation of literalism so frequently levelled at its decisions is absurd. Watson and Haldane in particular overtly and deliberately enhanced provincial powers in partial defiance of the BNA Act itself.[101] The Privy Council's solicitous regard for the provinces constituted a defensible response to trends in Canadian society.

Prior to the great outburst of criticism against the Privy Council in the Depression of the thirties, strong approval for its decisions and their consequences was voiced by a variety of commentators. In 1909 J.M. Clark pointed out "what is too well known to require argument, namely, that the earlier decisions of our Supreme Court would have rendered our Constitution quite unworkable," a fate prevented by the existence of appeals to the Privy Council.[102] A few years later another writer praised the Privy Council for the political astuteness it combined with its legal abilities: "Better for the Canadian Constitution that the highest tribunal is composed of judges who are also politicians, rather than of lawyers who are merely judges. The British North America Act is nearly forty-nine years old and works more easily every year; the American Constitution, admittedly a more artistic but less elastic document, is daily falling behind."[103]

In 1921 another supporter strongly criticized the opponents of the Privy Council "whose interpretations have evolved for us all that is great, splendid and enduring in the Constitution under which the Dominion has flourished."[104] An unsigned, eulogistic editorial in the *Canadian Law Times* (1920) sums up the approbation with which many viewed the work of the Judicial Committee:

> I have read many of the decisions of the Privy Council relating especially to the Constitutional questions of Canada which have come before it; and I say that if it never did anything else for the purification of our legal conceptions, it has by its interpretations of the BNA Act rendered services to this country which should assure to it an abiding and grateful memory. With steady, persistent, and continuous adherence to the true lines of demarcation it has kept the Province and Dominion apart; and it has built up the Provincial fabric into a semi-sovereignty independent alike of the Dominion and of the United Kingdom. Its declarations on the Provincial Legislative powers alone are worthy of our gratitude and endless admiration. They are reverberant of that splendid independency which the several entities of Canada enjoy. These powers which the Dominion at one time thought subject to its control and doubtless would have striven to make them so, the Privy Council has declared are not delegated at all or subordinate to any authority except the Crown, but on the contrary that they are powers granted and surrendered by the Imperial Parliament directly in favor of the Legislature of each Province of Canada, and not even through the medium of the confederate Dominion.
>
> How splendid an inheritance! This is not the letter of the BNA Act but its spirit interpreted or declared for us by the Sovereign through his Privy Council in the light of aspirant freedom and of future nationhood.
>
> Well may the upholder of our Constitution who stands aghast at the invectives of the would-be demolisher of the Privy Council say: *Si quaeris monumentum circumspice.*[105]

Any plausible defence of the Privy Council must come to grips with the *cause célèbre* that more than any other indicated to its critics its incompetence and insensitivity as a final appeal court. In 1937, in a series of decisions, the Privy Council largely invalidated the New Deal legislation of the Bennett government. By so doing it indicated, to the fury of its critics, that even the emergency of a worldwide depression provided insufficient justification for central government authority to grapple with a devastating economic collapse. In these broad terms the case of the critics seems irrefutable. The New Deal decisions, more than any other, are responsible for the general hostility to the Privy Council in the literature of recent decades. The critics, however, have ignored a number of factors that place the action of the Privy Council in a much more favourable light.

The constitutionality of most of the New Deal legislation was in doubt from the moment of its inception.[106] Further, the final decisions by the courts were entirely predictable to a number of critics. Ivor Jennings's British law class "correctly forecast five of the decisions; and we were wrong on the sixth only because we took a different view of 'pith and substance.' "[107] W.P.M. Kennedy anticipated every New Deal decision but one before they went to the Supreme Court or the Privy Council.[108] The decisions therefore were not wayward, random, or haphazard. The judges did what men trained in the law expected them to do.

Any impression of an aloof court slapping down a determined Canadian leadership backed by widespread support is wrong.[109] R.B. Bennett, the initiator of the legislation, was decisively beaten in the federal election of 1935. The victor, Mackenzie King, had questioned the constitutionality of the legislation from the outset, never displayed any enthusiasm for its retention on the statute books, forwarded it willingly, almost eagerly, to the courts for their opinion, and uttered no anguished cries of rage when the decisions were announced.

In brief, the decisions were legally predictable and politically acceptable. In addition, there were extremely powerful centrifugal forces operating in the Depression. Hepburn in Ontario, Duplessis in Quebec, and Aberhart in Alberta symbolized the developing regionalism unleashed by massive economic breakdown. French-Canadian separatists loudly resisted the claim that the Depression could only be fought by centralization.[110] In these circumstances it is at least arguable that the political situation of the time was scarcely the most apposite for the enhancement of federal authority. The centralist bias of the critics ignored this fact. They unquestioningly assumed that the scale and nature of the problems facing the Canadian people could only be handled by the central government, and that no other considerations mattered. The critics were supported by the contribution of the Statute of Westminster in 1931 to Canadian autonomy. They were also encouraged by the dramatic development of "an astonishing number of voluntary, non-political, national associations" dealing with social, cultural, and intellectual affairs.[111] Given these factors the critics' position is understandable and defensible. Equally so, however, is the conduct of the Privy Council. The real controversy is not over the performance of the Judicial Committee but over the proper criteria for the evaluation of judicial decisions.

The Weakness of the Judicial Committee

The Judicial Committee laboured under two fundamental weaknesses, the legal doctrine that ostensibly guided its deliberations, and its isolation from the setting to which those deliberations referred.

The basic overt doctrine of the court was to eschew considerations of policy and to analyse the BNA Act by the standard canons for the technical construction of ordinary statutes. The objection to this approach is manifold. Numerous legal writers have pointed out that the rules of statutory construction are little more than a grab bag of contradictions. It is also questionable whether a constitution should be treated as an ordinary statute, for clearly it is not. In the British political system, with which judges on the Privy Council were most acquainted, it is at least plausible to argue that the doctrine of parliamentary supremacy, and the consequent flexibility of the legislative process, provides some justification for the courts limiting their policy role and assigning to Parliament the task of keeping the legislation of the state appropriate to constantly changing circumstances. The BNA Act, however, as a written constitutional document, was not subject to easy formal change by the amending process. Consequently, the premise that the transformation of the Act could be left to lawmaking bodies in Canada, as in the United Kingdom, was invalid. A candid policy role for a final appeal court seems to be imperatively required in such conditions.

Even in the absence of this consideration it is self evident that no technical analysis of an increasingly ancient constitutional document can find answers to questions undreamt of by the Fathers. The Privy Council's basic legal doctrine was not only undesirable, therefore, it was also impossible. In reality, as already indicated, the Privy Council obliquely pursued a policy of protecting the provinces. The clear divergence between the Act as written and the Act as interpreted makes it impossible to believe that in practice the Privy Council viewed its role in the narrow, technical perspective of ordinary statutory construction. The problem of the court was that it was caught in an inappropriate legal tradition for its task of constitutional adjudication. It partially escaped from this dilemma by occasionally giving overt recognition to the need for a more flexible, pragmatic approach, and by covertly masking its actual policy choices behind the obfuscating language and precedents of statutory interpretations.

The covert pursuit of policy meant that the reasoning process in their decisions was often inadequate to sustain the decision reached. This also helps to explain the hypocritical and forced distinguishing of previous cases criticized by several authors.[112] Further, the impossibility of overt policy discussion in decisions implied the impossibility of open policy arguments in proceedings before the court. Inevitably, the court experienced severe handicaps in its role as policy-maker.

Caught in an unworkable tradition the Judicial Committee was unable to answer the basic question of constitutional jurisprudence, that is, how it should apply the discretion it unavoidably possessed. The application of a constitution to novel conditions provides a court with the opportunity for creative statesmanship. To this challenge the Judicial Committee evolved no profound theories of its own role. Its most basic answer was silence, supplemented by isolated statements of principle dealing with the federal system and occasional liberal statements concerning its role in contributing to the growth and evolution of the constitution. The confusion in Privy Council philosophy was cogently described by MacDonald:

> Uncertainty and inconsistency in . . . matters which lie at the very threshold of the problem of interpretation have played a large part in making the ascertainment of the meaning of the Canadian constitution the precarious task that it is today; for the chief element of predictability of legal decision inheres in a known and uniform technique of approach. It is a prime criticism of the Privy Council that it has had no uniform technique of approach to the act; for it has sought now the intention of the framers of the act, now the meaning of its terms; sometimes excluding, sometimes being influenced by, extraneous matters, and sometimes interpreting the terms of the act as speaking eternally in the tongue of 1867, and sometimes in the language of contemporary thought and need.[113]

The second main weakness of the Privy Council was its isolation from the scene to which its judgements applied. Its supporters argued otherwise by equating its distance from Canada with impartiality. Judges on the spot, it was implied, would be governed or influenced by the passions and emotions surrounding the controversy before them. British judges, by contrast, aloof and distant, would not be subject to the bias flowing from intimate acquaintance.

The logic of this frequently espoused position was curious. The same logic, as J.S. Ewart satirically observed, implied the desirability of sending British cases to the Supreme Court at Ottawa, but no such proposals were forthcoming. "Local information and local methods," he continued, "are very frequently essential to the understanding of a dispute. They are not disqualifications for judicial action."[114]

The critics were surely right in their assertions that absence of local prepossessions simply meant relative ignorance, insensitivity, and misunderstanding of the Canadian scene, deficiencies that would be absent in Canadian judges. "The British North America Act," Edward Blake had asserted in 1880, "is a skeleton. The true form and proportions, the true spirit of our Constitution, can be made manifest only to the men of the soil. I deny that it can be well expounded by men whose lives have been passed, not merely in another, but in an opposite sphere of practice. . . ."[115] The same argument was reiterated by succeeding generations of critics until the final elimination of appeals.[116]

The weakness flowing from isolation was exacerbated by the shifting composition of the committee, which deprived its members of those benefits of experience derived from constant application to the same task. "The personnel of that Court," stated a critic in 1894, "is as shifting as the Goodwin Sands. At one sitting it may be composed of the ablest judges in the land, and at the next sitting its chief characteristic may be senility and general weakness."[117] This instability of membership contributed to discontinuities in interpretation as membership changed. It also allowed those who sat for long periods of time, as did Watson and Haldane, to acquire disproportionate influence on Privy Council decisions.

The professed legal philosophy of the Judicial Committee helped explain away the disadvantages allegedly flowing from isolation, by stressing the mechanical, technical, legal character of the judicial task. This minimized the advantages of local understanding for judges. Conversely, the position of the critics was strengthened when they stressed the policy component in judicial interpretation. While a plausible case might be made that technical, legal matters could be handled as well, or even better, by a distant court, the same argument could scarcely be made of policy matters, where local understanding was obviously of first-rate importance. It necessarily followed that the Supreme Court of Canada, composed of men thoroughly conversant with Canadian social and political conditions, had a greater capacity to be a more sophisticated and sensitive court of appeal.

The understanding of Canadian politics held by British judges was well summarized by a sympathetic observer, Jennings:

> The Atlantic separates them from the political disputes of Canada. Their information about the controversies of the Dominion is obtained from the summary cables of the London press, which is far more interested in problems nearer home. If Mr. Dooley came to London he could not say that the Judicial Committee followed the Canadian election returns. Unless their functions make them particularly interested in Canadian news, they are probably as uncertain of the politics of the governments in power as is the average Englishman. The controversies which appear to them to be merely legal disputes as to the meaning of Sections 91 and 92 of the Act often have a background of party strife and nice political compromises. The judges may know enough to realize that politics are involved, but not enough to appreciate exactly why and how.[118]

These considerations add a special cogency to Vincent MacDonald's plea for abolition of appeals on the ground that "even in matters of dry law decision is affected by the national character and personal background of the judiciary." One could not ignore, he continued, "the temperament, the experience, the social background and training of the final court," especially when interpretation dealt with policy matters.[119] Tuck's argument was equally to the point:

> Resort to the Privy Council is unnecessary where the two tribunals agree; and where they disagree, since constitutional interpretation turns largely on matters of policy, its development would be best directed by a Canadian court with first-hand experience of Canadian conditions and needs. The Privy Council, with its constantly shifting personnel, working always at a distance from

the scene of operations, is hardly the appropriate body for this kind of work. . . . It is unlikely, therefore, that the board will ever be thoroughly familiar with the spirit of the Canadian constitution, or the environment necessary to its successful working.[120]

Given the difficulties that inevitably flowed from its London location, and given the sterilities of the legal tradition it espoused, the decisions of the Privy Council were remarkably appropriate for the Canadian environment. The Privy Council, in its wisdom, was partially able to overcome some of the dangers caused by its own ignorance. That it did so imperfectly was only to be expected. Watson and Haldane have been criticized by McWhinney on the ground that if they were consciously influenced "by a bias in favour of provincial powers, their approach seems nevertheless to have been a vague, impressionistic one, without the benefit of a detailed analysis and weighing of the policy alternatives involved in each case."[121] Essentially the same criticism is made by MacGuigan, who criticizes the abstract natural law approach adopted by the Privy Council in coming to its policy decisions. They were policy-makers without the necessary tools of understanding.[122] These criticisms, while valid, reflect failings that were inevitable for a body of men who adjudicated disputes emanating from the legal systems of a large part of the world, and who could not be expected to become specialists in the shifting socio-economic contexts in which each legal system was embedded.[123] This particular weakness could not be overcome by a body of British judges. If local knowledge was a necessary attribute of a good court, the Privy Council could only be a second-best interim arrangement.

The context in which the Privy Council existed deprived it of the continual feedback of relevant information on which wise and sensitive judging depends. Superficially this could be described as a deficiency of local knowledge. This deficiency, however, is sufficiently complex and important to require elaboration.

An effective court does not exist in a vacuum. It is part of a complicated institutional framework for the amelioration of the human condition through the device of law in individual nation-states. Law is unavoidably national. It cannot be otherwise as long as the basic political unit is the nation-state. Laws are not designed for men in general, but for Canadians, Americans, Germans, etc. Within these national frameworks a variety of procedures has been developed to make law sensitive to the needs of particular communities. This is readily recognized and admitted for legislatures and executives. For courts, however, the attributes of objectivity and impartiality, combined with the status of judicial independence, tend to distract attention from the task similarity between judges and legislators. Both, however, are concerned with the applicability of particular laws to particular communities. There is consequently an important overlap in their mutual requirements. Both must be provided with the institutional arrangements that facilitate an adequate flow of the relevant information for their specific tasks.

A strong and effective court requires a variety of supporters. It must be part of a larger system that includes first-class law schools, quality legal journals, and an able and sensitive legal fraternity – both teaching and practising. These are the minimum necessary conditions for a sophisticated jurisprudence, without which a distinguished judicial performance is impossible. Unless judges can be made aware of the complexities of their role as judicial policy-makers and sensitively cognizant of the societal effects of their decisions, a first-rate judicial performance will only occur intermittently and fortuitously. In brief, unless judges exist in a context that informs their understanding in the above manner, they are deprived of the guidance necessary for effective decision-making. Most of the conditions required as supports for a first-class court were only imperfectly realized in Canada prior to the abolition of appeals to the Privy Council. A shifting body of British judges, domiciled in London, whose jurisdiction covered a large part of the habitable globe, existed in limbo. This isolation of the court not only reduced its sensitivity to Canadian conditions but rendered it relatively free from professional and academic criticism.[124] A related part of the problem was noted by Ewart in his observation that the Privy Council either had the assistance of English barristers devoid of an intimate understanding of Canadian circumstances, or "Canadian barristers, who speak from one standpoint and are listened to from another."[125]

The position of the Judicial Committee at the apex of a structure of judicial review of global extent virtually necessitated the conceptualizing approach found offensive to so many of its critics. The court was not, and could not be, adequately integrated into a network of communication and criticism capable of transmitting the nuances and subtleties a first-class appeal court required.

The single opinion of the court, while it possibly helped to sustain its authority and weaken the position of its critics,[126] had serious negative effects. Jennings pointed out that "the absence of a minority opinion sometimes makes the opinion of the Board look more logical and more obvious than it really is. The case is stated so as to come to the conclusion already reached by the majority in private consultation. It is often only by starting again and deliberately striving to reach the opposite conclusion that we realize that . . . there were two ways of looking at it."[127] The absence of dissents hindered the development of a dialogue over the quality of its judgements. Dissents provide a lever for the critic by their indication of a lack of judicial unanimity, and by their provision of specific alternatives to the decisions reached. Unanimity of its published opinion thus made its own contribution to the isolation of the court. In addition, as a final appeal court, it had "no dread of a higher judicial criticism."[128] Finally, much of the debate that swirled around its existence and performance was so inextricably intertwined with the larger controversy between nationalism and imperialism that the question of the judicial quality of its task was not faced head on. These extraneous considerations partly account for the extremes in the evaluations made of the court, ranging between "undiscriminating praise and . . . over-criticism."[129]

The Confusion of the Critics

For the better part of a century the performance of the Judicial Committee has been a continuing subject of academic and political controversy in Canada. Even the elementary question of whether its work was basically good or fundamentally bad has elicited contrary opinions. The distribution of favourable and critical attitudes has shifted over time. From the turn of the century until the onset of the Depression of the thirties, informed opinion was generally favourable. Subsequently, English-Canadian appraisals became overwhelmingly critical. It is a reasonable speculation, sustained by Browne's recent volume,[130] by the contemporary strength of regional forces in Canadian society, and by the fact that Canadian judicial autonomy is now in its third decade, that more favourable evaluations of the Judicial Committee will begin to appear. For example, the Labour Conventions case (1937), which so aroused the ire of the critics who feared the emasculation of Candian treaty-making, now seems to present a defensible proposition in contemporary Canadian federalism.

In the period up to and subsequent to the final abolition of appeals in 1949 there was a consistent tendency for opposed evaluations of the Judicial Committee to follow the French-English cleavage in Canada.[131] This divergence of opinion was manifest in French-Canadian support for the Judicial Committee,[132] with opposition on grounds of nationalism and its provincial bias largely found in English Canada. Many English-Canadian writers hoped that the Supreme Court, as a final appeal court, would adopt a liberal, flexible interpretation, eroding at least in part the debilitating influence of *stare decisis*. In practical terms, their pleas for a living tree approach presupposed a larger role for the central government than had developed under the interpretations of the Judicial Committee. In essence, one of the key attitudes of the predominantly English-Canadian abolitionists was to view a newly independent Supreme Court as an agent of centralization.[133] The very reasons and justifications that tumble forth in English-Canadian writings caused insecurity and apprehension in French Canada, which feared, simply, that if English-Canadian desires were translated into judicial facts the status and influence of the provinces fostered by British judges would be eroded.[134] The American-style Supreme Court sought by the constitutionalist critics of the Privy Council was justifiably viewed with apprehension by French-Canadian observers. They assumed, not unfairly, that if such a court heeded the bias of its proponents it would degenerate into an instrument for the enhancement of national authority. These contrary English and French hopes and fears are closely related to the present crisis of legitimacy of the Supreme Court.

An additional significant cleavage in Canadian opinion was between those fundamentalist critics who opposed the Judicial Committee for its failure to provide a technically correct interpretation of a clearly worded document and the constitutionalists who castigated it for its failure to take a broad, flexible approach to its task.

The fundamentalist approach, already discussed, imposed on the courts the task of faithfully interpreting a document in terms of the meanings deliberately embodied in it by the Fathers of Confederation. This approach was replete with insuperable difficulties:

1. If the task of the courts was to provide a literally correct interpretation of the agreement of 1867 it is possible to differ on the degree of their success or failure. The standard interpretation adhered to by MacDonald, O'Connor, and numerous others is that

the performance of the Judicial Committee, from this perspective, was an abject failure. Recently, however, a new analysis by Professor G.P. Browne has lauded the Privy Council for the consistency of its interpretation and has categorically asserted that refined textual analysis of Sections 91 and 92 indicates that they were given a proper judicial interpretation. According to Browne, British judges were not acting out a bias in favour of the provinces, but were simply applying the logic of the BNA Act to the legal controversies that came before them for adjudication.[135] Browne's revisionist thesis has been both praised and harshly criticized.[136] Its truth, if such a word can be applied to such a subject as constitutional interpretation, is not germane to our purposes.[137] What is germane is the fact that a century after Confederation the question of the technically correct interpretation of the Act can still produce violently opposed positions among serious, competent scholars. One is tempted to ask if the pursuit of the real meaning of the Act is not a meaningless game, incapable of a decisive outcome.[138]

2. There is controversy over the relationship between the intentions of the Fathers and the BNA Act they created. The centralist argument is that the Fathers both intended and produced a centralized federal system. It has, however, been asserted by Professor Philippe Ferland that there is a discrepancy between the intentions and the result. This approach claims that the pre-Confederation statements of the Fathers favoured a legislative decentralization, but they drafted a text that devoured the provinces. The judges then, according to Ferland, concentrated on the text, ignored the external evidence, and thus damaged the interests of the provinces.[139] It is impossible to overlook the fact that here, as elsewhere, legal scholars have displayed an ingenious ability to locate evidence for the kind of intentions they sought.

3. LaBrie noted that even if it could be assumed that the Fathers of Confederation did have views on the newer areas of government, "there remains the question whether, in the light of our own greater experience in the problems of federal government, these intentions ought to rule us at the present day."[140] By implication the fundamentalists attempted to tie succeeding generations of Canadians down to the constitutional assumptions of a small body of men in the 1860s. For a completely static society, in which the original settlement was perfectly suited to existing social values and needs, such an approach has some plausibility. But as society changes, it seems evident that the faint glimmers of insights of the Fathers

should be overruled by the more comprehensive understandings of their successors. Literalism, consequently, is an inadequate guide for judges. This was tacitly admitted by those fundamentalist critics who applied their literalism to the division of powers, but often proudly noted the flexibility of other portions of the Act. They were, for example, happy to accept the evolving conventions that transformed the roles of the Governor General and the Lieutenant-Governor. They tended to be literalist only when it suited their purposes.

Further, literalism, either as a description of what judges can or should do, is so clearly preposterous that its frequent employment as a tactic of criticism is, to say the least, surprising. M.R. Cohen's comment dealing with judicial review in the United States is no less applicable to Canada: "The pretence that every decision of the Supreme Court follows logically from the Constitution must . . . be characterized as a superstition. No rational argument can prove that when the people adopted the Constitution they actually intended all the fine distinctions which the courts have introduced into its interpretation. Nor can we well deny the fact that judges have actually differed in their interpretations. . . ."[141]

4. Most obvious, and noted by various writers, was the fact that the new and developing areas of government activity, where uncertainty was greatest, could not be fitted into the intentions of a previous generation ignorant of the problems involved.[142] The courts themselves have had to recognize the novelty of the issues they frequently encounter. When the Privy Council faced the question of whether a Canadian legislature could regulate appeals, the judgement stated that "it is . . . irrelevant that the question is one that might have seemed unreal at the date of the British North America Act."[143]

5. It can be argued that the relevant intentions of the Fathers include not only their specific intentions for the Canadian political system as they visualized it in 1867, but also their attitudes to the possibility that future generations might wish to transform the nature of their creation. Lord Haldane, for example, argued that the Fathers intended the courts to work out the constitution.[144]

6. The question of the intentions of the Fathers is part of the larger controversy over the desirability of going beyond the wording of the Act to a variety of pre-Confederation material that conceivably could throw light on its meaning.[145] Many critics recommended the use of the historical material surrounding Confed-

eration as an aid to interpretation. Others asserted that not only was it the custom of the courts to exclude such materials, but that they were correct in doing so.[146] They agreed with Lord Sankey in the Edwards case that in interpreting the BNA Act "the question is not what may be supposed to have been intended, but what has been said."[147] Evan Gray, a critic of O'Connor, asserted that all pre-Confederation material "is illusory and inconclusive. It is not merely because a rigid rule of legal procedure binds our courts that we reject such material, but because as a matter of common sense we know that any other method of enquiry is unreliable, being speculative rather than logical and adding to uncertainty instead of resolving it."[148] The use of such materials was also undesirable, according to Vincent MacDonald, because the tying down of interpretation to the intentions of the Fathers "allows the horizon of that year [1867] to restrict the measures of the future." It was wiser, he argued, to interpret the words of the statute, which allowed flexibility and the incorporation of new meanings.[149]

The use of pre-Confederation material to document the intentions of the Fathers as an aid to interpretation would not have improved the Privy Council's performance. In addition to the much greater ambiguity of pre-Confederation speeches and resolutions compared to the BNA Act itself, their use is subject to all the criticisms of those who resist the binding of future generations by the restricted foresight of their predecessors. A living constitution incorporates only so much of the past as appears viable in the light of new conditions. A further weakness of the use of pre-Confederation material is that its contribution to understanding the BNA Act was greatest at the general level of the nature of the Act as a whole, and weakest in the more specific areas covered by constitutional cases. It is significant that critics of the Privy Council tended to focus on pre-Confederation statements about the nature of the political system as a whole. Judges inevitably interpreted particular powers rather than the entire BNA Act, "because there was no machinery for the interpretation of the constitution as such."[150]

In summary, the intellectual rigour of the fundamentalist critics of the Privy Council leaves much to be desired. Their case is destroyed by its essential shallowness.

The constitutionalist critics of the Privy Council based themselves on a much more promising normative and analytic stand. They welcomed and recognized a policy role for the courts in judicial review. They appreciated both the impossibility and undesirability of complete fidelity to a statute conceived in former times by men who lacked the gift of foresight. To this extent, they were judicial realists. They could easily document, when so inclined, the inevitable policy content of judicial decisions and by so doing could puncture the slot machine theory of law. This was their achievement. Their recognition of a policy-making role helped to initiate normative discussions on what a final appeal court should do with the discretion inherent in its task.[151] However, their own prescriptive statements were frequently shallow and seldom placed in a carefully articulated philosophy of the judicial role. An important contributing reason for the inadequacy of their normative contribution was that they were not clearly distinguished in policy objectives from the fundamentalists. Unlike the United States, where the advocates of strict constitutional construction were usually state rightists,[152] Canadian centralists could and did find in the 1867 agreement constitutional support for their position. Thus the distinctions between the constitutionalists and the fundamentalists were blurred by the fact that both were centralists.[153] Constitutionalists, accordingly, could always fall back on literalist justifications for their centralist policy position. They were not therefore under an obligation to prescribe a carefully defined policy justification, either for their centralization or for the role of the court in helping to attain it. They thus lapsed into uncritical support for centralization on the general ground that it was required by the needs of the time.[154] This, however, as B.N. Cardozo pointed out, is not even the beginning of judicial philosophy:

> I have no quarrel, therefore, with the doctrine that judges ought to be in sympathy with the spirit of their times. Alas! assent to such a generality does not carry us far upon the road to truth. In every court there are likely to be as many estimates of the "Zeitgeist" as there are judges on its bench. . . . The spirit of the age, as it is revealed to each of us, is too often only the spirit of the group in which the accidents of birth or education or occupation or fellowship have given us a place. No effort or revolution of the mind will overthrow utterly and at all times the empire of these subconscious loyalties.[155]

The critics did not develop a consistent and meaningful definition of the judicial role in constitutional review. The much maligned Judicial Committee was criticized on two mutually exclusive grounds.[156] The fundamentalists, fluctuating back and forth between the Act itself and pre-Confederation material, charged it with departing from the clear meaning of the Act and the obvious intent of its framers. The constitutionalists, concerned with policy, charged it with a failure to interpret the Act in the flexible manner appropriate to a constitutional document. Their policy approach tended to be based on whether or not a given decision, or series of decisions, agreed with their values, which usually meant whether or not it facilitated government action regarded as desirable, or inihibited government action regarded as undesirable. The fundamentalists castigated the Privy Council for reaching decisions that every historian knew to be untrue, the very kind of decision the logic of the constitutionalists invited the bench to make. The fundamentalists demanded a technically correct performance of a mechanical act, the interpretation of a clearly worded document. The constitutionalists appealed less to the Act than to the contemporary conditions to which it was to be applied. While they did not write off the BNA Act as irrelevant, the constitutionalists tended to be hostile when the Act, or its judicial interpretation, stood in the way of their objectives. Their prime purpose was to allow the federal government to grapple with problems they deemed to be beyond provincial competence, or which they expected provincial governments to handle in some undesirable way. The simultaneous or sequential employment of these divergent fundamentalist and constitutionalist rationales was effective as a debating device. It was productive of great confusion over the basic question of the proper role for the court.

The critics of the Judicial Committee were moved more by the passions of nationalism and desires for centralization than by federalism. By the mid-thirties the two main perspectives on the judicial role agreed that the Act, as interpreted, was increasingly irrelevant to the environment to which it applied. Both groups of critics "took it as axiomatic that the application of the appropriate techniques of interpretation of the BNA Act, whether in the form of a larger dose of knowledgeable judicial statesmanship or greater fidelity to the true meaning of the constitutional text, could only be achieved by transferring the highest judicial power from English to Canadian judges."[157] Both groups of critics were centralists, although they found different constitutional justifications for their position. Neither group wrote favourably of the provinces, or expected much of them. They pinned their hopes on Ottawa. They shared Underhill's evaluation of the provinces: "The only province," he wrote in 1931, "which has not been subject to the regular alternation between short periods of comparatively good government and long periods of decay is Quebec. In Quebec they enjoy bad government all the time."[158] The critics assumed that industrial, technological, urban, or some other set of conditions required centralization. They stressed the difficulties of divided jurisdiction as barriers to the effective regulation of an interdependent economy. They placed great emphasis on the national structure of an economy no longer capable of meaningful delimitation by provincial boundaries. They assumed economic forces to be uncompromisingly centralist and never regionalist in impact. They shared Laski's thesis that federalism was obsolete, paid little attention to the varying kinds of pluralism rooted in non-economic factors, and were hostile to the institutional arrangements that preserved and protected federalism. They were prone to stress the national-local distinction as crucial to the proper understanding of the BNA Act, and thus they tended to employ a national dimension or general-interest justification for federal legislation. This was an approach to which French Canadians took strong exception because of its obvious threat to provincial autonomy.[159]

The really dramatic cleavage between the supporters and opponents, especially the constitutionalists, of the Privy Council was, as hinted above, in their opposition over the kinds of non-legal facts that should be of significance in constitutional adjudication. The supporters stressed either the governmental pluralism of the federal system or the underlying, regionally grouped diversities on which it was deemed to be based. Judicial decisions that protected and fostered this pluralism were praised. Judicial interpretation hostile to pluralism was opposed. The constitutionalists, by contrast, downplayed the significance of pluralism, which they frequently saw as a cover for vested interests seeking to avoid regulation. To them the paramount extra-legal factors were the ties of economic and technical interdependence and the corporate power behind them. These, by implication, had either undermined the sociological supports for pluralism or, by generating problems of national importance or scope that imperatively required central government authority for their resolution, had reduced pluralism to secondary significance.

There is no easy way by which these contrary definitions of relevant extra-legal facts can be categorized as more or less true. Both provided plausible justifications for the kind of federal system their advocates sought and the kind of judicial review required to achieve or sustain it.

Several speculations are in order. With the passage of time since 1867, ties of interdependence have been generated and have helped to knit the Canadian economy together. It seems clear, however, that an economic interpretation of Canadian history which presupposes that this economic interdependence has undermined pluralist values is largely wrong. Canadians have remained pluralist in spite of economic change.

Economic interdependence is an omnibus concept that conceals as much as it reveals. To the extent that it does exist it is not always seen as beneficial by all the parties caught in it. The National Policy incorporated the Prairies into the Canadian economy in a manner that has generated disaffection ever since Manitoba began to fight the railway monopoly of the CPR shortly after being constituted as a province. French-Canadian politicians have not been notably pleased with a system of interdependence in which capital and management were English and the workers were French.

The concept of interdependence is thus too general to be helpful in describing the nature of the Canadian economy or the kinds of political authority necessary to manage it. The concept also contributes to a disregard for the distinctive nature of the regional economies that have grown since Confederation. The importance of provincial control of natural resources and the foreign markets to which these resources are sent sustain distinct regional or provincial interests frequently hostile to a national approach. The nature of the Canadian economy has never been such as to offer unequivocal support for central government authority.

It is also probable that the alleged disastrous effects of Privy Council support for the provinces have been exaggerated. In recent years, at least, the provinces, particularly the larger and wealthier ones, have not been the impotent units of government that critics of the Privy Council assumed. They are neither synonyms for reaction nor backwaters of ineptitude. In the long view judicial support for the provinces has contributed to the formation of competent governments. It is also clear that the paralysing effect of judicial decisions on the federal government has been overstressed. For a decade and a half after the Second World War Canada was run in a highly centralist fashion despite nearly a century of judicial interpretation that was claimed to have reduced Ottawa to a powerless nonentity. Judicial review scarcely seems to have been as important a determinant of constitutional evolution as has often been imagined. Professor Corry has indeed speculated that judicial interpretation adverse to Ottawa precipitated the "spectacular refinement of the techniques of economic and fiscal powers after the war" on which post-war centralization was based. "Perhaps the Privy Council interpretations have, in the sequel, pushed effective centralization further and faster than it would otherwise have gone."[160]

Professor McWhinney is critical of the quality of the controversy over the Privy Council because it too frequently proceeded "in the form of a dispute over alternative rules of statutory construction, rather than in terms of the actual consequences to Canadian national life flowing from the individual decisions."[161] This is neither entirely true nor entirely fair. At bottom, the critics, of whatever school, were motivated by a concern for the consequences of constitutional interpretation. Especially in the Depression of the thirties, the perceived consequences of the New Deal decisions aroused their ire.

Hostility to the Judicial Committee was fed by the inability of Canadians to develop an amending procedure to facilitate transfers of power from the provinces to the central government. In this situation the courts were viewed as the last resort. When they failed to respond to the challenge in the thirties, their critics retaliated with passionate hostility as the federal system appeared impotent when confronted with economic breakdown and social dislocation. In general, criticisms resulted from an antipathy to the negative effects of Privy Council decisions on the capacity of Canadians to pursue certain objectives. The Privy Council left Canadians, in the phrase of one critic, with a "hardly workable polity."[162] In area after area, argued the critics, the situation was intolerable in terms of administrative efficiency, the scope of the problem, or the power of the interests requiring regulation.[163]

The constitutionalists, in particular, were much concerned with the consequences of judicial decisions. They inevitably sought legal justification for the decisions they favoured, but they can scarcely be faulted for that. They were simply playing the game in the accustomed manner. As indicated above, they exaggerated both the harmful consequences of the decisions and the role of the Judicial Committee in the evolution of Canadian federalism. They cannot, however, be criticized for a lack of concern with policy. Their chief weakness lies elsewhere, in their failure to produce a consistent, comprehensive definition of what can legitimately be expected from a particular institution, a definition necessarily related to the specific task of that institution in the complex of institutions that make up the political system as a whole. In a discussion of the Privy Council's handling of the New Deal, A.B. Keith asserted that from a "juristic point of view" he was able to accord "cordial appreciation" to the decisions. It was, he continued, a "completely different question" whether the constitution was an apt instrument for the solution of new problems; but this, he concluded, was "a work for the statesmen and people of the Dominion, and not for any court."[164] The particular distinction made by Keith may or may not be valid. What is relevant is that he made a distinction. It is not necessary to fall into the textbook simplification between those who make the laws, those who administer them, and those who interpret them to suggest that different institutions are entrusted with different tasks. The failure to make any kind of differentiation denies the validity of the institutional division of political labour painfully evolved over centuries of Western history. To blame the milkman for not delivering bread or the doctor for the mistakes of the laundryman is a recipe for chaos. The basic, prior, and determining question is simply what can properly be expected of judicial review. In a constitutional system the function of judicial review must be more than simply allowing desirable policies to be implemented by whatever level of government so wishes. A worthwhile court of final appeal is bound on occasion to prevent one level of government from doing what a group of temporary incumbents or its supporters would like to do. Criticism of a court based on the fact that is has prevented a desirable objective from being attained is not good enough. Like the American legal realists, with whom the constitutionalists had some affinity, Canadian critics were effective at the task of demolition and weak at telling the judge what he should do.[165]

In sum, Canadian jurisprudence was deeply divided on the question of the relevant criteria for the guidance of judges in the difficult process of constitutional interpretation. Neither critics nor supporters of the Judicial Committee were able to develop consistent and defensible criteria for judicial review. Admittedly, Canadians were not alone in their confusion. Professor Corry asserted in 1939 that "one would have to search far to find a more confused portion of the English law" than "the rules to be followed in interpreting statutes and constitutions." He continued:

The text writers and judges all insist that the basic rule is to find the "expressed intention" of the makers of the constitution and that, in the case of constitutions, this intention is to be liberally rather than narrowly construed. The trouble is that constitutions often do not have "expressed intentions" about many of the situations to which they must be applied. The Fathers of Confederation could not express any intention about aviation and radio. At best then, in such circumstances, the court can only argue by analogy, making inferences as to what the framers would have said if they had thought about the problem. Even then, there are numerous situations where no compelling inferences can be found by logical processes. Nor does it help to propose that the constitution should be liberally construed, for one must still ask for what purpose and to what end. Liberal construction of Dominion power is, at the same time, strict construction of provincial power and *vice versa*.[166]

In brief, if the performance of the Privy Council was, as its critics suggested, replete with inconsistencies and insensitivity, the confused outpourings of the critics displayed an incoherence completely inadequate to guide judges in decision-making. To contrast the performance of the Judicial Committee with the performance of its opponents is to ignore the dissimilarity of function between artist and critic. It is clear, however, that the Judicial Committee was much more sensitive to the federal nature of Canadian society than were the critics. From this perspective at least the policy output of British judges was far more harmonious with the underlying pluralism of Canada than were the confused prescriptive statements of her opponents.[167] For those critics, particularly on the left, who wished to transform society, this qualified defence of the Judicial Committee will lack conviction. However, such critics have an obligation not only to justify their objectives but also the role they advocated for a non-elected court in helping to attain them.

Whether the decline in the problem-solving capacity of governments in the federal system was real or serious enough to support the criticism the Privy Council encountered involves a range of value judgements and empirical observations of a very complex nature. The purpose of this paper has been only to provide documentation for the minimum statement that a strong case can be made for the Judicial Committee, and to act as a reminder that the basic question was jurisprudential, a realm of discussion in which neither the Privy Council, its critics, nor its supporters proved particularly illuminating.

The Abolition of Appeals and an Inadequate Jurisprudence

It is valid, if somewhat perverse, to argue that the weakness and confusion of Canadian jurisprudence constituted one of the main justifications for ending appeals to the Privy Council. The attainment of judicial autonomy was a prerequisite for a first-class Canadian jurisprudence.[168] Throughout most of the period of judicial subordination the weaknesses in Canadian legal education produced a lack of self-confidence and a reluctance to abolish appeals.[169] As long as the final court of appeal was an alien body the jurisprudence that did exist was entangled with the emotional contest of nationalism and imperialism, a mixture that deflected legal criticism into side issues. In these circumstances the victory of nationalism was a necessary preliminary to the development of an indigenous jurisprudence that has gathered momentum in the past two decades.

It is also likely that the quality of judicial performance by Canadian courts was hampered by subordination to the Privy Council. The existence of the Privy Council undermined the credibility of the Supreme Court and inhibited the development of its status and prestige. The Supreme Court could be overruled by a superior, external court. In many cases it was bypassed as litigants appealed directly from a provincial court to the Privy Council. Finally, the doctrine of *stare decisis* bound the Supreme Court to the decisions of its superior, the Privy Council. The subject status of the Supreme Court and other Canadian courts was further exacerbated by the absence of dissents, which reduced the potential for flexibility of lower courts in subsequent cases. In spite of the quality of its performance the dominant position of the Privy Council in the Canadian judicial hierarchy was an anomaly, incompatible with the evolving independence of Canada in other spheres, and fraught with too many damaging consequences for its elimination to be regretted.

The inadequate jurisprudence, the legacy of nearly a century of judicial subordination, which accompanied the attainment of judicial autonomy in 1949, has harmfully affected the Supreme Court in the last two decades. The Supreme Court, the law schools, the legal profession, and the political elites have been unable to devise an acceptable role for the court in Canadian federalism. Shortly after the court attained autonomy the institutional fabric of the Canadian polity, the court included, began to experience serious questioning and challenges to its existence. The Diefenbaker Bill of Rights was succeeded by the Quiet Revolution with its confrontation between rival conceptions of federalism and coexistence. Additional uncertainty has been generated by the proposed Trudeau Charter, which, if implemented, will drastically change the significance of the judiciary in our constitutional system. In the unlikely event that a significantly different BNA Act emerges from the present constitutional discussions, the court will face the task of imparting meaning to a new constitutional document delineating a division of powers different from the existing division. To these factors, as indications of the shifting world of judicial review, can be added the possibility that the court may be reconstituted with a new appointment procedure, with a specific entrenched status, and perhaps even as a special court confined to constitutional questions.

It would be folly to suggest that the above problems would not exist if Canadian jurisprudence had been more highly developed. Their source largely lies beyond the confines of the legal system. On the other hand, the confused state of Canadian jurisprudence documented in this article adds an additional element of difficulty to their solution.

PART II

ELECTORAL POLITICS

Editor's Introduction

In representative democracies, political parties derive their legitimacy and authority from a system of competitive elections conducted in the context of open debate. As such, they are the most obvious and widely shared practice through which citizens express their preferences and influence the general orientation and complexion of government. The two essays reprinted in this section constitute important contributions to a now massive literature exploring the changing nature of the party system, its support base in the electorate, its efficacy as an instrument of change, the institutional factors that influenced its development, and its relation to the recent constitutional crisis, both as a possible cause and, suitably reformed as a partial response.

In "The Electoral System and the Party System in Canada, 1921-1965," several aspects of the conventional wisdom are challenged concerning the integrative capacity of the party system as it is influenced by the single-member plurality electoral system. While foreign scholars such as E.E. Schattschneider, S.M. Lipset, M. Duverger, and V.O. Key, among others, had long recognized the relevance of electoral systems for the understanding of political parties, studies of Canadian parties had seriously neglected this dimension prior to the provocative intervention by Cairns. The essay thus makes one of the first contributions to an understanding of the potentially dysfunctional consequences of some of our most important political institutions.[1] Not surprisingly, his analysis quickly precipitated controversy and alternative interpretations—sure signs of the growing maturity of the discipline and of the role his work

86

frequently has played in its evolution.[2] As one would expect, the alternative explanations that appeared typically utilized behavioural methodologies and frequently less stringent tests of an effective opposition and level of representation than the more normative, "civics approach" of Cairns.[3]

The second piece, "The Constitutional, Legal, and Historical Background to the Elections of 1979 and 1980," originally was commissioned by the American Enterprise Institute for Public Policy Research, "a publicly supported, non-partisan research and educational organization," while Professor Cairns held the Mackenzie King Chair of Canadian Studies at Harvard University. Evidence of the fact that the existing electoral system continued to exacerbate regionalism and weaken the national government was undeniably clear in the elections of both 1979 and 1980. More recently, the clean sweep to power of the Liberal government of Frank McKenna, transforming New Brunswick's parliamentary democracy into a single-party legislature, underscores the continuing relevance of these analyses to our understanding of representative democracy at the provincial no less than the national level of government.

Chapter Three

The Constitutional, Legal, and Historical Background to the Elections of 1979 and 1980

In the first general election in the Dominion of Canada, in 1867, 268,217 Canadians voted. In the thirty-first general election, in 1979, 11,455,702 Canadians cast valid ballots.[1] Eighteen of the thirty-one elections were won by the Liberals[2] and thirteen by the Conservatives.[3] Since 1921 the Liberals' electoral superiority has been especially pronounced, with thirteen victories in eighteen contests. The Liberal hegemony has been even more decisive in terms of years in office. The Conservatives have held office only twice since 1921, from 1930 to 1935 and from 1957 to 1963.[4] While there has been a third party in the field for the past sixty years, the two original parties that emerged at the time of Confederation have maintained their position as the leading contenders for national power. In recent federal elections third parties have consistently taken about one-quarter of the popular vote.

By virtue of this long experience of competitive politics and free elections, Canada has one of the oldest continuously functioning democratic political systems in the world. Canadians have always been able to change their rulers by electoral means. At the federal level, incumbent governments are defeated and replaced about one-third of the time. In the 1970s provincial governments were overturned in nine of the ten provinces. Only in Ontario, where the Conservative Party has held office continuously since 1943, has the party of government escaped electoral repudiation.

In the 1979 election, 35.9 per cent of the valid votes gave the Conservatives a minority government of 136 seats. The defeated Liberals, who had controlled the government since 1963 and were supported by 40.1 per cent of the voters, received only 114 seats and became the official opposition. This capricious result, an illustration of the perverse capacity of the Canadian electoral system to bestow the gift of power on the voters' second choice, was accepted with no serious questioning as the verdict of the people, as had been the results in 1896 and 1957, when the party with the most seats, which formed the new government, had come in second in the popular vote. Indeed, so habituated are Canadians to assessing the victor almost exclusively in terms of seats that the fact that the Liberals received nearly half a million more votes than the Conservatives was scarcely noted, especially in English Canada, where the Liberals ran a clear second to the Conservatives. The change of government was procedurally smooth. Joe Clark and the Conservative Party he had led since 1976 took power with 136 of the 282 seats in the House of Commons.

Its national government now controlled by the Conservatives for the first time since 1963, Canada was in the middle – or perhaps only at the beginning, or perhaps nearing the end – of a period of profound internal tension and malaise. Part of the frustration of leaders and disillusion of followers reflected the same perplexities, confusions, and contradictions that bedevil the governors and the governed elsewhere in Western democracies. The diverse conventional wisdoms that had provided adequate answers to yesterday's questions now seemed dated and irrelevant in a country beset simultaneously by inflation and unemployment, an energy crisis, and a weakening of political confidence. In addition, a constitution that had weathered a century of profound change, including war and depression, was now on the defensive. To many, not only in Quebec, it seemed little more than a museum piece. The constitution was criticized by some for its age, by others for its lack of appropriate democratic rhetoric; reformers said it stood in the way of a more effective management of public affairs, and the government of Quebec denounced it for shackling the Quebec people in an unrewarding relationship with an English-speaking majority. As the new Conservative government took office, it was clear that reality had finally caught up with the hitherto unfounded, somewhat indulgent assertion that Canada was a difficult country to govern.

In Canada as elsewhere, the ability of government to manage the complexities of the modern world was more frequently called into question. The resultant widespread attack on big government was the most visible aspect of a profound pause in the political and intellectual evolution of the Western world. In Canada "a binge of state-worship,"[5] based on an exaggerated belief in the efficacy and potency of governments, was coming to an end.

More threatening, however, than this pervasive uncertainty about political activity in the 1970s was the Canadian version of yet another ubiquitous phenomenon – the explosion of ethnic feeling or nationalism, which, to the surprise of social scientists no less than politicians, challenged the existing constitutional order of virtually every developed political system in the world. The Canadian experiment in French-English accommodation could no longer be taken for granted as a modest success story. The breakup of the country through its inability to contain the aggressive nationalism of Francophone Quebecers was a serious possibility that had to be entertained even by the most cautious scholar and politician. The politics of the second-largest country in the world, which only two decades earlier had seemed stable to the point of boredom, had become confused, tense, and exciting.

Federalism

Maintaining agreement on a common political system for French- and English-speaking Canadians has been a constant challenge to Canadian political leaders for more than a century, and federalism has been largely responsible for their success in meeting that challenge until recently. The choice of federalism in 1867, rather than a unitary government on the British model, was an unavoidable response to the political necessity of accommodating Nova Scotia, New Brunswick, and Ontario, as well as Quebec. The opposition of the French-Canadian population of Quebec to a unitary state, however, was much more deeply based than superficially similar sentiments elsewhere in British North America in the mid-nineteenth century.

French-Canadian opposition was based on language difference, cultural distinctiveness, Catholicism, and collective memories of the victory of the English over the French a century earlier. The preservation of some significant government authority under their own control was self-evidently necessary to the geographically concentrated French-speaking minority surrounded by an expansive, commercial Anglo-Saxon civilization.

The federalism developed out of the pre-Confederation discussions was an attempt to deal with the breakdown of the political system established by the 1840 Act of Union, which had brought English and French from Upper and Lower Canada (the future

Ontario and Quebec) together in what was designed as an essentially Anglo-Saxon unitary state. That polity, which combined the English-speaking majority from Upper Canada and the French-speaking majority from Lower Canada under a common government in the United Province of Canada, was a response to Lord Durham's analysis of what he saw as the backward, unprogressive character of French Canada. In his *Report on the Affairs of British North America* (1839), Governor General Durham had advocated institutional engineering to submerge and obliterate the distinctive nationality of French Canada within the framework of a united colony, where the progressive, superior, commercial civilization of English Canada would overwhelm the less competitive culture of the French-speaking inhabitants, to the benefit of both.

By the mid-1860s the inadequacies of Durham's diagnosis were evident in the continuing French-Canadian sense of nationality, the emergence of aggressive French-Canadian leadership, and the developing recognition of French-Canadian rights. The faltering political system of the colony was becoming unworkable. The inability of governments to survive hindered economic expansion. A new constitutional arrangement was necessary.

The power of ethnic feeling had triumphed over the institutions of a formally unitary political system, and constitutional engineering had failed to hasten the disappearance of French Canada. The next phase of constitutional craftsmanship showed greater sensitivity to the enduring national consciousness of the minority.

From an ethnic perspective, Confederation was designed to minimize competition between French and English by splitting the United Province of Canada into two provinces, Quebec and Ontario, to be dominated by French and English majorities respectively. Indeed, for many French Canadians, the significance of Confederation – an event never as symbolically important to them as to English Canadians – was the opportunity it allowed for an escape into provincialism.

The colonial societies of British North America and their local political elites did not insist on federalism out of any abstract conception of the desirability of diffusing and checking power. Their separate histories led them to oppose any constitutional arrangement that would have required them to submerge their individuality in a majoritarian political system governed by a single central government. Federalism, with its tolerance for diversity, was for them a precondition of acceptance of the other part of the Confederation package, the creation of an overriding central government endowed with predominant authority over the great affairs of state. For the leading English-Canadian Fathers, particularly John A. Macdonald and Alexander Galt, the latter was the essential objective, for the attainment of which they reluctantly conceded certain minimum powers and taxing capacities to the provinces. They sought and created a powerful central government to undertake the task of nation-building, which was their central purpose.[6]

Thus, like all complex arrangements, the federal system of 1867 was valued for different reasons by different people. In particular, there was an implicit division of labour along ethnic lines between the governments of the federal system. The central government, viewed as the key instrument of nation-building, economic growth, and territorial expansion, derived its impetus from the commercial culture of English Canada, while the provincial government of Quebec became one behind which the population could shelter under the protective guidance of the Catholic Church. It was not a government expected to lead its people.

The Monarchy

The choice of federalism in 1867 was the only significant institutional borrowing from the United States. Apart from federalism, the basic components of the political system were derived from the British tradition. Canada, as the preamble to the British North America Act stated, was to have a "Constitution similar in Principle to that of the United Kingdom." The features of the British constitution the colonists borrowed were those with which they had already had experience.

The monarchy, represented by a governor general at the federal level and by lieutenant-governors in the provinces, was not a matter of contention in the Confederation debates of the 1860s. There was no support for republicanism. On the contrary, the monarchy was valued as a bulwark for elitist tendencies against the possibly contagious heresy of democracy that had infected Canada's tumultuous neighbour to the south. The monarchy reflected the conservatism of the Fathers, "the social doctrine that public order and tradition, in contrast to freedom and experiment, were central to the good life."[7] In the North American context, it also symbolized Canada's distinctiveness and its continuing links with Europe.

In the 1970s the crown occupied a less central place. From the very beginning the monarchy in Canada was unavoidably weaker than in the United Kingdom: the representatives of the crown in Canada are appointed, not born to office, their tenure is limited, and they lack the aura of royalty. Recent developments have further reduced the significance of monarchical institutions. The decline of the British Empire and its transformation into the Commonwealth, the diminished political role of the United Kingdom in world affairs, the greatly reduced importance of Britain as an export market for Canadian products and as a supplier of capital, and Britain's entry into the European Common Market have eroded both the utilitarian and the sentimental bases for the British connection.

Canada's evolution from colony to independent nation and the increasing ethnic diversity of English Canada have also contributed to the weakening of the monarchical tradition. Indeed, given the indifference or hostility of many Francophone Quebecers and the republican sentiment spilling across the border, it is arguable that the monarch, governor general, and lieutenant governor are no longer unifying factors in the country. What is beyond question, however, is that attempts to eliminate or officially downgrade the constitutional monarchy, no matter how subtle, are highly divisive and counter-productive.

In any case, in addition to their useful ceremonial, ritual, and social roles, governors general and lieutenant-governors have an overall responsibility for the constitutional health and the constitutional morality of the political process that might in certain circumstances require their personal intervention. The constitutional monarch is more than a link with the past, to be cherished or deplored as temperament dictates. The governor general possesses reserve powers essential to the smooth functioning of the Canadian parliamentary system, which might have to be wielded against the advice of his constitutional advisers in order to safeguard the constitution.[8] The election of minority governments in six of the last nine federal elections increases the possibility of the governor general's involvement in delicate and sensitive political situations.

Responsible Government

Responsible government, cabinet government, or parliamentary government – different names for the same phenomenon viewed from varying perspectives – was, like the monarchy, not selected in 1864-1867, but simply continued. Responsible government had been achieved in 1848 in Nova Scotia and in the province of Canada and shortly afterward in New Brunswick, Prince Edward Island,

and Newfoundland. Canadians, according to Professor Brady's evocative summary, "could henceforth feel confident that the essential fabric of the British constitution was their own acquisition, secured through their persistent advocacy, fitted to their peculiar circumstances, and fostered as the substance and symbol of their political identity in North America."[9]

By the time of the Charlottetown, Quebec, and London conferences, which fashioned the Confederation agreement, responsible government, with its requirement that the political executive remain in office only as long as it received the support of a majority in the legislative assembly, was part of the habitual institutional environment of politicians in British North America. It was valued not only because it was British but for the practical contribution it could make to the decisive executive leadership required by a new country that faced daunting problems.

Although Canada was conceived when laissez-faire ideas were at their height in the United Kingdom, the Canadian Fathers were unimpressed by the idea of the state as night watchman or umpire, holding the ring for the contending social forces of a developing society. On the contrary, the state, especially the central government, was to play a leading role in territorial expansion across half a continent and in the political incorporation and economic development of the frontier. Given this orientation, there was negligible interest in establishing checks and balances on the American pattern of a separation of powers, which might hinder the decisive exercise of executive authority by the prime minister and his cabinet.

The Canadian polity was not shaped either by fear of the state as an enemy of liberty or by awe of it as the enduring, mystical expression of the transient generations over whose destiny it presided. In fact, the very concept of the state (until recently in Quebec) has been somewhat alien to the Canadian political vocabulary. The idea of an active government playing a leading role has been widely accepted, however, and has justified the concentration of executive authority in a party-dominated cabinet.

The Fathers revealed their political elitism in their preference for a cohesive cabinet, based on an assured legislative majority, wielding the authority of a strong central government. This authority was to be employed in the creation of a Canadian society, a Canadian economy, and ultimately a new Canadian political identity. The cabinet-dominated central government was to be not a mirror to the social and economic facts of 1867, but the chief instrument for the transformation of the northern half of the continent into a great new transcontinental country.

The Senate
The blend of federalism, responsible government, and the monarchy that constituted the primary institutional fabric of the polity was supplemented by a diluted bicameralism. The establishment of the Canadian Senate was an essential part of the Confederation agreement, especially for the smaller provinces. Nevertheless, various features of its composition assured it a distinctly secondary role, reducing it almost to the status of spectator of the political battles fought out by the cabinet and the Commons.

The creation of an upper house satisfied both the desire to duplicate the British constitution where possible and a wish to placate the territorial interests that had necessitated federalism.[10] With its entire membership appointed by the central government, originally for life, the Senate clearly could not be an influential advocate of regional perspectives in the central government arena. It lacked the prestige that election brings in a democratic polity (a consideration much more important now than in 1867); yet it was devoid of the aura aristocracy can bestow in a society with residual pre-bourgeois elements like the United Kingdom. Its sideline status was ensured by the conventions of responsible government that gave the lower house the power to make and unmake governments. Its most astonishing feat has been to survive and perform various useful functions in a society embarrassed at its continuing existence. It has combined weakness and longevity in a most impressive manner.

Institutions and Society: Part One
The institutional framework–federalism, responsible government, monarchical institutions, and bicameralism–has undergone little formal change since 1867. The functioning of Canada's institutions, however, is significantly different from that originally intended. The interaction between an evolving society and a network of institutions established in simpler times has inevitably transformed their meaning and modified their working. Since 1867 the population has grown from 3.5 million to nearly 24 million, and a predominantly rural nation has become predominantly urban, all within a formally unchanged constitutional order.

The political evolution of more than a century is a product of interactions too complex for detailed description. Only a general indication of the most important changes will be attempted.

The four provinces of 1867 had soon become seven, with the addition of Manitoba in 1870, British Columbia in 1871, and Prince Edward Island in 1873. Two more provinces, Alberta and Saskatchewan, were carved out of the Northwest Territories in 1905. Finally, Newfoundland, after a long history of rejecting association with Canada, became the tenth province in 1949 after two referendums, the second of which produced a narrow victory for the pro-Confederation forces led by Joseph Smallwood.

The federalism that was a necessary guarantee for the original participants in 1867 was no less necessary for the later arrivals. A unitary Canada would have encountered much more local resistance to its expansionist ambitions. Furthermore, as the nation expanded, distance became a consideration: Canada's new territories and new peoples needed governments closer at hand than Ottawa. They also needed governments attuned to their diverse interests. The great agrarian community specializing in the production of wheat for international markets, which comprised Alberta, Saskatchewan, and Manitoba, had economic interests often in conflict with those of central Canada. Prince Edward Island, British Columbia, and finally Newfoundland were each more distinctive in economic interest, way of life, and political tradition than would have been compatible with a unitary state.

The development and expansion of the federal system altered the conditions of competition in the party system. The original two-party system, which had firmly established itself at the national level by 1900 in central and eastern Canada, was unable to take root with equal success in the agrarian communities of Alberta, Saskatchewan, and Manitoba that grew so rapidly in the early years of the twentieth century. Their special economic interests, heterogeneous population base, and developing political tradition were not well served by a party system that had developed in response to the very different requirements of Canada east of the Great Lakes. In 1921 the Progressive Party returned sixty-five members to the House of Commons, including thirty-eight of the forty-three MPs from the three Prairie provinces. Support for farm movements in provincial politics and the successes of third parties in both federal and provincial politics in this area have been further indications of the contribution of regional diversity to the weakening hold of the two-party system.

Federalism has provided outlets for regional discontent at the provincial level and in doing so has increased the staying power of third parties, especially those able to gain control of provincial governments. Alberta had third-party government for fifty consecutive years, from 1921 to 1971, and British Columbia has been governed by third parties continuously since 1952. Since 1944 the New Democratic Party, originally the Co-operative Commonwealth Federation, has held office for twenty-nine years in Saskatchewan, and since 1922 Manitoba has had thirty-six years of a shifting coalition government and eight years of NDP rule. In the periods 1936-1939, 1944-1960, and 1966-1970, Quebec was governed by the Union Nationale, and since 1976 it has been governed by the Parti Québécois, neither of which participates in federal politics. Only in the Atlantic provinces and Ontario (except from 1919 to 1923) have the old parties remained in control of government.

Some of the third parties operate only at the provincial level; the Parti Québécois in Quebec and Social Credit in British Columbia are the prime current examples. The different receptivity of national and provincial arenas to third-party activity has been one of the key factors in driving the federal and provincial party systems apart. Many voters express very different partisan preferences in successive federal and provincial elections. On the other hand, there is a spillover in both directions: more third-party activity in national politics and more traditional party activity at the provincial level than would occur if weak parties at one jurisdictional level were not sustained by their stronger namesakes at the other level.

There is a peaceful but never-ending struggle between institutions in Canada for power and influence. Those most capable of responding to the shifting imperatives of democracy, representativeness, efficiency, expertise, and leadership have gained power, while the less capable, such as the Senate and the crown, have lost it. It is powerfully argued, in Canada as in the United Kingdom, that recent prime ministers, partly because of the media's stress on personality politics, have acquired an exalted leadership role based on a direct relation with the electorate, which gives them a pre-eminence in cabinet and party not enjoyed by their predecessors.

The power of the House of Commons has been transformed by party discipline from a capacity to defeat and replace governments to a more diffuse ability to influence the climate of opinion on which success or failure at the next election depends. Ordinary MPs, lacking expertise, burdened by constituency duties, and treated as voting machines by their party leaders, are not significant actors in devising, criticizing, or controlling the passage of legislation or in influencing its subsequent administration. "In 'normal' circumstances of majority government," writes Mallory, "once a parliament is elected it is no longer independent, but a groaning beast of burden for the government's legislative program."[11]

Responsible government no longer means the location in the House of Commons of an effective capacity to defeat and replace the incumbent executive. Its contemporary meaning has been suggestively described by a close student as follows:

> The constitutional essence of responsible government in Canada today probably includes the following: the government must command a regular majority in the House of Commons; the government must attempt to answer questions and criticisms in Parliament; the government must allow the Opposition to scrutinize government action and to debate urgent and important matters at periods both timely and lengthy enough to expose the major arguments; and elections must be held at least once every five years.[12]

Far more important than any of the preceding changes has been the general drift of power and decision-making from the market to government. The displacement of the market and the politicization of everyday life reflect the collectivist view that societies and economies, like factories, can and should be managed and manipulated. The evidence is ubiquitous. It is manifest in the scale of government employment, with federal, provincial, and local governments directly responsible for the employment of more than one of every nine Canadians in the work force (a ratio that has changed little in the last two decades) and indirectly responsible for many more.[13] Total government expenditures as a percentage of gross national product increased from 28.6 per cent in 1958 to 41.1 per cent in 1978, and detailed government regulations affect ever more spheres of activity.[14]

The expansion of government activity rearranges the relations of power and influence between the key actors in policy-making and administration. A direct consequence of the transformation in the role of government has been the steady accretion of power in the non-elected administrative branch. Every advance in the role of government tends to increase the indispensability, power, and autonomy of the civil service. The day-to-day administration of the minutiae of policies instituted by the legislators of yesterday inevitably escapes political scrutiny in all but the rarest of times. At the highest levels of the civil service, senior officials have a crucial say in policy-making as a result of their expertise, administrative skills, and political adroitness. That their nominal political superiors can often exercise only nominal control is not surprising.

The cumulative result of an expansion of government intended to serve the needs and hopes of society is a system that threatens to escape the control of the political strata possessed of formal power and therefore significantly to erode the capacity of the electorate to give direction to government. The report of the recent Royal Commission on Financial Management and Accountability concluded:

> After two years of careful study and consideration, we have reached the deeply held conviction that the serious malaise pervading the management of government stems fundamentally from a grave weakening, and in some cases an almost total breakdown, in the chain of accountability, first within government, and second in the accountability of government to Parliament and ultimately to the Canadian people.[15]

There is widespread agreement that the expenditure side of government is out of control and that many government operations have become almost immune to elementary considerations of economy. Cabinet ministers have more obligations than they can meet, including the normal constituency duties of MPs, performance in the House of Commons, the supervision and leadership of their departments, and participation in the cabinet.[16] Further, as Stewart points out, the reality is not that of spendthrift governments evading the control of tight-fisted legislators. The latter, no less than the former, see greater political gains in expenditure than in cutbacks.[17] As a result of these deep seated pressures for expansion, government has become a major instrument for the misallocation of resources.

The impact of big government on the performance of cabinet and Commons is devastating. According to Robert Stanfield, the former leader of the official opposition, both the cabinet and the House of Commons are overloaded to the point where they are incapable of doing their job. The cabinet cannot control the bureaucracy, and the Commons cannot control the cabinet. "What is involved is recognition that democratic responsible government and all-pervasive government in Ottawa are not compatible. They cannot exist together."[18] The expansion of government, as we shall see, has also compounded the difficulty of making the federal system efficient.

Institutions and Society: Part Two

Federalism has made an indispensable contribution to the peaceful functioning of the Canadian polity. Nevertheless, it has proved impossible to keep all matters on which French and English differ safely within provincial jurisdiction. On key occasions the contending ethnic groups have disagreed over vital federal policies. In both world wars, the different meaning of the European connection for English- and French-speaking Canadians occasioned significant variations in their willingness to fight and die on foreign soil. Federal involvement in the construction of the welfare state in the past half century has been less warmly received in Quebec than elsewhere. Divergent attitudes toward the role of the state, toward the federal system, and toward democracy itself have exacerbated French-English relations since Confederation. Canadian history has been punctuated by ethnic crises pertaining to language, education, civil liberties, military service, foreign policy, and other areas of government activity.

Nevertheless, until comparatively recently these divergences of belief and practice did not threaten the survival of the political system. Federalism, with disputes at the margin over the desirable degree of centralization and decentralization, seemed capable of responding flexibly to changing pressures for action by the provincial governments and the federal government in Ottawa. The fluctuation between periods of centralization and decentralization in response to the shifting strength of centripetal and centrifugal forces has, in fact, been a dominant theme for students of Canadian federalism.

The periods of unquestioned central government ascendancy have been limited essentially to the first decades after Confederation, both world wars, and the period of reconstruction from 1945 to the mid-1950s. This last period was shaped by the war experience and post-war conditions but also by the "lessons" of the Great Depression. The latter had a profound effect on the intellectuals of English Canada and the governing elites in Ottawa, who have had to grapple in recent years with the erosion of a federal hegemony they once thought destined to last.

The contrast between the Depression of the 1930s, when government was paralysed, allegedly because of the divided power structure of the federal system, and the war and post-war periods, with their notable successes in management and economic rehabilitation under the lead of a clearly dominant central government, made it easy for English Canadians to conclude that centralization was the wave of the future. In those halcyon days, which were really only yesterday, it was widely believed that a range of social forces and tendencies vaguely clustered under the label of modernization or secularization were driving the federal system toward centralization and reducing or eliminating the underlying diversity on which, it was thought, provincial power rested.

The numerous descriptions, predictions, and exhortations from the 1930s to the mid-1960s pointing to a more centralized future have, at least in the short run, been repudiated by the new reality of growing provincial power and a relatively weak central government. The attenuation of federal dominance in the last two decades has attracted varying explanations, the intricacies of which cannot be pursued here.[19] What must be noted is that the perception of a central government gravely weakened and in retreat is widespread. The recent report of the Task Force on Canadian Unity claimed that fifteen years ago the central government was regarded with respect, sustained by loyalty, and recognized as efficient and competent.

> Today, that is much less true; "Ottawa," as we found on our tour, is for many Canadians synonymous with all that is to be deplored about modern government – a remote, shambling bureaucracy that extracts tribute from its subjects and gives little in return . . . an unfair stereotype . . . but this view has . . . a widespread appeal today.[20]

Conversely, the escalating importance of the governments of the large or wealthy provinces is universally attested. In recent decades there has been an indisputable increase in the power and status of the provinces, to which, accordingly, citizens are increasingly linked by a network of laws, services, benefits, and duties. The realities of the situation are inextricably intermingled with the fads and fashions of the intelligentsia responsible for explanation and evaluation. To compensate for the errors of their elders, who viewed the provinces as anachronisms, many contemporary schol-

101

ars are almost blinded by provincialism and overlook the continuing power and responsibilities of Ottawa.

The attack on the central government is most vigorously mounted by the Parti Québécois government. Other provincial governments, however, are far from pleased with the functioning of a federal system they feel pays too little attention to their singularities, gives inadequate recognition to their competence, and provides insufficient opportunities for regional perspectives to be brought to bear on central government policy-making.

The frustrations of both levels of government are directly related to that expansion of government activities of which they are simultaneously the major beneficiaries and the prime victims. Both levels of government are active and entrepreneurial in attempting to implement their competing visions of a desirable future. Both intervene vigorously in the overlapping societies and economies under their jurisdiction in the pursuit of divergent grand designs.

In a unitary state the decline of the market results in a straightforward displacement of private by public decision-making. In a federal system with strong governments at both levels, the result is much more complex. What was hitherto handled by the processes of markets and by non-political decision-makers, for whom the federal division of powers was irrelevant, is not only politicized but federalized as well. Federal and provincial jurisdictional differences penetrate ever deeper. The sphere of activity outside the political, and therefore outside the federal, system constantly shrinks. Much of this federalization from above, which claims an ever-expanding ratio of citizen activity as federal or provincial, is a result of the internal dynamics of Leviathan at both levels of government. Much of the emphasis on regionalism, for example, reflects not any underlying territorial diversities but the power of provincial governments to structure the political world in terms of their self-interest.

In a federal state the displacement of the market generates intergovernmental conflict. The success of governments in enhancing their own authority multiplies the potential for intergovernmental conflict over anything from regulatory details to the most profound issues of public policy. To minimize the actual incidence of conflict, there has been a vast proliferation of federal-provincial committees with subject matters ranging from the most specific issues, which are handled by civil servants, to the most general questions of the economy and the constitution, which are on the agenda when the prime minister and the premiers of the eleven governments meet. The complexities of the system produce policy rigidities, bottlenecks that cannot be eliminated by the exercise of hierarchical authority, a decline in effective control by legislatures and electorates, and, frequently, serious costs to the citizenry the system is supposed to serve.[21]

In spite of the undeniable importance of these structural tensions, it is clear that the core of the threat to Canada's survival is elsewhere, in the area of Quebec/Ottawa or French/English relations. Since 1960 a succession of Quebec governments has constructed and employed the Quebec state as a powerful instrument of social and economic transformation. The institutional predominance of the Catholic Church was quickly eliminated, and its link with the English business classes in Quebec, with whom it shared an interest in a weak provincial state, was broken. The bureaucracy was transformed into an efficient agency for the pursuit of public purposes; welfare was transferred from the Church to government professionals; and the educational system was expanded, secularized, and taken over by the provincial state. In sum, a process was stimulated by which French-Canadian Quebecers were transformed into a political people, whose nationalism no longer cast government as an enemy. On the contrary, state and society in Quebec were drawn into an intimate embrace.

From the mid-1960s on, and particularly in the Trudeau years from 1968 to 1979, the federal government fought to preserve its authority and legitimacy with Francophones both within and outside Quebec. The basic strategy has been to increase the presence and visibility of French Canadians in the federal bureaucracy by extending the use of French as a language of work and by making services available, where numbers warranted, in either official language. The federal government has also attempted, with less success, to increase the availability of education in the French language in provincial education systems. The central government's objective has been to preserve the viability of Francophone communities outside Quebec, in order to redress the tendency of Quebec Francophones to see Quebec, not Canada, as their homeland.

Concurrently with the central government's attempts to strengthen the attachment of French Canadians, wherever located, to Ottawa, the internal politics of the province of Quebec were convulsed by the rapid growth of the Parti Québécois, which was formed in 1968 and attained power in 1976. After its severe defeat in the 1973 elections, the Parti Québécois deliberately severed its position on independence from the issue of good government. The party realized that its independence program hindered its bid for power in the province by frightening off many voters who were seeking a low-risk defeat of the unpopular incumbent government, the Liberal regime of Robert Bourassa. In the 1976 provincial election campaign the party stated that it would conduct itself in office as a provincial government and would give the electorate a separate opportunity in a post-election referendum to vote for or against independence.

The success of that strategy in its first phase – the attainment of office – precipitated a situation of profound constitutional uncertainty. The party used its assumption of provincial government power for an unrelenting assault on federalism, employing all the weapons that office makes available.

The Parti Québécois won its first provincial election on November 15, 1976, one of the great turning points in Canadian history. Since 1960 a succession of Quebec prime ministers had chipped away at the federal regime and made it clear that Quebec's allegiance to the idea of Canada was less than wholehearted. Nevertheless, all of them, from Jean Lesage to Bourassa, had been prepared to go along with federalism. With the victory of the Parti Québécois the old game of incrementalism, of ad hoc advances, was discarded. After 1976 political strategy in Quebec City responded to a set of guiding objectives that postulated an independent Quebec.

The Parti Québécois sought to make itself the only legitimate spokesman for the powerful nationalism that had long existed in Francophone Quebec. To do so it had to convince the electorate that federalism and nationalism were incompatible and that the latter must be clothed in the garments of an independent state.

The Electoral System and National Unity

The Canada that went to the polls on May 22, 1979, was not a nation in a state of equilibrium. It was widely assumed that major constitutional changes would be necessary to induce the people and government of Quebec to remain within Canada and that the constitution would have to be adapted to the new realities of provincial power. Canadians had just been told by a major government task force that time was running out[22] and that unless quick action were taken the fragmentation of the country was probable, some said inevitable.

Thus from November 15, 1976, when the Parti Québécois was elected to govern Quebec, up to the federal election in May, 1979, there was an unusual amount of introspection: conferences on "whither Canada?" proliferated, academic assessments of the country's condition and prospects multiplied, federal-provincial conferences on the constitution were held, and parliamentary committees conducted hearings on constitutional changes proposed by the Trudeau government. The public was extensively consulted in a series of open meetings between September, 1977, and April, 1978, held all across the country by the Task Force on Canadian Unity. The commissioners' efforts to stimulate grassroots feedback and to let the people speak produced "some 900 briefs and close to 3,000 letters."[23]

In Quebec, meanwhile, the provincial government was approaching the referendum to be held in the spring of 1980, in which the people of Quebec would be asked to contribute to the decision on their collective future. The wording of the referendum question had not been determined by the time of the national election, but it was bound to reflect the blend of integrity, partisan self-interest, and strategic advice from pollsters characteristic of political decisions in a democracy.

In these circumstances,[24] it might have been expected that the general election would be infused with high drama, as the parties confronted the electorate with clear, alternative constitutional futures. But no detailed proposals appeared. The Liberals identified Trudeau with strong leadership and national unity. The Conservatives portrayed Clark as a consensual leader with good relations with the Conservative premiers of six provinces. The NDP did not treat national unity as a priority issue, and it reduced the constitutional question to a superstructural reflection of economic problems caused by inept political leadership. The election made almost no contribution to Canadians' education in the causes and possible cures of the country's constitutional ailments.

Only loosely, therefore, could it be said that the election was about the constitution. On the other hand, concerned observers invested the outcome with great significance for the constitutional future of the country, not because of variations in the constitutional policy of the two major parties and only partly because of differences of personality and character in the party leaders, Clark and Trudeau. Concern was focused on the constitutional consequences expected to flow from the regional and ethnic biases of whichever governing party emerged when the votes were counted. In the graphic language of William Johnson, the Quebec correspondent of the leading English-Canadian newpaper:

> With foreboding I see the arrival of this election day, 1979. . . . French Canada will vote one way, English-speaking Canada another. The political process will reflect in the federal Government the drawing apart of the country's two language communities, who recognize themselves in different parties. The Progressive Conservatives and the NDP will by tonight be the only really significant political expressions of English Canada. . . . The rift in the country along the language fault line, where the tension has been building for years, opens tonight. . . . If Pierre Trudeau manages to form a minority government, with the massive support of French Canada, it will be seen as an outrage, a kind of alien occupation, by much of English-speaking Canada. The bitterness will go deep.
>
> [Or] Joe Clark [will] . . . form a government without significant representation in French Canada. The composition of the House of Commons [will] divide largely according to language. René Lévesque [will] anoint himself the political spokesman for all Francophones. He will say . . . that the two nations of Canada are now politically visible, the reality of the country no longer obscured by the masking presence of a French Canadian Prime Minister.[25]

Johnson's view that the election outcome would be disastrous for national unity was widely shared. It reflected a developing body of opinion, not yet a consensus, that some of the most destructive tendencies in the Canadian polity could be attributed to the bias in the transformation of votes into seats by the electoral system.

The electoral system, like much else in Canadian political life, had been taken over from Great Britain before Confederation and retained afterward with little thought for possible alternatives. Although proportional representation has always had a sprinkling of support in Canada and there has been occasional experimentation with other electoral systems in the provinces, the first-past-the-post system in single-member constituencies – known as ridings in Canada – has been little challenged at the federal level. It was

British and good enough for the Mother of Parliaments. It was simple and easy for voters and candidates to understand. Finally, until 1957 it contributed to one-party legislative majorities and hence to executive stability.

From 1921 to 1957 the electoral system discriminated savagely against the Conservative Party in Quebec and thus deprived one of the two main parties in the country of effective contact with French Canada, but this consideration was secondary. The Conservatives for all but five years had been confined to the opposition, where the regional and ethnic bias of their caucus apparently had minimal negative consequences for the political system. By contrast, the Liberal government in power for most of the period from 1921 to 1957 effectively straddled the two great language communities and also, with occasional exceptions, had politically adequate representation from western Canada.

From this and earlier historical experience going back to Confederation, a particular role in maintaining national unity was attributed to the party system. The governing party, in particular, and the federal cabinet were held responsible for the aggregation and conciliation of regional interests at the centre. Conventional wisdom had it that it was in these two bodies, which were, of course, intimately linked, that political compromises and regional brokerage took place. Here, if anywhere, was the genius of Canadian politics – the power to reconcile French and English, centre and periphery, provincial perspectives and national perspectives.

The period from 1957 to 1974, covering eight general elections, cast doubts on the contribution of the party system to political stability and national integration and by implication contributed to the erosion of support for the electoral system. Five of these eight elections produced minority governments. This undermined one of the prime virtues attributed to the electoral system, its capacity to manufacture a one-party legislative majority for a party receiving less than a majority of votes. More serious was the effect of the electoral system on the regional distribution of party members in the House of Commons. During this period the Liberals received on average only 32 per cent of the seats "merited" by their electoral support from the Prairie provinces. The Conservatives in the same period received only 64 per cent of their "entitlement" from Quebec, or 40 per cent if their breakthrough in 1958 is excluded. Particularly significant was the fact that basic shortfalls in provincial representation now affected governing parties, the Conservatives in Quebec in 1957-1958 and 1962-1963 and the Liberals in one or more Prairie provinces, especially Alberta, from 1963 to 1979. Under the first-past-the-post electoral system, therefore, not only did parties move in and out of government, but regions and provinces, including the Francophone community concentrated in Quebec, also underwent the abrupt transition from the government to the opposition side of the House.

According to several analysts, a major aspect of the political weakness of the central government was the lack of significant representation for whole provinces and regions on the government side of the House. This in turn contributed to a developing provincialism, led by the governments of those provinces deprived of effective input into the governing party at Ottawa. Thus, as time ran out on the Liberal government, politicians and analysts became increasingly apprehensive about the possibility that a Conservative government with negligible representation from Quebec would be elected. This result, which evidence indicated was the outcome coveted by the Parti Québécois government, became known as the doomsday scenario. It was feared that this outcome, with English Canada apparently in control of the central government, would further mobilize Francophone Quebecers behind the banner of a provincial government possessed of new proof of the insensitivity, ineffectiveness, and illegitimacy of the Ottawa government.

More generally, as Watts noted,

> where the parties have become primarily regional in their bases, the parliamentary federations have been prone to instability. . . . In this respect one of the most ominous signs in the present Canadian scene is the apparent inability of each of the major political parties to attract support from some major regions of the country and thus to be truly representative of an interregional consensus.[26]

Even outside Quebec, the representational imbalances in the national party system were given extra salience by the centrifugal pressures at work in the federal system. Various provincial governments, possessed of a heady confidence, chipped away at a central government with weak representative credentials. Since it was becoming increasingly difficult to deny that the electoral system made a major contribution to the regionalization of the national party system, which in turn eroded the legitimacy of the central government, the electoral system itself was on trial in the recent

election. The results gave little solace to the defenders of the existing system and further diminished the taken-for-granted quality it
had previously enjoyed. Electoral reform is bound to remain a live
issue as long as the existing system proves incapable of producing
majority governments representative of the nation.[27]

The objective of electoral reformers is a more reasonable relationship between the percentage of votes and the seats received by
each party in each province and region of the country. This goal is
pursued not in the interests of justice, but in the cause of national
unity. A more regionally representative central government would
be a more legitimate and effective central government.

The thirty-first general election, on May 22, 1979, was fought
under the old rules – what a recent Quebec government study
sympathetic to proportional representation pointedly called the
"English system."[28] The election results provide a textbook illustration of the inequities and negative consequences the existing system is capable of producing. The defeated Liberals received nearly
half a million more votes, and twenty-two fewer seats, than the
party that replaced them in office. Although the new Conservative
government was generally favoured by the electoral system, the
Conservatives were harmed in Quebec. They received 432,000
votes in Quebec, more than they received in six other provinces,
but only two seats. In Prince Edward Island, by contrast, 34,147
votes gave the party four seats. Thus, although the Conservatives
received 10.5 per cent of their total vote from Quebec, only 1.5
per cent of their seats were from that province. The Liberals, with
15 per cent of their vote west of the Great Lakes, received only
three seats, 2.6 per cent of their total seats, in the four provinces
of Manitoba, Saskatchewan, Alberta, and British Columbia.

The new Conservative government emerged from the May election to confront the nationalist demands of the Parti Québécois
with fewer members from Quebec than any government party since
1867. The Conservatives also had fewer popular votes than the
Liberals they replaced and the lowest percentage of the popular vote
of any governing party since Confederation. The minority status
of the Conservative Party and the bias in the regional and ethnic
composition of its caucus and cabinet not only would impinge on
the legislative-executive relationship in Ottawa. They would also
weaken the central government in that larger federal-provincial system of intergovernmental bargaining so crucial to the evolution of
Canadian federalism. As it turned out, the country was saved from

the consequences of an unrepresentative Conservative government by the return to power a year later of an unrepresentative Liberal government.

It was indeed a curious outcome. As noted earlier, the effective capacity of the House of Commons to control the government is minimal. In principle an elementary capacity to reward and punish belongs to the electorate. In reality the exercise of that capacity can be rendered nugatory by an inefficient electoral system that turns losers into winners and winners into losers, as it did on May 22, 1979. Few seem to have noticed this fact. Even fewer seem concerned. That the results of an election are easier to justify by the principles of a lottery than by any principle of equity is not, however, a trivial matter.

Chapter Four

The Electoral System and the Party System in Canada, 1921-1965

This paper investigates two common assumptions about the party system: (1) that the influence of the electoral system on the party system has been unimportant, or non-existent; and (2) that the party system has been an important nationalizing agency with respect to the sectional cleavages widely held to constitute the most significant and enduring lines of division in the Canadian polity. Schattschneider, Lipset, Duverger, Key, and others[1] have cogently asserted the relevance of electoral systems for the understanding of party systems. Students of Canadian parties, however, have all but ignored the electoral system as an explanatory factor of any importance. The analysis to follow will suggest that the electoral system has played a major role in the evolution of Canadian parties, and that the claim that the party system has been an important instrument for integrating Canadians across sectional lines is highly suspect.

Discussion of the respective merits of single-member constituency electoral systems and various systems of proportional representation is frequently indecisive because of an inability to agree on the values that electoral systems should serve. Advocates of proportional representation base their arguments on democratic fundamentalism. They simply argue that each vote should have equal weight, and that the distortion of the voters' preferences by single-member constituency systems is no more to be justified than the use of false scales by a butcher. This idealistic argument is countered by the opponents of proportional representation with the assertion that executive stability is a more basic consideration, and that it is well served by the propensity of Canadian-type systems to

111

create artificial legislative majorities. This controversy will not concern us further.

It may be noted, however, that critical analysis of the single-member constituency system encounters a cultural bias in the Anglo-Saxon world because of the pervasive hostility shown to systems of proportional representation,[2] and the executive instability to which they allegedly contribute. Proportional representation has not been seriously considered as a possible alternative to the existing system. It exists in a limbo of inarticulate assumptions that it is responsible for the ills of the French political system, but it is given no credit for the sophistication and maturity of the Swedish political system.

Given this bias there is, no doubt, a tendency to transform a critique of the existing system into advocacy of proportional representation. The purpose of this paper, however, is not to advocate proportional representation but simply to take a realistic look at some of the consequences of the prevailing system that have received insufficient attention. In any case, the habituation of Canadians to the existing system renders policy-oriented research on the comparative merits of different electoral systems a fruitless exercise.

The Basic Defence of the System and Its Actual Performance

If the electoral system is analysed in terms of the basic virtue attributed to it—the creation of artificial legislative majorities to produce cabinet stability—its performance since 1921 has been mediocre. Table 1 reveals the consistent tendency of the electoral system in every election from 1921 to 1965 to give the government party a greater percentage of seats than of votes. However, its contribution to one-party majorities was much less dramatic. Putting aside the two instances, 1940 and 1958, when a boost from the electoral system was unnecessary, it transformed a minority of votes into a majority of seats on only six of twelve occasions. It is possible that changes in the party system and/or in the distribution of party support will render this justification increasingly anachronistic in future years.

If the assessment of the electoral system is extended to include not only its contribution to one-party majorities, but its contribution to the maintenance of effective opposition, arbitrarily defined as at least one-third of House members, it appears in an even less

Table 1

Percentage of Votes and Seats for Government Party, 1921-1965

	% Votes	% Seats		% Votes	% Seats
1921	40.7	49.4 (L)	1949	49.5	73.7 (L)
1925*	39.8	40.4 (L)	1953	48.9	64.5 (L)
1926	46.1	52.2 (L)	1957	38.9	42.3 (C)
1930	48.7	55.9 (C)	1958	53.6	78.5 (C)
1935	44.9	70.6 (L)	1962	37.3	43.8 (C)
1940	51.5	73.9 (L)	1963	41.7	48.7 (L)
1945	41.1	51.0 (L)	1965	40.2	49.4 (L)

*In this election the Conservatives received both a higher percentage of votes, 46.5 per cent, and of seats, 47.3 per cent, than the Liberals. The Liberals, however, chose to meet Parliament, and with Progressive support they retained office for several months.
SOURCES: The data for this and the following tables have been compiled from Howard A. Scarrow, *Canada Votes* (New Orleans, 1963), and from the *Report of the Chief Electoral Officer* for recent elections.

satisfactory light. On four occasions, two of which occurred when the government party had slightly more than one-half of the votes, the opposition was reduced to numerical ineffectiveness. The coupling of these two criteria together creates a reasonable measure for the contribution of the electoral system to a working parliamentary system, which requires both a stable majority and an effective opposition. From this vantage point the electoral system has failed on ten of fourteen occasions, a failure rate of 71 per cent.

This unimpressive record indicates that if other dysfunctional consequences of the electoral system exist they can be only marginally offset by its performance with respect to the values espoused by its advocates. In this paper discussion of these other consequences is restricted to the effect of the electoral system in furthering or hindering the development of a party system capable of acting as a unifying agency in a country where sectional cleavages are significant. Or, to put the matter differently, the stability of concern is not that of the cabinet in its relations to the legislature but of the political system as a whole. Has the electoral system fostered a party system that attenuates or exacerbates sectional cleavages, sectional identities, and sectionally oriented parties?

The Effect on Major and Minor Parties

Table 2 indicates an important effect of the electoral system with its proof that discrimination for and against the parties does not become increasingly severe when the parties are ordered from most votes to least votes. Discrimination in favour of a party was most pronounced for the weakest party on seven occasions and for the strongest part on seven occasions. In the four elections from 1921 to 1930 inclusive, with three party contestants, the second party was most hurt by the electoral system. In the five elections from 1935 to 1953 inclusive the electoral system again worked against the middle-ranking parties and favoured parties with the weakest and strongest voting support. In the five elections from 1957 to 1965 inclusive there has been a noticeable tendency to benefit the first two parties, with the exception of the fourth party, Social Credit in 1957, at the expense of the smaller parties.

The explanation for the failure of the electoral system to act with Darwinian logic by consistently distributing its rewards to the large

Table 2

**Bias of Electoral System in Translating Votes into Seats:
Rank Order of Parties in Terms of Percentage of Vote**

Year	1		2		3		4		5	
1921	Libs.	1.21	Cons.	0.70	Progs.	1.20				
1925	Cons.	1.017	Libs.	1.015	Progs.	1.09				
1926	Libs.	1.13	Cons.	0.82	Progs.	1.55				
1930	Cons.	1.15	Libs.	0.82	Progs.	1.53				
1935	Libs.	1.57	Cons.	0.55	CCF	0.33	Rec.	0.05	Socred	1.68
1940	Libs.	1.43	Cons.	0.53	CCF	0.39	Socred	1.52		
1945	Libs.	1.24	Cons.	1.00	CCF	0.73	Socred	1.29		
1949	Libs.	1.49	Cons.	0.53	CCF	0.37	Socred	1.03		
1953	Libs.	1.32	Cons.	0.62	CCF	0.77	Socred	1.06		
1957	Libs.	0.97	Cons.	1.087	CCF	0.88	Socred	1.091		
1958	Cons.	1.46	Libs.	0.55	CCF	0.32	Socred	0		
1962	Cons.	1.17	Libs.	1.01	NDP	0.53	Socred	0.97		
1963	Libs.	1.17	Cons.	1.09	NDP	0.49	Socred	0.76		
1965	Libs.	1.23	Cons.	1.13	NDP	0.44	Cred.	0.72	Socred	0.51

Independents and very small parties have been excluded from the table.

The measurement of discrimination employed in this table defines the relationship between the percentage of votes and the percentage of seats. The figure is devised by dividing the former into the latter. Thus 1–(38% seats/38% votes), for example–represents a neutral effect for the electoral system. Any figure above 1–(40% seats/20%votes) = 2.0, for example–indicates discrimination for the party. A figure below 1–(20% seats/40% votes) = 0.5, for example–indicates discrimination against the party. For the purposes of the table the ranking of the parties as 1, 2, 3 . . . is based on their percentage of the vote, since to rank them in terms of seats would conceal the very bias it is sought to measure–namely, the bias introduced by the intervening variable of the electoral system that constitutes the mechanism by which votes are translated into seats.

114

parties and its penalties to the small parties is relatively straightforward.[3] The bias in favour of the strongest party reflects the likelihood that the large number of votes it has at its disposal will produce enough victories in individual constituencies to give it, on a percentage basis, a surplus of seats over votes. The fact that this surplus has occurred with only one exception, 1957, indicates the extreme unlikelihood of the strongest party having a distribution of partisan support capable of transforming the electoral system from an ally into a foe. The explanation for the favourable impact of the electoral system on the Progressives and Social Credit from 1921 to 1957, when they were the weakest parties, is simply that they were sectional parties that concentrated their efforts in areas of strength where the electoral system worked in their favour. Once the electoral system has rewarded the strongest party and a weak party with concentrated sectional strength there are not many more seats to go around. In this kind of party system, which Canada had from 1921 to Mr. Diefenbaker's breakthrough, serious discrimination against the second party in a three-party system and the second and third party in a four-party system is highly likely.

Table 3 reveals that the electoral system positively favours minor parties with sectional strongholds and discourages minor parties with diffuse support. The classic example of the latter phenomenon

Table 3

Minor Parties: Percentage of Seats and Votes

	Progressives		Reconstruction		CCF/NDP		Soc. Credit		Créditiste	
	votes	seats	votes	seats	votes	seats	votes	seats	votes	seats
1921	23.1	27.7								
1925	9.0	9.8								
1926	5.3	8.2								
1930	3.2	4.9								
1935			8.7	0.4	8.9	2.9	4.1	6.9		
1940					8.5	3.3	2.7	4.1		
1945					15.6	11.4	4.1	5.3		
1949					13.4	5.0	3.7	3.8		
1953					11.3	8.7	5.4	5.7		
1957					10.7	9.4	6.6	7.2		
1958					9.5	3.0	2.6	—		
1962					13.5	7.2	11.7	11.3		
1963					13.1	6.4	11.9	9.1		
1965					17.9	7.9	3.7	1.9	4.7	3.4

is provided by the Reconstruction Party in the 1935 election. For its 8.7 per cent of the vote it was rewarded with one seat and promptly disappeared from the scene. Yet its electoral support was more than twice that of Social Credit, which gained seventeen seats, and only marginally less than that of the CCF, which gained seven seats. The case of the Reconstruction Party provides dramatic illustration of the futility of party effort for a minor party that lacks a sectional stronghold. The treatment of the CCF/NDP by the electoral system is only slightly less revealing. This party with diffuse support, which aspired to national and major-party status, never received as many seats as would have been "justified" by its voting support, and on six occasions out of ten received less than half the seats to which it was "entitled." The contrasting treatment of Social Credit and the Progressives, sectional minor parties, by the electoral system clearly reveals the bias of the electoral system in favour of concentrated support and against diffused support.[4]

Distortion in Party Parliamentary Representation

No less important than the general differences in the way the electoral system rewards or punishes each individual party as such, is the manner in which it fashions particular patterns of sectional representation within the ranks of the parliamentary parties out of the varying distributions of electoral support they received. This sectional intra-party discrimination affects all parties. The electoral system consistently minimized the Ontario support of the Progressives, which provided the party with 43.5 per cent, 39.7 per cent, and 29.4 per cent of its total votes in the first three elections of the twenties. The party received only 36.9 per cent, 8.3 per cent, and 10 per cent of its total seats from that province. Further, by its varying treatment of the party's electoral support from Manitoba, Saskatchewan, and Alberta, it finally helped to reduce the Progressives to an Alberta party.

An analysis of CCF/NDP votes and seats clearly illustrates the manner in which the electoral system has distorted the parliamentary wing of the party. Table 4 reveals the extreme discrimination visited on Ontario supporters of the CCF from 1935 to 1957. With the exception of 1940, CCF Ontario voting support consistently constituted between 30 and 40 per cent of total CCF voting support. Yet, the contribution of Ontario to CCF parliamentary representation was derisory. During the same period there was a marked over-representation of Saskatchewan in the CCF caucus. The 1945

Table 4

Percentage of Total CCF/NDP Strength, in Seats and Votes from Selected Provinces

	N.S.	Que.	Ont.	Man.	Sask.	Alta.	B.C.
1935 votes	—	1.9	32.7	13.9	18.8	7.9	24.8
seats	—	—	—	28.6	28.6	—	42.9
1940 votes	4.5	1.9	15.6	15.6	27.0	8.9	26.2
seats	12.5	—	—	12.5	62.5	—	12.5
1945 votes	6.4	4.1	31.9	12.5	20.5	7.0	15.4
seats	3.6	—	—	17.9	64.3	—	14.3
1949 votes	4.3	2.3	39.2	10.6	19.5	4.0	18.6
seats	7.7	—	7.7	23.1	38.5	—	23.1
1953 votes	3.5	3.7	33.4	10.1	24.6	3.7	19.7
seats	4.3	—	4.3	13.0	47.8	—	30.4
1957 votes	2.4	4.5	38.7	11.6	19.8	3.8	18.6
seats	—	—	12.0	20.0	40.0	—	28.0
1958 votes	2.7	6.6	37.9	10.8	16.3	2.8	22.2
seats	—	—	37.5	—	12.5	—	50.0
1962 votes	3.8	8.9	44.0	7.4	9.0	4.1	20.4
seats	5.3	—	31.6	10.5	—	—	52.6
1963 votes	2.6	14.6	42.6	6.4	7.3	3.4	21.5
seats	—	—	35.3	11.8	—	—	52.9
1965 votes	2.8	17.7	43.0	6.6	7.6	3.2	17.3
seats	—	—	42.9	14.3	—	—	42.9

Percentages of votes do not total 100 horizontally because the table does not include Newfoundland, Prince Edward Island, New Brunswick, or the territories where the CCF/ NDP gained a few votes but no seats.

election is indicative. The 260,000 votes from Ontario, 31.9 per cent of the total CCF vote, produced no seats at all, while 167,000 supporters from Saskatchewan, 20.5 per cent of the total party vote, were rewarded with eighteen seats, 64.3 per cent of total party seats. In these circumstances it was not surprising that observers were led to mislabel the CCF an agrarian party.

The major parties are not immune from the tendency of the electoral system to make the parliamentary parties grossly inaccurate reflections of the sectional distribution of party support. Table 5 makes it clear that the electoral system has been far from impartial in its treatment of Liberal and Conservative voting support from Ontario and Quebec. For fourteen consecutive elections covering nearly half a century there was a consistent and usually marked overrepresentation of Quebec in the Liberal caucus and marked underrepresentation in the Conservative caucus, with the exception of 1958. For ten consecutive elections from 1921 to 1957, Ontario was consistently and markedly overrepresented in the Conservative caucus, and for eleven consecutive elections, from 1921 to 1958, there was consistent but less marked underrepresentation of Ontario in the Liberal caucus. Thus, the electoral system, by pulling the parliamentary Liberal Party toward Quebec and the parliamentary Conservative Party toward Ontario, made the sectional cleavages between the parties much more pronounced in Parliament than they were at the level of the electorate.

The way the electoral system affected the relationship of Quebec to the parliamentary wings of the two major parties is evident in the truly startling discrepancies between votes and seats for the two parties from that province. From 1921 to 1965 inclusive the Liberals gained 752 members from Quebec and the Conservatives only 135. The ratio of 5.6 Liberals to each Conservative in the House of Commons contrasts sharply with the 1.9 to 1 ratio of Liberals to Conservatives at the level of voters.[5]

Given the recurrent problems concerning the status of Quebec in Canadian federalism and the consistent tension in French-English relations, it is self-evident that the effects of the electoral system

Table 5

Liberals and Conservatives: Percentage of Total Parliamentary Strength and
Total Electoral Support from Quebec and Ontario

| | Conservatives | | | | Liberals | | | |
| | Ontario | | Quebec | | Ontario | | Quebec | |
	seats	votes	seats	votes	seats	votes	seats	votes
1921	74.0	47.1	—	15.5	18.1	26.6	56.0	43.8
1925	58.6	47.4	3.4	18.4	11.1	30.1	59.6	37.8
1926	58.2	44.9	4.4	18.7	20.3	31.7	46.9	33.4
1930	43.1	38.9	17.5	24.0	24.2	33.7	44.0	30.6
1935	62.5	43.1	12.5	24.7	32.4	34.4	31.8	31.5
1940	62.5	48.6	2.5	16.4	31.5	34.4	33.7	31.2
1945	71.6	52.7	3.0	8.3	27.2	34.6	42.4	33.3
1949	61.0	43.6	4.9	22.6	29.0	31.9	35.2	33.2
1953	64.7	44.2	7.8	26.0	29.8	32.6	38.6	34.2
1957	54.5	42.9	8.0	21.7	20.0	31.1	59.0	38.1
1958	32.2	36.2	24.0	25.7	30.6	33.3	51.0	37.8
1962	30.2	36.9	12.1	21.6	44.0	39.2	35.0	28.6
1963	28.4	37.8	8.4	16.0	40.3	39.1	36.4	29.3
1965	25.8	37.4	8.2	17.3	38.9	38.6	42.7	30.0

noted above can be appropriately described as divisive and detrimental to national unity. Brady and Siegfried, among others, have stressed the dangers that would arise should the lines of partisan division coincide with the "lines of nationality and religion,"[6] the very direction in which the electoral system has pushed the party system. This consequence has been partially veiled by the typically plural composition of the government party. In parliamentary systems, however, the composition of the chief opposition party, the almost inevitable successor to governmental responsibilities over time, is only moderately less significant. The electoral system has placed serious barriers in the way of the Conservative Party's attempts to gain parliamentary representation from a province where its own interests and those of national unity coincided on the desirability of making a major contender for public office as representative as possible.[7] The frequent thesis that the association of the Conservatives with conscription in 1917 destroyed their prospects in Quebec only becomes meaningful when it is noted that a particular electoral system presided over that destruction.

The following basic effects of the electoral system have been noted. The electoral system has not been impartial in its translation of votes into seats. Its benefits have been disproportionately given to the strongest major party and a weak sectional party. The electoral system has made a major contribution to the identification of particular sections/provinces with particular parties. It has undervalued the partisan diversity within each section/province. By so doing it has rendered the parliamentary composition of each party less representative of the sectional interests in the political system than is the party electorate from which that representation is derived. The electoral system favours minor parties with concentrated sectional support and discourages those with diffuse national support. The electoral system has consistently exaggerated the significance of cleavages demarcated by sectional/provincial boundaries and has thus tended to transform contests between parties into contests between sections/provinces.

In view of the preceding, it is impossible to accept any assertion implying that the electoral system has had only trivial consequences for the party system. The Canadian party system in its present form would not exist had it not been for the highly selective impetus the electoral system gave to its development. In more specific terms, it is evident that one of the most basic aspects of Canadian politics, its sectional nature, becomes incomprehensible if attention is not constantly focused on the sectional bias engendered by the single-member constituency system.

Party System as a Nationalizing Agency

The ramifications of sectional politics are highly complex. Given the paucity of literature on Canadian parties it is impossible to make categorical statements about these ramifications in all cases. Where evidence is sparse, the analysis will of necessity be reduced to hypotheses, some of which will be sustained by little more than deduction.

One of the most widespread interpretations of the party system claims that it, or at least the two major parties, functions as a great unifying or nationalizing agency. Canadian politics, it is emphasized, are politics of moderation, or brokerage politics, which minimize differences, restrain fissiparous tendencies, and thus over time help knit together the diverse interests of a polity weak in integration.[8] It is noteworthy that this brokerage theory is almost exclusively applied to the reconciliation of sectional, racial, and religious divisions, the latter two frequently being regarded as simply more specific versions of the first with respect to French-English relations. The theory of brokerage politics thus assumes that the historically significant cleavages in Canada are sectional, reflecting the federal nature of Canadian society, or racial/religious, reflecting a continuation of the struggle that attracted Durham's attention in the mid-nineteenth century. Brokerage politics between classes is mentioned, if at all, as an afterthought.

The interpretation of the party system in terms of its fulfilment of a nationalizing function is virtually universal. Close scrutiny, however, indicates that this is at best questionable and possibly invalid. It is difficult to determine the precise meaning of the argument that the party system has been a nationalizing agency, stressing what Canadians have in common, bringing together representatives of diverse interests to deliberate on government policies. In an important sense the argument is misleading in that it attributes to the party system what is simply inherent in a representative democracy, which inevitably brings together Nova Scotians, Albertans, and Quebecers to a common assemblage point, and because the majoritarian necessities of the parliamentary system require agreement among contending interests to accomplish anything at all. Or, to put it differently, the necessity for inter-group collaboration in any ongoing political system makes it possible to claim of any party system compatible with the survival of the polity that it acts as a nationalizing agency. The extent to which any particular party system does so act is inescapably therefore a comparative question or a question of degree. In strict logic an evaluation of alternative types of party systems is required before a particular one can be accorded unreserved plaudits for the success with which it fulfils a nationalizing function.

Assistance in grappling with this issue comes from an examination of a basic problem. In what ways does the party system stimulate the very cleavages it is alleged to bridge? The question can be rephrased to ask the extent to which an unvarying sectionalism has an autonomous existence independent of the particular electoral and party systems employed by Canadians. The basic approach of this paper is that the party system, importantly conditioned by the electoral system, exacerbates the very cleavages it is credited with healing. As a corollary it is suggested that the party system is not simply a reflection of sectionalism, but that sectionalism is also a reflection of the party system.

The electoral system has helped to foster a particular kind of political style by the special significance it accords to sectionalism. This is evident in party campaign strategy, in party policies, in intersectional differences in the nature and vigour of party activity, and in differences in the intra-party socialization experiences of parliamentary personnel of the various parties. As a consequence, the electoral system has had an important effect on perceptions of the party system and, by extension, of the political system itself. Sectionalism has been rendered highly visible because the electoral system makes it a fruitful basis on which to organize electoral support. Divisions cutting through sections, particularly those based on the class system, have been much less salient because the possibility of payoffs in terms of representation has been minimal.

Parties and Campaign Strategy

An initial perspective on the contribution of the parties to sectionalism is provided by some of the basic aspects of campaign strategy. Inadequate attention has been paid to the extent to which the campaign activities of the parties have exacerbated the hatreds, fears, and insecurities related to divisive sectional and ethnic cleavages.[9]

The basic cleavage throughout Canadian history concerns Quebec, or more precisely that part of French Canada resident in Quebec, and its relationships with the rest of the country. The evidence suggests that elections have fed on racial fears and insecurities, rather than reduced them.[10] The three post-war elections of 1921, 1925, and 1926 produced overwhelming Liberal majorities at the level of seats in Quebec, 65 out of 65 in 1921, 59 out of 65 in 1925, and 60 seats out of 65 in 1926. The Conservatives' weakness in Quebec derived from their identification with conscription, the hanging of Riel, and the punitive treatment they received from the electoral system. A contributory factor of considerable importance, however, especially in 1921 and 1925, was the vituperative tirade the Liberals waged against Meighen and the Conservatives, stressing the 1917 crisis and exaggerating the dangers to Quebec should the Conservatives be successful. The 1925 campaign was described by Meighen as one in which "our candidates faced a campaign of hatred and racial appeal even more bitter than that of 1921. Paid organizers went from house to house advising the voters, particularly the women, that if Meighen were elected Prime Minister a war with Turkey would be declared and that the entrails of their sons would be scattered on the streets of Constantinople."[11] In view of the ample evidence documented by Graham and Neatby of the extent to which the Liberal campaigns stirred up the animosities and insecurities of French Canada, it is difficult to assert that the party system performed a unifying role in a province where historic tensions were potentially divisive. The fact that the Liberals were able to "convince Quebec" that they were its only defenders and that their party contained members of both ethnic groups after the elections scarcely constitute refutation when attention is directed to the methods employed to achieve this end, and when it is noted that the election results led to the isolation of Canada's second great party from Quebec.[12]

More recent indications of sectional aspects of campaign strategy with respect to Quebec help to verify the divisive nature of election campaigning. The well-known decision of the Conservative Party in 1957, acting on Gordon Churchill's maxim to "reinforce success not failure," to reduce its Quebec efforts and concentrate on the possibilities of success in the remainder of the country provides an important indication of the significance of calculations of sectional payoffs in dictating campaign strategy.[13] The logic behind this policy was a direct consequence of the electoral system, for that system dictated that increments of voting support from Quebec would produce less payoff in representation than would equal increments elsewhere where the prospects of Conservative constituency victories were more promising. The electoral results were brilliantly successful from the viewpoint of the party, but less so from the perspective of Quebec, which contributed only 8 per cent of the new government's seats, and received only three cabinet ministers.[14]

In these circumstances the election of 1958 was crucial in determining the nature and extent of French-Canadian participation in the new government, which obviously would be formed by the Conservatives. Group appeals were exploited by the bribe that Quebec would get many more cabinet seats if that province returned a larger number of Tory MPs.[15] Party propaganda stimulated racial tensions and insecurities. A Conservative advertisement showed an outline map of Canada deeply cleft by a hatchet at the Quebec-Ontario border. Above it were the words: "The newspapers predict a shattering triumph for Diefenbaker." Below it the words: "Let us not isolate Quebec." Liberal propaganda retaliated with an advertisement consisting of twelve outline drawings of Diefenbaker comparing him to previous Conservatives who were stereotyped as anti-French.[16] Neither appeal was well designed to foster easy cordiality and an absence of suspicion and fear between French- and English-speaking Canada.[17]

The significance of Quebec representation in explaining the nature of the Canadian party system has often been noted. Meisel states that the federal politician is faced with the dilemma of ignoring the pleas of Quebec, in which case "he may lose the support of Canada's second largest province without the seats of which a Parliamentary majority is almost impossible. If he heeds the wishes of Quebec, he may be deprived of indispensable support elsewhere."[18] Lipson describes Quebec as the "solid South" of Canada whose support has contributed at different times to the hegemony of both parties, a fact that is basic in explaining the strategy of opposition of the two major parties.[19] An important point is made by Ward in his observation that Liberal dominance in Quebec contributes to "internal strains in other parties." He adds the fundamental point that the electoral system, "by throwing whole blocks of seats to one party," fosters for that party a "special role as protector of the minority," while other parties are baffled by their inability to make significant breakthroughs in representation. Prophetically, as it turned out, he noted the developing theory that opposition parties should attempt to construct parliamentary majorities without Quebec, thus facing French Canadians with the option of becoming an opposition minority or casting themselves loose from the Liberals.[20]

Ward's analysis makes clear that the special electoral importance of Quebec and the resultant party strategies elicited by that fact are only meaningful in the context of an electoral system that operates on a "winner take all" basis, not only at the level of the constituency but, to a modified extent, at the level of the province as a whole. It is only at the level of seats, not votes, that Quebec became a Liberal stronghold, a Canadian "solid South," and a one-party monopoly. The Canadian "solid South," like its American counterpart, is a contrivance of the electoral system, not an autonomous social fact that exists independent of it.

The electoral system is to politicians as the the price system is to businessmen. If the latter found marked differentials in the returns they received for their commodities in different sections of the country this would have, to say the least, important consequences for the staff in the salesroom. It seems clear that the staff in the salesroom of the political parties is importantly conditioned in its conduct by the imperfections of the political market in which the parties sell their goods.

Quebec constitutes the most striking example of the sectional nature of party strategy, electoral appeals, and electoral outcomes. It is, however, only a specific manifestation of the general principle that when the distribution of partisan support within a province or section is such that significant political payoffs are likely to accrue to politicians who address themselves to the special needs of the area concerned, politicians will not fail to provide at least a partial response.[21] The tendencies of parties "to aim appeals at the nerve centres of particular provinces or regions, hoping thus to capture a bloc geographical vote,"[22] and to emphasize sectional appeals are logical party responses within the Canadian electoral framework.

Electoral System and Party Policy

The effect of the electoral system on party policies has already been suggested in part in the preceding indication of its impact on election campaigns. The inquiry can be extended by noting that the electoral system affects party policies both directly and indirectly. The direct effect flows from the elementary consideration that each party devises policy in the light of a different set of sectional considerations. In theory, if the party is viewed strictly as a maximizing body pursuing representation, party sensitivity should be most highly developed in marginal situations where an appropriate policy initiative, special organizational effort, or a liberal use of campaign funds might tip the balance of sectional representation to the side of the party. Unfortunately, sufficient evidence is not available to assert that this is a valid description of the import of sectional considerations on party strategies. The indirect effect of the electoral system is that it plays an important role in the determination of who the party policy-makers will be.

The indirect effect presupposes the pre-eminence of the parliamentary party and its leaders in policy-making. Acceptance of this presupposition requires a brief preliminary analysis of the nature of party organization, especially for the two major parties. The literature has been unanimous in referring to the organizational weakness of the Liberals and Conservatives. Some of the basic aspects and results of this will be summarily noted.

The extra-parliamentary structures of the two major parties have been extremely weak, lacking in continuity and without any disciplining power over the parliamentary party. The two major parties have been leader-dominated with membership playing a limited role in policy-making and party financing. Although there are indications that the extra-parliamentary apparatus of the parties is growing in importance, it can be safely said that for the period under review both major parties have been essentially parliamentary parties.

Some suggestive explanations of this situation have been offered, particularly by Regenstreif. These include the absence in Canada of several important stimuli that have facilitated the development of party organization in the United States and Great Britain. The stimuli resulting from a powerful mass-membership left-wing party and by serious restrictions on campaign expenditures, as in Great Britain, are absent in Canada. Unlike the American situation, Canadian parties are not responsible for voter registration. Compared to the United States, Canada also has a paucity of elections and elective offices, and party spoils have constituted a less attractive inducement to organizational work for the party.

In these circumstances of weak extra-parliamentary organization, it is evident that the parliamentary party, or more specifically the leader and his trusted parliamentary colleagues, has had few institutional party restraints to contend with in the development of policy.[23] Thus, the contribution of the electoral system to the determination of the parliamentary personnel of the party becomes, by logical extension, a contribution to the formation of party policies.[24] Scarrow has asserted that "it is the makeup of the parliamentary party, including the proportional strength and bargaining position of the various parts, which is the most crucial factor in determining policy at any one time."[25] While this hypothesis may require modification in particular cases, it is likely that historical research will confirm its general validity. For example, the antithetical attitudes of Conservatives and Liberals to conscription in both world wars were related not only to the electoral consequences of different choices, but also reflected the backgrounds and bias of the party personnel available to make such key decisions.[26] The generally much more solicitous treatment of Quebec and the French Canadians by the Liberals than by the Conservatives is similarly explicable. It is not accidental that bitter criticisms of family allowances as bribes to Quebec came from the Conservatives, while the recent emphasis on unhyphenated Canadianism has also been a Conservative contribution.[27]

The significance of the electoral system for party policy is due to its consistent failure to reflect with even rough accuracy the distribution of partisan support in the various sections/provinces of the country. By making the Conservatives far more of a British and Ontario-based party, the Liberals far more a French and Quebec party, the CCF far more a prairie and B.C. party, and even Social Credit far more of an Alberta party up until 1953 than the electoral support of these parties "required," they were deprived of intraparty spokesmen proportionate to their electoral support from the sections where they were relatively weak. The relative, or on occasion total, absence of such spokesmen for particular sectional communities seriously affects the image of the parties as national bodies, deprives the party concerned of articulate proponents of particular sectional interests in caucus and in the House, and, it can be deductively suggested, renders the members of the parliamentary party personally less sensitive to the interests of the unrepresented sections than they otherwise would be. As a result the general perspectives and policy orientations of a party are likely to be skewed in favour of those interests which, by virtue of strong parliamentary representation, can vigorously assert their claims.

If a bias of this nature is consistently visited on a specific party over long periods of time it will importantly condition the general orientation of the party and the political information and values of party MPs. In such ways, it can be argued that the effect of the electoral system is cumulative, creating conditions that aggravate the bias it initially introduced into the party.[28] To take the case of the Conservative Party, the thesis is that not only does the electoral system make the party less French by depriving it of French representation as such, but also by the effect that absence of French colleagues has on the possibility that its non-French members will shed their parochial perspectives through intra-party contacts with French co-workers in parliament.[29]

The Conservatives have experienced great difficulty in recruiting capable French-Canadian representation into the hierarchy of the parliamentary party, a difficulty partly related to the discrimination of the electoral system that gave the party only a small pool of talent to work with. It has also been suggested that the parliamentary party has provided a most uncongenial habitat for those few French Canadians who did survive the rigours of electoral competition to take their seats as Conservative MPs. John R. Williams claims that the Ontario-dominated parliamentary group played an important role in the decline of the Conservative Party in the King era.[30] The caucus, with its disparaging comments about Quebec and miserable treatment of French-Canadian colleagues, seriously damaged the party in Quebec. French-Canadian Conservatives refused to run for re-election or crossed the floor to join the Liberals. On at least two occasions the departing French Canadians "publicly renounced the party because of the parliamentary group's hostility toward them and their race."[31] In marked contrast is the evidence of Ward that French-English relations within the Liberal Party are "regarded by both as good," although they seem to be based on peaceful co-existence rather than on mutually intimate understandings.[32]

While a lengthy catalogue of explanations can be adduced to explain the divergent orientations of Liberals and Conservatives to Quebec and French Canada, the electoral system must be given high priority as an influencing factor. A strong deductive case therefore can be made that the sectional bias in party representation engendered by the electoral system has had an important effect on the policies of specific parties and on policy differences between parties.[33] In addition, the electoral system has helped to determine the real or perceived sectional consequences of alternative party policy decisions. Politicians engaged in party organization and electoral work are, in Chubby Power's words, "inclined to gauge policies and administrations primarily in the light of their effect on the voting proclivities of the population, and to assess their value in terms of electoral success or failure, rather than on any other consideration."[34] This thesis, a practitioner's echo of Schumpeter's suggestion that politicians are individuals who deal in votes,[35] is far from constituting a total explanation of the factors influencing policy, but it is clear that no politician in a competitive party system can overlook the electoral consequences of his actions. In particular instances, the desire to win over a section in which the party is weak may lead to neglect of an area in which the party already has strong representation. King's courting of the Prairie provinces and neglect of the Maritimes in the first half of the twenties constitutes a revealing instance of this phenomenon.[36] Whether a party directs attention to the sections where it is strong, as a result of the assertiveness of intra-party spokesmen, or whether attention is lavished on a section where a major breakthrough is deemed possible, is a matter for investigation in each case. From our perspective the basic point is that both reflect the politics of sectionalism as stimulated by the single-member constituency system.

In some cases the sectional nature of party support requires politicians to make a cruel choice between sections, a choice recognized as involving the sacrifice of future representation from one section in order to retain it from another. This, it has been argued, was the Conservative dilemma in deciding whether or not Riel was to hang and in determining conscription policy in the First World War. Faced with a choice between Quebec and Ontario, in each case they chose Ontario. It should be noted that these either/or sectional choices occasionally thrown up in the political system are given exaggerated significance by an electoral system capable of transforming a moderate loss of votes in a section into almost total annihilation at the level of representation. If only votes were considered, the harshness of such decisions would be greatly mitigated, for decisions could be made on the basis of much less dramatic marginal assessments of the political consequences of alternative courses of action.

Electoral System and Perceptions of the Polity

A general point, easily overlooked because of its elementary nature, is that the electoral system has influenced perceptions of the political system. The sectional basis of party representation the electoral system has stimulated has reduced the visibility of cleavages cutting through sections. The effect of this on the perceptions and conduct of political activists has already been noted. Academics have also been misled and frequently have imputed a monolithic partisan unity to the sectional particularisms of Canadian society.[37] The resultant misconception has identified particular sections with particular parties and particular parties with particular sections.[38]

It has been argued that the fragmentation of the electoral struggle into several hundred individual constituency contests, in contrast to the American system, prevents Canadians from identifying a "genuine regional influence" on election outcomes.[39] The fact is, however, that commentators have been far from reluctant to interpret election phenomena in sectional terms. A hasty survey of political literature finds Quebec portrayed as "the solid Quebec of 1921," western Canada described as "once the fortress of protest movements," since transformed "into a Conservative stronghold," eastern Canada depicted in the 1925 election as having "punished King for his preoccupation with the prairies," and the Conservative Party described in 1955 as "almost reduced into being an Ontario party,"[40] when in the previous election 55.8 per cent of its voting support came from outside that province.

The use of sectional terminology in description easily shades off into highly suspect assumptions about the voting behaviour of the electorate within sections. One of the most frequent election interpretations attributes a monolithic quality to Quebec voters and then argues that they "have instinctively given the bulk of their support" to the government,[41] or it is claimed that "the voters of Quebec traditionally seem to want the bulk of their representation . . . on the government side of the House. . . ."[42] Several authors have specifically suggested that in 1958 Quebec, or the French Canadians, swung to Diefenbaker for this reason. To Regenstreif this was because otherwise he would have formed a government without French support, which would have meant "that their entire way of life would be at stake. . . . Their solution was to help form the new government that was obviously going to be created anyway and thereby avoid the much-feared isolation that would otherwise be their lot."[43] A recent analysis of New Brunswick politics argues that the strong tendency for MPs from that province to be on the government side of the House "must be" because "it seeks to gain what concessions it can by supporting the government and relying on its sense of gratitude."[44]

The tendency of the electoral system to create sectional or provincial sweeps for one party at the level of representation is an important reason for these misinterpretations. Since similar explanations have become part of the folklore of Canadian politics it is useful to examine the extremely tenuous basis of logic on which they rest. Quebec will serve as a useful case study. The first point to note is the large percentage of the Quebec electorate that does not vote for the party that subsequently forms the government, a percentage varying from 29.8 per cent in 1921 to 70.4 per cent in 1962, and averaging 48 per cent for the period 1921 to 1965 as a whole. In the second place, any government party will tend to win most of the sections most of the time. That is what a government party is. While Quebec has shown an above-average propensity to accord more than 50 per cent of its representation to the government party (on eleven occasions out of fourteen, compared to an average for all sections of just under eight out of fourteen[45]), this is partly because of the size of the contingent from Quebec and its frequent one-sided representation patterns. This means that to a large extent Quebec determines which party will be the government, rather than exhibiting a preference for being on the government or opposition side of the House. This can be tested by switching the representation Quebec gave to the two main parties in each of the eleven elections in which Quebec backed the winner. The method is simply to transfer the number of seats Quebec accorded the winning party to the second main party and to transfer the latter's Quebec seats to the former. This calculation shows that had Quebec distributed its seats between the two main parties in a manner precisely the opposite to its actual performance it would have been on the winning side on seven out of eleven occasions anyway.[46] It is thus more accurate to say that parties need Quebec in order to win than to say Quebec displays a strong desire to be on the winning side.

One final indication of the logical deficiencies of the assumption that Quebec voters are motivated by a bandwagon psychology will suffice. The case of 1958 will serve as an example. In 1957, when there was no prediction of a Conservative victory, Quebec voters gave 31.1 per cent of their voting support to the Conservative Party. In 1958 that percentage jumped to 49.6 when predictions of a Conservative victory were nearly universal. On the reasonable assumption that most of the Conservative supporters in 1957 remained with the party in 1958, and on the further assumption, which is questionable, that all of the increment in Conservative support was due to a desire to be on the winning side, the explanation is potentially applicable to only one Quebec voter out of five.

In concluding this critical analysis of a segment of Canadian political folklore, it is only necessary to state that the attribution of questionable motivations to Quebec or French Canada could easily have been avoided if attention had been concentrated on voting data rather than on the bias in representation caused by the single-member constituency system. The analysis of Canadian politics has been harmfully affected by a kind of mental shorthand, which manifests itself in the acceptance of a political map of the country that identifies provinces or sections in terms of the end results of the political process – partisan representation. This perception is natural since elections occur only once every three or four years while the results are visible for the entire period between elections. Since sectional discrepancies between votes and seats are due to the electoral system, it is evident that the latter has contributed to the formation of a set of seldom questioned perceptions that exaggerate the partisan significance of geographical boundaries.

Electoral System, Sectionalism, and Instability

Individuals can relate to the party system in several ways, but the two most fundamental are class and sectionalism.[47] The two are antithetical, for one emphasizes the geography of residence, while the other stresses stratification distinctions for which residence is irrelevant. The frequently noted conservative tone that pervades Canadian politics is a consequence of the sectional nature of the party system.[48] The emphasis on sectional divisions engendered by the electoral system has submerged class conflicts, and to the extent that our politics has been ameliorative it has been more concerned with the distribution of burdens and benefits between sections than between classes. The poverty of the Maritimes has occupied an honourable place in the foreground of public discussion. The diffuse poverty of the generally underprivileged has scarcely been noticed.

Such observations lend force to John Porter's thesis that Canadian parties have failed to harness the "conservative-progressive dynamic" related to the Canadian class system and to his assertion that "to obscure social divisions through brokerage politics is to remove from the political system that element of dialectic which is the source of creative politics."[49] The fact is, however, that given

131

the historical (and existing) state of class polarization in Canada the electoral system has made sectionalism a more rewarding vehicle for amassing political support than class. The destructive impact of the electoral system on the CCF is highly indicative of this point. It is not that the single-member constituency system discourages class-based politics in any absolute sense, as the example of Britain shows, but that it discourages such politics when class identities are weak or submerged behind sectional identities.

This illustrates the general point that the differences in the institutional contexts of politics have important effects in determining which kinds of conflict become salient in the political system. The particular institutional context with which this paper is concerned, the electoral system, has clearly fostered a sectional party system in which party strategists have concentrated on winning sections over to their side. It has encouraged a politics of opportunism based on sectional appeals and conditioned by one-party bastions where the opposition is tempted to give up the battle and pursue success in more promising areas.

A politics of sectionalism is a politics of instability for two reasons. In the first place it induces parties to pay attention to the realities of representation that filter through the electoral system, at the expense of the realities of partisan support at the level of the electorate. The self-interest that may induce a party to write off a section because its weak support there is discriminated against by the electoral system may be exceedingly unfortunate for national unity. Imperfections in the political market render the likelihood of an invisible hand transforming the pursuit of party good into public good somewhat dubious.

Secondly, sectional politics is potentially far more disruptive to the polity than class politics.[50] This is essentially because sectional politics has an inherent tendency to call into question the very nature of the political system and its legitimacy. Classes, unlike sections, cannot secede from the political system, and are consequently more prone to accept its legitimacy. The very nature of their spatial distribution not only inhibits their political organization but induces them to work through existing instrumentalities. With sections this is not the case.

Given the strong tendency to sectionalism found in the very nature of Canadian society, the question can be raised as to the appropriateness of the existing electoral system. Duverger has pointed out that the single-member constituency system "accentuates the geographical localization of opinions: one might even say that it tends to transform a national opinion . . . into a local opinion by allowing it to be represented only in the sections of the country in which it is strongest." Proportional representation works in the opposite manner for "opinions strongly entrenched locally tend to be broadened on to the national plane by the possibility of being represented in districts where they are in a small minority." The political significance of these opposed tendencies "is clear: proportional representation tends to strengthen national unity (or, to be more precise, national uniformity); the simple majority system accentuates local differences. The consequences are fortunate or unfortunate according to the particular situation in each country."[51]

Sectionalism and Discontinuities in Party Representation

It might be argued that the appropriate question is not whether sectional (or other) interests are represented proportionately to their voting support in each party, but simply whether they are represented in the party system as a whole proportionately to their general electoral strength. This assertion, however, is overly simple and unconvincing.

An electoral system that exaggerates the role of specific sections in specific parties accentuates the importance of sectionalism itself. If sectionalism in its "raw" condition is already strong, its exaggeration may cause strains beyond the capacity of the polity to handle. By its stimulus to sectional cleavages the electoral system transforms the party struggle into a struggle between sections, raising the danger that "parties . . . cut off from gaining support among a major stratum . . . lose a major reason for compromise."[52]

This instability is exacerbated by the fact that the electoral system facilitates sudden and drastic alterations in the basis of party parliamentary representation. Recent changes with respect to NDP representation from Saskatchewan, Social Credit representation from Quebec, and the startling change in the influence of the prairie contingent in the Conservative Party, with its counterpart of virtually eliminating other parties from that section, constitute important illustrations. The experience of Social Credit since 1962 and more recent experience of the Conservative Party reveal that such changes may be more than a party can successfully handle.

Sudden changes in sectional representation are most pronounced

133

in the transition from being an opposition party to becoming the government party. As Underhill notes,[53] it is generally impossible to have more than one party with significant representation from both French and English Canada at the same time. That party is invariably the government party. This has an important consequence that has been insufficiently noted. Not only are opposition parties often numerically weak and devoid of access to the expertise that would prepare them for the possibility of governing, but they are also far less national in composition than the government party. On the two occasions since the First World War when the Conservatives ousted Liberal governments, 1930 and 1957, their opposition experience cut them off from contact with Quebec at the parliamentary level. Even though the party was successful in making significant breakthroughs in that province in 1930 and especially in 1958, it can be suggested that it had serious problems in digesting the sudden input of Quebec MPs, particularly in the latter year.

The transition from opposition to government therefore is a transition from being sectional to being national, not only in the tasks of government, but typically in the very composition of the party itself. The hypothesis that this discontinuity may have serious effects on the capacity of the party to govern is deserving of additional research. It is likely that such research will suggest a certain incongruity between the honorific status symbolically accorded Her Majesty's Loyal Opposition and an electoral system likely to hamper the development in that party of those perspectives functional to successful governing.

The Electoral System as a Determinant of the Party System

Students of Canadian politics have been singularly unwilling to attribute any explanatory power to the electoral system as a determinant of the party system.[54] Lipson has argued that the electoral system does not mould the party system, but rather the reverse. Essentially his thesis is that parties select the type of electoral system most compatible with their own interest, which is self-perpetuation. He admits in passing that once selected the electoral system "produces a reciprocal effect upon the parties which brought it into being."[55]

Lipson's interpretation is surely misleading and fallacious in its implication that because parties preside over the selection, modification, and replacement of particular institutions the subsequent feedback of those institutions on the parties should not be regarded as causal. In the modern democratic party state, parties preside over the legal arrangements governing campaign expenses, eligibility of candidates, the rules establishing the determination of party winners and losers, the kinds of penalties, such as loss of deposits, which shall be visited on candidates with a low level of support, the rules establishing who may vote, and so on. Analysis is stifled if it is assumed that because these rules are made by parties the effect of the rules on the parties is in some sense to be regarded as derivative or of secondary interest or importance. Fundamentally, the argument concerns the priority to be accorded the chicken or the egg. As such, it can be pursued to an infinite regression, for it can be asserted that the parties making a particular set of rules are themselves products of the rules that prevailed in the previous period, which in turn. . . . It might also be noted that parties presiding over particular changes in electoral arrangements may be mistaken in their predictions about the effect of changes. It is clear that the introduction of the alternative ballot in British Columbia in 1952 misfired from the viewpoint of its sponsors, with dramatic effects on the nature of the provincial party system that subsequently developed.

The only reasonable perspective for the analyst to adopt is to accept the interdependence of electoral systems and party systems and then to investigate whatever aspects of that interdependence seem to provide useful clues for the understanding of the political system.

In a recent article Meisel explicitly agrees with Lipson, asserting that parties are products of societies rather than of differences between parliamentary or presidential systems, or of electoral laws.[56] This argument is weakened by its assumption that society is something apart from the institutional arrangements of which it is composed. It is unclear in this dichotomy just what society is. While it may be possible at the moment when particular institutions are being established to regard them as separate from the society to which they are to be fitted, this is not so with long-established institutions that become part and parcel of the society itself. Livingston's argument that after a while it becomes impossible to make an analytic distinction between the instrumentalities of federalism and the federal nature of the society they were designed to preserve or express is correct and is of general validity.[57] To say, therefore, that parties are products of societies is not to deny that they are products of institutions. The only defensible view is once again to accept the interdependence of political and other institutions that comprise society and then to establish the nature of particular patterns of interdependence by research.

Confirmation of the view that electoral systems do have an effect on party systems is provided by logic. To assert that a particular electoral system does not have an effect on a particular party system is equivalent to saying that all conceivable electoral systems are perfectly compatible with that party system and that all conceivable party systems are compatible with that electoral system. This is surely impossible. Any one electoral system has the effect of inhibiting the development of the different party systems that some, but not necessarily all, different electoral systems would foster. To accept this is to accept that electoral systems and party systems are related.

Approaches to a Theory of the Party System

This paper has suggested that the electoral system has been an important factor in the evolution of the Canadian party system. Its influence is intimately tied up with the politics of sectionalism it has stimulated. Sectionalism in the party system is unavoidable as long as there are significant differences between the distribution of party voter support in any one section and the distribution in the country as a whole. The electoral system, however, by the distortions it introduces as it transforms votes into seats, produces an exaggerated sectionalism at the level of representation. In view of this, the basic theme of the paper in its simplest form, and somewhat crudely stated, is that statements about sectionalism in the national party system are in many cases, and at a deeper level, statements about the politics of the single-member constituency system.

The suggested impact of the electoral system on the party system is relevant to a general theory of the party system but should not be confused with such a general theory. The construction of the latter would have required analysis of the import for the party system of such factors as the federal system, the relationship of provincial party organizations to the national party, the nature of the class system, the underlying economic and cultural bases for sectionalism, a parliamentary system of the British type, and many others. For this discussion all these have been accepted as given.

136

They have been mentioned, if at all, only indirectly. Their importance for a general theory is taken for granted, as are the interdependencies they have with each other and with the electoral system. It is evident, for example, that the underlying strength of sectional tendencies and the weakness of class identification are interrelated with each other and with the electoral system as explanations of sectionalism in Canadian politics.[58] For any one of these to change will produce a change in the outcomes their interactions generate. We are not therefore suggesting that sectional tendencies are exclusive products of the electoral system, but only that that system accords them an exaggerated significance.

Concentration on the electoral system represents an attempt to isolate one aspect of a complex series of interactions that is only imperfectly understood, and in the present state of our knowledge these cannot be handled simultaneously with precision. In such circumstances the development of more systematic comprehensive explanations will only result from a dialectic between research findings at levels varying from that of individual voters through middle-range studies, such as Alford's recent analysis of class and voting, to attempts, such as those by Scarrow and Meisel,[59] to handle a complex range of phenomena in one framework.

We can conclude that the capacity of the party system to act as an integrating agency for the sectional communities of Canada is detrimentally affected by the electoral sytem. The politicians' problem of reconciling sectional particularisms is exacerbated by the system they must work through in their pursuit of power. From one perspective it can be argued that if parties succeed in overcoming sectional divisions they do so in defiance of the electoral system. Conversely, it can be claimed that if parties do not succeed this is because the electoral system has so biased the party system that it is inappropriate to call it a nationalizing agency. It is evident that not only has the electoral system given impetus to sectionalism in terms of party compaigns and policy, but by making all parties more sectional at the level of seats than of votes it complicates the ability of the parties to transcend sectionalism. At various times the electoral system has placed barriers in the way of Conservatives becoming sensitively aware of the special place of Quebec and French Canada in the Canadian polity, aided the Liberals in that task, inhibited the third parties in the country from becoming aware of the special needs and dispositions of sections other than those represented in the parliamentary party, and frequently inhibited the parliamentary personnel of the major parties from becoming attuned to the sentiments of the citizens of the Prairies. The electoral system's support for the political idiosyncrasies of Alberta for over two decades ill-served the integration of that provincial community into the national political system at a time when it was most needed. In fact, the Alberta case merely illustrates the general proposition that the disintegrating effects of the electoral system are likely to be most pronounced where alienation from the larger political system is most profound. A particular orientation, therefore, has been imparted to Canadian politics that is not inherent in the very nature of the patterns of cleavage and consensus in the society, but results from their interplay with the electoral system.

The stimulation offered to sectional cleavages by the single-member constituency system has led several authors to query its appropriateness for national integration in certain circumstances. Lipset and Duverger have suggested that countries possessed of strong underlying tendencies to sectionalism may be better served by proportional representation that breaks up the monolithic nature of sectional representation stimulated by single-member constituency systems.[60] Belgium is frequently cited as a country in which proportional representation has softened the conflict between the Flemish and the Walloons, and the United States as a country in which the single-member constituency system has heightened cleavages and tensions between North and South. Whatever its other merits, the single-member constituency system lacks the singular capacity of proportional representation to encourage all parties to search for votes in all sections of the country. Minorities within sections or provinces are not frozen out as they tend to be under the existing system. As a consequence, sectional differences in party representation are minimized or, more accurately, given proportionate rather than exaggerated representation – a factor that encourages the parties to develop a national orientation.

PART III

THE FEDERAL SYSTEM AND THE INTERGOVERNMENTAL DIMENSION

Editor's Introduction

For all their differences, pluralist, structural-functionalist, cybernetic, and neo-Marxist theories of the state share the assumption that public policies are principally the product of societies rather than governments. Until quite recently, a similar assumption dominated most discussions of federalism. A classic statement of such a view was W.S. Livingston's study, *Federalism and Constitutional Change*. The institutions of government, Livingston argued,

> do not provide an accurate index of the federal nature of the society that subtends them; they are only the surface manifestations of the deeper federal quality of the society that lies beneath the surface. The essence of federalism lies not in the constitutional or institutional structure but in the society itself. Federal government is a device by which the federal qualities of the society are articulated and protected.[1]

In the first essay of this section, Cairns's 1977 Presidential Address to the Canadian Political Science Association, readers will find one of the earliest and most provocative challenges to such views. The type of society-centred perspective and reductionism advocated by Livingston and others could not, Cairns claims, explain the survival and growth of dynamic provincial governments, particularly in English Canada. The essay then proceeds to probe some of the more worrisome implications of the realization that, as Samuel H. Beer once poignantly observed, "government itself may be a source of what government does."[2] The increasing functional specialization of the modern welfare state entails the

139

development of a sprawling professional bureaucratic complex; the spatial, territorial specialization unique to federal societies fuels a vast intergovernmental lobby at national, provincial or state, and local levels; the combined effect of these two mutually reinforcing centres of power and influence poses serious difficulties for citizen control and responsible government in liberal democracies such as Canada.

Concern over the declining capacity for the effective use of government authority for the attainment of public goals constitutes the principal theme of the second essay in this section, "The Other Crisis of Canadian Federalism," initially presented in 1977 as his Inaugural Lecture at the University of Edinburgh's Centre of Canadian Studies. Drafted during the height of the pessimism so characteristic of the period between the 1976 election of the Parti Québécois and the referendum on sovereignty-association in 1980, "The Other Crisis" contends that "the working constitution of Canadian federalism can no longer control and channel the activities of governments in order to minimize their self-defeating competition with each other. Far from existing in splendid policy-making isolation from each other, these governments jostle and compete in an ever more destructive struggle, which reduces the beneficial public impact of the massive public sector produced by their conflicting, overlapping, and discordant ambitions."[3] Always alert to the ironies of political life and the unintended consequences of our designs, Cairns here challenges us to shed several of our most cherished illusions and grapple with the realization that "The very effort to maximize public control over our fate by the device of big government at two levels has undermined the federal system and produced a situation in which we are in imminent danger of being victimized by our own creations."[4]

Hardly a study of Canadian federalism has appeared in the last decade that has not found it necessary to address the powerful and frequently iconoclastic perspective of these essays. Their place in future debates over the nature of Canadian federalism and the role of the state seems equally secure.[5]

Chapter Five

The Governments and Societies of Canadian Federalism

If you marry the Spirit of your generation you will be a widow in the next.

— *Dean Inge*

The Canadian political system, now in its second century, can no longer be taken for granted. It is altogether possible, some would say probable, and some would say desirable, that major institutional change, not excluding the fragmentation of Canada, is on the immediate horizon. It is therefore an opportune time to reflect on the century-long interaction between government and society in Canada. I use the word "reflect" advisedly, for this is not the type of interaction about which hard statements can be confidently made.

The impact of society on government is a common theme in the study of democratic polities. Less common is an approach stressing the impact of government on the functioning of society. I have chosen the latter for the guiding theme of my remarks, because I am convinced that our approach to the study of Canadian politics pays inadequate attention to the capacity of government to make society responsive to its demands.

With some exceptions, my remarks will be confined to senior governments operating in the institutional framework of federalism. Particular institutions, such as the electoral system, the Senate, and many others will be ignored or given only minor attention.

Since the Depression of the thirties, the analysis, criticism, and defence of federalism have been the major stock-in-trade of political

141

scientists attempting overall perspectives on the Canadian political system. Rising and changing political expectations in Quebec, culminating in the victory of the Parti Québécois in November, 1976, have set us on the path toward yet another brooding inquiry into our federal condition. Unfortunately, our capacity to make wise choices for the future is seriously curtailed by our limited understanding of the political system we are urged to leave behind. In the last half century students of Canadian federalism have been consistently taken aback by the unexpected transformation of the subject matter to which their expertise applied. There is no compelling reason to believe that our scholarly fate will be different.

We occasionally hear of tribes that consult the writings of their anthropologist when in doubt about the customs they should follow. This reuniting of social science description and actual behaviour is most gratifying to the tribal scholar who, understandably, may fail to see that this apparently positive feedback is independent of the correctness of his original analysis. The anthropologists of Canadian federalism have no such real or imaginary consolation for, whether or not political actors read what we write, we observe with chagrin that federal reality monotonously disconfirms our predictions. It is even so with the predictions of our present Prime Minister, a keen student of federalism, who has had the misfortune to become the chief of a tribe that consults the works of other anthropologists.

I do not expect the remainder of this paper to provide an analysis of Canadian federalism that will not be belied by the future; nor do I intend to join the army of constitution writers who will bedazzle or bedevil us in the next few years with the fertile products of their imagination. My task is simply to try and identify the major shortcoming in the approaches we employ in the analysis of federalism and to propose an alternative perspective.

The reaction against traditional political science, with its alleged overemphasis on the formal, legal aspects of the polity at the expense of the social forces that worked it, was given striking emphasis for students of federalism in W.S. Livingston's famous assertion in 1956 that "Federalism is a function not of constitutions but of societies."[1] The dynamic of the system was to be sought not in government, or in features of the constitution, but in society. In the elaboration of this sociological perspective, political systems are seen as superstructures devoid of autonomy and lacking independent coercive and moulding power vis-à-vis their environment.

Two decades before the appearance of Livingston's seminal piece, the Depression produced a great outburst of federalist literature, or, more properly, anti-federalist literature, in English Canada, which presupposed "The Obsolescence of Federalism."[2] This literature viewed the central government as the fortunate and necessary beneficiary and provincial governments as the hapless victims of overwhelmingly powerful socio-economic forces. In essence, it was argued that technological interdependence and the evolution of a national market made centralized leadership necessary for planning purposes and destroyed the sociological basis for the vitality and meaningful survival of the provinces. Provincial governments, considered out of tune with fundamental requirements and urgent imperatives rooted in society and economy, apparently had no resources adequate to stay the execution decreed for them by scholars with the future in their bones.

The centralization predicted in the thirties seemed firmly and securely in place in the forties and for much of the fifties. It was explained in 1957 by Professor J.A. Corry as a product of technological necessity. Corry, responding to prevailing interpretations of the nature and direction of socio-economic change, produced a polished epitaph for any significant future role for provincial governments. The growth of "giant corporations, national trade associations, and national trade unions"[3] created a nationalizing of sentiment among elites who backed the central government and thus contributed to the centralization of authority in Ottawa. The most a province could hope for, he asserted, "is freedom for minor adventure, for embroidering its own particular patterns in harmony with the national design, for playing variant melodies within the general theme. . . . [I]t is everywhere limited in the distance it can go by having become part of a larger, although not necessarily a better, scheme of things."[4]

To the distress of a later generation of liberal-left critics of federalism, Corry's predictions of a nationalization of politics and the continuing centralization of authority in federal hands proved premature. For John Porter, writing in the mid-sixties, when the centralizing impulse born of depression, war, and post-war reconstruction had faded, the federal system was little more than a pious fraud devoid of real meaning for the citizenry, and sustained by academics with a vested interest in their esoteric knowledge of the system's functioning, and by political and bureaucratic elites happy to place federal roadblocks in the way of class politics. To Porter, reiterating an argument widely employed in the thirties, the "conditions of modern industrial society and international relations . . . [made] it . . . almost essential that the central government acquire power at the expense of the provincial . . . governments."[5] Canada, however, was relatively exempt from this necessary and beneficial trend. The cause of this regrettable backwardness was located in the political system, with its exaggerated obsession with national unity and its bias in favour of provincial rights. Reduced to essentials, Porter's position was simply that the class cleavage, based on the economic system, was the true, natural, and dynamic cleavage, while regional cleavages stimulated and fostered by the political system were fundamentally artificial, meaningless, and accordingly undeserving of respect. A well-functioning, modern political system, in marked contrast to the existing federal system, would serve, above all else, as an instrumentality for the expression of creative politics founded on the class struggle of advanced industrial society, with regional considerations shunted to the sidelines. This may be called the sociologist's ideal political system, for it awards primacy to his subject matter.

The unavoidable briefness of my remarks obviously does not do justice to the complexity and diversity of the extensive literature on Canadian federalism, and inevitably oversimplifies the views of those few writers mentioned above. What I have tried to do is to highlight their relative failure to perceive the degree of autonomy possessed by governments and the ongoing capacity of the federal system to manufacture the conditions necessary for its continuing survival. Where such is partially noted, as it is by Porter, the admission is grudging and is accompanied by pejorative adjectives that cloud the analysis.

In a sense, Livingston's plea to search for the determinants of a changing federalism in society, not constitutions, was not needed in Canada. From the mid-thirties to the present we have not lacked sociological approaches to federalism. The weakness of our understanding lies elsewhere, in a failure to treat government with appropriate seriousness. The remainder of this paper is an attempt to redress the balance by arguing, contrary to Livingston, that federalism, at least in the Canadian case, is a function not of societies but of the constitution, and more importantly of the governments that work the constitution.[6]

The great mystery for students of Canadian federalism has been the survival and growth of provincial governments, particularly those of English Canada. Sociologically focused inquiries, with Quebec as an implicit model, have looked for vital, inward-looking provincial societies on which governments could be based and, finding none, have been puzzled why these governmental super-structures, seemingly lacking a necessary foundation, have not faded away.

The sociological perspective pays inadequate attention to the possibility that the support for powerful, independent provincial governments is a product of the political system itself, that it is fostered and created by provincial government elites employing the policy-making apparatus of their jurisdictions, and that such support need not take the form of a distinct culture, society, or nation as these are conventionally understood. More specifically, the search for an underlying sociological base, whatever its nature and source, as the necessary sustenance for viable provincial political systems, deflects us from considering the prior question of how much support is necessary. Passivity, indifference, or the absence of strong opposition from their environment may be all that provincial governments need in order to thrive and grow. The significant question, after all, is the survival of provincial governments, not of provincial societies, and it is not self-evident that the existence and support of the latter is necessary to the functioning and aggrandisement of the former. Their sources of survival, renewal, and vitality may well lie within themselves and in their capacity to mould their environment in accordance with their own governmental purposes.

In the analysis of contemporary party systems much has been made of the extent to which today's parties represent the historic residue of the cleavages of yesteryear. In the Canadian case the freezing of party alternatives fades into insignificance compared with the freezing by the federal system of initially five and now eleven constitutionally distinct and separate governments. The enduring stability of these governments contrasts sharply with the fluctuating fortunes of all parties and the disappearance of many. Governments, as persisting constellations of interests, constitute the permanent elements of the Canadian polity that thus far have ridden out the storms of social, economic, and political change.

The decision to establish a federal system in 1867 was a first-order macro decision concerning the basic institutional features of the new polity. It created competitive political and bureaucratic elites at two levels of government endowed with an impressive array of jurisdictional, financial, administrative, and political resources to deploy in the pursuit of their objectives. The post-Confederation history of Canadian federalism is little more than the record of the efforts of governing elites to pyramid their resources and of the uses to which they have put them. Possessed of tenacious instincts for their own preservation and growth, the governments of Canadian federalism have endowed the cleavages between provinces, and between provinces and nation that attended their birth, with an ever more comprehensive political meaning.

The crucial, minimum prerequisites for provincial survival and growth have been the preservation of jurisdictional competence and of territorial integrity. In terms of the former, it is notable that explicit change in the constitutional responsibilities of the two levels of government has been minimal, in spite of strong centralizing pressure on occasion. The division of powers has been altered to federal advantage only three times, in each of which unanimous provincial consent was obtained, and in two of which provincial paramountcy was respected. Provincial pressure has ensured the *de facto* acceptance of the principle that the concurrence of all provincial governments is necessary for any amendment that would reduce their formal constitutional authority. Even in their periods of greatest weakness provincial governments steadfastly resisted and thwarted all efforts to accord explicit constitutional recognition to a more flexible amendment procedure dealing with the division of powers. By their self-interested obstinacy they preserved their basic bargaining power for the future and formally protected the jurisdictional integrity essential for subsequent increases in their governmental potency. Although the proposed amendment procedures in the Victoria Charter of 1971 departed from the principle of provincial unanimity for formal changes in the distribution of legislative powers, the Charter was rejected by the Bourassa government of Quebec.[7] The principle of unanimous provincial consent for constitutional amendments in this area thus remains as part of the operating constitution. The paucity of amendments dealing with the division of power and the long-standing opposition of provincial governments to any formally agreed amendment procedures that might diminish their lawmaking authority without their express consent strikingly reveal an entrenched governmental conservatism where the constitutional base of provincial governing capacity is concerned.

Equally indicative of provincial tenacity in self-preservation is the integrity of provincial boundaries. No province has given up territory to which it had clear and undisputed possession. Where territorial "loss" has occurred, as in the 1872 case of the San Juan boundary settlement by the German Emperor, which denied the claims of British Columbia, or in the case of Labrador decided by judicial determination in favour of Newfoundland in 1927, provincial frustrations have been pronounced, and in the latter case long-lived. Half a century later the claim of Quebec to Labrador remains a live issue to the Quebec government.[8] Disputed cases, such as offshore mineral resources caught between the counterclaim of federal and provincial governments, illustrate the vigour with which provincial positions are defended, even in the face of adverse court decisions. Where the possibility of territorial expansion has existed, or still exists, with respect to contiguous territory outside provincial boundaries, the provinces have consistently manifested a revolution of rising expectations not yet dead. It has not only been the federal government assiduously extending the range of its jurisdiction from the limited Canada of 1867 to the ten-province Canada of 1949, and now extending its effective writ over Canada's Arctic frontiers, which displays a well-developed drive for territorial acquisition. The original boundaries of Quebec, Ontario, and Manitoba contained only a small portion of the land masses they now control. On occasion, interprovincial controversy over disputed territory has even produced mini border conflicts, as in the case of Manitoba and Ontario in the thirty-year period preceding the final determination of their boundary in 1912.[9]

The three Maritime provinces, doomed by location to be deprived of attainable territorial ambitions, have been tenacious in not giving up the political control over defined territories they individually possess. They resisted amalgamation in the 1860s, and in spite of the urgings of the Deutsch Report, they resist it today. "By any administrative logic," stated *The Economist*, "the three provinces should be bundled into one. But nobody will be crazy enough to try."[10] The hostile stance of Newfoundland to any possible reopening of the Labrador case by an independent Quebec further attests to the territorial conservatism of the provinces, tightly holding on to what they have won in the historical lottery of land acquisition. The provincial protection of and search for *Lebensraum* comprise a relatively unexamined aspect of federal-provincial history deserving as much scholarly investigation as their better-known safeguarding of their formal jurisdictional authority.

The protection of jurisdictional authority and the protection and expansion of provincial territory have been accompanied by an ever more vigorous employment of provincial legislative competence. Related to this as both cause and effect has been a concomitant increase in government personnel. A similar expansion of personnel and a no less aggressive exploration of the limits of its constitutional responsibilities have been displayed by the federal government.

It would be a serious mistake to view these governmental mountains as molehills. The several hundred political officeholders constitute only a trivial minority of those who wield government power and/or derive their income directly from public positions. The growth of one federal and ten provincial governments has produced large and powerful complexes of institutions and personnel with their own professional and personal interests, and their own official purposes for the provincial and federal populations they govern. At the elementary level of numbers, the figures are staggeringly impressive. Total provincial government personnel, including provincial government enterprises, as of September, 1976, reached 519,000,[11] while the federal government sustains a veritable army of various shades and categories of civil service and crown corporation personnel, totalling 557,000 persons, a figure that includes the armed forces.[12] Nearly one out of every nine members of the Canadian work force is employed by the two senior levels of government,[13] while municipal government employs a further 256,000.[14] They are not indifferent to the fate of the governments they serve.

The astute observation of Alexander Hamilton in Federalist Paper No. 1, two centuries ago, has not declined in relevance: "Among the most formidable of the obstacles which the new Constitution will have to encounter may readily be distinguished the obvious interest of a certain class of men in every State to resist all changes which may hazard a diminution of the power, emolument, and consequence of the offices they hold under the State establishments."[15] Another certain class of men has attached itself to the central government.

It makes little sense to think of these impressive concentrations of power and personnel as superstructures whose existence and purposes are largely derivative of the electorate, the class structure, the pressure group system, or whatever. Even if we ignore their functions, the more than one million Canadians who work for federal and provincial governments, and their dependents, constitute an immense component of Canadian society directly tied to government. When we do consider their functions of policy-making, service-provision, regulation, and protection, extending to the most specialized activities where government monopolizes the expertise in a given field, we are made aware that we live in a period of convulsive change in government-society relations. In the evolution of the division of labour between those who govern and those who are governed, the energizing, proselytizing, and entrepreneurial role increasingly rests with those civil servants and politicians with the capacity to influence policy and its administration.

While the sheer fact of large numbers directly dependent on government should not be underestimated as a crucial, if elementary, factor in government survival, that contribution is multiplied by the ramifying effects of the institutional and organizational complexes in which these employees work and have their being. The ministries, departments, agencies, bureaus, and field offices to which they daily report constitute partially self-contained entities, valued for their own sake, and possessed of their own life and interests. Their minimum desire is for a steady level of activity. Typically, however, they seek to enlarge the scope of their functions. If the environment offers new opportunities for expansion in emergent problem areas they will compete with other bureaucracies for the prizes of status and growth offered by enhancement of their activity. If major challenges are made to their organizational identity, purpose, or cohesion, they will fight back against unsympathetic political superiors and other menacing figures and forces in their environment.[16] If their functions decline in social utility or their expertise becomes obsolescent, they will scan the horizon of alternative possibilities in an aggressive search for new justifications for continued existence.[17] While they are subject to political control and direction they have impressive capacities to get their own way and to bend their political superiors to their will. Although their functions relate them to particular sectors of society, they are not puppets or simple reflections of the interests of the groups they control, regulate, or service. "[B]oth the sector served and political leaders come to be forces in the environment which public servants must manage and manipulate so that they will demand or agree to expansion of the bureaucracy."[18] Their basic strength resides in the expertise that makes them indispensable to their political superiors and in the support of the external interests that have positively adapted to their policies. They represent a permanent, expansive aspect of government. They are the necessary instruments of an administered society that could not, without major disruption, survive their disappearance from the scene.

The presence in the Canadian federal system of eleven governments, each honeycombed with bureaucratic interests and desires of the nature just described, helps explain the expansion of each level of government, the frequent competition and duplication of activity between governments, and the growing impact of government on society. It is impossible to think clearly about Canadian federalism without devoting extensive attention to the one million Canadians parcelled out in eleven jurisdictions and committed by loyalty, the terms of their employment, and self-interest to the particular government they serve.

These pyramids of bureaucratic power and ambition are capped by political authorities also possessed of protectionist and expansionist tendencies. The eleven governments of the federal system endow the incumbents of political office with the primary task of defending and advancing the basic interests of crucial sectors of the provincial or national economy and society. Each political office, particularly those of prime ministers and premiers, has a history that influences and constrains the succession of incumbents who briefly possess it. Thus, as André Bernard says: "No political leader in Quebec would ever dare voice a doubt about the sacrosanct objective of 'la survivance française en Amérique'. Survival of the French-Canadian people is an obligation, an article of faith. It has been so for 200 years. It is basic, fundamental."[19] Since 1871 the political leaders of British Columbia have consistently pressed economic claims on Ottawa demanding compensation for the chronically alleged financial maltreatment they have suffered from the federal government. The special needs and expenses associated with the harsh facts of geography and a primary resource-based economy have been reiterated in countless briefs. Other provinces also have "fairly durable and persisting interests"[20] reflecting the relatively unchanging factors of society, economy, and basic position in the federal system. The claims derived from the preceding are nourished by the constantly refurbished memory of past grievances.

Provincial political elites not only seek to further the long-range interests of their society and economy, they also have "a vested interest in provincial status and power which the several provincial electorates perhaps do not share fully."[21] Their policy determinations reflect a varying mix of goals for their provincial citizenry and an institutional concern for the long-term survival of the political and bureaucratic power of government itself. On the other side of the bargaining table they encounter Ottawa, a larger version of their own expansionist tendencies, which, in the slightly jaundiced words of Claude Morin, "is quite simply loyal to a solidly-rooted historical tradition, the unmistakable outlines of which could already be discerned in John A. Macdonald's remarks at the time the federation was put together."[22]

The inertia of the political and bureaucratic momentum of the governments they join inducts new recruits into prevailing definitions of the situation. This is instanced by the frequency with which staunch provincialists, from Joseph Howe onwards, become staunch federalists on entering the federal government. Thus, it is not surprising that the representatives of "French power" in Ottawa will seek solutions to French-English problems by policies that do not weaken the central government. They will try and make the federal government and, indeed, the whole country a more congenial environment for Francophones rather than opt for a solution that enhances the power of the government in Quebec City. It is also not surprising that such efforts are looked on with little favour by government elites in Quebec City. French Canadians in federal politics and in the federal civil service are conditioned to see the world through different eyes than their Quebec City counterparts.[23] What is attractive to the latter is often a direct threat to the political and bureaucratic needs of the former. Profound governmental contraints minimize the possibility of ethnic solidarity across jurisdictional boundaries.

Federal and provincial governments are not neutral containers, or reflecting mirrors, but aggressive actors steadily extending their tentacles of control, regulation, and manipulation into society – playing, in Deutsch's terminology, a steering role – and thus fostering sets of integrated relationships between themselves and the various socio-economic forces and interests in their jurisdictions. Governing elites view their task as the injection of provincial or federal meaning into society, giving it a degree of coherence and a pattern of interdependence more suited for government purposes than what would emerge from the unhindered working of social and market forces. Each government's policies pull the affected interests into relations of dependence and attachment to the power centre that manipulates their existence. Each government seeks policy coherence in order to minimize internal contradictions leading to the frustration of its own policies. The inadequacies of the theory and advice on which decision-makers rely produce major discrepancies between governmental ambition and actual achievement. The byzantine complexity of internal government structures and the sluggishness of the diffuse bureaucratic instrumentalities on which policy-makers depend create additional obstacles to the coherence in policy and society that each government seeks. Nevertheless, given these limitations, each government transmits cues and pressures to the environment, thus tending to group the interests manipulated by its policies into webs of interdependence springing from the particular version of socio-economic integration it is pursuing. Provincial governments work toward the creation of limited versions of a politically created provincial society and economy, and the national government works toward the creation of a country-wide society and economy.

Federal policies are responses to nation-wide considerations. From the perspective of Ottawa the provinces constitute concentrations of governmental power whose manipulation is difficult but nevertheless must be attempted where necessary. In pursuing its mission as a national government from 1867 to the present, Ottawa has not hesitated to interfere with provincial policies by the disallowance of provincial legislation and, more recently, by the adroit and extensive employment of the spending power. The mission of provincial political elites is necessarily more restricted, being territorially confined by provincial boundaries, often restrained by weaknesses of financial capacity, and, formerly, hampered by administrative shortcomings. Nevertheless, the British North America Act gives the provinces jurisdictional authority in functional areas of expanding significance, and, most importantly, gives them control of the natural resource base of their economies. While the jurisdiction of a province lacks the comprehensive coverage enjoyed by the government of a unitary state, it is a sufficiently impressive base of governmental power to elicit visions of futures to be pursued. It cannot be doubted, to cite only the more obvious examples, that Lesage, Smallwood, Douglas, W.A.C. Bennett, and Manning had coherent sets of public purposes for the provincial societies they governed. From their perspective the federal government and its policies constituted environmental uncertainties that had to be managed, exploited, or reduced, and in some cases bitterly attacked in the defence of the provincial futures whose creation they envisaged.

As they pursue their specific goals, federal and provincial elites unwittingly serve the profound trend toward the increasing politicization of society. What Léon Dion calls the "political invasion of our daily lives . . . a new phenomenon in history,"[24] has a particular significance for a federal polity. In almost every conceivable aspect of our existence, from the workaday world of our daily occupation to the private intimate worlds of sex and love, our conduct is affected by the larger, pervasive world of federal and provincial competition and co-operation. We are light years away from the relatively apolitical, non-governmentalized societies of 1867. No national society existed in 1867, and provincial societies were expected to be relatively free from extensive government controls by the newly created provincial governments. A century later we have governmentalized societies, both federal and provincial, interwoven with each other in relations of competitive interdependence.

The institutionalization of government,[25] the construction of a sphere of political and bureaucratic existence differentiated from other spheres of collective life, automatically reduces the relative importance of non-government groups, interests, and individuals in policy-making. There is impressive unanimity from students of Canadian government that members of the public are little more than spectators, mobilized by competing elites at three- to five-year intervals for electoral purposes and then returned to their accustomed role as objects of government policy. "Canada," observes Richard Simeon, "combines the British tradition of a strong executive and centralized leadership with a *relative* freedom from mass pressure and popular constraint."[26] Even bitter and well-publicized intergovernmental conflict may take place in the face of almost complete public indifference or ignorance, as Claude Morin asserts was true of the recent Ottawa-Quebec hostilities over the latter's role at international conferences.[27]

Paradoxically, the institutionalization process acting as a barrier to public influence on decision-making is the instrumentality for political and bureaucratic elites to bring society under ever more comprehensive government control and guidance. If socialism is about equality, contemporary Canadian federalism is about governments, governments that are possessed of massive human and financial resources, that are driven by purposes fashioned by elites, and that accord high priority to their own long-term institutional self-interest. We should not be surprised, therefore, to be told that in the early years of the Lesage regime "most governmental activity . . . was initiated by the government itself,"[28] to be reminded of the various federal government programs introduced by political and bureaucratic elites in the absence of strong demands,[29] and to read that the "demands on government have been in large part self-created."[30] It is abundantly clear that the massive impact of government on society at the output stage does not require a prior massive impact of society on government at the input stage.

By and large, the above analysis also applies to Quebec. The Quebec government, like the others, attempts to mould society in terms of its conception of a desirable future. Here, too, bureaucrats and politicians have the same disproportionate capacity to influence policy evident in other jurisdictions. But important differences exist. In recent years the political system they manage has been repeatedly shaken by social transformations, often government induced. Further, the society to which elites respond is not simply the provincial segment of an English-speaking North American culture that, with variations, dominates the rest of the country and the neighbour to the south. Although clusters of French culture exist elsewhere in Canada, its primary concentration in the province of Quebec necessarily involves the government of that province in a host of specific national questions. The government of Quebec is not in the business of controlling and directing the provincial segment of a larger society but of fostering and stimulating a "full blown society"[31] infused with nationalistic fervour by two centuries of minority status. This is a society in which the major groups, associations, and organizations increasingly "tend . . . to fall back on the Quebec government."[32]

The singular importance of provincial government in contemporary Quebec is partly a delayed compensation for the long era of negative government under Duplessis and his predecessors, which bequeathed the modernizing governments of the past two decades a heritage of daunting problems. Also, the relative weakness of the Francophone role in the private economic sector generates pressure to employ the majority-controlled provincial state to redress this no longer acceptable ethnic imbalance. Thus, although in contemporary Quebec, as elsewhere in Canada, the political debate centres on the precise nature of the leading role to be played by government, it is a debate with a difference. In recent years it has focused with growing intensity on the fundamental question of the relationship of the people and government of Quebec with the rest of Canada. Specifically, the debate centres on the question of whether a sovereign Quebec government is the best instrument to satisfy the profound desire of Francophone Quebecers for a modern, secure community. The existing system of political authorities is not taken for granted. The opponents of Confederation claim that it constitutes a mobilization of governmental bias hostile to national survival.

As a consequence of the particular circumstances just outlined, government-society relations in Quebec are characterized by a special intensity and passion. Further, the commitment of the present provincial leadership to hold a referendum on the constitutional future of the province involves the provincial population in the determination of the most crucial issue facing the society. The situation, therefore, is fundamentally different from the first sixty years of this century when the goal of provincial autonomy was standard fare in elite political rhetoric but left the masses "largely unmoved."[33] Nevertheless, in the process leading up to the referendum a key role will be played by the political leaders of the government. Their clear and professed task is to employ the levers of government power to persuade a majority of the population to support independence. They will control the wording and the timing of this carefully controlled exercise in democratic participation. And, confident that time is on their side, they have told the population of Quebec, and Canadians outside the province, that if the first effort fails they will try and try again.

The vanguard role of the governing Parti Québécois in actively changing attitudes to the political system is, from the perspective of this paper, no more than a particular manifestation of the managerial role I have attributed to all governments of the federal system. The creative leadership role of the Quebec government is a necessary consequence of the simple fact that it is deeply committed to an objective for which popular support is, in relative terms, lacking.

Before the referendum there will be intergovernmental competition of a particularly aggressive nature, for the issues at stake relate not to a particular program or to the next election, but to opposed constitutional futures. The erosion of support for the federal regime involves the federal government in extraordinary efforts to preserve its legitimacy,[34] particularly by maximizing direct links with individuals clearly seen to be profitable by the Quebec citizenry. The federal system, as Morin observes, "divides Quebecers against themselves."[35] The constitutional referendum that has been under way in Quebec for a decade and a half, which accelerated in tempo after November 15, 1976, and which will be formalized in the near future, involves a competition orchestrated by the government elites in Quebec City and Ottawa to shift or stabilize the dividing line in individuals and in the society as a whole. Further, it is evident that whatever its outcome the referendum will only constitute an ephemeral plebiscitarian interruption of the intergovernmental contest that will resume immediately after the votes are counted. The results of the referendum will instantly be transformed into political resources by federal and provincial prime ministers and cabinet ministers who will fasten conflicting interpretations on the nature of the message the electorate has transmitted. And even should that message be unequivocally positive in support of independence it will still be the task of governments to manage the next stage of partial or complete disengagement.

Thus far this paper has portrayed the federal political process from the perspective of political and bureaucratic actors in government. This section will look upwards, a revealing change of direction, from the perspectives of citizens, interest groups, and parties to show the impact of the federal system on the character of their political activity.

Our approach to the study of politics focuses disproportionately on the problems posed for governments by the transformation of society, and too little on the problems posed for society by the escalating demands of government. Society, constantly challenged by new public policies ranging from education, economy, and welfare to the basic questions of life, death, and human meaning, devotes more and more resources to the task of responding to government. In a narrow, superficial sense this is most visible at the level of the taxpayer compelled to finance the numerous ill-conceived government ventures that litter the contemporary landscape of public choice. In recent years he has been burdened by the chaotic and unplanned introduction of automobile insurance in British Columbia, a system of railway passenger transportation whose escalating expenses produce less and less service, dramatic overruns on the Olympic installations in Montreal, and the burgeoning costs of the

James Bay developments. Our Weberian conceptions of efficiency, economy, and rationality seem increasingly difficult to transfer from our lecture notes to the reality outside our window.[36]

These spectacular escapades, however, constitute only the tip of the government iceberg. A recent Ontario study found that the time from the submission of an application for subdivision approval to its final acceptance had increased from an average of 1.9 years in 1973 to 2.1 years in 1974 and 2.3 years in 1975.[37] In general, the ever more elaborate regulatory role of government greatly increases "the overhead (compliance) costs of industry, trade unions and other groups in either protecting or extending their interests."[38]

To those affected by its actions, contemporary government is correctly viewed as both a potential resource and a threat. It is always a powerful presence in the environment to be exploited, attacked, or evaded as self-interest and citizen duty dictate. In the complex contest between provincial governments seeking control and individuals and organized interests seeking a favourable environment, the latter may respond by exit, taking advantage of the gap between the limited geographic reach of particular governments and the area of free movement that constitutes the federal system, to move to more congenial jurisdictions.[39] Capital knows no loyalty. Its easy mobility across provincial and national boundaries exerts a strong pressure on each province not to deviate in its tax system from the other provincial systems with which it is in unavoidable competition, and on Canada not to impose a more burdensome or discriminatory system of taxes than exists in the United States.[40] In British Columbia, polarized by a free enterprise versus socialism rhetoric for half a century, the claim that investment would dry up if the CCF-NDP formed the government has been a standard election threat by big business and the various partisan opponents of the left.

The social and economic interests of Canadian society, seeking their own advantage, work the federal system in their search for the optimum relationship with its double layer of governments.[41] J.R. Mallory, writing of an earlier era, noted that powerful economic interests sought to stem collectivist inroads on their freedom by resort to extensive litigation to weaken the constitutional competence of the governments attempting to regulate them.[42] Conversely, as Trudeau observed and deprecated, those interests seeking advantage and/or protection knocked on any government door, hoping to benefit from the confusion of jurisdiction and to elicit a positive response, "regardless of the constitution," from whichever level of government would listen.[43]

There is contemporary evidence that pressure groups attempt to influence the workings of the federal division of power by having the government closest to the centre of their organizational strength, and to which they have easiest access, handle the concerns affecting them.[44] Thus the Quebec-based Confederation of National Trade Unions "attempted to weaken the federal government in order to strengthen the provincial governments, the Quebec government in particular. The [Canadian Labour Congress], on the other hand, has striven mightily to restore or preserve the authority of the federal government and to cajole it into regaining the initiative."[45] In a period when the distribution of power was in flux, it "was found that the leadership of both groups made demands which, if adopted, would have resulted in the strengthening of 'their' level of government."[46] Yet another study reveals the success of the extractive industries in mobilizing provincial governments to fight the Carter Commission's proposals for higher taxes. The localization of the industries, their dominance of particular communities, and "their success in identifying their own prosperity with the prestige of particular regions"[47] contributed to the intense and successful pressure they induced provincial governments to bring on their behalf at the federal level. The real victors, however, were the provinces, whose success in thwarting Ottawa confirmed the dependent, client status of the extractive industries at the provincial level,[48] subsequently evidenced by heavy provincial tax and royalty increases.

There is, as just indicated, some manoeuvrability in the relationship between organized pressure groups and the governments of the federal system. Nevertheless, the overriding tendency is for such groups to structure their associational life in accordance with the relatively stable jurisdictional location of the legislative authority affecting them. The increasing politicization and governmentalization of society elicits a proliferation of pressure groups struggling to fit the federal system's requirements for influencing policy. Canadian experience testifies to the basic astuteness of the observation of Roy. C. Macridis that "[w]herever the political governmental organization is cohesive and power is concentrated in certain well-established centres, the pressure groups become well-organized with a similar concentration of power and vice versa."[49]

However, the working out of the process suggested by Macridis is often imperfect. Most groups affected by both federal and provincial governments, or where jurisdiction is unclear, have a federated group structure, but it is one in which the central, national executive is often made up of provincial or regional representatives and is dependent on provincial organizations. The latter reflect the local concerns of their members, who often identify with the provincial agency that administers the provincial policies affecting them. As a result, the national executive is sometimes reduced to an aggregation of contradictory provincial particularisms unable to agree on a position toward proposed Ottawa policies. Further, the distrust of a distant government centre which, here as elsewhere, affects the workings of the Canadian polity, produces an antipathy to the national office and an occasional reluctance to staff and finance it at adequate levels.[50] In the party system, as is noted below, this federal tension is reduced by the increasing separation and independence of provincial and national parties from each other. Inadequate resources and low levels of institutionalization make it difficult for interest groups to develop and sustain a similar degree of federal-provincial organizational differentiation and specificity. As a consequence, their national efficacy, beset by the centrifugal pressures of divergent regional interests, is often weakened by internal contradictions.[51]

The impact of federalism is also evident in the workings of the party system.[52] The general tendency in federal regimes, as Carl Friedrich observes, is that "parties tend toward paralleling the government setup. . . . Political science has recognized for some time that the organizational structure of parties tends to correspond to the governmental pattern under constitutional democracy. This is only natural, since it is one of the purposes of parties to gain control of the government; therefore, if the government is federally structured, parties must adapt themselves to such a structure."[53]

In the contemporary era the structuring effect of federalism has generated a pronounced trend to the separation of federal and provincial party systems. This is manifested in tendencies toward distinct political careers at both levels, separate national and provincial organizations, and separate sources of party finance. Of particular significance is the development of public schemes of provincial election financing that reduce financial dependence on the national parties. The employment of the public resources of autonomous provincial governments to foster the autonomy of their party systems is an impressive illustration of federalism's capacity for self-reinforcement.

The federal system contributes to party system separation by its provision of discrete provincial arenas in which sectionally based parties can capture power while the same parties are weak in the country as a whole. The federal system also stimulates ideological differentiation between federal and provincial parties bearing the same name. This combines with divergent strategy requirements at the two levels to generate recurrent tensions between the federal and provincial branches of the party.[54] The parties at different levels of the federal system exist in different socio-economic environments, respond to different competitive situations, and are products of particular patterns of historical development and historical accidents. They fight elections under different leaders, at different times, and on different issues before different electorates in separate jurisdictions endowed with distinctive constitutional responsibilities. Numerous voters respond to this catalogue of differences by deliberately switching their votes as they move from one arena to another, particularly where a third party with a limited or non-existent federal presence is provincially strong, as in B.C. The complicated translation of these differences into the strength or weakness of individual parties frequently results in striking dissimilarities between the federal and provincial party system in a particular province.

The circumstances in which provincial parties in power will support their federal counterparts almost entirely reflect strategic considerations.[55] From the federal perspective incumbent national parties of whatever persuasion recognize that the intergovernmental conflict and collaboration involved in the working of contemporary federalism are only minimally affected by purely partisan considerations.[56] "From the federal point of view, whatever parties are in power provincially will press provincial interests."[57] And from the provincial point of view the same holds true of power-holding parties at the federal level.

Given the unavoidable fact of different parties in office federally and provincially, it would be damaging to the federal system for an incumbent national party to be integrally linked with and overtly supporting its provincial counterparts. In the case of the federal Liberal Party in 1977 this would mean an intimate collaboration with eight opposition parties, mostly weak, and only two government parties, both in the Atlantic provinces. A hands-off policy and organizational structure separate from its own provincial namesakes are far more functional to a national governing party for that intimate collaboration with provincial governments required for the effective working of executive federalism. Party solidarity across jurisdictions is sacrificed for the greater good of intergovernmental agreement. Thus, the knitting together of governments induces the federal-provincial separation of parties.[58]

The structuring effect of federalism on parties and interest groups has crucial consequences for the political system. The federal system was originally conceived as a layer of provincial governments representing territorial diversities and a central government with responsibilities for creating the national society it was to serve. It has become a system of powerful governments, sustained by interest groups and parties that, with imperfections, mirror the governmental structure in which they exist. The chain of federal influence, commencing with the elemental fact of a federal constitutional system, has successfully exerted strong pressure to align parties, interest groups, and individual voters behind the distinct governments that are the essence of federalism. Federal and provincial governments, federal and provincial parties, and federal and provincial pressure groups reinforce each other, and they reinforce federalism.

The fleshing out of the governmental structure of federalism by interest groups and parties contributes to the vitality of the system by attaching powerful supports to each level of government that resists any diminution of its authority. "[G]roups organized on a local or regional basis will tend to strengthen local awareness, local loyalties and local particularism," while nationally organized groups foster "national awareness . . ., feelings of identification with the national institutions of government, . . . [and] heighten feelings of efficacy and involvement with those institutions and thus promote national integration."[59] The symbiotic relationship between interest groups and the governments they interact with produces strong mutualities of interest in which each sustains and feeds on the other.[60]

Accordingly, the deliberate creation and fostering by governments of interest groups[61] to whose induced demands they wish to respond is a primary weapon for government survival in circumstances of aggressive intergovernmental competition. As already noted, however, special difficulties attend the organization of interest groups on a national level, raising the possibility that the expanding role of provincial governments and the more homogeneous environments they face may elicit a pressure group bias in favour of the provinces.

Systems of power-seeking parties have the same reinforcing effect for the level of government whose control they seek. Here, too, however, there are powerful tendencies working on behalf of the provinces. The regionalization of the national party system, with neither Liberals nor Conservatives capable of encompassing the sectional heterogeneity of the country, with the Conservatives suffering continuing weakness in Quebec and the Liberals a like weakness on the Prairies, complicates the party support base of federal authority.[62]

The national party system operates under a much more difficult set of constraints than the provincial in generating parties consonant with the needs of its level of government for support and legitimation. Governing provincial parties have a much smaller range of diversities to encompass than their federal counterpart. Further, a section or geographically concentrated interest left out of a provincial government party lacks the political force and focus that provincial governments can provide for sections unrepresented at Ottawa. Finally, the provinces are protected by their numbers. A weak, minority, or unrepresentative government in a province is partially protected against federal competition by strong, aggressive provincial governments elsewhere in the system. No such safety in numbers was available to console the minority governments of Diefenbaker and Pearson, or to protect the Trudeau Liberals from the consequences of their weakness on the Prairies. Accordingly, the "absolutely critical latent function of the party system . . . the development and fostering of a national political culture . . . [and] generating support for the regime"[63] have been performed well below the optimum level in recent years.

A federal system of governments, supported by parties and pressure groups that parallel the governmental structure and infused with conflicting federal and provincial visions of economy and society held by competing political and bureaucratic elites, requires a language of political debate appropriate to its fundamental political concerns.[64] Hence, the dominant political language since Confederation has been geared to the making of claims and counterclaims by the federal and provincial spokesmen for territorially defined societies. In an indirect way, and with the passage of time, the federal language of political discourse became a vehicle for the standard normative controversies that concern modern political systems, questions dealing with equality, the socio-economic rights of citizens, and social justice. Inevitably, however, the pressure of existing language contributed to the clothing of new controversies in federal garments and their emergence in claims on behalf of provincial communities and governments, or charter members, or founding races, or the national interest as defined by Ottawa.[65]

Clearly, the political language of federalism, and the federal political system with which it is intertwined, have encouraged a politics in which provincial particularisms have been accorded special prominence. Provincial governments, as the claimants for and recipients of federal bounty, have acted as surrogates for the communities they govern. In the dialectical process of federal-provincial controversies, the claims of provincial governments encounter the rival claims of the central government with its constitutional authority to speak for all Canadians, for the national community stretching from Bonavista to Vancouver Island. The political incentives for the federal government to couch its claims in the language of individual citizen rights and obligations[66] engender a direct conflict with provincial claims on behalf of territorially based communities,[67] the reconciliation of which is worked out in the federal process.

Formerly, many of these conflicts derived sustenance from specific clauses in the British North America Act, from the terms of admission of individual provinces to the federal system, or from certain alleged intentions of the Fathers relating to the rights of particular provinces or communities. The resultant language of political debate was fundamentally stabilizing in its emphasis on rights and claims that presupposed continuing membership in an ongoing political system. Under the impact of the constitutional crisis of the past two decades, essentially precipitated by the changed objectives of Quebec political elites and the concomitant allocation of the political decisions of 1867 to a distant and irrelevant past, the language of political debate has undergone a dramatic change. The historic, rooted language of the various versions of the compact theory has virtually disappeared, as have other backward-looking justifications that appealed to a common past. They have been replaced by a confusion of newly developing political languages, more nakedly power-seeking, which reflect the ambitions of some political elites to refashion their position, inside or outside the federal system, as the past fades into insignificance, and the induced obligation for other elites to respond in kind. In Quebec the forward-looking language of national self-determination has replaced the traditional elite emphasis on prescriptive rights derived from history and the constitution. The new attitude was graphically expressed by Claude Morin when he was deputy minister of federal-provincial affairs in the Lesage government. "Quebec's motto is: We're through fooling around! It seems rediculous to me to invoke the Constitution. It is like invoking St. Thomas."[68]

The destruction of a customary historical language was accelerated by the recent process of constitutional review that downgraded the Canadian constitutional heritage and promised new beginnings it failed to deliver. The present language situation is clearly in flux[69] as disputants talk past each other, rather than to each other. No new linguistic paradigm in which debate can be couched has emerged.[70] Linguistic instability and federal instability reinforce each other.

The political language of federalism, a language for conducting political competition and co-operation between territorially based groups and their governments, is necessarily hostile to the nation-wide politics of class. The politics and language of class assume that the conditioning effects of capitalism have washed out identities and political perspectives based on socialization into provincial frames of reference. This has not yet happened. In spite of the auspicious depression circumstances of its birth, its early antipathy to the provinces, and its long-standing attempts to create a new politics and language of class at the national level, the CCF and its successor the NDP have made only minor dents in the non-class language of federalism.

For nearly half a century left-wing academic analysis has stressed the allegedly inexorable logic of capitalist development in producing class polarization and a modern class-based politics, described as "creative politics" by its more recent exponents. Indeed, by constant repetition this perspective has become the time-honoured traditional language of a dissenting minority that updates the old arguments and the standard predictions decade after decade. Elections and surveys have been carefully monitored since the thirties in numerous attempts to detect the always imminent emergent trend of class mobilization and polarization, the assumed hallmarks of a maturing economy. The failure of reality to conform to the canons of this version of social science has evoked fulminations against federalism and an adroit use of the concept of false consciousness. These have had minimal impact on the non-class world view of elites and masses involved in the political world of federalism. The political language of territorially based group competition derived from the federal system, and socialized into the consciousness of political actors since Confederation, has prevailed over the twentieth-century challenge from the weakly developed language of class based on the economy.

Contrary to virtually all predictions, post-World War II Canadian politics has not displayed an irreversible trend to centralization, nor the manifestations of capitalist contradiction in polarized class politics, creative or otherwise. Instead, the provinces, aided by secular trends that have enhanced the practical significance of their constitutionally based legislative authority, and by the deliberate improvement of their own bureaucratic power and capacity, have given a new salience to the politics of federalism and the territorially based diversities it encompasses, reflects, and fosters. The present crisis of Canadian federalism, indeed, is caused not by the politics of class but by the passionate politics of territorially based nationalism espoused by the incumbent government in Quebec City. In a logical sense the politics of the Quebec journey toward independence is simply an extended development of the traditional federal concept of provincial autonomy carried to an anti-federalist conclusion.

Canadian scholars have frequently noted, and almost as frequently regretted, that political elites have been unable to free themselves from the seemingly eternal burden of working the federal system and preventing disintegration of the country. That burden continues to be our fate. If the Parti Québécois succeeds in its objectives, the burden of governing the northern half of North America will not go away. It will remain, albeit in altered form.

Success in grappling with the special burdens of governing a federal state does not come easily. The eleven governments of the provincial and country-wide societies of Canada require an effective co-ordinating capacity if each is not to frustrate the efforts of the others in their joint governing of the country.

The fact that the federal-provincial political arena is not restricted in scope to only a few matters of peripheral concern for society and economy enhances the importance of the task. Almost without exception, every crucial issue, including the constitutional framework of the country itself, eventually ends up at the conference table for resolution. "In few policy areas," according to Richard Simeon, "except perhaps defence, the post office or garbage collection – does one government act alone."[71]

Unfortunately, the contemporary search for intergovernmental co-ordination confronts a set of conditions inimical to conflict resolution. Reconciliation of federal and provincial objectives is facilitated when one or the other level of government is passive, when one level of government is clearly dominant, when the scope of government activity is minimal, or when the two levels deal with discrete, separable sectors of society and economy. Thus, in the early years of the federation there were few administrative conflicts related to jurisdictional divisions. "Both provinces and dominion, in the formative years, found quite enough to occupy their limited administrative resources without trespassing on the other's preserves."[72] This jurisdictional isolation is gone forever, and none of the other agreement-facilitating situations now prevails, or is likely to do so in the future. Both levels of government are strong. Neither can dominate the other. Both pursue increasingly comprehensive and integrated goals with a consequent decline in their willingness to defer to the interests of external governments. Provincial willingness to defer to Ottawa has diminished with the development of administrative skills and professional competence in the provincial capitals.

This pessimistic appraisal is given extra weight by the developing integration of governments and societies in Canadian federalism. The competitive coexistence of provinces and central government has especially profound consequences in an era of expanded government bureaucracies, strong pressures for policy coherence by each government, and the massive extension of the tentacles of government regulation, control, and public ownership. The economy and society of each province are confronted with competing and sometimes opposing government directives emerging from separately conceived national and provincial plans for making sense of the same socio-economic order. The national and provincial perspectives, although they frequently encompass the same interests, inevitably take into account a different set and range of considerations. A coast-to-coast perspective based on the federal authority granted by the BNA Act, and especially sensitive to the existing relations between the federal government and Canadian society produced by past and continuing federal policies, confronts the provincial perspective, restricted in geographic coverage, based on a different assignment of constitutional authority, and responsive to the current relationships between the provincial government and provincial society.

In these circumstances, contemporary intergovernmental co-ordination is not a simple matter of agreement between a handful of political leaders and their staff advisers. It requires the co-ordination of powerful bureaucracies with deep policy roots in their societies and of "the publics that are implicated in their normal functioning."[73] It requires, therefore, the containment of ineradicable tendencies to conflict between the federal vision of a society and economy and ten competing provincial visions, each building on the pervasive links between government and its environment forged by its predecessors.

The premises of 1867 were that federal and provincial governments could go their own separate ways with the provinces assuming only limited functions. Further, the then-divergent French and English definitions of the good life minimized the possibility of fundamental French-English conflict between the governments of Quebec and Ottawa. This nineteenth-century recipe for intergovernmental and interethnic harmony is gone.[74] In Quebec, according to Léon Dion, "culture, politics, and economic activity . . . will . . . have to develop new organic interrelationships," and federal policies will be judged by their contribution to this objective.[75] Contemporary federalism, consequently, is more than an arena for a debate between abstract ideas of the public good or for the conducting of competition between either governments or societies detached from each other. It is an arena in which the political and bureaucratic leaders of governmentalized societies and economies hammer out the next stage in the further evolution of the eleven distinct yet interdependent political economies and politicized societies that are the gifts of the past to the present. From this perspective it is no longer meaningful or appropriate to think of these economies and societies at the provincial and national levels as logically prior to governments. To an indeterminate but undoubtedly significant extent, they are the consequences of past government activity and will increasingly be so in the future.

Parliamentary government and federalism have contributed to a flexible, non-ideological, pragmatic style of politics that facilitates intergovernmental agreement. Federal politics, in particular, has always required political leaders with well-developed bargaining skills, capable of encompassing the profound diversities of the country in their appeals, politics, and leadership. One of Mackenzie King's "robust convictions," doubtless born of long experience, was "his belief that the really important people in the world were the *conciliators*."[76]

Formerly, pragmatism and expediency at the political level of cabinets allowed a high degree of bureaucratic autonomy for specialists to work out agreements with counterpart civil servants in the other jurisdiction. Under this system of functional federalism, which was characteristic of the conditional grant era, federal-provincial relations were handled in discrete categories by specialists, guided by professional norms, and relatively independent of hierarchical superiors concerned with overall policy coherence and the opportunity costs of fifty-cent dollars. Under the new regime of political federalism, to employ Smiley's terminology, effective decision-making capacity has drifted upwards to politicians and bureaucrats "with jurisdiction-wide concerns."[77] The desire of each level of government to put its own house in order by establishing central executive control over policy priorities and fiscal decisions has primarily focused on the elimination of intragovernmental contradictions, incoherences, and uncontrolled spending. The inevitable side effect, however, has been an attempt to manage the external environment in the interest of the same objectives. This has led Ottawa and most of the provinces to establish federal-provincial ministries, bureaus, or agencies to eliminate the uncertainty and disturbances of an *ad hoc* approach to intergovernmental relations.[78] The effort by each government to integrate its policy outputs is a reaction to the contradictions in the extensive existing policy grip of government on society, as well as a necessity for the many plans still germinating in myriad committees. The successful introduction of the latter requires deft manoeuvring through the minefield of existing policies.

Although societies can stand a great deal of chaos, the economic and social costs of contradictory policies generate pressures to minimize their incidence. Since this can be most effectively done within a single jurisdiction where only one overall political decision-making authority exists, there will be a tendency for intrajurisdictional clashes to be controlled or moderated at the expense of flexibility in handling interjurisdictional concerns. The playing out of this bias will result in a relative and absolute increase in irreconcilable policy clashes between governments.

The dynamics and weaknesses of political federalism are rendered more explicable if it is recognized that we have stumbled into a peculiar Canadian version of the American separation of powers. Agreement on the innumerable major issues that clog the federal-provincial agenda requires the approval of independent political authorities with distinct and separate bases of electoral, party, group, and bureaucratic support. They are not constitutionally beholden to each other and they are aligned with large and powerful constituencies of interests that can be mobilized behind the evocative labels of provincial rights and the national interest. Indeed, the Canadian version of the separation of powers may be more difficult to work than its American counterpart, for it involves not just the separate legislative and executive strata of the policy-making process but governments, conscious of their historic position, jealous of their prerogatives, and aggressively enterprising in the performance of their managerial responsibilities for their societies.

By implication this paper has suggested that to look at the literature of Canadian federalism historically makes clear how much has been a response to particular climates of academic and intellectual opinion, how much has been characterized by an anti-federalist mentality, and how the wish has too frequently fathered the thought. Studies of Canadian politics have suffered from a disciplinary mobilization of bias that grossly underestimates the autonomy of elites, the weight of government, and the moulding effect of institutions on political behaviour. A form of sociological reductionism common to North American political scientists has stressed society at the expense of the polity and either devalued, ignored, or denied an autonomous role for government.[79] Democratic assumptions have elicited analyses that focus on the popular impact on government and neglect the reverse. Egalitarianism has had similar effects by undervaluing and underweighting the extent, significance, and unavoidability of elite discretion. Further, the search for class politics has entailed a stress on elections, an excessive interest in parties, and a deflection of attention from the overriding reality of government.

Developments in comparative politics have played a part in our miseducation. The evanescence and crumbling of political systems in the post-independence states of the Third World have contributed to a brutal awareness of the fragility of political structures incompatible with the historic social systems they confront. The study of the latter and their impact on the polity has elicited a strong sociological thrust in Third World studies. However, the sociological perspective appropriately applied to the "soft states" of Africa, Asia, and Latin America has been uncritically and inappropriately extended to the study of the highly institutionalized political systems of the Western world. Finally, the weakly developed idea of the state in the English-speaking world[80] has reduced the visibility of government and no doubt contributed to the academic underestimation of its central political role. Accordingly, the enterprise of assessing the creative, formative, and coercive capacities of government, authority, and institutions requires us to overcome the biases of sociological reductionism, democratic mythology, egalitarian levelling, incorrect Third World analogies, and the disciplinary errors to which they contribute. Success in the enterprise will provide much needed understanding of "the reality of structures, the extent of their 'grip' over society, and the true importance of constitutions in shaping behaviour."[81]

Chapter Six

The Other Crisis of Canadian Federalism

. . . I have called my talk "The Other Crisis of Canadian Federalism." Accordingly, I will not focus on that most fashionable contemporary topic of Canadian after-dinner speakers, the French-English or Quebec-Ottawa manifestations of our lengthening winter of discontent. The other crisis, which constitutes my theme, is the crisis of a political system with a declining capacity for the effective use of the authority of government for the attainment of public goals. This, too, is a constitutional crisis in the sense that the working constitution of Canadian federalism can no longer control and channel the activities of governments in order to minimize their self-defeating competition with each other. Far from existing in splendid policy-making isolation from each other, these governments jostle and compete in an ever more destructive struggle that reduces the beneficial public impact of the massive public sector produced by their conflicting, overlapping, and discordant ambitions.

In Canada direct concern with the role and efficiency of government has been relatively sidetracked for two decades by the overwhelming application of limited political energies to the task of either keeping Quebec in Confederation or getting it out. In this situation of an apparently irresistible concentration on the issue of survival, other equally important but less visible problems are left unattended by our political leaders, who, try as they may, cannot escape the pressures of the immediate and the short run.

The crisis of which I speak is of recent vintage–essentially a product of the last two decades. Therefore a brief historical survey of

171

happier times in the evolution of Canadian federalism may provide helpful background to our present impasse.

Historical Background

The evolution of Canadian federalism is frequently described in terms of alternations between periods of centralization and decentralization. While this perspective has been primarily descriptive, it has captured basic tendencies in our history. Periods of centralization are customarily considered to be the early post-Confederation years, both world wars, and the post-World War II period up to 1957. In these periods Ottawa's ascendancy is held to reflect the necessary performance by the central government of tasks that by their nature could not be performed by the provincial governments and that, because of their compelling importance or urgency, gave to the only government capable of their undertaking an unchallenged priority in the political system. In the immediate post-Confederation period the task of fleshing out the incipient and weak political community, of nation-building under the leadership of centralist-inclined politicians in Ottawa, gave the national government a precarious hegemony, subsequently eroded by the relative failure of its policies to produce the thriving economy that was a prime *raison d'être* of its dominance. In both world wars the ascendancy of Ottawa was a response to the need for centralized authority in periods of international crisis. The continuing dominance of the central government after World War II was sustained by the momentum built up by its successful administration of a wartime economy, concurrent with extensive military involvement on the side of the victorious allies. The post-war rationale for Ottawa's continuing leadership was found in the demanding task of converting a wartime economy to peacetime and of performing the new economic management role publicly assumed by the central government in response to Keynesian theories.

The intervening periods, from the breakdown of centralized leadership in the late 1880s and 1890s to World War I, during the 1920s, and from the late 1950s to the late 1960s, are variously described as periods of provincial ascendancy or as periods in which both government levels handled important responsibilities with neither enjoying a clearly dominant position.

Most English-Canadian scholarship, imbued with a central government bias, has tended to view with alarm those periods in which Ottawa did not play a leading role. The provinces, with the important exception of Quebec and the French-Canadian scholars who addressed themselves to the relation between French-Canadian survival and provincial autonomy, have found few defenders in the social science community and, indeed, have been viewed with contempt. From an historical perspective, however, it is evident that central government ascendancy hitherto has been restricted to periods of emergency and crisis, while the provincial role has always re-emerged in periods of relative normality.

Growth of Big Government at Both Levels

The federal-provincial contest and the resultant periodic alternations of the relative *de facto* significance of the two levels of government previously took place in eras when the task of governments and the scope of the joint public sectors they managed were, as can now be seen in retrospect, limited. Nevertheless, the general tendency through time has been a growth in the effective power, scope, and responsibilities of each level of government, a growth not always proceeding at the same rate for each level, a growth occasionally glacial, sometimes interrupted, and sometimes rapid, but always, and unmistakably, growth. This growth of government at each level necessarily affects the patterns of competition and co-operation between governments. We have now reached a stage where the necessity of intergovernmental co-ordination and collaboration is not matched with an equivalent capacity for its attainment. We are approaching a condition of federal-provincial paralysis if existing trends continue.

The evidence of big government is ubiquitous. It is manifest in the total size of the taxing bite, which is now a much larger share of GNP, at 33 per cent, than at its highest level in the Second World War, of 27 per cent.[1] It is revealed in the extent of public employment, with both levels directly responsible for the employment of more than one of every ten Canadians in the work force, and indirectly responsible for many more. It is reflected in the profusion of experts and professionals who guide our lives from their niches in the byzantine complexity of the multiplying bureaus and agencies of the modern federal state. Its most important and emphatic indication, however, is found in the fact that the central government and major provincial governments now view their task as the direct management of the economies and societies under their respective jurisdictions. For all of these indicators of big government, the proportion falling under provincial jurisdiction has increased steadily for a quarter of a century. The new circumstances of Canadian federalism now include, therefore, the coexistence of powerful, *dirigiste* government at both levels. As a result, as I will subsequently indicate, the ratio of co-operative to competitive tendencies has shifted to the detriment of the former, and the stakes of that competition have increased. In addition, future cyclical changes in the responsibilities and powers of the governments of Canadian federalism will occur at a higher threshold of government activity than in the past. Quite distinct, therefore, from the Quebec crisis, although impinging on it, is this larger crisis that has transformed Canadian federalism in the direction of an increased incidence of federal-provincial conflict.

This pessimistic appraisal is strengthened by a recent study of political cleavages in Canada. The three most salient cleavages in Canada, according to Professor John Meisel – the ethnic cleavage pitting French against English, the regional cleavage setting the peripheries against the centre, and the economic-regional cleavage pitting poor provinces against rich provinces – all produce clashes between governments.[2] Clearly, it is not because these cleavages are the most important that they acquire government sponsorship, but they are the most important because they have government sponsorship, which reflects the profound interest of governments in the outcome of the contests they generate. The consequences of government sponsorship are most strikingly illustrated by the dramatic increase in the intensity of the controversy over French-English Quebec-Ottawa relations following the election of the Parti Québécois government on November 15, 1976.

Useful background for understanding our present situation is provided by the economic crisis of the Great Depression of the thirties and the reaction of Canadian academics and intellectuals to it. In its most general terms the Depression gave an immense boost to the belief that both society and economy could and should be planned. The future was to be tamed and brought under human control by the exercise of political authority. The planning task required, it was taken for granted, a major change in Canadian federalism. The English-speaking academic community agreed with Harold Laski's famous article "The Obsolescence of Federalism,"[3] which asserted that the planning imperative required the concentration of planning capacity in a single government, and hence the attrition of provincial powers of self-government. The economic crisis of the 1930s was transformed by numerous Canadian commentators into a political, constitutional crisis. The inadequacies of political leadership were attributed to the divided power structure of the federal system, which prevented that single-minded mobilization of resources by Ottawa that the resolution of economic paralysis required. There was a tendency to assume that federalism was an appropriate form of government only for bygone periods of laissez faire when the tasks of government were light and the economy was largely self-regulating. Thus, not only did the Depression erode the belief in the beneficence of the liberal economic order, but by necessary implication it also focused hopes for secular salvation on a single central government and consequently undermined the long-standing belief in the virtues of federalism. The possibility of powerful collectivist governments coexisting at both levels was not foreseen by would-be planners.

In spite of the then prevalent hostility of English-Canadian intellectuals to the provinces, the Depression did not produce a decisive shift in the balance of power to Ottawa. Among its many consequences, it contributed to demagogic political leadership in several provinces, notably Quebec, Ontario, and Alberta, whose premiers vigorously espoused provincial autonomy and resisted pressures to centralization.

The culmination of the centralist dream finally emerged not in the Depression but in the Second World War when the federal authorities ran the country virtually as a unitary state. Although the peak of federal dominance receded after the Allied victory, the central government continued to play the leading role in economic management and welfare provision. To many observers the federal system appeared to be tilted permanently in a centralist direction. In the mixed economy fleshed out in the post-war years the central government was benignly viewed as a good and faithful servant of the public interest – controlling capitalist excess, engaged in the piecemeal construction of the welfare state, and fostering full employment with a nonchalant competence that elicited the profound respect and gratitude of those whose memories extended to the pre-war Depression years.

Although the government of Quebec continued to fight ritual battles for provincial autonomy, this was easily disregarded. A minority nationalism that could be labelled reactionary and conservative, and that was embodied in a corrupt governing party, could be ignored by the centralists in Ottawa and their supporters in the universities of English Canada.

Nevertheless, the provinces had numerous factors working in their favour. They possessed impressive constitutional responsibilities in areas of expanding government concern, notably welfare, education, highways, and natural resources. Further, and belatedly, their own administrative competence experienced major improvement in the post-war years. Several of them came to be headed by ambitious political leaders who sought to manage their provinces in the pursuit of enlarged public purposes. They took full advantage of the historical accident that gave them jurisdictional control of the growth areas of government. The provinces were no longer the overblown municipalities that the Fathers of Confederation had intended them to be. The leaders of the larger provinces managed mini-states, impressive in wealth and geographic extent. They saw their tasks as positive and managerial, and they developed visions commensurate with their enlarged responsibilities. They began to take deliberate control of their provincial societies and economies. They took up the slack in their constitutional powers and extended them into new domains.

One of the most impressive examples of this new breed of provincial leaders, Premier Lougheed of Alberta, recently asserted the need for Albertans "to reduce the dependency for our continued quality of life on governments, institutions or corporations directed from outside the province."[4] A recent analysis locates the source of this demand for provincial "long-range economic planning . . . and a consistent strategy of economic development"[5] in the governing elite of the province.

> Confident of its administrative competence to manage the huge revenue surpluses of the 1970s and committed to provincial economic planning, this state-bureaucratic elite sees the province as the logical arena for the advancement of its career opportunities and . . . is fiercely loyal to the province as a semi-sovereign economic and political unit and deeply engaged in the process of province-building. Much of the pressure to use Alberta's remaining energy resources as a catalyst for industrialization appears to originate within the public bureaucracy.[6]

Further evidence of the increasingly extensive reach of provincial governments is provided by Ontario, which, by 1972 had trade offices in Dusseldorf, Brussels, Vienna, London, Stockholm, Tokyo, New York, Boston, Atlanta, Cleveland, Minneapolis, and Los Angeles.[7]

Provincial histories in the last two decades are replete with grandiose plans for development, manifested in mammoth hydroelectric schemes, nationalization, massive highway programs, and ambitious strategies for economic growth. This transformation of the role of provincial governments has been particularly evident in Quebec. The ancient values of agriculturalism, anti-statism, and spirituality no longer serve as guides to the new political leaders of a province bent on rapid modernization under the aegis of the provincial state. It is not nationalism that is new in Quebec, for in some form that has been a constant, but its new linkage with the provincial state, viewed as a prime lever for the attainment of national goals. The traditional anti-statist attitudes of Duplessis have been replaced by a philosophy that has consistently advocated the vigorous use of state power since the first Lesage government of the early sixties. The state, asserted René Lévesque in 1963, was to be "a creative agent," the chief instrument of the French-Canadian people of Quebec in a society in which the bulk of private economic power was in English hands.[8] Although provincial leaders elsewhere employed less resounding language and grappled with different problems, their basic orientation was similar.

From the mid-fifties to the late sixties the weak leadership of Diefenbaker and the minority governments of both Diefenbaker and Pearson, his Liberal successor, seemed to indicate a concurrent eclipse of the federal government. This tendency was thwarted by the renewed vigour of the federal role under Trudeau, who came into politics for the express purpose of redressing the drift of power to the provinces. Thus, the assertiveness of the provinces, after a brief transition period, was met by a renewed countervailing assertiveness of the federal role.

The resultant federal system can no longer be captured under yesterday's labels as either centralized or decentralized. Rather, it is characterized by strong government at two levels, with the admitted exception of the weaker provincial governments of the Atlantic region.

The chief hallmark of the new federalism is the attempt of both levels of government to mould the society and economy under their jurisdiction for specific purposes. Both levels of government now control and manipulate impressive public sectors, and both are less willing than formerly to conduct their affairs in an *ad hoc* manner. Governments at both levels have tried to systematize their own policy process to eliminate contradictions and to exercise control over the centrifugal forces in their own administration. The resultant intergovernmental struggle is not a minor battle between small platoons of politicians and administrators but a contest between big battalions with often opposed plans for the societies and economies for which they hope to play an enlarged steering role.

The Bias in Favour of Bigness

As the crisis of federalism is a product of the big governments that have evolved in its midst, a brief overview of the factors contributing to the growth of government is essential.

Any historical overview of the process of expansion of the public sector runs the risk of imputing to the key actors a degree of far-seeing deliberateness they clearly lacked. It must be made clear, therefore, that a process is not a plan. What we observe is not the fulfilment by successive generations of a conscious plan articulated by a founder. On the contrary, we observe little more than the efforts of particular groups of political and bureaucratic decision-makers to grapple with the cluster of problems, in society and in their own governments, placed on the public agenda at their point in time. The future beyond the next election is often conspicuously absent from their deliberations. Indeed, in many cases it is inappropriate to describe the frequently chaotic process of decision-making as characterized by deliberation.

To speak of a process is to imply the existence of an enduring pervasive bias of pressure, opinion, or "logic" that moulds and skews the responses of elites in ways they may not comprehend. One of the tasks of social science is to raise to the level of consciousness the determining or influencing factors at work. While it is unlikely that the clarification of the sources or causes of underlying tendencies will easily allow their reversal, where such is deemed appropriate, it does at least enhance the possibility, however slim, of modifying the forces that have us in their grip. Even if, as often will be the case, the possibility of changing direction is minimal, there remains an intellectual satisfaction in understanding how we have reached our present situation.

In the Canadian case the simultaneous coexistence of big government at two levels is not attributable to left-wing governments in office or to any well-articulated or conscious philosophy of collectivism. With the partial exception of contemporary Quebec, big government represents the end result of the incremental collectivism characteristic of the modern social democratic state. The *ad hoc*, piecemeal advance of the state at both federal and provincial levels is powered by the general bias of a political process in which the benefits of state action are seldom contrasted with the costs; by an ingenious tax system that makes the raising of revenues by governments as painless and invisible as possible and makes the provision of benefits highly visible; by the outbidding process of competitive elections at frequent intervals; by the tendency of every past advance to build up quickly a coterie of supporters in those who benefit from its existence;[9] by a process in which for governments "means become elevated into ends in themselves . . . [and] achieving the goals of policy becomes less important than maintaining past policies";[10] by the supporting propensity of decision-makers and administrators to "acquire political and psychological stakes in their own decisions and [to] develop a justificatory rather than a critical attitude towards them";[11] by the bureaucratic self-interest that dictates a continuing expansion of personnel and budgets as the tools to improvements in power, status, and salary; and by the existence of a level of affluence capable of supporting both the efficiencies and inefficiencies of a large public sector through increased taxes. In view of the above, Galbraith's much-cited claim of a bias against the public sector generated by the stimulus to private consumption elicited by the engines of capitalist advertising[12] is a reversal of the truth. The bias of the modern social democratic state is hostile to the existence of autonomous decision-making by key social and economic centres of competing non-state power.[13]

Public opinion and the electoral process may hold back the expansion of old programs or the creation of new ones, but they have little capacity to roll back existing programs. In any case, as the late Harry Johnson observed, we are influenced by a pervasive climate of opinion sympathetic to collectivism:

> At the general philosophical level – the level of fundamental presumptions about the nature of organised human social life – the new synthesis can be summarised in the view that the market is guilty until proved innocent, while the government is never guilty, however criminally or irresponsibly particular governments may have behaved.[14]

Even if Johnson is wrong and a newer synthesis is slowly crystallizing, the political agenda is nearly always forward-looking, always querying what is to be done, and almost never asking what is to be undone. The incredible inertia and rigidity of government, sustained by this bias, provides indiscriminate support for both the policy achievements and the policy blunders of our governing predecessors. Also, as Dicey astutely observed long ago, legislation often reflects the received opinions of the thinkers and writers of yesterday, "when in the world of speculation a movement has already set in against ideas which are exerting their full effect in the world of action and of legislation."[15]

Further, the role of government responds not only to the world of ideas, but to the facts of power and self-interest. Collectivist policies have tied the welfare position of countless citizens, the economic profitability or survival of innumerable firms and organizations, and the self-interest of a legion of administrators to the status quo to which their fortunes are intimately linked.

It is easy to exaggerate the public pressures for collectivism and equally easy to underestimate the extent to which new programs reflect the interests and ambitions of political and bureaucratic elites,[16] not only for their societies, but for their own political and bureaucratic significance, prestige, and roles in the political system. Much of what is justified in the public interest reflects that species of organizational pathology by which means become ends, by which the power of government acquires its own justification to our governors. Regulations become more valuable to the administrators than to the administered,[17] and agency filing cabinets are ransacked for possible expenditures because a surplus is available and the end of the fiscal year approacheth.

The interests of governments only partially coincide with the interests of the population they govern. Two centuries ago Adam Smith observed that businessmen seldom met but for the purpose of conspiring against the public. While Smith's thesis has lost none of its validity as a description of business behaviour, it is no less applicable to the behaviour of governments. The decisions made by governments are no less likely than business decisions to sacrifice public interests for the varied interests of those who make the decisions.[18] This is particularly so in Canadian federalism, the very complexity of which contributes to elite dominance since inevitably only few can be well informed of its intricacies and its jargon.[19]

The size of governments on the landscape of Canadian federalism is, therefore, sociologically understandable, but only partially justified in terms of democratic responsiveness to popular demand. It is not even clear that our political masters could control, if they wished, the process of expansion over which they seem to preside.

It is grudgingly admitted at the highest level that it is virtually impossible for politicians to hold back the bureaucratic pressures for growth.[20]

In the Canadian case a conventional acceptance of a vaguely collectivist philosophy has been characteristic of opinion leaders for nearly half a century. The displacement of the intellectual hegemony of collectivism is, therefore, not an imminent possibility. Thus, although the image of government efficiency has been badly battered by a series of well-publicized misadventures in the public sector in recent years, and although there is growing disinclination to attribute unquestioning virtue to state action, the complexity and multiplicity of the overlapping and reinforcing factors supporting big and bigger governments are likely to provide irresistible impetus to at least the retention of the present extent of government activity, and more probably to its continued incremental growth. This growth, it is evident, has little to do with individuals and everything to do with the system, which distributes incentives and disincentives to conduct that reflects the biases just described.[21]

The Decline of the Constitution

What, it may well be asked, has become of the constitution? Surely the BNA Act, as amended and as interpreted, with its written division of powers, exercises a significant constraint on intergovernmental competition. While the BNA Act cannot yet be described as completely irrelevant, it clearly cannot be described as determining.[22] After all, the fluctuations over more than a century in the *de facto* power and responsibilities of the two levels occurred with only minimum explicit change in the Act.

Dicey asserted in 1885 that federalism means litigation rather than legislation, the predominance of the legal mind in the working of a federal system, and the substitution of legal arguments for policy arguments in the rhetoric of federal debate.[23] However, it can be argued persuasively that Dicey's thesis no longer applies. Since World War II necessary flexibility has been obtained by a developing willingness to override legal considerations by a pragmatic approach. This has transformed the federal system from an instrument for increasing lawyers' incomes into a political arena for the free play of contending socio-economic, political, and governmental forces, which, in the pursuit of self-interest, vie with each other to influence the system's working.

Viewed as a political arena it is not surprising that political actors

181

have approached the BNA Act from the strategic perspective of the requirements for effective intergovernmental competition. This manifests itself in the self-interested allocation of the most extensive meaning to those responsibilities over which one's own government has control, and the most restricted meaning to those assigned to the other level of government.[24] The resultant never-ending word game is irritating to those who seek certainty in human affairs and amusing to those who delight in human ingenuity, but above all it is unavoidable to those who work the system. It is simply one of the ways of playing the federal game.

The BNA Act, and particularly the division of powers, has always been approached in a spirit of political calculation by those who worked it. Attitudes to the courts and to judicial review have not been immune from strategy considerations determined by the possibility of winning or losing in that cloistered arena of decision-making. More generally, the division of powers has been exploited by partisan governments intent on enhancing their freedom of action whenever openings for manoeuvre presented themselves. However, until recently, these stratagems have occurred within at least a diluted tradition of constitutionalism, an underlying assumption that the BNA Act, for all its age and rigidities, was, in the last analysis, a constitutional document to be approached with at least a mild deference.

Up to a point the flexibility attained by these strategies served the country well, but the contemporary success in playing fast and loose with the division of powers has begun to produce diminishing returns. Flexibility now looks dangerously like intergovernmental anarchy. The federal-provincial game has gotten out of hand, and we are in danger of being left not with a flexible division of powers but a non-existent division.

In the last analysis the sources of this change lie in the minds of those who work the constitution. There is adequate evidence to suggest that key political and bureaucratic actors now accord even less concern to the intended restrictions of the BNA Act on their sphere of action than hitherto, and stress their own capacity to roam beyond its hampering confines with little likelihood of a check by the courts.

This decline in the aura of the constitution is partly the product of the lengthy French-English crisis in the Canadian polity. That crisis has produced one major process of constitutional review, which had the effect of diminishing the authority of the existing constitution but proved incapable of replacing it. Nearly ten years ago Prime Minister Trudeau stated that "the whole Constitution is up for grabs,"[25] and it has been up for grabs ever since. Such a constitution elicits little respect. Indeed, it is not clear that it can any longer be properly called a constitution. Since November 15, 1976, there has been in power in Quebec a government deeply committed to some form of independence of Quebec from Canada and thus prepared to accord only a conditional and short-run allegiance to a constitution it is pledged to destroy.

In this climate of accelerating constitutional uncertainty the leaders of Canadian governments almost inevitably respond by adopting strategies less and less determined by an ancient statute whose future is questionable. For example, it can no longer be taken for granted that Supreme Court decisions will be accepted as binding by governments whose "rights" are adversely affected. More significant is a tendency for governments to devise policies for which little constitutional support can be found. Thus, a recent Ottawa task force on urban policy deliberately disregarded the federal-provincial division of powers with an "uncompromising assertion of a strong and legitimate federal role in urban affairs."[26] In the area of social security the policy advisers of Prime Minister Pearson were prepared to act "without being intimidated by the federal constitution."[27] The DREE program of regional economic development treated "constitutionally assigned jurisdictions . . . as expendable luxuries."[28] According to a recent analysis, justification for government action no longer springs from the constitution, or from "the rights and privileges derived from a federation supposedly respecting diversity as well as unity," but from "sheer economic or fiscal power."[29] In summary, according to the same author, "Governments at both levels have freely chosen to set aside the BNA Act and interpret spontaneously what they feel to be their mandates arising from their commonly-shared populace . . . . The dynamic between governments has tended to turn upon each level's broad-scale policy initiatives, noble in the scope of response to problems, but consciously poor in recognition of the objectives of federalism or clarity of government mandates."[30]

Thus the existing constitution is a lame-duck constitution, cursed with increasing impotence as it awaits its eventual allocation to the dustbin of history. A basic feature of our present troubles, therefore, is a diminished respect for the constitution manifested in a serious decline in its capacity to regulate the competitive conduct of governments, which, in turn, produces further disrespect.

Federalist Causes of the Federal Crisis

The prevailing constitutional weakness in the Canadian polity is only partially caused by the French-English crisis of recent decades. An additional contribution comes from the steady growth of governments in the past half century. But this growth occurs within a particular federal system that makes its own contribution both to the generation of demands and to the effectiveness of the response to them. In this sense we are experiencing not only a crisis of federalism but a crisis to which federalism has contributed.

Stated simply, the increase in demands is a product of the multiplication of political arenas with its attendant increase in the points of citizen and interest group access to the political system. In earlier times, particularly in the thirties, the simultaneous access of groups to the different levels of government in the federal system thwarted the capacity of governments to act. The confusion and multiplication of jurisdictions were transformed into instruments of delay or blockage by interests seeking to avoid the regulatory tentacles of incipient collectivism.[31] That era has been succeeded by new circumstances and philosophies that have transformed access into a vehicle for increasing rather than blocking government output. The overall result is to enhance the pressure on governments to act. Probably more important is the fact that federalism increases the opportunity for what Easton calls "withinputs." It multiplies the incidence of discrete and separate political and bureaucratic pressures for a larger level of services and for ever more extensive regulation. Eleven governments pursuing visions instead of one, two hundred ministers building empires instead of twenty-five, several hundred distinct departmental hierarchies of civil servants seeking expansion of their activities instead of a tenth as many – all these provide an extensive supplementary impetus to the normal pressures for expansion of the public sector present in other polities.

It might be argued that this is simply an optical illusion: that one strong government presiding over a unitary state would combine the present aggregation of dispersed demands into an equivalently sized demand from one government. Even if this were true, which I doubt, Canadian federalism contributes to the generation of pressure for government action in other ways. The nature of the federal system, with its fuzzy lines of jurisdictional demarcation and extensive overlapping of the potential for government response, means that in innumerable fields there is, in fact, an intergovernmental competition to occupy the field, and slackness by one level of government provides the occasion for a pre-emptive strike by the other.[32] Further, the prevailing French-English crisis of Canadian federalism, with the federal and Quebec governments vying for the allegiance of the Quebec voter, encourages an elaborate competition between governments not just for party support but for regime support. Thus, contemporary Canadian federalism reduces the likelihood of unoccupied or only lazily exploited fields and often encourages wasteful competition.

A further consequence must not be overlooked. The diminution of respect for those constitutional procedures and rules of the game capable of policing the boundaries of federal and provincial jurisdiction adds to the insecurity of all governments. The security and certainty of jurisdictional responsibilities that cannot be gained by reference to the constitution are sought by the exercise of sheer power, the staking of claims for popular support by the manufacture of constituencies of allegiance tied by free-wheeling policies and expenditures to a government seeking to maintain its position. Ottawa's regional economic development policies, for example, are based on a political desire, regardless of the BNA Act, to increase the number of satisfied consumers of federal services beyond those satisfied by provincial governments.[33]

So much for the contribution of federalism to the generation of demands for government activity.[34] What of its capacity to produce effective responses to those demands? The answer to this question is ambiguous. The traditional justification for federalism, that it increases the sensitivity of policy-making in a regionally diversified society, undoubtedly retains some cogency even in our second century of existence. The capacity to allow local majorities in provincial settings to go their own ways without having to consider the wishes of residents of other jurisdictions clearly contributes to sensitivity in policy and its administration. However, this virtue has been eroded in several areas by federal-provincial programs that inhibit the freedom of response available to provincial governments.

A further traditional advantage of federalism merits brief discussion: its capacity to reduce the management burden on any single government and thus facilitate political control and policy coherence by restricting the range of interests it is necessary for a particular government to juggle. This, however, like the above-mentioned reputed advantage, presupposes a form of classical federalism in which governments do not get in each other's way and do not subject their respective societies, which, after all, are composed of the same people and the same interests, to conflicting objectives.

But such a federalism no longer exists. Thus, a recent analysis of economic nationalism noted the inadequacy of assuming that only Ottawa pursues nationalistic policies vis-à-vis the economy under its jurisdiction. In addition, powerful provincial economic nationalisms reflect the desire of incumbent provincial elites to plan their own economic development in terms of specific provincial values, with reference to the particularities of the various provincial economies, and employing the set of policy instruments under provincial control. The provinces accordingly have "embarked on policies usually associated with sovereign states – provincial fiscal policies toward full employment and growth; various kinds of restrictions on the free movement of people, goods and capital between provinces; [and] economic relations outside Canada apart from the supervision and control of the national government."[35] The result is a competition of objectives capable of frustrating the aims of both levels of government in such fundamental policy areas as energy, resource development, foreign investment, full employment, and inflation.

Even within areas of supposed intergovernmental agreement, competitive tendencies often outweigh co-operative tendencies. It is understandable and was probably unavoidable for classical federalism to break down under the weight of problems that could not be handled by a single level of government. This has led to an intermeshing of jurisdictions, typically of a nature in which Ottawa provides funds to the provinces on condition that their expenditures meet federal criteria of performance even where legislative jurisdictions are provincial. In two of the most expensive areas covered by such programs, medicare and hospital insurance, federal criteria have contributed to excessive expenditures by providing severe disincentives to provincial governments to economize by the employment of paramedical personnel and the use of cheaper institutional forms than hospitals, for these less expensive responses were not eligible for federal payments. These federal programs also militated against the desire of both Ontario and Quebec governments to integrate health services with other aspects of social policy.[36]

Federal-provincial competition is not abnormal or sporadic. It is frequent and widespread. Thus, in the late sixties major federal proposals for tax reforms affecting the mineral industry were successfully thwarted by the provinces who feared that implementation would slow down resource development crucial to provincial economies.[37] On a smaller scale, recent federal attempts to change the regulations relating to the extra-provincial trucking industry were fought to a standstill by the provinces.[38] A recent case study of a federal-provincial arrangement for adult occupational training in Ontario described it as a vehicle for a clash between the competing grand designs of the federal and Ontario governments and their respective officials. "The clash of these designs can be likened to a collision of ships at sea that results in both vessels remaining afloat and steaming off on their respective courses, taking water, displaying gaping holes in their superstructure, and relatively oblivious to the number of passengers and crew crushed by the impact."[39]

The contribution possible under classical federalism to simplifying the managerial task of governments disappears under a system of big *dirigiste* governments at both levels. Like lumbering mastadons in tireless competition, these governments are possessed of an infinity of weapons capable of wreaking deliberate and inadvertent harm on each other, but incapable of delivering a knockout blow.

The federalism of contemporary big government at both levels can best be understood in terms of the tendency of each government to seek to minimize the policy contradictions in its own jurisdiction and reduce the environmental uncertainty emanating from the conduct of other governments.[40] Hundreds of officials at both levels are employed in this enterprise. Each government, in brief, strains, to exaggerate somewhat, to attain and exercise the powers of a unitary state. This tendency is unavoidable as long as each government views the conduct of the other governments as threatening to its own pursuits.

It is logically impossible for each government simultaneously to succeed in controlling the environmental uncertainties caused by its rivals. The effort to do so produces struggles between governments and innumerable "co-operative" ventures that are serious failures.[41] The dramatic emergence of this previously concealed structural incompatibility in Canadian federalism constitutes the "other crisis" of Canadian federalism. Whereas Lévesque himself has described the conflict of two nations in Canadian federalism as equivalent to "two scorpions in the same bottle,"[42] I consider it more accurate to speak of eleven elephants in a maze. The uncertainties confronting policy-makers in Canadian federalism come not so much from private groups, or even from competing ethnic-linguistic communities, but from other governments in the system. I have described this situation elsewhere in the following terms:

> We have stumbled into a peculiar Canadian version of the American separation of powers. The reaching of agreement on the innumerable major issues which clog the federal-provincial agenda requires the approval of independent political authorities with distinct, and separate bases of electoral, party, group, and bureaucratic support. They are not constitutionally beholden to each other and they are aligned with large and powerful constituencies of interests that can be mobilized behind the evocative labels of provincial rights and the national interest. Indeed, the Canadian version of the separation of powers may be more difficult to work than its American counterpart, for it involves not just the separate legislative and executive strata of the policy-making process but governments, conscious of their historic position, jealous of their prerogatives and aggressively enterprising in the performance of their managerial responsibilities for their societies.[43]

Conclusion

The situation just described portrays major barriers to a viable federalism of big governments. The political thought underlying the evolutionary collectivism of the past half century was inspired by the noble aim of disciplining private concentrations of power and making them accountable to the community. The collectivist solution has left us with the problem of how to make public concentrations of power accountable to the community.

An argument addressed to the problems of big governments can be applied, with only minor modifications, to the governments of contemporary unitary states. Governments that combine bigness with inefficiency, that manage pyramids of power never before experienced by mankind and yet elicit widespread frustration and cynicism in their citizenry, are indeed the veritable hallmarks of our era. Big government now joins the lengthening queue of gods that failed, yet one more noble aspiration shattered by the world it was intended to uplift.

In the Canadian case, the crisis of big government has produced a crisis of federalism. The federal system served Canadians well in simpler times of more limited government. It proved capable of accommodating big government at one level, notably during World War II and its aftermath. But contemporary Canadian federalism founders on the coexistence of big government at both levels. Contemporary Canadian federalism cannot restrain big government, and big governments do not respect federalism. It was probably inevitable that as governments extended their reach into every nook and cranny of our lives they would view the federal system itself as no less amenable to manipulation than the other legacies of a simpler order now subject to political discretion and control. As recently as twenty years ago the language of constitutional debate referred constantly to the intentions of the Fathers of Confederation. Now the language of the original Confederation settlement is a dead language, replaced by a more pragmatic language that speaks of needs, interests, and functions. The handiwork of the Fathers of Confederation recedes into history.[44]

The federal aspects of the BNA Act no longer serve their intended purpose of clarifying and controlling the exercise of power by competing governments. Whether it is even technically feasible to devise a federal system capable of containing strong governments at both levels, of facilitating effective administration by each level where possible and effective joint policies where unavoidable, is open to question. The provinces in Canadian federalism, especially those combining wealth and resources with impressive jurisdictional capacity, are more powerful than the states or provinces of any existing federal system. They are more powerful than most of the member states of the United Nations. Hence, we cannot look elsewhere for successful models. There is no way of reducing the provinces to the position of comparative impotence they previously experienced. We have reached an impasse. We are left with an overloaded political system that has gotten out of control, a system of competitive big governments which, increasingly incapable of effective governing, burdens the societies it is supposed to serve.

In 1964 a Canadian economist praised the authors of the Rowell-Sirois Report for their intellectual achievement in providing a history appropriate for their times, a history that gave "their contemporaries a coherent picture of themselves – of where they had been and how they had got where they were; of where they stood in relation to each other and to the rest of the world; and where they seemed to be going."[45] But more than that they provided a blueprint for the future and a modest optimism that our fate was to be more than a plaything of circumstances.

From the vantage point of the late seventies the Depression generation of social scientists had an easy task. It is much more difficult in the 1970s to define an equivalent set of compelling public purposes for this generation. For those Québécois intellectuals and government elites attracted by the vision of independence the problem does not exist. The presence of visionary possibilities for those who believe in the independence of Quebec, however, destroys the possibility of an equally strongly held vision for those who believe in Canada. The future for the latter is a long twilight struggle of coping, compromising, revising, and adapting. Success in the endeavour is likely to be fragile. A new, enduring harmony will probably elude us, and English Canada will be fortunate to achieve the more limited goal of keeping the frustrations of Québécois down to a level where the short-run future, but not more, partakes of a shaky security.

This is the optimistic scenario. Even less attractive, if somewhat less likely, is that Canadians outside Quebec will find themselves against their wills in the remnant of a ruptured political system they did not seek and whose coming they tried to forestall. This scenario provides even fewer building blocks for a vision, for it will represent a future the believers in Canada tried, and failed, to avoid.

Even if we leave the Québécois nationalist pressures aside, as this paper has largely done, the grounds for optimism are slim. If the other crisis of Canadian federalism is as I have portrayed it, the agency to which we customarily turn for a solution, government, in some federal form, is so much the cause of our problems that one can only half-heartedly visualize it as the instrumentality for alleviating the strains to which it has so markedly contributed. The very effort to maximize public control over our fate by the device of big government at two levels has undermined the federal system and produced a situation in which we are in imminent danger of being victimized by our own creations.

At such a conjuncture there is a clear danger of privatization, of a retreat to cultivating one's garden or succumbing to despair over the apparent passing of a hitherto durable, beneficent, and competent political order that has buoyed up our spirits for more than a century. Neither gardening nor despair will help. We have no alternative but to give up our illusions and go back to the study to grapple with the present reality of that no longer mythical assertion that Canada is a difficult country to govern.

PART IV

CONSTITUTIONAL AND POLITICAL CHANGE

Editor's Introduction

Since time immemorial, social and political theorists have recognized the qualitative difference between the language and imagery appropriate to an understanding of the routine acts that occur in the daily life of a polity, on the one hand, and those foundational activities that characterize periods of constitutional choice and fundamental institutional design, on the other. The latter type of activity, giving a form or constitution to collective life, is quintessentially a question of political presuppositions and is best described as an exercise in "ontological politics," typically characterized by a process of generational imperialism and theory destruction inappropriate to more "profane" political activities.[1] In a presentation to the Royal Society of Canada, Cairns expressed this distinction when he observed that "a constitutional system undergoing crises will . . . encourage macro, holistic thinking of a kind hitherto uncharacteristic of Canadian political science."[2] The remaining two essays to this volume are, above all else, studies in the ontology of Canadian constitutional change and the type of holistic, normative understanding appropriate to its unique place in our history.

"The Canadian Constitutional Experiment" originally was delivered as one of the 1983 Dorothy J. Killam Lectures presented at the Dalhousie Law School. One of its initial concerns is to explore a variety of respects in which our political identities and boundaries of community have changed radically since World War II. In light of such profound changes, Cairns asks, "Can we respond with vision to the urgent task of making moral sense of our collective existence? Can that vision of community extend to the creation

192

of more effective participatory links between the citizens and the governments of Canadian federalism?"[3]

The essay goes on to contend that the harrowing constitutional process of reform we have endured, the continuation of which we confront in the Meech Lake/Langevin Accord, has "changed our understanding of our political system, modified our civic identities, and adjusted our overall relationship to our constitutional arrangements. We have been simultaneously made aware of the fragility of our constitutional system, with its possible breakup only narrowly averted, and of the tremendous difficulty of fundamental, far-reaching reform despite the titanic efforts of strong-willed leaders."[4] While it will not be easy to reconcile the increasing role of bureaucracy in our lives, the traditional elitism of cabinet government, and a more democratic polity, Professor Cairns here finds several hopeful signs that the functional requirements of the state for legitimacy and efficacy can be harnessed to and constrained by the participatory values of democracy. Elitism and hierarchy, he reminds us, are "less compatible with the people we have become than the people we were. A failure to respond will leave us worse off, for our expectations have been raised, and the Charter will, in all probability, not let them die."[5]

While "The Canadian Constitutional Experiment" underscores the political dynamics of constitutional change, "The Politics of Constitutional Conservatism" seeks to explain "why there was so little formal change when so many were convinced that the Canadian constitutional system was about to be turned upside down, and so many directed their efforts to extensive reform."[6] Against those who contended that the resulting limited outcome of the changes that emerged as the Constitution Act can be explained deterministically as the result of some inexorable logic of social and political development, Cairns's analysis highlights the precarious aspects of "a byzantine process in which accidents, personality, skill, and sheer willpower were central to the final outcome."[7] True to the imagery and dominant concerns of his earliest contributions to our understanding of Canadian constitutionalism, Cairns concludes here that "the bias of established systems is to favour continuity. The existing system thus illustrates the reach of the past into the present. In the same way, the new amending formula, the Charter, and other components of our recent constitutional change will be our gift to our successors and will confront future generations as givens, incapable of easy modification."[8]

In contrast to constitutions, social and political theories are regularly exposed to the scrutiny and criticism of the peers and publics to which they are addressed. Never "givens," they must be able to withstand the ravages of continuous debate no less than that of time. The mark of significant scholarship, the likes of which these essays consistently embody, is that they withstand the test of both.

Chapter Seven

The Politics of Constitutional Conservatism

Tradition means giving votes to the most obscure of all classes—
our ancestors. It is the democracy of the dead. Tradition refuses
to submit to the small and arrogant oligarchy of those who
merely happen to be walking around.

— G.K. Chesterton

The dust is slowly settling on the battlefield of intergovernmental
warfare over a new or revised constitution. The truce called the
Constitution Act has produced an uneasy peace. The retrospective
stage, of the use and abuse of history, is now upon us. The search
for truth and the search for partisan advantage vie for our attention.
The race is on between those who seek to uncover what happened
and those who prefer to conceal yesterday's realities and so plant
false clues to mislead the unwary. For, as always, there are votes
to be won, reputations to be made and destroyed, and causes to be
served. In these matters truth is not always as serviceable as fiction,
and may be jettisoned by the politically minded if it gets in the way
of advantage. It is, accordingly, not much easier to keep one's feet
on the ground now that the first phase of our constitutional renewal
has begun to fade into history than it was when we were caught up
in the drama of its unfolding.

Those who profess objectivity may only be practising a more
subtle partisanship, possibly unbeknownst to themselves. Academics, who pride themselves on being above or outside politics, may
be caught up in a war of the schools in their own discipline and
thus suffer from their own special brand of disrespect for what

really happened and why. So, in what follows, we are treading on treacherous ground. There is no other place to walk.

This essay has two objectives. First, it will underscore and attempt to explain the conservatism of the Canadian constitutional system, manifested in the remarkable difficulties it places in the way of advocates of formal change. Second, it will also argue that the package of changes that finally got over all the hurdles and emerged as the Constitution Act cannot be explained in any deterministic fashion as the result of some inexorable unfolding. On the contrary, it was the precarious result of a byzantine process in which accidents, personality, skill, and sheer willpower were central to the final outcome.[1]

Introduction

There is no lack of competing perspectives that can be fruitfully employed in attempting to make sense of our recent constitutional struggles. Perhaps the most obvious approach is to focus on the modifications to the constitution made by the Constitution Act and to seek their explanation in terms of various antecedent conditions and the strategies of the main actors. This emphasis on change, especially congenial to the social science community, is unquestionably a necessary part of an inclusive assessment of the great chess game of constitutional politics that both entertained and exhausted Canadians in recent years. The package of changes now embodied in the revised constitution, particularly the Canadian Charter of Rights and Freedoms and a new amending formula, clearly surpasses in significance any previous amendment in Canadian history. It is not unacceptably far-fetched, therefore, to suggest that the 1982 additions to the constitution will have major effects on the Canadian polity.

Nevertheless, an exclusive stress on change and its determinants has serious drawbacks. It too easily leads to an overlooking of the constitutional continuities, which dwarf change in extent and significance. Certainly the recent constitutional changes, if not trivial or minuscule, seem relatively modest when placed alongside the slowly evolving traditions and long-established constitutional practices deriving from Confederation and before. Our constitutional system was only modified, not overthrown by our recent constitutional renewal.

The limited nature of the change is readily apparent from several perspectives. The twelve-item constitutional agenda established by the first ministers after the Quebec referendum proved to be far too ambitious. Of the twelve items, only resource ownership and inter-provincial trade, equalization and regional disparities, the Charter of Rights, and patriation with an amending formula got past all of the roadblocks to achieve some kind of constitutional resolution. Eight other items – communications, the Senate, the Supreme Court, family law, fisheries, offshore resources, powers over the economy, and a statement of principles – were put aside for the future.

Not only did this twelve-item agenda experience severe attrition as the constitutional process developed, but it was originally said to represent only the first of a several-stage process of constitutional reform. Now, with only a limited portion of the first stage achieved, the momentum for a further major burst of constitutional renewal seems all but dissipated. The requirement to hold a constitutional conference by April, 1983, with the accompanying requirement of an agenda item "respecting constitutional matters that directly affect the aboriginal peoples of Canada," is unlikely to elicit exten-sive further constitutional change.

This limited outcome, it must be stressed, was achieved after constitutional efforts unparallelled in Canadian history. No other period since Confederation manifested a concentration of energy on constitutional reform even remotely equivalent to that of the past few years.

Furthermore, the constitutional system possessed by Canadians at the time of the Quebec referendum, and which still survives in its essentials, had been the subject of widespread denigration and scorn from a variety of actors and commentators for the previous two decades. Few would have speculated only a few years ago that the Canadian constitution, never endowed with the symbolism and majesty of the American constitution, could have emerged so rel-atively unscathed from the battering of so many diverse opponents. Then, too, especially in the sixties when worlds were made and unmade by pamphleteers and gurus, constitutional change seemed so easy, little more than a matter of good intentions, a pencil, and a notepad. Against such facile assumptions the revealed reality of the almost impregnable barriers to large-scale formal change attests to the discrepancy between the flexibility of language and the inflexibilities of the world to which it is addressed.

In retrospect, it is evident that the constitutional process had a remarkable capacity to elicit a striking diversity and extent of pro-

197

posals for constitutional change. By comparison, the constitutional thinking of the thirties was cribbed and confined. Equally striking in our recent efforts, however, was the ruthless winnowing process that resulted in such a limited constitutional outcome. No extraordinary insight is required to observe how much remains the same, to assert that our major constitutional problems survive almost untouched, and to note with varying degrees of surprise, sadness, or anger that the Parti Québécois government of Quebec, whose accession to power in 1976 was the major catalyst of the drive for constitutional change, was left embittered on the sidelines when the constitution came home, deprived of its veto and with a weakened jurisdiction.

The Parti Québécois goal of sovereignty-association was never discussed at the bargaining table, as the Quebec electorate decisively refused to authorize the provincial government to see what terms, if any, could be struck with the other governments of the country it hoped to leave. The competing Quebec constitutional proposals of the provincial Liberal Party never attained the status of an official government position, as Claude Ryan was unable to unseat the Lévesque government. Thus the behaviour of the Quebec electorate in defeating the PQ's sovereignty-association proposals, but refusing to elect a provincial Liberal government with alternative proposals, greatly reduced the Quebec impact in the constitutional discussions that followed the referendum. By a profound irony, which may have long-run tragic consequences, the decisive stages of a process of constitutional renewal originally undertaken primarily to respond to Quebec had only an ineffectual provincial representation from Quebec. Lévesque and his colleagues were on the defensive, toothless tigers in the struggle for a renewed federalism they neither believed in nor thought attainable.

The Quebec experience is not unique. It is not only sovereignty-association and Quebec independence that were jettisoned in the confusing march to the Constitution Act. The road is littered with proposals that fell by the wayside, reflecting aspirations raised and then shattered in a bruising process of accommodation to the narrow limits of the attainable. The proposals of the Task Force on Canadian Unity (Pépin-Robarts), in spite of praise from various political commentators, languished on the sidelines as they never received endorsement from any of the governments that dominated the process. Fifth-region status for British Columbia, a transformed Senate, proportional representation, a referendum role for the people in the amending procedures, Supreme Court reform, and innumerable other projects and proposals have been put back on the shelf to await the political maestro of the future once again capable of breathing life into them.

The major lesson to be drawn from recent Canadian constitutional experience, then, is the truly impressive capacity of the existing constitutional system to survive, to outlast its detractors, and to frustrate those who seek its fundamental transformation. The constitutional exercise of recent years is a practical lesson in the politics of constitutional conservatism, which deserves no less explanation than the politics of constitutional change. Each interacts with the other. However, in spite of the general academic predisposition to be more attracted to understanding the exciting phenomenon of change than the stodginess of stability, the next two sections of this paper seek to explain why there was so little formal change when so many were convinced that the Canadian constitutional system was about to be turned upside down and so many directed their efforts to extensive reform.

Sources of Conservatism

Conflicting Objectives: The capacity of the constitutional system to survive in spite of widespread dissatisfaction with its functioning was partly due to basic divergences of opinion over the desired direction of change. This served the interests of the status quo. The constitutional goals of the competing governments and the incompatibility of many of their objectives have been described elsewhere[2] and need not be given detailed repetition here. An illustration of the extent and nature of the profound differences that surfaced in the constitutional struggle is, however, necessary to an understanding of the barriers to consensual change.

At the very core of the intergovernmental conflict was a profound difference of opinion over the relation of constitutional change to the societies and economies of the country and over the direction in which the federal system should go. A pervasive assumption, verging on a new conventional wisdom, was that the federal government had lost contact with the vigorous nationalism of post-Duplessis Quebec and the only slightly less demanding regionalism of English Canada in the sixties and seventies. From this perspective, constitutional renewal was designed to make the federal system more congruent with the underlying realities of a politically assertive Quebec and a provincialized English Canada. This perspective was also fed by the widespread belief that Canadian federalism was in a long-run decentralizing phase due to a variety of socio-economic, cultural, and political considerations. The task of constitutional renewal was to accommodate these underlying forces. Society was the master, the political system was the superstructure. Accordingly, the new federalism had to be a positive response to the province-building forces based on the powerful realities of dualism and regionalism.

Since the reality of the country had come to be defined in terms of a developing realignment of social forces behind provincial governments, proposals for accommodative constitutional change inevitably favoured the provinces. This was most strikingly the case with respect to Quebec. The fact that the Parti Québécois was committed to independence logically seemed to imply that a constitutional response within federalism, and responsive to Quebec concerns, would result in enhanced jurisdiction for the Quebec government. So powerful and widespread was this climate of opinion that it was almost universally assumed that the unspecified constitutional renewal promised by Trudeau in the 1980 Quebec referendum would mean more power for the Quebec government.

There was, however, a competing definition of an appropriate constitutional response to provincial aggressiveness. From the perspective of the federal government under Trudeau, although not under the short-lived Clark government, the purpose of constitutional change was to strengthen Ottawa by giving it new resources to overcome the centrifugal tendencies threatening to break up the country. Thus the federal proposals for constitutional change from the late sixties to the First Ministers' Conference in 1981 were consistently informed not by a desire to respond in an accommodative fashion to provincialism but by an urge to weaken it and to build a resurgent Canadianism and a stronger Ottawa to fight it.

The task of constitutional change from this perspective was not to transform the constitutional system to make it more consonant with the allegedly dominant regionalism of Canadian society. Instead, the challenge was, by an act of political will, supported by all the jurisdictional levers commanded by Ottawa, to transform Canadian society in support of federal ambitions to be once again the senior government in Canadian federalism. This posture was given an extra stimulus by the return of the Liberals to power in 1980, followed shortly after by the decisive defeat of the Parti Québécois referendum. As Bruce Doern astutely observed, this federal effort at reassertiveness was not confined to the constitutional front, but was also displayed in the energy field, in intergovernmental fiscal relations, and elsewhere. The 1981-82 Liberal spending priorities reflected "what is perhaps the most coherent assertion of political belief and principle by the Liberals since the early years of the Pearson Government." The guiding Liberal belief was simply "that there is a sense of Canadian nationhood and that it is fundamentally based on an identification by individual Canadians with their national institutions, including the federal government."[3] The task of government policy, accordingly, was sedulously to foster and cultivate that identification. In the constitutional field the Liberals acted on the premise that the provincial governments were far more weakly rooted than the strident provincialism of provincial premiers suggested, and that a coast-to-coast nation was struggling to find a constitutional expression that Ottawa was more than willing to provide.

This general federal-provincial conflict was supplemented by an additional conflict over the appropriate future relationship of the Anglophone and Francophone communities to the governments of the federal system. Ottawa sought to define Canada as a coast-to-coast community in which the French language was not confined to Quebec but had a national extension, and in which the English language was equally protected and thriving in Quebec. This Liberal vision of Canada required for its implementation a profound wrenching of Canadian history in a new direction, resulting in serious confrontations with many of the provinces. It required the provinces to adopt a national perspective in their provincial language policies.

The difference in federal-provincial perspectives was cogently summed up by the Pépin-Robarts commission:

Canada, seen from the federal government's perspective, is a linguistically dual federal state composed of two societies – one French-speaking and one English-speaking – which extend geographically beyond the borders of any one province. Thus the federal government believes that it is necessary that this linguistic duality be more fully reflected in Canada's central political institutions and in federal policies and programs.

To the provincial governments, the picture is different. With one exception [New Brunswick], each of them serves a provincial population whose vast majority shares one language.[4]

The Trudeau objective of protecting and fostering linguistic duality at the provincial level, specifically in education and in the use and enjoyment of a range of provincial government services, required the provinces to be subordinated to certain national principles. This necessarily precluded a sensitive response by provincial cabinets to the cues and pressures deriving from their own provincial milieus. Parliamentary supremacy and majoritarianism at the provincial level were to be restrained in the interests of official language minorities. Provincial governments were to become servants of national purposes. This bilingualism goal required the successful imposition on the provinces of English Canada of a limited acceptance of dualism, which was far more natural to any federal government than to provincial political elites and electorates outside of New Brunswick and, possibly, Ontario. The Liberal goal of fostering linguistic duality within Quebec also directly confronted the persistent thrust of a succession of Quebec governments in the sixties and seventies to secure and extend the primacy of the French language. The differences between the Liberals and the Parti Québécois over the nature of community within Quebec spilled over into differences over the linkages between Francophones inside and outside Quebec. The Parti Québécois objective was to separate Francophones in Quebec, relabelled Québécois, from French Canada as a whole. The federal Liberal goal was to keep the concept of French Canada alive, for it had the useful property of crossing provincial borders and linking Francophones together regardless of their provincial location. It was thus hostile to Quebec nationalism.

At the heart of the Quebec-Ottawa confrontation was a basic difference of assumption as to the boundaries of linguistic communities in Canada and their relationship to the governments of the federal state. The Parti Québécois, in its pursuit of sovereignty-association, sought total political responsibility for the preservation and nourishment of the French fact in an independent Quebec. The goal of the federal Liberals was to protect French Canadians throughout the country by means of entrenched constitutional rights binding on all levels of government. In its purest form, the Parti Québécois goal required the elimination of the federal government role in Quebec. In its more restricted form after the referendum defeat, the Lévesque government sought to ensure that Quebec was the primary government of the Québécois nation it was fostering. The Liberal goal, by contrast, required a reduction in the power of the Quebec government to shape the linguistic evolution of Quebec, by constitutionally shoring up the existence of the Anglophone community in the demographic heartland of French Canada. The overall federal purpose was thus clear, consistent, and public. Ottawa sought to preserve linguistic duality in Quebec in order to counter tendencies to equate Quebec exclusively with its Francophone majority and to keep alive the possibility of a French Canada not confined to Quebec, but vital and flourishing in Ontario, New Brunswick, and possibly with more hope than realism, in small pockets of settlement elsewhere.

These profound differences in the major premises of the desirable shape of future government-society relationships constantly got in the way of constitutional agreement. The compromises that can be fairly easily developed when differences concern matters of technique or detail are much less attainable when large issues of principle animate the parties seeking agreement.

The Procedural Bottleneck: The procedures available for constitutional change compounded the difficulties deriving from competing government objectives. The possibility of reaching an acceptable compromise was indelibly affected by the ill-defined procedures for constitutional change bequeathed to the main constitutional actors by their predecessors. The inability of previous generations to regularize, and thus constitutionalize, the amending procedure had an overwhelmingly deleterious effect on the constitutional renewal process. The available procedures for formal change were made up of a cluster of accepted rules and an uncharted, shadowy area where conflicting opinion was rife. The ambiguity of the amending procedures helped to turn the constitutional process into a brutal power struggle that undermined civility and trust. The disagreement over what was included under the domestic amending authority available exclusively to Ottawa under section 91(1)[5] of the British North America Act, and the contradictory assertions of what degree of prior political consent was necessary to legitimate a federal request to Westminster for constitutional change falling outside of section 91(1), profoundly embittered the reform process and eventually turned the courts into prominent participants.

The uncertainty attending the amending process was, of course, far from being total. It was less serious and less pervasive with respect to the domestic amending authority available to Ottawa than with respect to the amending route that involved Westminster.

For the former, controversy was relatively focused and, at least in terms of legality, restricted to rival interpretations of the precise scope of an explicit amending authority possessed by Ottawa. The capacity of Ottawa to stray beyond the core of meaning of section 91(1) was limited and, in relative terms, fairly easily controllable by the courts.

The Westminster route was much more contentious, partly because the scope of the amending authority here was much more threatening to the provinces, and partly because it involved competing interpretations of convention. The stakes were higher, and the procedures were cloudier – an almost certain recipe for tension and bitter disagreement. Acrimony was also heightened over the British route to constitutional change because the ultimate federal resort to unilateralism in the autumn of 1980 was a clear rebuff to the provincial governments, who had been intimately involved with Ottawa over the previous four months in a co-operative intergovernmental search for constitutional agreement.

Somewhat paradoxically, uncertainty and conflict over the method of obtaining constitutional change increased rather than diminished with the passage of time, and reached its highest levels in the post-referendum period. This was partly because the main federal government effort in the period leading up to the referendum was its draft Constitutional Amendment Bill (Bill C-60), which in its first stage was based on section 91(1) rather than on the potentially much more contentious resort to the British Parliament. Although in the seventies there were several federal trial balloons intimating the possibility of a unilateral approach to Westminster, these did not erode the widespread assumption that unanimous provincial consent was required for constitutional changes affecting the division of powers and the rights or privileges of the provinces.

The assumption that unanimity prevailed in these crucial areas had a decisive centrifugal effect, for by giving a veto to each government, it undermined the possibility of any overarching focus on a set of commonly agreed problems requiring solution. It gave each government the option of total selfishness without having to pay a price. It discouraged compromise by not penalizing obstinacy. It made the possibility of agreement conditional on the support of the most recalcitrant or demanding government, and since one government was committed to removing its province from Canada, any adherence to unanimity was a recipe for stalemate. Unanimity, which maximized the power to block, provided an almost unbeatable defence of the existing system wherever it could be invoked. Ironically, this made it most useful to the government least committed to Canadian federalism, for it gave the Quebec government the power to block any possible changes that might tie its people more effectively to Canada and to Ottawa.

Ottawa's search for constitutional change in the period following the election of the Parti Québécois in 1976 until the Quebec referendum was governed by the necessity of avoiding a Quebec government veto. On two previous occasions – the Fulton-Favreau amending formula of the mid-sixties and the Victoria Charter of 1971 – Quebec alone dissented, and Ottawa had not proceeded with the proposed constitutional amendments. There was no reason to believe that a Quebec government seeking independence would be more co-operative than the previous Liberal administrations of Lesage and Bourassa. Lévesque, it could reasonably be assumed, was not going to co-operate in any scheme of renewed federalism that would disprove his criticism of the rigidities and insensitivities of the existing system and thus weaken the case for sovereignty-association in the build-up to the referendum. In any event, Trudeau's preferred brand of renewed federalism was essentially hostile to the interests of the Parti Québécois governing elite, for it did not stress the jurisdictional aggrandisement of the Quebec government, the only kind of constitutional change within federalism of any interest to Lévesque and his supporters.

The federal Liberal government response to this limitation on its manoeuvrability had several facets. One was to chip away at the concept of unanimity as an impossible and unacceptable straitjacket, and thus to pave the way for a full-fledged future assault should that prove necessary. This was coupled with a floating of the idea that referenda might be an acceptable alternative to intergovernmental agreement for constitutional change, for Ottawa believed with some justification that the people were more likely to be supportive of federal government ambitions than were the provincial governments. Lurking in the background was the possibility that Ottawa might petition the United Kingdom unilaterally for those amendments incapable of being implemented by Ottawa's domestic amending authority under section 91(1). Although different versions of this approach surfaced intermittently in the last half of the seventies, the possibility acquired its greatest prominence after the return of Trudeau to power in 1980.

The federal government made two major, explicit efforts to escape the paralysing consequences of the unanimity requirement. In its first effort in 1978, with Bill C-60, Ottawa tried to achieve a limited measure of reform under the domestic authority it had under section 91(1). The constitutional matters covered by the bill included a revised Senate, to be called the House of the Federation, the Supreme Court, certain aspects of the federal executive, a preamble to the constitution and a statement of aims, and a Charter of Rights and Freedoms.

There was a certain awkwardness and incompleteness to the 1978 federal proposals, not only in what was excluded but even with respect to what was ostensibly included. For example, initially the Charter of Rights and Freedoms would be binding only on the federal government. It would become applicable to the jurisdiction of a province only when adopted by that province, and would become entrenched only when endorsed by a formal amending process. Similarly, the provisions relating to the Supreme Court would be part of the constitution upon enactment of the bill, but would become entrenched only after appropriate constitutional amendment processes involving the provinces had been undertaken. Even the proposed preamble and the statement of aims would become entrenched only after provincial approval, although they would become part of the constitution and applicable to Ottawa on passage of the bill.

There were additional complications attendant upon Ottawa's choice of this route to constitutional renewal. In an attempt to maximize its freedom of action, Ottawa was induced to assert a very generous interpretation of what was within the latitude of its domestic amending power, where it could act alone. On the other hand, and revealing the political complexities of the process, Ottawa agreed to discuss its proposals with the provinces while simultaneously denying that any provincial agreement was necessary on those aspects of the bill it claimed fell under section 91(1). Consultation with the provinces was defined as a political courtesy, not as a recognition of any formal provincial right to veto the federal proposals.

The most controversial component of this 1978 package was the inclusion of a complex scheme of Senate reform. Sufficient doubts existed about the legality of attempting Senate reform, which obviously directly concerned the provinces, without their concurrence that Ottawa agreed reluctantly to refer the matter to the

Supreme Court. Long after the federal proposals had been sidelined by political opposition in Parliament and from the provincial governments, and when the Liberal government was no longer in office, the Supreme Court ruled that the Senate reform proposal was not within the scope of Ottawa's domestic amending authority.

This attempt to bypass the provinces had the inevitable effect of skewing the contents of the federal package in a particular direction, thus avoiding many of the issues on the constitutional agenda of the provinces, particularly the division of powers. Central to the federal effort here, of course, was the necessity of making a response to the people of Quebec that did not require the consent of the government of Quebec.[6]

The procedures of constitutional change and the controversies that surrounded them thus had a significant influence on what reforms it was feasible to pursue. To the extent that Ottawa tried to avoid provincial consent by utilizing the amending authority it possessed under section 91(1), it had only a very restricted range of manoeuvre. Many of the weaknesses and awkward features of Bill C-60 reflected Ottawa's tortuous efforts to squeeze the maximum amount of constitutional reform out of section 91(1). To the extent that resort to Westminster was the preferred strategy, the subject matter of potential amendments was greatly increased. But if unanimity was respected as an unbreakable rule, this version of the amending process tilted the scales in favour of conservatism and against significant reform.

The frustrations that flowed from unanimity were most pronounced for the federal government. Unanimity deprived Ottawa of the leadership role in constitutional change that the national government felt was rightfully hers. Furthermore, no one questioned the existence of a federal veto over constitutional change.[7] So Ottawa, secure in its legal ability to prevent constitutional change it disliked, was concerned to reduce impediments to change it sought. Accordingly, it was in Ottawa's interest to downgrade any requirement of provincial consent preceding resort to the British Parliament to a mere convention, or occasional practice, and certainly not binding.

Federal government frustration was also fed by the commitment it had given to the Quebec electorate in the referendum to achieve some measure of unspecified constitutional renewal. Consequently, once the September, 1980, First Ministers' Conference had ended in a failure Ottawa could partially attribute to the unanimity assumption, there were powerful incentives for the Liberal cabinet to commence a process of unilateral patriation and limited amendment. Ottawa sought to exploit its privileged access to Westminster for amendments by claiming the unilateral right in law to request the British Parliament to amend the BNA Act, with no questions asked, in a manner dictated by the federal government, with or without provincial consent.

Ottawa's willingness to resort to unilateralism was also based on a developing mistrust of and retreat from executive federalism. Co-operative federalism seemed to be long ago and far away as Ottawa mandarins and ministers came to view intergovernmental diplomacy, especially of first ministers and before television cameras, as a no-win situation for the federal government. It was a forum in which they were publicly lambasted on national television by provincial governments whose appetites for "more" were considered insatiable.

This attempted unilateralism, described by the Prime Minister as a necessary act to break the logjam of unanimity, had convulsive effects on intergovernmental relations, on the subsequent development of the constitutional struggle, and on the contents of the package that ultimately gained the agreement of all provinces but Quebec more than a year later.

Once the federal government decided to proceed with less than unanimous provincial consent, the constitutional reform process fragmented. For the dissenting provinces, questions of substance were replaced by controversy about the methods by which the proposed reforms were being pursued. Thus those provinces opposed to the idea of a Charter, which was consistently supported by decisive majorities of the Canadian electorate, focused their criticisms not on the Charter itself but on the safer ground of the unilateralism by which it was to come into effect. On the other hand, the unilateral reform process elicited a very different response in the Special Joint Committee of the Senate and the House of Commons, to which the federal resolution was sent for examination. In the committee, whose proceedings were televised, questions of substance almost completely displaced concern for the procedural constitutionality of Ottawa's methods.

The fragmentation of the reform process engendered by Ottawa's push for unilateral change produced a partial division of constitutional labour that was to have a profound impact on the final constitutional package. The dissenting provinces, initially six, then eight, not only tried to block the federal effort but also undertook the refinement of an alternative amending formula, based on earlier Alberta proposals, so that their effort would not appear totally negative.

Throughout the autumn and winter of 1980-81, two distinct constitution-making arenas emerged with separate personnel and only partly overlapping agendas. The go-between, compromise role attempted by Saskatchewan and the sideline role of Nova Scotia could not survive the polarization between the two camps, and both ultimately joined what then came to be known as the provincial "Gang of Eight." In this provincial arena, where there was no public input and no federal presence, the Alberta amending formula was worked on, refined, and eventually subscribed to by the eight provinces as their constitutional Accord. The Gang of Eight then invited Ontario, New Brunswick, and Ottawa to join and thus end the constitutional impasse. The Accord, which was simply an amending formula that as a by-product would allow patriation, was unquestionably constructed as a protective device to defend the interests of provincial governments. When released in a staged television ceremony in April, 1981, it was savagely criticized by federal spokesmen as viewing Canada as no more than a nation of shopping centres. Generally, the media treated this achievement of the Gang of Eight with little enthusiasm and much derision.[8]

Little is known about the politics of the constitutional Accord, which was fashioned in secret meetings. But its workings were probably governed by an implicit veto based on the need to appear united in the face of the federal juggernaut and to respond to Trudeau's reiterated taunts that the Gang of Eight could not agree on anything. Furthermore, it would have been politically impossible for the eight provincial premiers to have insisted on a unanimity requirement for eleven governments to proceed to Westminster if they could not attain it in the less demanding context of eight allegedly like-minded governments. The unanimity assumption had the inevitable effect of giving strong leverage to the most provincialist-minded members of the shaky coalition—Alberta, Manitoba, and Quebec. The influence of Quebec in toughening the Accord was enhanced after the decisive re-election of the Lévesque government just a few days before the Accord was to be publicly released. Some of the premiers had tried to make it more difficult for provinces to opt out of future constitutional amendments by requiring a two-thirds vote of the provincial legislature, a requirement that would have made the amending formula somewhat more attractive to Ottawa. Lévesque, fresh from a decisive election victory, led the fight against the two-thirds rule, which was defeated, and a simple majority requirement for opting out was retained.[9] Several months later, Premier Bennett of British Columbia noted that Quebec had been far more amenable to compromise after the Parti Québécois loss in the referendum than it was after Lévesque won the subsequent provincial election a year later.[10]

The need for unanimity of the Gang of Eight also precluded a more comprehensive approach to constitutional reform, for any attempt to widen the provincialist agenda would generate fissures in the provincial camp and thus be counterproductive. Thus, a response to the federal desire for a Charter was incompatible with the continued allegiance of several provinces, particularly Manitoba and Quebec, to the provincialist front.

The provincial constitutional Accord, fashioned without any public input, with no federal government involvement, and without the moderating influence of the two provinces (Ontario and New Brunswick) closest to the federal position, inevitably reflected a provincialist vision of Canada. The eight provincial signatories were further pulled away from compromise by the need to placate the most unyielding of their colleagues: Alberta and Quebec on the amending formula, and Premier Lyon of Manitoba on the Charter. The possibilities of an olive branch being offered to Ottawa were further damaged by the political weakness of Premier Blakeney, the most plausible candidate for a mediating role, whose provincialist credentials had been sullied by his flirtations with Ottawa. Accordingly, the constitutional Accord, which was essentially a province-protecting amending formula, contained nothing to entice Ottawa to give up its unilateral drive. By its nature and its limits the Accord revealed the fragility of the Gang of Eight, whose precarious unity was based more on opposition to a common federal enemy than on any overriding constitutional vision capable of encompassing national as well as provincial concerns.[11]

In the highly visible federal arena of Parliament and the Special Joint Committee, an alternative constitutional package, reflecting the interests of a different set of actors, took shape. Building on the original Liberal government resolution, the overt parliamentary process, supplemented and partly orchestrated by the behind-the-scenes manoeuvres of the federal cabinet and officials in the Federal-Provincial Relations Office and the Department of Justice, worked on the Charter, an amending formula, the taxation and regulation of provincial resources, and several other items. The original federal amending formula was modified slightly in deference to provincial concerns, particularly those of Saskatchewan, and clauses dealing with the regulation and taxation of natural resources were inserted to maintain the parliamentary support of the New Democratic Party and to go some way toward appeasing the western provinces.

Overall, however, the federal political process, especially in the Special Joint Committee, focused on the Charter. The form of the Charter originally presented to Parliament was weak and conciliatory to its provincial government opponents, reflecting both the lengthy intergovernmental constitutional process from which Ottawa had just emerged and the continuing federal hope that some provincial governments might yet come on side. But the dissenting provinces did not respond to this implicit concession, and Ottawa was in danger of antagonizing its potential civil rights constituency. Far better to offend the provinces and gain the support of the aggressive lobbyists for a stronger Charter, who had negligible concern for provincial rights or for abstractions such as parliamentary supremacy.

Four provincial premiers appeared before the committee, while four other provincial governments submitted briefs. Several provincial opposition parties also presented their views to the committee. On the whole, however, the provincial perspective was distinctly in the minority of the ninety-seven witnesses who gave evidence to the committee and the 962 written submissions made to it.[12] The complete federal package, therefore, and particularly the Charter and the amending formula, reflected a vision of the country insensitive to the expressed wishes of eight provincial governments. Ottawa, intent on exploiting the loophole of unilateralism, preferred to respond to its own pan-Canadian vision of the country, supported by the lobbyists for a tougher Charter, than to the provincial premiers it considered to be balkanizing a people aspiring to clothe itself in national garments.

When the Supreme Court decision threw the two sides back together there was a confrontation of two antithetical philosophies of federalism embodied in two explicit constitutional reform packages. Given the intense pressure to compromise and the different components of the two packages, the most plausible bargain was a provincial concession on the Charter, to which Ottawa was wedded, and a federal concession on the amending formula, which was the only developed proposal to which the Gang of Eight was committed. But given the long build-up of antipathy between the two groups, the hothouse atmosphere of the bargaining, and the uncompromising stance of Quebec, one more failure was a distinct possibility and was only narrowly averted. The federal government gave up its amending formula and injected some national concerns into an amending formula originally tailored with provincial interests in mind. The dissenting provinces, with Quebec left out, succeeded in weakening a nation-building Charter to make it more compatible with their desires to be as unhampered as possible in their pursuit of policy goals. They saw the Charter less as an attack on parliamentary supremacy at the provincial level than as an attack on the ongoing creation of provincial diversities by the exercise of provincial jurisdiction. The language of parliamentary supremacy was a rhetorical device to protect province-building against the nationalizing philosophy of the Charter. Thus, the basic compromise resulted in the partial provincialization of a nationalizing charter and the partial nationalizing of a province-protecting amending formula.[13]

The impact of the process on the outcome was complex. In general, the curious mix of rigidities and ambiguities in the reform process had a profoundly dampening effect on the scope and substance of constitutional change it was possible to pursue. It deflected immense resources and psychic energy away from the substance of change to an exhausting controversy about the legitimacy of the process. On the other hand, given the political context, the availability of a questionable right of unilateralism had a catalytic effect that produced a degree of constitutional change that otherwise would almost certainly not have been achieved.

The final package sent to Westminster and subsequently enacted is a strikingly inconsistent document reflecting the competing visions of Canada that went into its making. Its two basic components—the Charter and the amending formula—emerged through different routes and were the creation of different actors. They were brought together in a blunt and brutal compromise in which each was tugged marginally in the direction of the spirit that animated the other. However, the last-minute concessions produced a very particular kind of compromise. A different kind of compromise, which would doubtless have reflected a more philosophically integrated view, would have emerged had the final package been the end product of a series of piecemeal adjustments in an ongoing bargaining process.

The constitutional package reflects the cumulative biases built up in two separate arenas, in each of which the main actors proceeded with negligible attention to the sensitivities of the other side. In each arena there was a certain congealing and consolidation of a one-sided perspective from the time the federal government decided to proceed unilaterally to the final crash course in constitution-making more than a year later, in four days in November, 1981. By this time, positions were too entrenched and time was too short for a fundamental change of direction by either the Gang of Eight or the "Gang of Three" – New Brunswick, Ontario, and Ottawa. Consequently, those who seek the guiding spirit or the real intentions of the Fathers of our limited re-Confederation will search in vain for a dominant animating vision. There is none to be found. The Constitution Act does not transcend competing visions of the country; it only entrenches them in the constitution and provides new arenas in which the battles of the future will be fought. Our constitutional discontents are not yet behind us, although the exhaustion of the actors and the imperatives of a collapsing economy may produce a lull of considerable duration.

Opposition Within: The conservatism of the reform process was based not only on the struggles between governments in the context of unwieldy and unsettled procedures for amendment, but also on the power of interests and institutions within governments to block change they considered repugnant. These intragovernmental barriers to reform were most evident on the federal side, especially with respect to Senate reform and, although the issue was not pressed and is not formally constitutional in nature, with respect to electoral reform.

Since the late sixties, the Senate has been high on the list of candidates for reform, but it has possessed an almost invincible resource – the capacity to veto any change not to its liking. The federal 1978 Bill C-60, which recommended extensive changes in Senate representation and a reduction of its veto power to a delaying power of sixty days, was given severe treatment by the senators, and it was far from clear that it would have passed the Senate hurdle had it not been dropped for other reasons. It is also widely understood that one reason Trudeau was reluctant to embrace Senate reform in the summer of 1980, although it was strongly demanded by some provinces, was his unwillingness to take on the Senate again and thus risk the delay or thwarting of his plans in other areas more central to his objectives. The power and willingness of the Senate to block any changes designed to diminish its influence were further revealed when the Liberal government attempted in its parliamentary resolution of October, 1980, to reduce the Senate's participation in constitutional amendments from its existing veto to a delaying power of ninety days. This was not major Senate reform as such, but it would have paved the way for future Senate reform without Senate concurrence. The opposition of an organized majority of Liberal senators to this proposed reduction in their power and influence led to an unsuccessful government attempt at appeasement by doubling the time of the suspensive veto to 180 days. When it remained unclear that this revision would placate the Senate, the Liberal government reintroduced the absolute veto the Senate had historically possessed. The government was unwilling to jeopardize its larger package by risking a confrontation with the Senate for the sake of a secondary aspect of its constitutional proposals. The situation was graphically, but not inaccurately described by Svend Robinson, an NDP committee member, as follows:

[The Senate,] this nonelected body, this house of patronage accountable to no one, in a final stab at self preservation had made it very clear, apparently, that they do not intend to tolerate any interference with their powers; and that the only way this resolution will pass through Parliament is if there is a Senate amendment, a Senate preservation amendment appended.[14]

The remarkable capacity of the Senate, an institution widely considered to be without roots in Canadian society, to protect itself was built on the entrenched position derived from its veto power. Its veto gave it much greater defence against unwanted change than the Supreme Court possessed. The Supreme Court, unlike the Senate, had many defenders but a much more limited capacity of self-defence from its position on the side-lines.[15] The resistance of the Senate was finally overcome when the limitation of its veto power in amendments, which was built into the provincial constitutional Accord, survived the November, 1981, First Ministers' Conference and was contained in the final agreement of the ten governments. From the perspective of the Trudeau cabinet, it was a happy circumstance to be able to include an elimination of the Senate's protective veto in a larger constitutional package that no Senate, at this culmination of years of constitutional effort, could afford to block.[16]

While electoral reform, technically speaking, is not constitutional reform, Prime Minister Trudeau has viewed a measure of proportional representation as part of his overall political strategy to make the central government more representative of the regions of the country. Here, too, the power of interests built up around the existing system, which it is the function of reform to reduce, threatens to block reform. Electoral reform has to run the gauntlet of the very biases in House of Commons representation it is designed to overcome. While a generalized affection for the traditional ways of electing members has been a not unimportant support for the existing electoral system, the deepest opposition to change comes from Liberal members of Parliament from Quebec and Conservative MPs from the Prairies. On this matter the New Democratic Party is a party like the others. At its 1981 national convention the NDP, whose leader, Ed Broadbent, was publicly in favour of a limited use of proportional representation, voted against electoral reform at the behest of its western members who were fearful that such reform would reduce their party's power in the West, and the power of the West in the party.

Thus, the biases in the representative system, which it is the purpose of proportional representation to alleviate, are kept alive by the beneficiaries of those biases. Those who would benefit from the change are present neither in caucus nor in the House of Commons to argue their case. The goals of a strengthened Ottawa and national integration are clearly secondary concerns to those who are asked to make sacrifices. If the issue ever reaches the House of Commons, the prairie Liberals, Quebec Conservatives, and NDP supporters east of Ontario that electoral reform is designed to represent in the House will not have votes on the proposed measure.

In summary, then, the conservative resistance of the existing constitutional system to change was truly impressive. It derived from the conflicting goals pursued by the contending governments, the limitations and uncertainties of the amending procedures, and the veto power of particular interests within the federal government. In spite of these formidable barriers, some constitutional change was nevertheless achieved. Detailed examination of the particulars of that change is beyond the purview of this paper. What the next section attempts is not to provide additional historical analysis of the making of the Constitution Act, but to provide a perspective that stresses the essential arbitrariness and chancy nature of what has been newly added to the constitution to bind future generations of Canadians.

Determinism, Contingency, and Personality

A focus on the politics of constitutional change invites us to look backward from the particulars of the recent Constitution Act to the factors that went into its making. Such an approach subtly tempts the researcher to find an underlying determinism that inexorably led to what happened. That same determinism applied to the policies and proposals that failed to survive to the implementation stage explains their rejection as equally the result of some historical juggernaut, which cast them aside as inappropriate to the needs of the time, or some other alleged economic or social imperative.

To some twenty-first-century historian, falsely assuming that the passage of time and the cooling of passions have contributed to an Olympian objectivity that allows truth the more easily to be discerned, the constitutional struggles of the last fifteen years may seem to fall into place as the inevitable working out of some deterministic process. Such an interpretation, however plausible its neat and tidy patterns may appear, will be false to the historical record. The Constitution Act resulted from a chaotic process dominated by titanic contests of political will. It was deeply influenced by the byzantine procedures from which it ultimately emerged, and it was profoundly marked by the personalities of the key actors, by the skills they employed and the blunders they perpetrated, and by various historical accidents and ephemeral considerations. At every stage and in every arena the developing constitutional package was tugged and pulled by competing interests seeking advantage. In its final form it is a composite creation whose imperfections and contradictions reflect the compromises of the exhausted opponents who fashioned it.

To suggest that no other outcome was possible is to ignore the fragility of the delicate and precarious balance of interests that shaped the final agreement. It is also to overlook the chaos and contradictions, the accidents and miscalculations, which were an integral part of the long constitutional struggle, not only from the Parti Québécois victory in 1976, but going back to the 1960s.[17]

Prior to the November, 1981, First Ministers' Conference that frantically pieced together a constitutional package, it was quite unclear what agreement, if any, would be reached; and failing agreement, it was not clear what would have happened to the federal patriation package in the United Kingdom had the Liberal government proceeded unilaterally. Unilateralism, still available to Ottawa after the Supreme Court decision, might well have been accepted, albeit reluctantly, by a weary Westminster, resulting in a very different amending formula and Charter for the country. On the other hand, an attempted federal unilateralism in the face of extensive provincial opposition in the United Kingdom could have been defeated, either because of an ultimate failure of federal nerve or a firm, if unenthusiastic Westminster acceptance of a trusteeship role on behalf of the provinces. Either of these outcomes would have embittered federal-provincial relations for years to come.

The particular outcome of the Constitution Act, therefore, was underdetermined. Slight or major differences in one or more of dozens of prior events or political decisions could have nudged the constitutional process onto a different path, which would have led the country to another constitutional destination. The retention of power by the Clark government, a Parti Québécois referendum victory or the replacement of the Lévesque government by the Ryan Liberals, the non-leaking of the Kirby memorandum, a different Supreme Court decision which, given the general surprise that greeted its actual decision, can scarcely be rejected as a possibility[18] – any one of these or various other no less plausible happenings could have reshuffled the actors in the game, the resources at their disposal, and their perceptions of the possible. The constitutional struggles of the sixties and seventies do not lend themselves to explanations of social forces bending men and institutions to their dictates. The constitutional conflict occurred largely at the elite levels of the political system itself. The key actors were political leaders making choices and pursuing strategies in a situation of considerable fluidity.

The observations of Edward McWhinney, while somewhat cynical and even exaggerated, do not entirely miss the mark. The patriation exercise, he wrote,

seems to have been less a clash of contending, clearly defined, historical forces or of rival ideologies–a genuine dialectical operation–than an exercise in political theatre in which personalities were often more important than the ideas they claimed to represent. If it was not, at times, a dress rehearsal in the theatre of the absurd, some of the players seemed casual characters wandering on and off the stage in search of an author and a script, without always being certain about their lines or why they were there in the first place.[19]

This attribution of extensive happenstance to the final constitutional package is supported by the considerable discretion, autonomy, and manoeuvrability possessed by the leading political actors. The constitutional controversy was not rooted in enduring constellations of economic interests that dictated the constitutional options pursued by political elites. The relevant economic concerns were those defined by political elites who dominated the process. There was negligible constitutional input from the big battalions of management and labour.[20] While this partly reflected the particular issues on the agenda, several of the issues were far from irrelevant to the major actors in the economy. The issues on the twelve-item agenda in the summer of 1980 included resource ownership and interprovincial trade, communications, fisheries, offshore resources, powers over the economy, and equalization and regional disparities, subjects that by no stretch of the imagination could be defined as matters of indifference to corporate managers and union leaders. The federal paper on powers over the economy[21] introduced into the 1980 discussions was of great significance to the economic elites on both sides of the industry bargaining table. Yet even here business and labour elites, possibly due to internal divisions in their national organizations, were more akin to Wimbledon spectators than to backroom puppeteers manipulating federal and provincial Punch and Judies in a make-believe performance. The constitutional struggles, therefore, seem peculiarly resistant to any Marxist explanation that denies extensive autonomy to state political elites.

While the relative freedom of the political actors, which contributed to the unpredictability of the process, was partially due to the exclusion of established economic interests, it was also due to intra-governmental bureaucratic considerations. Particularly in the decisive unilateralism period, the items on the agenda were such that operating departments, with their normal bureaucratic goals of self-preservation and imperial expansion, and with ongoing programs linked to specific clientele groups, were shunted to the background. The stage was occupied by prime ministers and premiers, ministers of intergovernmental affairs, attorneys general, and other officials and ministers with jurisdiction-wide concerns. The issues of patriation, an amending formula, and the Charter were issues of high politics, of concern to governments as governments, and thus relatively insulated from the more specialized bureaucratic constraints that a constitutional agenda focusing on the division of powers might have elicited.

Policy proposals pertaining to these highly political areas, as well as to the Senate, the Supreme Court, equalization, and a constitutional preamble, often had an idiosyncratic quality, although they seldom conflicted with some conception of jurisdictional gain or defence. They are best seen as the products of particular political elites and their key advisers, rather than the inescapable consequences of viewing the world from the vantage point of Manitoba, British Columbia, or some other jurisdiction. Much of Manitoba's position, especially on the Charter, was due to the particular incumbency of Sterling Lyon rather than to some basic values in the Manitoba political culture. The defeat of the Lyon government in November, 1981, was partly attributed to "his negative position on the charter of rights." The defeat also "had a profound effect on the style of federal-provincial relations conducted between the province and Ottawa. . . . Lyon's outspoken opposition to Ottawa's constitutional proposals" contrasted with his successor, "Premier Pawley [who] ushered in a policy of friendly, co-operative dealings with Ottawa."[22] A British Columbia government led by Opposition Leader Dave Barrett would almost certainly not have ended up with the specifics of the constitutional positions so vigorously espoused by Premier Bill Bennett. To Bennett, Senate reform was the centrepiece of the British Columbia proposals. To Barrett, "the best reform of the Senate is to abolish it."[23] Barrett was a passionate supporter of the Charter, Bennett a cool defender of the British tradition of parliamentary supremacy.[24] The accident of who was in office made its own contribution to th˄ dynamics of constitutional renewal.

The staggered process of constitution-making Canadians have experienced since the mid-sixties, and especially since the election of the Parti Québécois in 1976, was an unusually hazardous undertaking for the participants. No single actor possessed sufficient power to ensure a favourable outcome. The possibility of a devastating defeat no matter how skillfully one played the game was a recurrent nightmare. The knowledge that even the shrewdest strategies might backfire accompanied each actor on his constitutional rounds.

The vagaries and waywardness of the process put an extraordinarily high premium on such traits as political skill, intelligence,[25] and willpower. The political game of constitution-making and unmaking did not have clear rules, with the result that the key actors devoted much effort to trying to get their definition of the game accepted. This involved various attempts to define who were the other relevant actors, what were the legitimate arenas, and what were the rules. Successful redefinitions of the game could greatly enhance one's bargaining position, increase the possibility of victory, and diminish the likelihood of defeat.

Given the conflicting objectives of the competing governments, acceptance of the unanimity requirement for constitutional change was, as already noted, a virtual guarantee of stalemate. Thus the two governments that possessed an especially strong concern for constitutional change sought to redefine the nature and rules of the game by taking charge, developing momentum on their side, and reducing the capacity of their adversaries to block their way. The two major efforts of this kind were the attempt of the Parti Québécois to break out of Canadian federalism by the use of a referendum, and the strategy of unilateralism announced by Trudeau four and a half months after the referendum defeat.

The Parti Québécois under Lévesque brilliantly redefined the rules of the Canadian constitutional game by asserting a self-declared right to a unilateral exit from the Canadian Confederation after a process of democratic consultation with its own electorate, a process in which Canadians outside of Quebec were turned into onlookers while one province pursued its own destiny. The Parti Québécois gained considerable support for the idea that should the Quebec people decide to leave Canada after an open and fair consultation of their opinions, force would not be used to prevent such an outcome.

This Quebec unilateralism, to be based on an act of collective will, was not justified by any reference to the extant procedures for constitutional change. To break up a country has its own imperatives, and they clearly would not include the requirement of unanimous consent of the other ten governments. Thus, in the period from 1976 to 1980, Quebec operated in terms of two sets of rules. With respect to the existing constitution Quebec conducted herself in the traditional way, as possessed of the historic right of veto she had exercised against the Fulton-Favreau amending formula and against the more comprehensive Victoria Charter. With respect to her proposed future exit from the constitution, Quebec asserted a unilateral right of departure. The legitimacy of secession, should events come to that, was founded almost entirely on plebiscitary consultations with the Quebec people, not on some explicit constitutional right of self-determination sanctioned by the existing constitution.

Quebec also pushed the view of Ottawa as the government of English Canada, and hence as the only government with whom an independence-seeking Quebec would have to deal in attempting to work out the sovereignty-association it was pledged to seek after a positive referendum result. The referendum defeat, however, produced a remarkable transformation of the Parti Québécois government's definition of the rest of Canada. The provinces of English Canada, treated prior to the referendum as little more than irrelevant subdivisions of an English Canada led from Ottawa, were transformed into the provincial brothers of a beleaguered Quebec badly in need of allies as a new round of constitutional discussions got under way. Devoid of any plans of its own for a renewed federalism, and hostile to the plans of Trudeau, the Parti Québécois government had no alternative but to adopt a defensive strategy in which safety lay in numbers. According to Claude Morin, the "no" vote left Quebec with no other choice but to "try and block Ottawa and form a common front with the other provinces. . . . Giving us a 'no' vote meant sending us to Ottawa with a terrible handicap."[26] Thus Quebec, for more than a year, and for strategic reasons, became a "province like the others." The Quebec bargaining position was simply to protect all existing rights and to repeat the "traditional" demands of previous Quebec governments.

The behaviour of the Quebec government in the constitutional discussions can only be understood in the light of the extremely difficult political position in which the Lévesque cabinet found itself. As Zukowsky succinctly expressed it,

> the Quebec government's options were quite limited. On one side, its representatives were constrained by their ideals and by their membership in a party dedicated, not to renewing federalism, but to sovereignty-association. On the other side, they were constrained by their role as representatives of a people who

had just rejected sovereignty-association. Thus, if the Quebec government could not appear to its party to be actively pursuing renewed federalism, neither could it be seen by the provincial electorate to be actively obstructing it. Only in this way could the PQ leaders retain the confidence of their party and maximize their chances for success in the next provincial election.[27]

With its own unilateral assault on federalism shattered by the Quebec electorate, the Lévesque government returned to the provincial fold as a stout defender of whatever federal principles could be mustered in her defence. The Quebec willingness to return to the provincialist camp and play the federal-provincial game once again required the acceptance of the Lévesque government as a legitimate partner and reliable colleague by at least some of the provincial governments of English Canada. Throughout the lengthy interministerial discussions in the summer of 1980, the Quebec delegation guided by Claude Morin carefully cultivated the other provincial delegations. By the time of the September, 1980, First Ministers' Conference, Quebec was a prominent actor in orchestrating the strategies designed to thwart Trudeau's plans. Quebec was influential in presenting an overwhelmingly provincialist package to Trudeau as the collective wishes of the provinces, a package so clearly destined for rejection that it seemed to have been designed with failure in mind.[28] In the subsequent unilateralism period, Quebec was a leading participant in the provincial camp that fought Ottawa's unilateralism before courts and before the public in Canada and in Great Britain. This dramatic and successful *volte face* by Quebec was a brilliant example of effective federal-provincial diplomacy. Seven of the English-Canadian provinces that had formed a common front with Ottawa against sovereignty-association moved into a provincialist camp whose main objective was to block Trudeau's version of constitutional renewal.

If the pursuit of the constitutional goals of the Quebec government in both pre- and post-referendum periods was the result of choices made by a small group of political actors, particularly Lévesque and Morin, federal goals and strategy were equally influenced by a small group of individuals, led by Prime Minister Trudeau. The constitutional vision pursued by Trudeau was not simply an automatic consequence of scanning the federal system from the vantage point of Ottawa. While it was clearly designed to serve federal government interests, it also reflected the particular view of federalism developed by Trudeau in an unusual sequence of theory and practice as he moved from the world of scholarship and political journalism to the world of action.

The indispensability of the role of particular individuals in explaining the constitutional outcome is highlighted by the federal decision in the fall of 1980 to pursue constitutional change unilaterally. While the availability of unilateralism as a possibility was an historical accident, seizure of this device to break the deadlock was a Gaullist act that found in Trudeau a willing agent. "Don't underrate the guy's commitment on the constitution," a senior federal adviser said of Trudeau. "He's not obsessed, he's monomaniacal."[29]

In the decisive post-referendum phase of the constitutional struggles, the Trudeau Liberal government's high morale and aggressiveness reflected the party's unexpected return to power in February, 1980, and the extent of the referendum defeat of the Quebec government's appeal for a mandate to negotiate sovereignty-association. From the federal perspective this conjuncture of events provided an unanticipated opportunity to redress the centrifugal drift of Canadian federalism toward a progressively weaker Ottawa. The defeat of the Progressive Conservatives was turned into a repudiation of Joe Clark's concept of Canada as a "community of communities." The referendum, which was to give the Lévesque government a mandate to dismember Canada, was interpreted as a mandate for the Trudeau government to restructure Canadian federalism in pan-Canadian terms and to define dualism on a country-wide basis, thus denying Quebec the exclusive role as spokesman of one-half of the Canadian duality. More generally, the federal government under Trudeau decided to act on the assumption that there was no irresistible determinism in the centrifugal trends that the conventional political and academic wisdom assumed must carry the day.

When the processes of executive federalism, with their assumption of a necessary unanimity of agreement, failed to produce an outcome acceptable to Ottawa, the decision was made to break with the past and proceed unilaterally. Federal government unilateralism, with the support of Ontario and New Brunswick, provided the dynamism in the face of massive opposition for fourteen months – from October 2, 1980, when Trudeau announced unilateral action, to early December, 1981, when the constitutional package received final parliamentary approval after receiving support from nine provincial governments.

In its unilateral efforts, Ottawa and its two provincial allies were

223

deflected but not sidetracked by the Supreme Court decision of September 28, 1981. Although its ruling on convention gave ammunition to the provinces, the Supreme Court sustained the legality of Ottawa's efforts. Furthermore, by its pointed unwillingness to support the proposition that unanimous provincial consent was necessary, the court changed the context of the next round of intergovernmental bargaining. By preserving the legal possibility of unilateralism and refusing to support a conventional requirement of provincial unanimity, the court greatly diminished the probability that unilateralism would be necessary. The tyranny of unanimity that had been used as a justification for unilateralism by Ottawa, and which had frustrated the possibilities of intergovernmental agreement, no longer existed as a cohesive force to keep the dissenting provinces in a common front of opposition. Unanimity had become, in Blakeney's words, no more than a "ghost of conferences past."[30] The disappearance of the unfettered power to block was replaced by the disturbing possibility of being left out. Furthermore, the overwhelming pressure of public opinion for an agreement, coupled with the evident willingness of Ottawa and her allies to compromise in this final bargaining session, made some of the premiers of English Canada fearful of being blamed for a breakdown of the talks. The federal capacity to split the Gang of Eight was thus enhanced, while the ability of Quebec and other hardliners to keep the Gang united was gravely attenuated. The conflicting purposes that had found a temporary home in the Gang of Eight and the provincial constitutional Accord could no longer be submerged once there was a return to the bargaining table, and unilateralism had been at least temporarily checked. "It's one thing to try to get eleven people to agree," stated Premier Blakeney, "but if only seven or eight have to agree and three can disagree then it makes for very, very different negotiations."[31]

The realignment of Ottawa and the nine provinces behind a compromise agreement that Quebec refused to sign was not inevitable, but it quickly emerged as one of several highly plausible outcomes. The final agreement can be explained in many ways. McWhinney's somewhat unfashionable judgement that Lévesque had simply been "out-smarted"[32] is not the kind of explanation customary in social science analysis, but in this case it has the virtue of reminding us of the significance of key individuals and the decisions they made.

The ethics of unilateralism in the Canadian federal context, and the judgement of the future on the quality of the constitutional achievement to which the threat of its employment contributed – two separate strands of evaluation that cannot be entirely disentangled–will be the subject of scholarship and political controversy for decades to come. Those evaluations will be unable to ignore the indispensability of unilateralism to any constitutional renewal in the post-referendum drive for constitutional change.

The major impact of unilateralism on the constitutional process is inexplicable without recognizing the support the Charter gave to the federal initiative. Bereft of the Charter, unilateralism would have been reduced to a simple power play lacking in popular support for the substance of the federal efforts. The immense popularity of the idea of a Charter gave the federal government a crucial support base in the country. In political terms this helped to compensate for the public disquiet over the procedure of unilateralism and greatly complicated the opposition of the Gang of Eight. The vulnerability of Ottawa in the area of procedure was counterbalanced by the vulnerability of the dissenting premiers who, however much they proclaimed their defence of the federal principle, could not claim to be representing the majority wish of their provincial electorates for a Charter.

The Charter and unilateralism were Siamese twins. Without the Charter the federal unilateral effort would surely have foundered. On the other hand, unilateralism, by removing the Charter from the intergovernmental arena where it had languished in the summer of 1980 and making it the centrepiece of federal proposals before the Special Joint Committee, mobilized both diffuse and specific support for the Charter. When the parliamentary package returned to the chambers of executive federalism after the Supreme Court decision on constitutionality, the Charter enjoyed too much momentum to be totally emasculated, even in private, by the provincial advocates of parliamentary supremacy. If the Charter kept the federal unilateral process alive, it is equally true that the political salvation of the Charter was the political support developed on its behalf by that same unilateral process.

Conclusions

What was in happier days described as the "living Canadian constitution" still lives, modified in some ways, but still essentially much as before. Its survival is due at least as much to the difficulties of change and the profound disagreement about the desirable direction of change as to any massive support by elites or masses for the particulars of the existing constitutional system. It survives because no other constitutional option enjoys enough first-choice support to replace it. It survives because in competition with its rivals it alone possesses the supreme advantage of existence, and its continuation does not spell chaos for the private and public interests whose affairs it regulates and channels.

If the existing constitutional system that confronted the blue-prints of its adversaries had been itself only a blueprint confronting some other historical, established reality, its triumph would have been unlikely. For in that case, those interests attaching themselves to any reasonably successful ongoing system would have been ranged against it. It is not, therefore, the abstract qualities of the Canadian constitutional system, its theoretical virtues so to speak, that account for its durability, but simply its monopolistic occupation of the field and the resultant advantage this gives it over all contenders.

The conservatism of the constitutional system and its marked resistance to far-reaching change are not due to an exalted reverence in which it is held, nor to any special logical consistency of its parts, nor even to some mystic entity called traditionalism whose enveloping spirit erodes the will of would-be reformers. A more basic explanation resides in the prosaic fact that any developed constitutional system acquires numerous supporters in the varied interests which have adapted themselves to it, and which resist change detrimental to themselves.

The prime interests, of course, are the federal and provincial governments, often radical in what they seek, but always bulldog-like in self-defence of what they have. The reiterated accusation that some of the provinces wished to barter their support for the symbol of patriation for increased provincial powers, or their acceptance of the Charter for jurisdiction over fisheries, was both true and not surprising. The guiding strategy here was to employ the blocking power derived from the claimed requirement of unanimous consent to advantage oneself elsewhere. Ottawa's veto power was no less selfishly employed in self-defence, as in the dismissal of the loose interprovincial Accord presented by all provinces to Ottawa at the close of the September, 1980, First Ministers' Conference.

On occasion, the conservatism of the process resulted not from the self-interest of government in some unitary sense, but from the capacity of particular institutions with key blocking power to defend themselves against unwanted change. Thus the Senate, as already noted, fully exploited its central position in the amending process to beat back changes detrimental to its own preferred image of its future role. Only when the pressures were irresistible, when the elimination of its veto on future amendments was embodied in a package that it would have been suicidal to resist, did its string of successful opposition finally run out. The defensive capacity of strategically placed institutions is not confined to the Senate. Reform of the House of Commons by proportional representation will undoubtedly encounter oppostion from the parliamentary beneficiaries of the regional imbalances in the party system it is intended to alleviate.

This conservatism and general resistance to major change can be dressed up in the language of functionalism. It can be viewed uncritically by admirers as a highly appropriate protective reaction of an integrated interdependent system preserving its clockwork harmony against barbarian *ad hocery*. Less false to reality is to view the conservatism as deriving from the mutually cancelling tendencies of competing powers with divergent goals. The result is a system in which the capacity to resist major constitutional change has far more leverage than can usually be mustered by the forces of innovation.

This conservatism means, however, not that constitutional change is impossible, but that it is supremely difficult. In the period of constitutional turmoil just ended, an idiosyncratic combination of circumstances, which included an almost obsessive firmness of constitutional purpose in Ottawa, was required to generate the limited breakthrough of November, 1981. While Ottawa hoped to employ the strategic advantages of unilateralism to generate an amending formula and Charter significantly beneficial in both practical and psychological terms to its long-run interest, such was not to be. Unilateralism was constrained by the politics of provincial opposition before the courts and the public. In the resultant compromise, no government enjoyed an undiluted victory, although the Parti Québécois government of Quebec was a clear loser. Thus, while change is possible, it requires Herculean efforts, and the outcome may be seriously disappointing. While the new amending formula will at least provide a set of known rules that can be followed, formal amendments will doubtless continue to be infrequent events in the evolution of Canadian federalism.

Constitutional change is seldom intended to be easy. The bias of established systems is to favour continuity. The existing system thus illustrates the reach of the past into the present. In the same way, the new amending formula, the Charter, and other components of our recent constitutional change will be our gift to our successors and will confront future generations as givens, incapable of easy modification.

These evolving constitutional givens can, at the extreme, be viewed either as a prison from which escape is unlikely, or as a rich tradition to be worked and cultivated. At the present juncture, the recent ferment of the search for change lends little credence to the idea that Canadians see themselves as the happy inheritors of a rich tradition. Eulogies seem fanciful and strained. On the other hand, at least in English Canada, it seems no less exaggerated to describe our constitutional situation as a prison.

In French-English relations, Quebec-Ottawa relations, and federal-provincial relations more generally, there is no resting place, no end to tensions and frustrations. There are no constitutional utopias. We have to be satisfied with the stumbling efforts of imperfect men to keep our problems at bay. From that perspective a restrained half cheer may be suggested as the appropriate response to the new Canadian constitution. It is the only constitution we have.

Chapter Eight

The Canadian Constitutional Experiment

Introduction

Amidst the staggering array of possible foci for an essay on the Canadian constitutional experiment I have chosen to stress the recent tumultuous struggles for identity and community that have engaged citizens and governments. My perspective is primarily from the bottom up, not because the recent constitutional exercise shows the Canadian peoples as masters of their fate, which it does not, but because who we are and to whom we relate as fellow citizens are important subjects in themselves. Further, the contemporary democratic state cannot function successfully in a vacuum. Its weight and its pressure are such, and its purposes are so intrusive of society, that what we now have is a state-society fusion in which a positive symbiosis between the two is a functional necessity. Otherwise the state will fall into disrepute and disrepair as it faces an indifferent populace. State purposes now require so much popular support and participation if they are to succeed that we have no alternative but to move in the direction of a more participant citizenry, which shares on a day-to-day basis in the task of governing itself. Thus the community toward which we work is a political community that simultaneously links us with each other and reduces the distance and the differentiation between the governors and the governed.

The first issue to be addressed is our complex evolution as a people. The political identities and boundaries of community that satisfied our grandparents are gone forever. We have been progressively set adrift from our former selves and we need to find a new resting place with meanings we can all share, which contains and accommodates our rampaging diversities in a framework of tolerance and civility, and which recognizes that older definitions of nations will no longer work. The world is too much with us, constantly washing over us with waves of interdependence, for us to choose anything other than a non-exclusive partial distinctiveness that attaches us simultaneously to Canada and to mankind.

My task, therefore, is to answer the questions of where we have come from, and who we are now as a people, thrown together in a common space, subject to the same political system, but with our historical senses of identity and community shattered by jolts of change we did not seek. Can we respond with vision to the urgent task of making moral sense of our collective existence? Can that vision of community extend to the creation of more effective participatory links between the citizens and the governments of Canadian federalism?

The Decline of Britishness and the Fragmentation of Community and Identity

The definition of who we are as a people has been a moving target for the last half century. The federal state and Canadian society have been caught up in a vortex of pressures between new identities emerging from below and struggling for recognition, and manipulatory government attempts from above to refashion collectivities in the light of state purposes. The transformations in political identity and conceptions of community since the Second World War have already been immense, but the end is not yet in sight.

The prevailing definition up to World War II of Canada as a British country–with a French-Canadian minority concentrated in Quebec, little concerned with the positive use of provincial state power, and excluded from all but token and symbolic representation in the federal political elite and the bureaucracy–has been relegated to the museum. The declining psychological significance of Britishness to the Canadian identity is a consequence of the reduced British role in world affairs, the transformation of the Empire into a diluted multiracial Commonwealth no longer bound by common allegiance to Westminster political traditions, and the diminished British interest in Canada as British attention shifted to Europe.

The ending of psychological tutelage to the mother country, proudly described as the move from colony to nation by liberal nationalist historians, left Canadians with the task of fashioning a more autonomous identity. For a heady but ephemeral interlude the post-war international role of Canada seemed to promise a new and pleasing definition of the country as a middle power whose international significance could provide a satisfying external role while an emerging domestic heterogeneity worked itself out. That interlude ended with the post-war recovery of Europe, the explosion of Third World states, and the relegation of Canada to a lower position in the international pecking order.

Domestic pressures emanating from a no longer quiescent Quebec further undermined the continued vitality of a British, Anglophone definition of Canada. Concurrent with this phenomenon was a more general ethnic assertiveness outside the two founding nations. The pan-Canadianism of Diefenbaker and the Diefenbaker Bill of Rights were responses to the latter; the dualist emphasis of the Liberals, leading to linguistic reconstruction of the federal bureaucracy and the new prominence of Francophone cabinet ministers, was the first stage of an ongoing response to the former. Since then, dualism and multiculturalism, which are not easily compatible, have diminished the Anglophone role in the collective image of Canadian society. Britishness is now only one of the images and traditions in an increasingly variegated and unstable blend of linguistic duality, ethnic pluralism, and social heterogeneity.

The declining Britishness of Canada is also reflected in shifts in the external political models to which we look for guidance. The diminished significance of Britain as a constitutional reference was strikingly evident in the recent constitutional debate. Symptomatic of that erosion was the inability and unwillingness of all but a few to defend the British virtues of parliamentary supremacy against the non-British, almost un-British practice of rights to the people. To a previous generation Sterling Lyon's defence of parliamentary supremacy would have seemed platitudinous and central to the derivative Canadian tradition, rather than a defensive last gasp of support for yesterday's verities, which earned him the label of redneck.

The constitution has grown away from its British roots, not just by the Americanism of the Charter, or by the final ending of the Westminster role in the amending process, but by the more general opening up of Canadians to the constitutional experience of other countries. The Westminster model has seemed of limited relevance to the problems of federalism that have dominated our agenda in recent decades.

Canadian political elites and academic analysts underwent a

recent crash course in comparative government as they ransacked the globe for ideas and institutional suggestions appropriate to the Canadian setting. A senatorial mission visited Australia to explore the possible utility of an elected Senate for Canada. The British Columbia government's constitutional proposals for Senate reform were inspired by the German Bundesrat, after on-the-spot study of German and Swiss experience. The search for a proportional representation system that might be employed to generate a more regionally balanced party system resulted in a canvass of continental European, not British, experience where such systems are commonly employed. Finally, in a startling reversal of the historic Canadian attitude of superiority to American political and constitutional practices, the American Congressional system is now often viewed positively. We no longer confidently and automatically consider the fusion of executive and legislative power and the strength of party discipline in the Canadian system to be superior to the American separation of powers and the greater freedom enjoyed by members of Congress.

The concurrent and related decline of the Britishness of our constitutional tradition and of our basic identities has been accompanied, in both cases, by an internationalization of the forces and ideas feeding into our constitutional system and our self-conceptions. Put differently, our particular Canadian past has a diminished hold on us as the contemporary world external to our border increasingly pervades our consciousness.

Our openness to the practices and experiences of the outside world is everywhere apparent. The aboriginal peoples, who can claim a prescriptive right to privileged treatment as the first Canadians, are deeply frustrated by their low socio-economic status. They are fortified in their demands by various aboriginal international organizations that meet periodically for consciousness-raising, the exchange of political information, and the generation of cross-national solidarities. Additional demands for equitable treatment are raised by the growing communities of non-white immigrants who reject white supremacy in all its forms, and whose emerging political importance is revealed by the existence of a House of Commons Special Committee now holding hearings on the Participation of Visible Minorities in Canadian Society.

The group pressures for recognition and for the redefinition of Canadianism do not stop here. The profound and powerful demands of the women's movement for a non-sexist society are a socio-political phenomenon immensely challenging to the status quo. They, too, feed on international roots. Finally, the explosion of alternative lifestyles born of the sexual revolution in the Western world elicits domestic claims for non-discriminatory treatment by lesbians, gays, single parents, and co-vivanting couples.

This bewildering procession of diverse demands for recognition is accompanied by the emergence into popular consciousness of group labels – Québécois, Inuit, Dene, Aboriginal Peoples, Gays and Lesbians–unknown to our grandparents but now part of popular discourse. The political significance of these identity transformations is not trivial, for they all result in claims on the state for recognition, for fair treatment, often for affirmative action, and for representation in the governing councils of the nation. Their successful accommodation into a new pluralist and integrated understanding of what it means to be a Canadian will not be easy, for each typically seeks a supportive use of state power, either to accelerate their movement to equality of status, or to provide temporary or permanent privileged treatment as compensation for past injustices.

These issues of identity and group rights may seem far removed from discussion of the health of that abstraction called the Canadian constitutional system, but they are not. To the extent they do not elicit positive responses, the citizen base of political authority will be fragmented and unstable. On the other hand, a maladroit response to the proliferating claims for recognition and group rights could result in a rigidified society of exclusive and often ascriptive group identities stressing the parts at the expense of the whole. The increasing use of the word "nation" – the Dene nation, the Inuit Nation, the Indian Nation of First Peoples, and the Quebec nation capped by the state of Quebec – is a key indicator of escalating group identities for which the comfortable label of "mosaic" is too insipid to be appropriate.

Since the satisfaction of these group claims typically involves refashioning and restricting the identities of others, as well as increasing the competition for public and private goods in circumstances in which not all can be winners, they are initially divisive in their impact. From the perspective of society and the state, therefore, these emergent group identities are not without their costs and ambiguities. The emphasis on dualism based on charter groups of British and French descent, for example, was not received with acclaim by the various Third Force groups, especially in western

Canada, who saw themselves as relegated to a second-class citizen status. Ottawa responded with its policy of multiculturalism, indicating the troubling tendency for each response to generate new sets of claims and a further set of responses.

For political authorities, these fissiparous tendencies, whatever their justification and sociological explanation, immensely complicate the state's task in generating consent and legitimacy. The psychic integration of these mushrooming diversities into a common harmonious Canadianism is one of the central contemporary challenges facing the Canadian federal state. The failure of the state to meet this challenge will not leave the populace unmoved. We will be left floundering if no overarching sense of community emerges.

The response to the societal fragmentation just described was, and is, conditioned by our political fragmentation. Concurrent with the developing fragmentation of community deriving from both domestic and international forces, the federal and provincial governments were engaged in often competing attempts to restructure the contours of community and identity for their own purposes.

Federalism and the Fragmentation of Community

Nothing in the three decades from the stock market crash of 1929 to the assumption of office in Quebec by Jean Lesage in 1960 prepared Canadians for the nature of the debate that has periodically convulsed the country in the last quarter of a century. The class-focused debate on the inequities of capitalism, for which we had been waiting since the thirties, never happened. As late as the mid-1960s, leading scholars continued to predict the demise of the provinces. Others predicted and hoped that a creative, country-wide class politics organized by a simplified two-party system – conservative versus democratic socialist – would break through the anachronistic barriers of a fossilized federal system. That system, it was held, sustained an irrelevant debate that exaggerated the significance of regionalism/provincialism. In the economic determinism of this analysis, capitalism and technological change were to be the dynamic agents. The class system would provide the relevant cleavages, and a new party system based on those cleavages would moderate the injustices of an economy based on the profit principle. Implicit in this perspective was the assumption that economic change had made us one people and that accordingly the central government was to be the ultimate and clearly dominant master of our collective fates. Neither provincial governments nor the sentiments of provincialism on which they allegedly were based were accorded any prominence in such analyses, except in the form of a scarcely concealed irritation at their inexplicable and too long delayed departure from the Canadian scene.

To explore the events that led to the unravelling of this vision, which was not without a certain nobleness of purpose, would be to write the history of the past half century, a task that limitations of time and space thankfully preclude. Briefly, however, the explanation is found at the intersection of two phenomena, the unpredicted quiescence and intellectual disorganization and weakness of the left, and the equally unpredicted growth of a positive state-centred nationalism in Quebec, which, in conjunction with a resurgent government-led provincialism in much of the rest of Canada, shattered the centralist federal framework we had been bequeathed by World War II.

Consequently, our controversies have been about federalism and the boundaries of community, not about the class system and the injustices of capitalism. For two decades our most vigorous public debates have sought answers to the pre-eminently political questions of who we are as a people and what constitutional framework is appropriate for a harmonious future co-existence of our national and provincial selves.

The debate was not a derivative of other issues. It was not a mask for a debate really about the role of the state in the economy – although the question of which state has clearly been central – nor, to put it slightly differently, was it a debate in which economic actors behind the scenes manipulated political puppets whose language concealed the real goals and purposes of competing economic interests. The debate was what it professed to be on the surface. It was a political debate about those political issues central to our existence – how our federal and provincial selves could be reconciled at the level of community and at the level of government.

The debate transformed our understanding of federalism. Since the Depression of the thirties the division of powers had been viewed as the essence of Canadian federalism. Debate about constitutional change was directed to jurisdictional questions, and it was a pervasive assumption that the provincial level was the outlet for provincial concerns. By contrast, national politics, focusing on the central government, was seen as an arena where Canadians debated their future as Canadians, where they analysed problems as a single people and focused on their national existence. There was an assumed, neat bifurcation of identities and communities. As the citizen lifted his eyes from the behaviour of politicians in the provincial capital and turned toward Ottawa, his provincial identity was thought to be left behind as he partook of a Canadianism that was different from and much more than the sum of its provincial parts.

This Canadianism was always more of an English than a French-Canadian phenomenon. Indeed, it rested on a too easy equation of Canadianism with the outlook and interests of the Anglophone side of duality. Nevertheless, until the Quiet Revolution challenged the centralization of power in the federal government, and by so doing drew attention to the insensitivity of Ottawa as a national capital and to the Anglophone bias of the national bureaucracy, the ethnic and linguistic composition of the federal government was not a salient issue. More general regional concerns were assumed to be adequately melded into a composite national policy in the privacy of caucus and cabinet. From the Depression until the early sixties, therefore, the sensitivity of the central government to provincial interests or linguistic dualism was not a major issue.

So profound was the subsequent transformation of basic assumptions that by the seventies a new conventional wisdom asserted that the major "structural weakness" in the federal system was the insensitivity of the institutions of the central government to the territorial particularisms of which the country was allegedly composed. Accordingly, one significant stream of proposals for constitutional change aimed to modify the institutions of the central government, such as the Senate, the Supreme Court, the bureaucracy, and various boards and commissions, so that provincial orientations would have a greater impact on policy decisions. This approach, labelled intrastate federalism by Donald Smiley,[1] was often described as "federalizing" central institutions.

A federal system viewed almost entirely in terms of the division of powers and one viewed from the intrastate perspective of the regional sensitivity or insensitivity of central institutions are very different animals. In the former, regional interests are confined to provincial containers. In the latter, they spill over into national politics, pervade the institutional structure of the central government, and in their most elaborate form threaten to transform the centre into little more than a broker for the resolution of inter-provincial or interregional conflict.

The joining of these debates produced a dramatic confrontation between rival conceptions of Canada. These conceptions structured the debate on the Charter, the amending formula, the economic union, official bilingualism, a reformed Senate, the position of Quebec within or without Canada, and other more peripheral issues.

The federal government position, after some hesitation, confusion, and vacillation (and discounting the short Conservative interlude), was to reassert the traditional Ottawa approach. This included the basic premise that Canada was more than the sum of its parts, not just an aggregation of provincial and sectional interests. Further, although sectional and provincial concerns might need to be more accurately reflected in reformed central institutions – including the bureaucracy – the federal government was to relate directly to Canadians as individuals and as members of provincial societies. To the extent that regional/provincial interests were to receive greater recognition, that was not to be done by making provincial governments their spokesmen in Ottawa in areas clearly subject to federal jurisdiction, but by enhancing the representativeness of federal government institutions. Also, given the new penetrative capacities of the provincial state to draw the communities and interests subject to provincial jurisdiction into networks of dependence on provincial authority, further decentralization of power to the provinces was to be shunned. Finally, since the positive state at the provincial level threatened to balkanize both the economic and the political union, the federal government sought institutional mechanisms to limit the ability of provincial governments to create territorial diversities of citizen treatment capable of subverting the overriding Canadianism dear to federal policymakers. Both the Charter and the federal desire to protect the economic union sprang from the same basic objective of limiting provincializing tendencies.

In essence, the federal strategy was one of contestation with provincial definitions of the country that threatened to undermine the centrality of the federal government in citizens' eyes. There was nothing novel about this approach. There has been a consistent, natural, almost inevitable federal tendency to protect and exalt the national community, the national identity, and the national interest whenever they are threatened by provincial fragmentation, even if the latter reflects the entirely legitimate use of provincial powers. In areas central to its evolving vision of Canada, the central government has recurrently tried to diminish the capacities of provincial governments to create provincial diversities of citizen treatment. For Ottawa to so act is like breathing, requiring no second thoughts as to purpose, but only careful calculation as to means and timing.

This policy tendency was inherent in the very meaning of Confederation with its creation of a central government that took possession of the key jurisdictional areas of the former colonies. The centralized federalism of 1867 was to provide a framework within which growing sentiments of loyalty and identification with the new central government would flow from the exercise of its authority. The subsequent National Policy was a set of policy instruments designed to integrate the separate societies and economies of the new country around a national transportation system and tariff which, along with massive immigration to the West, would tie the country together in networks of interdependence.

After the Rowell-Sirois Report and the onset of the Second World War, Ottawa moved to eliminate the clashing federal-provincial tax jungle of the thirties by pre-emptively occupying the direct tax field in return for payments to provincial governments. Ottawa took over unemployment insurance in 1940 after securing a constitutional amendment, and followed this in 1951 by gaining the constitutional authority to establish its own old age pension program, followed by another tidying up amendment in 1964 that added supplementary benefits such as survivors' and disability benefits to Ottawa's constitutionally legitimate base of legislative authority. The latter were all part of a basic drive to give the federal government leadership in the creation of the Canadian welfare state, although the basic jurisdictional authority for most of its component parts rested with the provinces. The federal government sought to minimize the centrifugal consequences of predominant provincial responsibility in the welfare area by purchasing, with conditional grants, a degree of uniformity that otherwise would not have prevailed, at the cost of a *de facto* weakening of provincial autonomy. These centralizing initiatives were legally based on the use of the spending power. Politically, they were based on the federal desire to provide a uniform base of welfare entitlements for Canadians regardless of province of residence. The consistent thrust of federal policy was to reduce the barriers to citizen mobility by eliminating the cost to citizens of crossing provincial boundaries.

In 1960 the Diefenbaker Bill of Rights represented a further attempt to mould a Canadian citizenry by providing an equal floor of rights for Canadians for matters in federal jurisdiction. This was followed by the Official Languages Act of 1969, a straightforward effort to legitimate the central government for French-speaking citizens in the face of a threatening province-based Quebec nationalism.

To look back at these major initiatives is to see a strong thread of basic purpose: the ever renewed federal effort to proceed incrementally to the evolutionary creation of the symbolic and practical attributes of a single Canadian citizenship. Federal policy in the recent constitutional review process was the contemporary expression of this historic and traditional federal government effort to strengthen the national community and to resist the provincialization of the Canadian people.

Since 1960 a counter, provincializing trend, concurrent with the more recent federal efforts, reflected a new aggressiveness of provincial governments. A province-building phenomenon born not only of the emergence of a positive state-centred nationalism in Quebec, but also of the ambitions of various other provincial governments, saw the latter strengthen their hold on their societies and economies, pulling their citizenry to the provincial sources of authority, discretion, and power.

The significance of the province-building phenomenon in general, and in its particular Quebec nationalist expression, was found not simply in the contest of power between the federal government and the provinces that it precipitated. More important was the development of a counter ideology to centralism. As the Smallwoods were replaced by the Peckfords, the Mannings by the Lougheeds, Duplessis by the Lesages and the Lévesques, and elder Bennetts by younger Bennetts, the emergent realities of provincial power came to be clothed in definitions of the country that emphasized provincial governments at the expense of the national government, and provincial communities and identities at the expense of the national community and the national identity. This provincializing perspective saw Canada more as an aggregation of provincial communities for whom provincial governments were the natural spokesmen, rather than seeing such communities merged and diluted in the larger encompassing and integrating national community responsive to the leadership of a dominant central government. By the late seventies the Pépin-Robarts Task Force described Canada primarily in terms of dualism and regionalism, while the first Conservative Prime Minister in nearly two decades viewed Canada as a vaguely defined community of communities. To the Parti Québécois the federal government was simply illegitimate. To Peckford, Ottawa was the child of the provinces. To Lougheed it was an alien, exploiting centre seeking to deprive Alberta of its new-found wealth.

By the time of the constitutional discussions of 1980-81, platform rhetoric had passed over into constitutional demands for a reconstruction of Canada based on these new provincial self-images.

The constitutional struggle, therefore, was a contest between competing definitions of Canada, which carried in their wake the potential restructuring of the psyche of Canadians. It was for possession of our souls that the contending governments fought. The competing actors sought not only a practical but a symbolic reconstruction of the Canadian constitutional system – a reconstruction designed over the long haul to transform our identities and perceptions and to direct our definitions of who we are and what Canada was all about in ways compatible with the new federalism they were bent on constructing, or in the case of the Parti Québécois, destroying.

The basic federal objective was to nationalize the environment from which the citizenry received its cues so that the future balance of federal-provincial loyalties and identities would shift to the advantage of the central government. The basic objective of the more aggressive members of the provincial "Gang of Eight" was to do the reverse. We, the citizenry caught in the middle of this constitutional Wimbledon, were mostly audience, occasionally players, and always uneasily aware that our future as a people was attached to the trophy the ultimate winner would triumphantly hold aloft.

The Amending Formula and the Charter: Competing Conceptions of Community

The process by which the recent constitutional settlement was reached has been described elsewhere. The settlement itself was not a triumph for any of the more extreme views contending for acceptance. Sovereignty-association was, of course, repudiated by the

Quebec electorate. The more provincialist versions of desired futures were basically thwarted, while the centralizing federal patriation package of 1980-81 was cast aside by the perceived need to obtain extensive provincial government support before proceeding to Westminster for the last time.

Not surprisingly, therefore, the constitutional settlement speaks with divergent voices about the nature of the Canada to which it is to apply and which it is to help create. Its contradictions reflect the clash and subsequent compromise between profoundly antithetical views about Canada. These contradictions are embedded in the Charter and the amending formula, the two major institutional modifications to emerge from our recent protracted struggle.

An intimate linkage between institutional advocacy and conceptions of community pervaded the constitutional debates. While this is self-evident for sovereignty-association, with its explicit purpose of sundering the Canadian community to the end of creating a new Québécois nation, it is no less applicable for the other major choices that confronted constitution-makers.

The preferred federal amending formula in the unilateralism package was clearly designed to diminish the role of provincial governments in amending procedures, to exalt the role of the people with their new referendum capacity, and generally to allow the national will to override recalcitrant provincial wills.

The federal formula was based on a four-region Canada – the West, Ontario, Quebec, and the Atlantic provinces – and was so constructed that an amendment could pass as long as it had the support of the governments of Ontario and Quebec, governments of any two Atlantic and any two western provinces, and the federal government. Clearly, such a formula did not respect the sovereignty of the provinces. Not only, therefore, was it a relatively flexible formula but it was also a decisive manifestation of a federal desire to give institutional expression to a national will triumphing over (up to four) recalcitrant provincial governments.

The diminished status Ottawa sought to accord provincial governments was even more emphatically present in a supplementary amending provision. If the requisite provincial government agreement was not obtained, the federal government could call a national referendum allowing a national voting majority, providing certain regional criteria for support were met, to bypass the opposition, in the extreme case, of all ten provincial governments. This was potentially an immensely significant symbolic and practical redefinition of the constituent parts of the Canadian federal polity. It located ultimate sovereignty in an alliance between the federal government and national referendum electorates conceivably responding to amending proposals mainly of interest to the federal government and answering questions worded by federal officials. It was an incredibly ambitious attempt to strengthen the central government, elevate the status of the people as constitutional actors, and reduce provincial governments to the status of initial, but no longer final spokesmen for provincial interests. The fundamental thrust of the proposal was nation-building, if need be, at the expense of provincial governments whose powers would henceforth be held on sufferance. The federal government, of course, preserved its own veto and had the exclusive power to activate the process, so there was no way in which it could be a loser.

In marked contrast, the Alberta amending formula, and the eight-province Accord based on it, was a protective package directed to making each province, for which the exclusive spokesman was to be its government, a fortress of rights immune to nationalizing and centralizing pressures that any provincial government wished to resist. The Alberta formula and the Accord were based on the triumph of province over region. Both were based on the equality of the provinces and their sovereignty. The formula explicitly repudiated all concepts of regions and regional majorities and denied power to a national majority, whether composed of governments or voters, to impose its will on a recalcitrant provincial government. Consequently, it expressed a view of Canada as an aggregation of provincial communities and provincial governments, with the latter endowed with indefeasible rights in perpetuity to the jurisdictional powers they possessed.

The ingenuity of the formula was in its combination of flexibility –seven provinces with 50 per cent of the population being sufficient to pass an amendment – with provincial protection. The Accord allowed up to three provinces to opt out of amendments, "derogating from the legislative powers, the proprietary rights, or any other rights or privileges of the Legislature or government of a province," and required the federal government to "provide reasonable compensation to the governments of such provinces." What was sacrificed in the Accord was the nation-wide uniform application of future amendments. The integrity of the national community was to be sacrificed to preserve the integrity of the component provincial parts.

The Charter and the provincial opposition to it were also based on conceptions of community. From one perspective the controversy over the Charter was simply a straightforward debate over the best way to protect rights, between supporters of a leadership role for the judiciary enforcing an entrenched Charter and supporters of leaving responsibility in the hands of parliamentarians who could respond flexibly to unpredictable future situations.

However, the real constitutional significance of the Charter becomes clearer when it is noted that those political actors who defended the supremacy of legislatures against an encroaching role of the courts were spokesmen for provincial governments. Nothing was more revealing of the situational determinants of policy position than the fact that, as discussion of the Charter moved back and forth between the federal parliamentary public arena and First Ministers' Conferences, it was alternately strengthened and weakened. From the perspective of provincial governments in the Gang of Eight, the Charter was seen not as an instrument that removed power impartially from both levels of government on behalf of the people, but as a tool for the achievement of federal government objectives at the expense of provincial governments. Inevitably, the Charter's goal of ensuring that Canadians had a category of rights immune from governmental interference at either level would restrict the possibility of provincial legislative experimentation with its resultant creation of diversities coincident with provincial boundaries. It was this balkanization of rights which Ottawa sought to prevent, and which parallelled its desire to prevent the balkanization of the economic union. The opposing provinces fought not only to preserve their capacity for legislative experimentation, including the creation of distinctive bundles of provincial rights for their citizens, but Quebec, Alberta, and Saskatchewan were also strongly opposed to the enhancement of judicial power the Charter would necessarily bring in its wake. They saw, or professed to see, the Supreme Court not as an impartial umpire but as an instrument of centralization.

The resolution of these contradictory positions on the Charter and the amending formula required compromises on both sides. The extent and direction of change were dictated by the fact that Ottawa's commitment to the Charter was stronger than its commitment to its amending formula. The Gang of Eight, by contrast, was more committed to its amending formula than it was opposed to the Charter. Consequently, the final week of bargaining was

devoted to a provincializing of the Charter and a limited nationalizing of the Accord amending formula. The latter contained an
opting-out clause, which was weakened by Ottawa's insistence that
the clause requiring financial compensation to opting-out provinces
be removed (later partly reinstated with respect to education and
cultural matters to placate Quebec). The Charter was weakened by
the insertion of a non-obstante clause with respect to specified sections of the Charter. Section 33 allows Parliament or any provincial
legislature to prevent the application of the Charter provisions dealing with Fundamental Freedoms, Legal Rights, and Equality Rights
to any federal or provincial Act or provision of an Act, for up to
five years, which can be extended for additional five-year periods
by re-enacting legislation.

Since the two major components of the constitutional settlement,
the Charter and the amending formula, derive respectively from
nationalist and provincialist positions, only partly modified by
concessions to the other side, it is not surprising that the overall
philosophic consistency of the constitutional settlement in which
they co-exist is negligible. Either the Alberta amending formula and
no Charter or the federal amending formula and a strong Charter
lacking a non-obstante clause would have been internally consistent
in their basic assumptions about the nature of community in Canada. The constitutional settlement that combines a nationalizing
Charter and a provincializing amending formula is a contradiction
posing as a compromise.

Was the Game Worth The Candle?

"But what good came of it at last?" quoth little Peterkin: "Why that
I cannot tell," said he, "but 'twas a famous victory."

Robert Southey is not around to pass his judgement on the Canadian version of the Battle of Blenheim. Little Peterkin's question,
however, deserves an answer.

The Constitutional Exercise
as a Collective Experience

A constitution is not just a bundle of machinery, a big tinker toy
with substitutable parts facilitating easy assembling and disman-
tling. It is also a body of understandings, norms, and identities of
those who live the ongoing constitutional life of the country. From
this perspective, we are all part of the constitution, and the evolution of our inner life has a constitutional component and signif-

icance. Although I cannot provide rigorous proof, I can at least plausibly argue that the world of inner meanings and understandings we carry in our heads, and which is no less important than the institutional framework, was profoundly transformed with major consequences for our constitutional future. It is not sufficient, therefore, to look outward to federalism and parliamentary government as if the skin of our bodies were a shell protecting our inner selves from major changes in the functioning of institutions. We must also look inward to the rearrangement of our constitutional psyches and assumptions, recognizing always that the overt world of constitutional machinery and our inner private worlds of meanings are connected, if not always harmoniously.

From this vantage point, the constitutional process produced more constitutional change than appears in the formal amendments. In its largest sense the constitution is a collective experience and a body of evolving understandings and assumptions that interacts with that experience. In this expanded sense there was significant, albeit elusive, constitutional change, which was not always deliberately sought but emerged as a by-product of the pursuit of other purposes.

The harrowing constitutional process of recent decades changed our understanding of our political system, modified our civic identities, and adjusted our overall relationship to our constitutional arrangements. We have been simultaneously made aware of the fragility of our constitutional system, with its possible breakup only narrowly averted, and of the tremendous difficulty of fundamental, far-reaching reform despite the titanic efforts of strong-willed leaders.

The taken-for-granted quality of the constitution characteristic of the immediate post-World War II decades and earlier periods has been eroded. We now know that our political identity, our sense of community, and the balance of our federal and provincial loyalties are all subject to potential modification by institutional change. Although we experienced extreme difficulties in generating formal change, the recognition that political systems can represent acts of choice is now much more widespread. We have come to agree with Renan, often quoted by Trudeau, that a nation is a plebiscite of every day. While this was most strikingly evident in Quebec with its traumatic referendum experience, there was a concurrent Canada-wide implicit ongoing referendum through which the entire country passed.

245

English Canadians were made aware that the comfortable frame of placid existence of the post-war King and St. Laurent years lacked the durability and stability that seemed to tinge it with eternity. As the transformation of Quebec politics proceeded through the post-Duplessis years to the installation of an *indépendantiste* government in 1976, followed by four years of constitutional cold war culminating in the 1980 referendum, those of us who lived outside of Quebec recognized that the Canada we knew might pass away, that we might be Pakistanized against our will. Further, this potential act of separation was driven by an internal dialectic in Quebec, which left those of us living elsewhere only the status of observers. We sat before our television screens and watched our collective Canadian future decided elsewhere. The Parti Québécois goal of destroying the Canadianism of Quebecers would, as a byproduct, destroy the Canadianism of the rest of us.

We even lacked an acceptable name for that new political self that might, unsought, have been thrust upon us. We were variously dignified by the label "the rest of Canada," or "Canada without Quebec," descriptions that did not make our hearts sing. Further than that, it was not clear that Canada without Quebec would continue as a single political entity. In an era of strident provincialism, with an independent Quebec separating East from West, and given the hypothesis of a shattered Ottawa that would follow Quebec's departure, it required little paranoia to see the future of Canada without Quebec as subject to a further fragmentation into a gaggle of provinces posing as states.

For Québécois the experience was very different. From 1976 to 1980 the political dynamism and direction of events seemed to be concentrated in Quebec. Here the great drama of Quebec's future, and therefore of Canada's, was played out. The interaction of the heady wine of nationalism and the charismatic leadership of René Lévesque produced the seemingly incontrovertible truism that Quebec's future would be somewhere in the spectrum from Quebec independence to a position within a revised Canadian federalism significantly more elevated than existing provincial status.

The political logic that turned English Canada into spectators of unfolding events in Quebec led Quebecers to believe that at least the first act in the political reconstruction of Canadian federalism was theirs alone to make in an atmosphere of nationalist introspection. Provincial leaders outside of Quebec participated tentatively and gingerly, if at all, in the Quebec referendum debate, thus providing implicit support for the thesis that they could only choose between being outsiders or intruders in a process designed to break up their country. Even Prime Minister Trudeau limited his major interventions to four speeches – although Quebec members of the federal cabinet were quite active – with the command of the "no" forces being handled by the Quebec provincial Liberal leader, Claude Ryan.

The Parti Québécois message was clear, that what was required was a great act of national will, after which Ottawa – the existence of the other provinces was scarcely noted – would bargain with a triumphant nationalist elite with a mandate to negotiate sovereignty-association. And yet when it was all over, the result was otherwise. Not only was sovereignty-association defeated in the referendum, but the very act of pursuing it, coupled with the surprising re-election of the Parti Québécois in the spring of 1981 (which kept the elaborate constitutional demands of the Quebec Liberals for renewed federalism off the bargaining table), deprived Quebec of effective representation in the constitutional process that followed the referendum. A massive psychological commitment to mobilizing nationalist forces behind the goals of a hoped-for independent state precluded the simultaneous preparation of a sophisticated fall-back position of a renewed federalism. The Parti Québécois dilemma rested on the inability to combine passion for their first choice with a carefully calculated strategy for a distant second choice. Admission of the possibility that the renewal of a decrepit federalism had to be prepared for was to admit the possibility of losing, which was politically out of the question.

Thus, in the same way that Canada outside of Quebec would have been unprepared to think of itself as a coherent entity bargaining with a victorious Parti Québécois government, the latter was unprepared for the federalist counter-offensive when Pierre Trudeau turned out to be the real winner of a referendum designed to break up the country over which he was Prime Minister. Quebec, because of the Parti Québécois re-election, was unprepared for what happened. For the rest of us, by a stroke of luck, our unpreparedness was innocuous as it applied to a future that did not happen – the post-referendum situation that would have followed a "yes" vote.

All Canadians, therefore, live in the aftermath of great political events – of aspirations dashed, of certainties eroded, of strategies that backfired, of too easy assumptions that the world north of the

49th parallel could easily be channelled in the direction of idealistic purposes. We have been alternately frightened by threatened change we did not seek, enraptured by constitutional visions seemingly within our grasp, and ultimately seared by the recognition of potentialities that continued to elude us.

The sense of loss, of pain, and of incredulity at the hardness of the world was given bitter lament by Claude Morin after the exclusion of Quebec from the agreement between Ottawa and the other nine provinces.

> An undeniable fact remains—we are faced with a situation where a (federal) government which is majority English-speaking, associated with nine English-speaking provincial governments, will ask another English-speaking government in London to reduce without its consent the integrity and authority of the only French-speaking government in North America. For 18 years now . . . I have been directly involved in the constitutional debate. At no time did I ever think Quebec would end up in the deplorable and painful situation in which we find ourselves today.[2]

His sentiments, if not his words, would have been uttered by a spokesman for the rest of Canada had the results of the referendum ballot been reversed.

It may be poetic exaggeration to say that we have all been indelibly marked by these revelations of our collective and individual impotence, to suggest that we now know that our immunity from the normal tribulations of our planetary colleagues accustomed to recurrent upheavals was and always will be contingent. I think otherwise. We have all felt the shaking of the earth, the memory of which will not quickly depart.

We have seen the ruthlessness of democratic politics when the stakes are high. We will not easily forget that major constitutional change is not a parlour game for the faint of heart. As our future was played out it was made brutally clear that constitutions and changes in them are instruments to fashion and to destroy peoples, and that as citizens and even as leaders we have only a limited capacity to move our little Canadian world in preferred directions or prevent its movement in directions of which we disapprove. A few short years ago many of us thought otherwise.

Some recent essays of Albert O. Hirschman,[3] organized around the general theme of the role of disappointment in private and public life, are relevant here. Hirschman reminds us of the oscillation in human affairs wherein major efforts that fail produce a counter-reaction. Exhausted, we depart the field of failure and retire to lick our wounds. Thus, many who have visited their hopes on the public sphere to improve the political management of our collective existence are induced by disappointment to retreat to family, to the private life, to cultivating their garden. But the taste of victory, too, can be flat and insipid, for the victors seldom win completely, wholly, and convincingly. Even if they do, the promised land remains elusive and still beyond their grasp.

So, we may expect a temporary abatement of our constitutional introspection. The subjects temporarily crowded off our public agenda by the constitutional exercise have returned. They combine with the changed people we have become, because of what we have been through, to move us on to other issues and to a new balance between our public and our private selves. We approach those other issues against the historical backdrop of a constitutional experience that may be as significant as memory, and hence as controlling, as was the Depression experience of the thirties to a previous generation.

Constitutionalism and Democracy

Quite independently, therefore, of the formal changes in the constitution, but rather reflecting the experiences we have lived through, we have become in subtle ways a new political people. Since the constitutional order does not exist in isolation from the evolving nature of its citizenry, this, too, is a constitutional change in its own way, albeit one difficult to measure and too easy to underestimate.

The changes in our knowledge, in our political dispositions, and in the feeling side of our political selves do not exhaust the constitutional transformations we have gone through as citizens. A larger question demands an answer it is difficult to give. Has the experience and its outcome enhanced that elusive quality of constitutionalism on which the most highly developed political systems depend for the moral quality, civility, and tolerance in the political behaviour of leaders and citizens?

A well-functioning constitution is, among other things, an overarching normative order that constrains and ennobles the major actors by relating their roles to the political traditions, contemporary meanings, and future goals of the overall system. Such a normative order strains toward coherence and equilibrium and is closely connected with ideas of legitimacy. The existence of such a normative order, whose moral dictates restrain and guide both citizens and leaders, is the essence of constitutionalism.

From this perspective, institutions are not simply pieces of machinery sustained by vested interests but the embodiment of particular values that in the aggregate define a political system in terms of procedures and goals. Thus, to rearrange the constitutional machinery of the state, as we have just done, is to rearrange the normative system of the polity, change the cues transmitted to political actors at both elite and mass levels, and in some cases to adjust the boundaries of political community and the content of political identity.

The capacity of the Canadian state to clothe itself in the garments of constitutionalism is unclear. We no longer have, and cannot return to, a liberal state ruling benignly in a limited fashion, asking little of its citizens and giving little in return. The modern Canadian state intertwines with society and economy in a multitude of ways. While this binds citizens and interests to the state in networks of benefits and obligations, it simultaneously enhances the state's dependence on the citizenry for the successful pursuit of public purposes.

Every increase in state-society interactions increases the requirement for the state to be sensitive, discriminating, and caring. Otherwise, a growing number of abrasive interactions between state, society, and economy can only work to the disadvantage of a constitutionalism that depends on mutual respect.

As is often the case, the need for a more comprehensive, fuller, and subtle expression of a particular value in human affairs emerges in inauspicious circumstances. So it is with the contemporary democratic state. It is a sprawling, diffuse, unco-ordinated leviathan whose very nature simultaneously requires and hinders that more developed sense of constitutionalism now necessary to keep the genie we have let out of the bottle amenable to our wishes. The centrifugal nature of the operation of the modern state produces a proliferation of unco-ordinated interactions with the citizenry. The absence of an effective directing core of power renders the efficacy of responsible government, competing parties, universal suffrage, and so on, no longer adequate to keep the state our servant.

In that reciprocal interdependence between state and society the state, as well as society, is imperilled if it comes to be judged as an inefficient, amoral actor. Democratic capitalist welfare states are challenged by the global interdependence of the modern condition in which capital, ideas, and, to a lesser but still significant extent, the citizenry are mobile. The citizens are bombarded with ideas and external models of private and public, individual and collective behaviour that take them out of the protective cocoon of an insulated existence. Many of these citizens are newcomers, immune to the bonds of tradition that help to sustain loyalties in the longer established. Many are potential emigrants prepared to vote with their feet if the possibility of pursuing life goals seems more fruitful elsewhere.

In other words, the citizens' relationship to the political authorities governing them is increasingly conditional. Not only our economy but also our society has been internationalized, as the composition of our metropolitan centres testifies. The state's relations to its citizens could, of course, become analogous to a great railway station in which all are passengers coming and going. No state, however, is likely to adopt this approach to a citizenry whose potential mobility is threatening to political authorities whose domain is fixed by geography.

The stratagems open to the state are various, but essentially they are reduced to the simple thesis that the state has to make its occupation of a particular corner of the world more attractive than other beckoning alternatives. The democratic state commences this task with certain advantages. Mobility is not costless. Further, the instruments of socialization bias the citizen in favour of the political order in which he lives. The more elaborate and complete the version of citizenship that exists in a given state, the more the citizen will identify with the state and be reluctant to leave it. In Hirschman's terms, the state must strengthen the mechanisms of voice and the sentiments of loyalty to limit resort to the mechanisms of exit.

From this perspective the recent constitutional settlement is a mixed blessing. The obtaining of a settlement, almost any settlement, was a positive good, since the total failure of such a massive effort at renewal would have been profoundly dispiriting. However, the process itself, with its incivilities, threats, and competitive brinksmanship was deeply disillusioning and disheartening. Frequent repetition of such intergovernmental acrimony undermines the citizens' confidence in political authority and reduces the hold of the state on the affections of its subjects. Nothing in the recent constitutional agreement addressed that profound weakness of our intergovernmental system, except the amending formula, which at least provides us with rules for that limited class of future inter-governmental controversies focusing on amendments. Another possible contribution lies in the constraining effect of the memories of future political leaders of that disfiguring episode of final bargaining in which our rights were publicly bartered and swapped like sides of mutton. These will not be enough. The world of executive federalism, especially at the summit, still awaits the devising of rules and norms capable of civilizing the intergovernmental process.

Elsewhere, however, there were some hopeful portents in our recent collective constitutional trauma. When brought together they are surprisingly positive for a regeneration of constitutionalism that will contribute to keeping government responsible, strengthening the Canadian community, and enhancing loyalty by elaborating the meaning and practice of citizenship.

Both in terms of its process and its outcome, the constitutional exercise strengthened the democratic component in Canadian constitutionalism and moved partially in the direction of vesting sovereignty in the people. This is not the standard interpretation of the process, which has been widely castigated by many critics (myself included) for its dominance and manipulation by elites. However, to pull some of the scattered threads together is to glimpse another deeper process at work, pregnant with possibilities for an increasing public role in the Canadian constitutional order.

The Quebec referendum is instructive here. Implicit in that daring exercise was the assumption that such a significant change in political status as a move to sovereignty-association could only be legitimized by a popular majority. Further, not only was the referendum itself an exercise in plebiscitary democracy, but the referendum question made it clear that any possible change in constitutional status as a result of bargaining, consequent on a government receipt of a positive mandate, would itself have to be supported in a second referendum.

A further instructive lesson of the Quebec referendum was the apparent willingness of Canadians elsewhere to allow the peaceful disintegration of the Canadian state as a consequence of a decisive affirmative vote in a free and fair referendum contest. Admittedly, this was stated more by indirection than explicitly by the federal government. Nevertheless, the almost universal assumption that force should not be employed to keep a recalcitrant Quebec majority in the federation was impressive testimony to the civility and

tolerance of a society prepared to allow its own peaceful disman-
tling. In a constitutional sense this contributes to the norm that the
Canadian political system is ultimately based on the freely given
consent of its citizenry.

Further indications of a democratizing process can be found in
the major impact of citizens' groups on the work of the Joint Committee of the Senate and the House of Commons, and the very
effective application of mass political pressure by aboriginal groups
and women for the restoration of rights removed in closed intergovernmental bargaining to placate some of the provincial
premiers.

An additional indication of a democratizing process was the elimination of an absolute veto for the Senate in constitutional amendments—an elimination that has paved the way for a reformed Senate
more compatible with contemporary assumptions about the necessity for a popular base for political officeholders possessed of discretion. Early anticipations of the democratizing consequences of
this elimination of a Senate veto capacity are found in the recent
government paper on Senate reform supporting elections and the
probability that the Special Joint Committee on Senate reform will
propose some version of an elected upper house.

More generally, not only was the elite domination of the constitutional process subject to extensive criticism, but there was a
developing intellectual current in the federal government, and in
academic commentary, to view the people as the ultimate arbiter
when an impasse is reached between governments on constitutional
issues. Thus, the federal government was seriously tempted to
bypass the intergovernmental mechanisms of executive federalism
and resort to the people at various stages in the recent constitutional
discussions.

The various federal referendum initiatives[4] were a mix of strategic considerations, governmental self-interest, and belief in the
sovereignty of the people. The fact remains that federal politicians
were willing to consider sacrificing elite dominance of the intergovernmental constitutional process by a profound redefinition of
the basis of ultimate authority in the Canadian constitutional
system.

Cynicism about federal government motives is somewhat allayed
by the reiterated assertions of Prime Minister Trudeau of the importance of the national will as the ultimate basis of a well-functioning
constitutional order. Strategically, the federal government's posi-

tion rested on the belief that there was a national community waiting to be tapped by Ottawa for nation-building purposes, in defiance of the centrifugal tendencies in the federal system that resulted from the monopoly position of provincial governments as spokesmen for provincial communities.

With the federal government's proposed amending formula, Trudeau sought to change the constitution from being a compact among governments to being a compact between the people and the national government, with provincial governments reduced to ineffective bystanders if they stood in the way of that alliance. In magnitude, the proposed change was almost as profound as the reconstruction of political and governmental power north of the 49th parallel sought by the Parti Québécois. That the referendum amending process might have been infrequently employed would have been less significant than the rearrangement of our constitutional norms that its simple existence would have brought in its wake.

Several other aspects of the constitutional process and its outcome were congruent with the popular role envisaged by the federal government. The rhetorical contrast in the "people versus powers" definition of the issues at stake in federal-provincial constitutional bargaining, with Ottawa's proposals designated as a people's package and the Gang of Eight characterized as only interested in jurisdictional power aggrandisement, was a shrewd, and relatively successful propaganda ploy to portray the demands of the opposing provincial governments as only the squalid interests of provincial government elites. This was perhaps a natural perspective for Ottawa – to portray the dissenting provinces as more interested in fish than the rights of the people – but its significance resides in the fact that it was effective. The only counter-claim of the opposing provinces was to assert that their demands were also people demands, and only fortuitously connected with what looked like a self-interested focus on the division of powers or a greater provincial government input into the institutions of the central government.

It may be that these democratizing tendencies and initiatives will turn out to be only ephemeral aberrations from the elitism characteristic of Canadian politics. On the other hand, the Canadian Charter of Rights and Freedoms is now part of our constitutional landscape. Its basic consequence is to give constitutional legitimacy in our political discourse to the language of rights residing in the people. The Charter will not be an unmixed blessing. If it takes hold, it may contribute to an aggressive rights-conscious individualism hostile to fraternity and solidarity. Further, the affirmative action sanctioned and even invited by the Charter may engender disruptive group antagonism.

On the other hand, in the modern world charters and bills of rights are useful mechanisms to attach the citizenry to the state and to generate loyalty both by their symbolism and by the capacity to redress grievances that they provide. Further, the citizens of a fragmented society may achieve an integrating collective sense of themselves from their common possession of rights and the availability of a common language of political discourse.

Finally, a society that is strongly rights-conscious is likely to step up demands for participation. This, of course, can be state-threatening. However, if it is the case that constitutionalism in the modern era demands more of governments and more of citizens at the same time, a participant, rights-conscious citizenry is a necessary, if not sufficient condition for a well-functioning constitutional order.

If the possibilities opened up by these democratizing tendencies are to be translated into fact, the federal and provincial governments of the country must facilitate further democratic input. Elitism and hierarchy are less compatible with the people we have become than the people we were. A failure to respond will leave us worse off, for our expectations have been raised, and the Charter will, in all probability, not let them die.

It will not be easy to reconcile the role of the bureaucracy, the elitism of cabinet government, and a more democratic polity. Utopia is not on our agenda. Incremental moves in the right direction are all that can reasonably be expected. Fortunately, if this analysis is correct, the functional requirements of the state for legitimacy and efficacy and the democratic value of participation are congruent. In this case, the recognition of necessity is not a burden to be borne but an opportunity to be grasped. At least at the margins and for once we are not in a zero-sum game.

In the absence of Robert Southey to answer little Peterkin's question of "What good came of it at last?" I cannot provide a ringing answer. However, the Charter and the democratizing tendencies described above are surely hopeful signs. They may help to bind us together by legitimizing the political process through which we resolve claims on each other. The holding of rights in common may help overcome the multiple fragmentations of community described earlier. Further, a rights-conscious community may reduce the distance between the governed and the governors and may contribute to more sensitive government. We may be disappointed, but we have a chance.

Was, then, the constitutional game worth the candle? Throwing academic caution to the winds, I respond with a resounding "Maybe!"

Acknowledgements

Permission to reprint the following articles is gratefully acknowledged from: "The Living Canadian Constitution," *Queen's Quarterly*, LXXVII, 4 (1970); *The Canadian Journal of Political Science:* "The Electoral System and the Party System in Canada, 1921-1965," I, 1 (March, 1968), "The Judicial Committee and Its Critics," IV, 3 (September, 1971), and "The Governments and Societies of Canadian Federalism," x, 4 (December, 1977); "The Constitutional, Legal, and Historical Background," American Enterprise Institute and Howard Penniman, ed., *Canada at the Polls, 1979 and 1980: A Study of the General Elections* (Washington: American Enterprise Institute, 1981); "The Other Crisis of Canadian Federalism," *Canadian Public Administration*, XXII, 2 (Summer, 1979); "The Politics of Constitutional Conservatism," Methuen Publications and Keith Banting and Richard Simeon, eds., *And No One Cheered* (Toronto: Methuen Publications, 1983); and "The Canadian Constitutional Experiment," *Dalhousie Law Journal*, IX 1 (November, 1984).

Notes

Editor's Preface

1. The materials for the contrast drawn here can be found in Stefan Collini, Donald Winch, and John Burrow, *That Noble Science of Politics: A Study in Nineteenth-Century Intellectual History* (Cambridge, 1983); Frank Underhill's Introduction to Siegfried's *The Race Question in Canada* (Toronto, 1966); J.A. Corry's memoirs, *My Life and Work: A Happy Partnership* (Kingston, Ontario, 1981); James Charlesworth, ed., *Contemporary Political Analysis* (New York, 1967); John Gunnell, *Philosophy, Science, and Political Inquiry* (Morristown, N.J., 1975); and David Ricci, *The Tragedy of Political Science: Politics Scholarship, and Democracy* (New Haven, 1984).

2. "Bringing the State Back In: Strategies of Analysis in Current Research." in P.B. Evans, D. Rueschemeyer, and T. Skocpol, eds., *Bringing the State Back In* (Cambridge, 1985), p. 4, italics in original.

3. "The Governments and Societies of Canadian Federalism," an address delivered at the annual meetings of the Canadian Political Science Association in Fredericton, New Brunswick, 1977, mimeo, p. 1; this passage was deleted from the published version of the text reprinted in this volume.

4. "Alternative Styles in the Study of Canadian Politics," *Canadian Journal of Political Science*, 7, 1 (March, 1974), p. 124. Cf. Melvin Richter, ed., *Political Theory and Political Education* (Princeton, N.J., 1980); Michael Oakeshott, "Political Education," in his *Rationalism in Politics* (London, 1962); Hannah Arendt, *Between Past and Future* (New York, 1961); and Manfred Stanley, "The Mystery of the Commons: On the Indispensability of Civic Rhetoric," *Social Research*, 50, 4 (Winter, 1983), pp. 851-83.

5. *Ibid*.

6. (Toronto, 1980), p. 332.

Author's Introduction

1. The symbolic and normative component of the American constitution is widely recognized. See Max Lerner, "Constitution and Court as Symbols," *Yale Law*

Journal, 46 (June, 1937). The best Canadian analysis is Raymond Breton, "The Production and Allocation of Symbolic Resources: An Analysis of the Linguistic and Ethnocultural Fields in Canada," *Canadian Review of Sociology and Anthropology*, 21 (May, 1984).

2. "The Canadian Constitutional Experiment," p. 240 above.

3. Bernard Crick, *The American Science of Politics* (London, 1959).

4. Published as *Prelude to Imperialism: British Reactions to Central African Society, 1840-1890* (London, 1965).

5. Alan C. Cairns, S.H. Jamieson, and K. Lysyk, *A Survey of the Contemporary Indians of Canada: Economic, Political and Educational Needs and Policies*, ed. H.B. Hawthorn. A Report submitted to the Department of Indian Affairs and Northern Development, Vol. 1 (Ottawa, 1966).

6. See the references in the various introductions to the parts of this volume.

7. "The Canadian Constitutional Experiment," p. 248 above.

8. Cited in Donald V. Smiley, "Rationalism or Reason: Alternative Approaches to Constitutional Review in Canada," paper presented to the Priorities for Canada Conference of the Progressive Conservative Party of Canada, October, 1969, mimeo, p. 7.

9. See K.N. Llewellyn, "The Constitution as an Institution," *Columbia Law Review* (1934), for a brilliant American discussion.

10. See the criticism in D.V. Smiley, *The Federal Condition in Canada* (Toronto, 1987), pp. 89-91.

11. J.A. Corry, "The Uses of a Constitution," in Law Society of Upper Canada, Special Lectures, *The Constitution and the Future of Canada* (Toronto, 1978).

12. William H. Riker, "Implications from the Disequilibrium of Majority Rule for the Study of Institutions," *American Political Science Review*, 74 (June, 1980), cited in Robert J. Jackson *et al.*, *Politics in Canada* (Scarborough, 1986), p. 12.

13. Karl R. Popper, *The Open Society and its Enemies*, Vol. 1 (London, 1945), p. 110, italics in original.

14. E.E. Schattschneider, *The Semi-Sovereign People* (New York, 1961), pp. 71-72, italics in original.

15. "The Politics of Constitutional Conservatism," p. 226 above.

16. Edward Shils, *Tradition* (Chicago, 1983), p. 213.

17. Karl R. Popper, *The Poverty of Historicism* (London, 1961), p. 157, italics in original.

18. *Report of the Royal Commission on the Economic Union and Development Prospects for Canada*, Vol. 1 (Ottawa, 1985), p. 27.

19. For an excellent comparative study, see Roger Gibbins, *Regionalism: Territorial Politics in Canada and the United States* (Toronto, 1982).

20. Albert O. Hirschman, *Essays in Trespassing: Economics to Politics and Beyond* (Cambridge, Mass., 1981), p. 265.

21. Eugene Forsey, *Freedom and Order* (Toronto, 1974), brings together many of his major essays.

The Constitutional Framework: Introduction

1. Frederick Vaughan, "Critics of the Judicial Committee of the Privy Council: The New Orthodoxy and an Alternative Explanation," *Canadian Journal of Polit-*

ical Science, 19, 3 (September, 1985), p. 495; cf. the responses to Vaughan's critique by Peter Russell and Alan Cairns, pp. 521-39.

2. Review of James G. Snell and Frederick Vaughan, *The Supreme Court of Canada, Canadian Bar Review*, 64 (December, 1986), pp. 764-70.

3. "Constitutionalism, Citizenship, and Society in Canada: an Overview," *Constitutionalism, Citizenship and Society in Canada* (Toronto, 1985), Volume 33 of the Research for the Royal Commission on the Economic Union and Development Prospects for Canada, p. 41.

The Living Constitution

1. For an excellent American discussion of the living constitution, see K.N. Llewellyn, "The Constitution as an Institution," *Columbia Law Review*, 34 (1934).

2. Cited in Archibald Macleish and E.F. Pritchard, Jr., eds., *Law and Politics: Occasional Papers of Felix Frankfurter* (New York, 1962), p. 71. The eloquence of Holmes can be supplemented by Marshall's famous description of "a constitution intended to endure for ages to come, and consequently, to be adapted to the various crises of human affairs."

3. Peter Joseph Thomas O'Hearn, *Peace, Order and Good Government* (Toronto, 1964), p.6.

4. *Globe and Mail*, April 13, 1966, p. 7.

5. Llewellyn, "The Constitution as an Institution," p. 6.

6. "Constitutional Monarchy and the Provinces," *Ontario Advisory Committee on Confederation: Background Papers and Reports* (Toronto, 1967), p. 180. Ronald I. Cheffins, *The Constitutional Process in Canada* (Toronto, 1969), provides a well-argued defence of the existing constitution. See especially chapter I and pp. 150-151, 167.

7. Llewellyn, "The Constitution as an Institution," p.3.

8. *The Supreme Court in Modern Role*, rev. ed. (New York, 1965), p. 192.

9. Arthur S. Miller and Ronald F. Howell, "The Myth of Neutrality in Constitutional Adjudication," *University of Chicago Law Review*, 27 (1960), p. 683.

10. Cited in Paul Abraham Freund, *The Supreme Court of the United States* (New York, 1965), p. 20.

11. *Report Pursuant to Resolution of the Senate to the Honourable the Speaker by the Parliamentary Counsel Relating to the Enactment of the British North America Act, 1867, any lack of consonance between its terms and judicial construction of them and cognate matters* (Ottawa, 1939), 11, Annex 1, p. 47.

12. Barry L. Strayer, *Judicial Review of Legislation in Canada* (Toronto, 1968), p. 156.

13. Learned Hand, *The Bill of Rights* (Cambridge, Mass., 1958), pp. 34-35.

14. Rufus Davis, "The 'Federal Principle' Reconsidered," in Aaron B. Wildavsky, ed., *American Federalism in Perspective* (Boston, 1967), p. 14.

15. *The Confederation of Tomorrow Conference: Proceedings* (Toronto, 1968), Appendix B, p. 8.

16. *The Federal-Provincial Conference, Quebec – Federal-Provincial Tax Structure Committee* (Ottawa, 1966), pp. 56-57.

17. Alfred Dubuc, "The Decline of Confederation and the New Nationalism," in Peter Russell, ed., *Nationalism in Canada* (Toronto, 1966), p. 131.

Judicial Committee

In writing this article I have received assistance from numerous friends and colleagues, including Leo Barry, Ed Black, Alexander Brady, Ronald Cheffins, Peter Finkle, Martin Levin, Susan McCorquodale, Donald Smiley, Paul Tennant, and Walter Young.

1. "Within the last twenty years in particular," wrote G.F.G. Stanley in 1956, "it has been the common sport of constitutional lawyers in Canada to criticize, cavil and poke fun at the *dicta* of the judges of the Privy Council and their decisions in Canadian cases. Canadian historians and political scientists have followed the legal party line with condemnations of 'the judicial revolution' said to have been accomplished by Lord Watson and Lord Haldane, and the alleged willful nullification of the true intentions of the Fathers of Confederation." "Act or Pact? Another Look at Confederation," in Ramsay Cook, ed., *Confederation* (Toronto, 1967), p. 112.

2. I have not confined my sources to the writings of the legally trained. Historians and political scientists are also considered. Their approach, although less influenced by technical considerations, did not differ significantly in orientation from that of the lawyers.

Canadian criticism of the Privy Council was part of the more general dissatisfaction present in many of the jurisdictions for which it was a final appeal court. See Hector Hughes, *National Sovereignty and Judicial Autonomy in the British Commonwealth of Nations* (London, 1931), for an analysis.

3. Peter H. Russell, *The Supreme Court of Canada as a Bilingual and Bicultural Institution* (Ottawa, 1969), pp. 34-35, identifies the same two streams of criticism singled out in this article. André Lapointe, "La jurisprudence constitutionnelle et le temps," *Thémis*, 7 (1956), pp. 26-27, adds a third main criticism, the failure to use adequate legal arguments, but this is clearly subsidiary and is not in fact discussed in his article.

4. V.C. MacDonald, "Judicial Interpretation of the Canadian Constitution," *University of Toronto Law Journal* (hereafter *UTLJ*), 1 (1935-36), provides a general centralist interpretation of the intentions of the Fathers and the BNA Act they created, which he contrasts with the judicial interpretation of the act. See also H.A. Smith, "The Residue of Power in Canada," *Canadian Bar Review* (hereafter *CBR*), 4 (1926), pp. 438-39.

5. MacDonald, "Judicial Interpretation," p. 267, after noting that a centralized federation was intended, observed "how closely the language of the act reproduces that intent . . ." W.F. O'Connor stated: "there are not any material differences between the scheme of distribution of legislative powers between Dominion and provinces as apparently intended at the time of Confederation and the like legislative powers as expressed by the text of Part VI of the British North America Act, 1867." *Report Pursuant to Resolution of the Senate to the Honourable the Speaker by the Parliamentary Counsel Relating to the Enactment of the British North America Act, 1867, any lack of consonance between its terms and judicial construction of them and cognate matters* (hereafter the *O'Connor Report*) (Ottawa, 1939), p. 11.

In his most recent publication, Donald Creighton states that the Fathers regarded federalism as a "suspect and sinister form of government . . . British American union, they admitted, would have to be federal in character; but at the same time it must also be the most strongly centralized union that was possible under federal forms. . . . This basic principle guided all the planning whose end result was the British North America Act of 1867." *Canada's First Century: 1867-1967* (Toronto, 1970), p. 10 (see also pp. 44-46).

The extent of Macdonald's centralist bias is evident in his prediction in a letter to M.C. Cameron, dated December 19, 1864: "If the Confederation goes on you, if spared the ordinary age of man, will see both local governments and all governments absorbed in the General Power." Cited in A. Brady, "Our Constitutional Tradition," mimeo, paper presented to the Progressive Conservative Party Policy Conference, Niagara Falls, Autumn, 1969, p. 16n.

For additional support for the thesis that a centralized federal system was both intended and embodied in the BNA Act, see R.I. Cheffins, *The Constitutional Process in Canada* (Toronto, 1969), p. 37; D.G. Creighton, *British North America at Confederation* (Ottawa, 1939); R.M. Dawson, *The Government of Canada*, rev. by Norman Ward (4th ed., Toronto, 1963), chapters 2 and 5; W.P.M. Kennedy, *The Constitution of Canada, 1534-1937: An Introduction to Its Development, Law and Custom* (2nd ed., London, 1938), chapter 19; Kennedy, *Some Aspects of the Theories and Workings of Constitutional Law* (New York, 1932), pp. 86-87; A.R.M. Lower, *Colony to Nation* (Toronto, 1946), pp. 329-31; E. McInnis, *Canada: A Political and Social History* (rev. ed., New York, 1960), chapter 13; *Report of the Royal Commission on Dominion-Provincial Relations* (hereafter the *Rowell-Sirois Report*) (Ottawa, 1954), I, pp. 32-35; F.R. Scott, "The Development of Canadian Federalism," *Papers and Proceedings of the Canadian Political Science Association* (hereafter *PPCPSA*), 3 (1931); Scott, "The Special Nature of Canadian Federalism," *Canadian Journal of Economics and Political Science* (hereafter *CJEPS*), 13 (1947); Scott, "Centralization and Decentralization in Canadian Federalism," *CBR*, 29 (1951); Scott, *Canada Today* (London, 1938), pp. 75-78; R. Tuck, "Canada and the Judicial Committee of the Privy Council," *UTLJ*, 4 (1941-42), pp. 41-43.

6. H.A. Smith, "The Residue of Power in Canada," p. 433. For additional assertions that the failure of the Judicial Committee to use pre-Confederation evidence was partially responsible for their misinterpretation of the BNA Act, see Tuck, "Canada and the Judicial Committee," pp. 40-41. V.C. MacDonald, "Constitutional Interpretation and Extrinsic Evidence," *CBR*, 17 (1939), is a helpful discussion of the actual practice of the Privy Council.

7. W.P.M. Kennedy, "The Terms of the British North America Act," in R. Flenley, ed., *Essays in Canadian History* (Toronto, 1939), p. 129.

8. *Can. H. of C. Debates*, April 5, 1937, pp. 2584-85.

9. *O'Connor Report*, pp. 11-14, and Annex 1.

10. R.W.S., "Criminal Appeals," *CBR*, 4 (1926), p. 410.

11. J.R. Mallory, *Social Credit and the Federal Power in Canada* (Toronto, 1954), p. 29, notes that generally historians, political scientists, and lawyers have argued that the courts misinterpreted the BNA Act. See, for example, Lower, *Colony to Nation*, pp. 376-77; D.G. Creighton, *Dominion of the North* (Boston, 1944), pp. 380-81; C.H. Cahan, *Can. H. of C. Debates*, April 5, 1937, p. 2575; W.P.M. Kennedy, "The Interpretation of the British North America Act," *Cambridge Law Journal*, 8 (1943), pp. 156-57, 160; V.C. MacDonald, "The Constitution in a Changing World," *CBR*, 26 (1948), pp. 29-30, 41; MacDonald, "The

Privy Council and the Canadian Constitution," *CBR*, 29 (1951), p. 1035; Smith, "The Residue of Power in Canada," p. 434.

12. Creighton, *Canada's First Century*, p. 49.

13. B. Laskin, " 'Peace, Order and Good Government' Re-examined," *CBR*, 25 (1947), p. 1054.

14. The vehemence that ran through many of these criticisms is evident in Laskin's assertion: "My examination of the cases dealing with the Dominion's general power does not indicate any inevitability in the making of particular decisions; if anything, it indicates conscious and deliberate choice of a policy which required, for its advancement, manipulations which can only with difficulty be represented as ordinary judicial techniques." *Ibid.*, p. 1086. Kennedy, "Interpretation of the British North America Act," pp. 153-56, and Tuck, "Canada and the Judicial Committee," pp. 56-64, describe the development of the misinterpretation of this clause. See also Creighton, *Dominion of the North*, pp. 380, 466-67; Dawson, *Government of Canada*, pp. 94-102; MacDonald, "The Constitution in a Changing World," pp. 33-34, 41; *O'Connor Report*, Annex 1, pp. 52-78; E.R. Richard, "Peace, Order and Good Government," *CBR*, 18 (1940); D.A. Schmeiser, *Civil Liberties in Canada* (London, 1964), pp. 8-9.

15. Kennedy, "Interpretation of the British North America Act," p. 156 and 156, n42. The situation was so anomalous that Anglin c.j. asserted that he found it difficult to accede to the proposition that "it should be denied all efficacy as an independent enumerative head of Dominion legislative jurisdiction." *King v Eastern Terminal Elevator Co.*, [1925] s.c.r. 434, at 441. Lionel H. Schipper, "The Influence of Duff c.j.c. on the Trade and Commerce Power," *University of Toronto Faculty of Law Review*, 14 (1956), discusses the influence of the provincial bias of Duff on the evolution of this clause. For critiques of the Privy Council interpretation, see B. Claxton, "Social Reform and the Constitution," *CJEPS*, 1 (1935), pp. 419-22; A.B. Keith, "The Privy Council and the Canadian Constitution," *Journal of Comparative Legislation*, 7 (1925), pp. 67-68; MacDonald, "The Constitution in a Changing World," pp. 36-42; M. MacGuigan, "The Privy Council and the Supreme Court: A Jurisprudential Analysis, "*Alberta Law Review*, 4 (1966), p. 421; F.R. Scott, "Constitutional Adaptations to Changing Functions of Government," *CJEPS*, 11 (1945), pp. 332-33; A. Smith, *The Commerce Power in Canada and the United States* (Toronto, 1963); Tuck, "Canada and the Judicial Committee," pp. 64-69.

16. Smith, "The Residue of Power in Canada," p. 433; H.A. Smith, "Interpretation in English and Continental Law," *Journal of Comparative Legislation*, 9 (1927), pp. 162-63; Creighton, *Dominion of the North*, p. 381; Dawson, *Government of Canada*, pp. 96-98; Thorson, *Can. H. of C. Debates*, April 5, 1937, p. 2584.

The critics asserted that the original and intended meaning of property and civil rights was much more restrictive than it came to be under judicial fostering. See W.F. O'Connor, "Property and Civil Rights in the Province," *CBR*, 18 (1940).

17. H. Carl Goldenberg, "Social and Economic Problems in Canadian Federalism," *CBR*, 12 (1934), p. 423.

18. *Hodge v The Queen* (1883), 9 App. Cas. 117; *Liquidators of the Maritime Bank of Canada v Receiver-General of New Brunswick*, [1892] a.c. 437; *A.G. Ont. v Mercer* (1883), 8 App. Cas. 767. See Cheffins, *Constitutional Process in*

Canada, pp. 38-39, 107-08. Ramsay Cook, *Provincial Autonomy, Minority Rights and the Compact Theory, 1867-1921* (Ottawa, 1969), pp. 21-22, discusses the successful attempt of Premier Mowat of Ontario "to make the lieutenant-governor as much the representative of the Queen in the province as the governor general was the representative of the Queen in federal affairs." See also G.F.G. Stanley, *A Short History of the Canadian Constitution* (Toronto, 1969), pp. 99-102, and J.C. Morrison, "Oliver Mowat and the Development of Provincial Rights in Ontario: A Study in Dominion-Provincial Relations, 1867-1896," in Ontario Department of Public Records and Archives, *Three History Theses* (Toronto, 1961), chapter 2.

19. This is the gist of comments by Mallory, *Social Credit and the Federal Power*, p. 29; Creighton, *Dominion of the North*, p. 381; J.M.S. Careless, *Canada: A Story of Challenge* (Toronto, 1963), pp. 364-65; MacDonald, "The Constitution in a Changing World," p. 44.

20. *Bank of Toronto* v *Lambe* (1887), 12 App. Cas. 575, at 579. Critics of the Privy Council for its adoption of a narrow legal approach were legion. See, for example, Creighton, *Canada's First Century*, p. 49; Lower, *Colony to Nation*, p. 334; MacDonald, "The Privy Council and the Canadian Constitution," pp. 1029-31; MacDonald, "Judicial Interpretation of the Canadian Constitution," pp. 267-70; Kennedy, "Interpretation of the British North America Act," pp. 151-52; Kennedy, *Some Aspects of the Theories and Working of Constitutional Law*, pp. 70-72; MacDonald, "The Constitution in a Changing World," p. 23; Thorson, *Can. H. of C. Debates*, April 5, 1937, p. 2582; F.R. Scott, "Section 94 of the British North America Act," *CBR*, 20 (1942), p. 530; E. McWhinney, *Judicial Review* (4th ed., Toronto, 1969), pp. 16-17, 29-30; Tuck, "Canada and the Judicial Committee," pp. 36-41.

Even supporters of the Privy Council agree that this was its approach. In the midst of the furore over the New Deal decisions, Ivor Jennings wrote: "It is not reasonable to expect that the members of the Judicial Committee of the Privy Council would interpret the Act in any way different from that adopted in the interpretation of other statutes. The Act is an ordinary statute, passed by Parliament at the request of certain rather troublesome and very remote colonists on the other side of the world. The judges did not think of themselves as determining the constitutional development of a great nation. Here was a statute in essence not different from many other pieces of legislation; and the judges naturally interpreted it in the usual way, by seeing what the statute said. They were concerned not with the desires of the Fathers, but with the progeny they had in fact produced." "Constitutional Interpretation: The Experience of Canada," *Harvard Law Review*, 51 (1937), p. 3 (see also p. 35).

21. Lord Sankey's bias was "clearly against pettifogging lawyers' arguments that interfered with the effective control of social life and the freedom of Dominion action, and this led him to infuse a new spirit into the process of interpretation." Jennings, "Constitutional Interpretation," p. 36. He also suggested (p. 36) that had he been on the court at the time, the New Deal decisions might have been sustained. He discusses Sankey's "liberal" approach on pp. 28-30. A "liberal" interpretation "implies a certain impatience with purely formal and technical arguments" (p. 31). "Liberal" decisions most frequently favourably cited by critics of the Privy Council were *Edwards* v *A.G. Can.,* [1930] A.C. 124; *In re Regulation*

and Control of Aeronautics in Canada, [1932] A.C. 54; *In re Regulation and Control of Radio Communication in Canada*, [1932] A.C. 304; *British Coal Corporation* v *The King*, [1935] A.C. 500; *A.G. Ont.* v *A.G. Can. and A.G. Que.*, [1947] A.C. 127.

22. MacDonald, "The Privy Council and the Canadian Constitution," p. 1034.

23. MacDonald, "The Constitution in a Changing World," p. 24.

24. *Ibid.*, p. 41.

25. Laskin, " 'Peace, Order and Good Government' Re-examined," p. 1087.

26. A. Brady and F.R. Scott, eds., *Canada after the War* (Toronto, 1943), p. 77.

27. Lower, *Colony to Nation*, p. 334.

28. MacDonald, "The Constitution in a Changing World," p. 45

29. Laskin, " 'Peace, Order and Good Government' Re-examined," pp. 1086-87.

30. Kennedy, "The British North America Act: Past and Future," *CBR*, 15 (1937), p. 399.

31. Kennedy, *Some Aspects of the Theories and Workings of Constitutional Law*, pp. 92-93.

32. MacDonald, "Judicial Interpretation of the Canadian Constitution," p. 282. See also MacDonald, "The Constitution in a Changing World," pp. 26, 44.

33. Michiel S.D. Horn, "The League for Social Reconstruction: Socialism and Nationalism in Canada, 1939-1945," (Ph.D. thesis, University of Toronto, 1969), p. 158.

34. Scott, "Development of Canadian Federalism," p. 247; see also Scott, *Canada Today*, pp. 32-33, 80-82.

35. Laskin, " 'Peace, Order and Good Government' Re-examined," p.1085.

36. In 1936 Vincent MacDonald wrote of the "inability of the Canadian constitution to meet the social, economic, and politicial needs of today and of the necessity for its revision . . . great problems affecting the social and economic life of the country demand legislative capacity and solution. The second great fact at the moment is that effective solution of these contemporary problems is, in part, handicapped, and, in part, rendered impossible by (*a*) the terms of the act of 1867, and (*b*) previous decisions thereon, which, together, withhold jurisdiction where it is necessary that jurisdiction should be, divide jurisdiction where unity of jurisdiction is essential, and in other cases, paralyse action because of doubt as to jurisdiction where certainty of jurisdiction is vital." "Judicial Interpretation of the Canadian Constitution," p. 282. According to A.R.M. Lower, "Objection to Privy Council appeals did not become considerable until about 1930, but it rapidly increased during the Depression when certain decisions visibly hampered the country's ability to cope with the situation." "Theories of Canadian Federalism–Yesterday and Today," in Lower *et al.*, *Evolving Canadian Federalism* (Durham, N.C., 1958), p. 30. J.A. Corry, *Law and Policy* (Toronto, 1959), p. 26, notes how "the Great Depression of the thirties came perilously close to a breakdown in public order." See also Jean Beetz, "Les attitudes changeantes du Québec à l'endroit de la constitution de 1867," in P.A. Crépeau and C.B. Macpherson, eds., *The Future of Canadian Federalism/L'avenir du fédéralisme canadien* (Toronto, 1965), pp. 134-35.

37. Horn, "League for Social Reconstruction," p. 468.

38. *A.G. Can.* v *A.G. Ont.*, [1937] A.C. 326, at 350.

39. Scott, "Centralization and Decentralization in Canadian Federalism," p. 1113.

40. Kennedy, "Interpretation of the British North America Act," p. 159.
41. MacDonald, "The Constitution in a Changing World," p. 42.
42. See Russell, *Supreme Court*, pp. 11-17, for the controversy attending the establishment of the court and the failure to eliminate appeals at that time.
43. J.S. Ewart, *The Kingdom of Canada* (Toronto, 1908), p. 227; see also p. 22, and Ewart, *The Kingdom Papers* (Ottawa, 1912), I, p. 88. For a study of Ewart, see Douglas L. Cole, "John S. Ewart and Canadian Nationalism," Canadian Historical Association, *Historical Papers, 1969.* "Canadian history as Ewart viewed it had but one chief theme – Canada's fight for freedom from imperial control" (p. 65).

Nationalist criticisms of the Privy Council waxed and waned up until the thirties. There was a brief flurry immediately prior to the First World War. See W.E. Raney, "Justice, Precedent and Ultimate Conjecture," *Canadian Law Times* (hereafter *CLT*), 29 (1909), p. 459; W.S. Deacon, "Canadians and the Privy Council," *CLT*, 31 (1911), p. 9, and "Canadians and the Privy Council," *CLT*, 31 (1911), pp. 126-27; J.S. Ewart, "The Judicial Committee," *CLT*, 33 (1913), pp. 676-77; also "Address by W.E. Raney," *Proceedings of the Canadian Bar Association* (hereafter *PCBA*), 5 (1920), pp. 221-24. McWhinney points out that the very low repute of Privy Council judges in the Depression represented not only dissatisfaction with "economically conservative judicial decisions . . . [but] . . . also, in part, an outpouring of local nationalism in that the court . . . was an alien (in the sense of English) tribunal . . ." *Comparative Federalism* (Toronto, 1962), pp. 21-22.
44. Scott, "Abolition of Appeals to the Privy Council: A Symposium," *CBR*, 25 (1947), p. 571; see also Scott, "The Consequences of the Privy Council Decisions," *CBR*, 15 (1937), pp. 493-94.
45. Hon. Stuart S. Garson (minister of justice), *Can. H. of C. Debates*, Sept. 20, 1949, pp. 69, 74-75.
46. Michel Brunet, "Canadians and Canadiens," in R. Cook, ed., *French-Canadian Nationalism: An Anthology* (Toronto, 1969), p. 289, discusses the war and post-war nationalist drive to centralism, of which the abolition of appeals was a part.
47. Scott, "The Development of Canadian Federalism," p. 245. See also J.A. Corry, review of G.P. Browne, *The Judicial Committee and the British North America Act* (Toronto, 1967), in *Canadian Journal of Political Science*, 1 (1968), pp. 217-18; *Rowell-Sirois Report*, I, pp. 57-59, and Browne, *The Judicial Committee*, pp. 40, 84, 158-59.
48. *Ibid.*, Browne.
49. As John Dafoe believed. See R. Cook, *The Politics of John Dafoe and the Free Press* (Toronto, 1963), p. 217. Modified versions of this view were also presented by A.R.M. Lower, "Theories of Canadian Federalism," p. 38; Jacques Brossard, *La Cour Suprême et la constitution* (Montreal, 1968), p. 172; and Guiseppe Turi, "Le déséquilibre constitutionnel fiscal au Canada," *Thémis*, 10 (1959-60), p. 38. Hughes, *National Sovereignty and Judicial Autonomy*, pp. 98, 104-05, discusses the possibility of Judicial Committee bias "where the issue is one between a Dominion and the British Government or between a Dominion person or firm and a British person or firm . . . This is based on its composition which is predominantly English and partly political . . ."

Unspecified allegations of political expediency are contained in Thorson, *Can. H. of C. Debates*, April 5, 1937, p. 2582, and MacDonald, "Judicial Interpretation of the Canadian Constitution," p. 285.

50. For discussions of the provincial bias of the Judicial Committee, see F.E. LaBrie, "Canadian Constitutional Interpretation and Legislative Review," *UTLJ*, 8 (1949-50), pp. 318-23; McWhinney, *Judicial Review*, pp. 51 n7, 67, 69; MacDonald, "The Privy Council and the Canadian Constitution," pp. 1030-32, 1035; MacDonald, "The Constitution in a Changing World," p. 23; MacGuigan, "The Privy Council and the Supreme Court," pp. 426-27. R.F. McWilliams, "The Privy Council and the Constitution," *CBR*, 17 (1939), p. 582, attempts to prove that the Privy Council was not a defender of the provinces or responsible "for whittling down the powers of the Dominion." See also Browne, *The Judicial Committee*, p. 77.

51. Privy Council treaty references are summarized in R. Arès, *Dossier sur le pacte fédératif de 1867* (Montreal, 1967), pp. 66-68, and criticized in MacDonald, "Privy Council and the Canadian Constitution," pp. 1030-31.

52. Cheffins, *Constitutional Process in Canada*, p. 130, provides a summary of the speculation on the reasons for the provincial bias of Watson and Haldane. Some interesting reflections on Haldane are contained in the "Address by the Right Honourable Sir David Maxwell Fyfe," *PCBA*, 37 (1954), pp. 149-51. Jonathon Robinson, "Lord Haldane and the British North America Act," *UTLJ*, 20 (1970), and Scott, *Canada Today*, p. 77, refer to the relevant writings of Haldane. Robinson attempts to explain Haldane's provincial bias as an outgrowth of his Hegelian philosophy. See also the obituary of Watson given by Haldane, *CLT*, 23 (1903), pp. 223-25.

53. See, for example, Creighton, *Dominion of the North*, p. 466; Thorson, *Can. H. of C. Debates*, April 5, 1937, p. 2585; Laskin, " 'Peace, Order and Good Government' Re-examined," p. 1077; MacGuigan, "The Privy Council and the Supreme Court," p. 425; Scott, *Canada Today*, pp. 77-78.

Jennings asserted that "Lord Watson held to the fixed idea that Canada was a true federation and that it was the function of the Board to maintain something called 'provincial autonomy' which was not in the Act." Jennings is an exception, however, in claiming that Haldane favoured the provinces reluctantly because of the "weight of the previous decisions." "Constitutional Interpretation," pp. 35-36, 21.

54. Lord Haldane, "The Work for the Empire of the Judicial Committee of the Privy Council," *Cambridge Law Journal*, 1 (1923), p. 150.

55. Cited in Ewart, *Kingdom of Canada*, p. 20.

56. *Can. H. of C. Debates*, Feb. 1, 1937, pp. 426, 444.

57. *Special Committee on British North America Act: Proceedings and Evidence and Report* (Ottawa, 1935), p. 82. R.M. Dawson, ed., *Constitutional Issues in Canada, 1900-1931* (London, 1933), pp. 343-44, reprints a 1912 editorial from the *Ottawa Journal* strongly critical of several decisions in which the Privy Council supported "vested right against the public weal," while the decisions of the Canadian courts had been "in favour of the public." These cases are briefly noted by C.G. Pierson, *Canada and the Privy Council* (London, 1960), p. 47. For Depression fears that business would seek to shelter behind the provinces, see R.A. MacKay, "The Nature of Canadian Federalism," in W.W. McLaren *et al.*, eds.,

Proceedings, Conference on Canadian-American Affairs (Montreal, 1936), p. 202. F.H. Underhill wrote that the use of provincial rights to obstruct social reform was "largely camouflage put up by our industrial and financial magnates. None of these worthy gentlemen wants a national government with sufficient constitutional power to be able to interfere effectively with their own pursuit of profits." "Revolt in Canadian Politics," *Nation*, 139 (December 12, 1934), p. 673, cited in Horn, "League for Social Reconstruction," p. 439.

58. Scott, "Centralization and Decentralization in Canadian Federalism," p. 1116; Scott, "The Consequences of the Privy Council Decisions," p. 492; J.R. Mallory, "The Courts and the Sovereignty of the Canadian Parliament," *CJEPS*, 10 (1944), pp. 166-73. Since the Revolution Settlement, asserted Mallory, British judges "have been activated by an acute suspicion of the motives of both the executive and the legislature and have conceived it their duty to confine the application of statute law to cases where its meaning could not be mistaken" (p. 167). "Upon occasion the very novelty of government expedients has seriously strained the impartiality of the type of judicial mind which is shocked by the unorthodox" (p. 173). See also Mallory, "The Five Faces of Federalism," Crépeau and Macpherson, *The Future of Canadian Federalism*, pp. 6-7, and *Social Credit and the Federal Power*, pp. 53-56 and chapter 3.

When Australia sought to restrict appeals to the Privy Council, the British Colonial Secretary, Chamberlain, stated: "The question of the right of appeal must also be looked at from the point of view of the very large class of persons interested in Australian securities or Australian undertakings, who are domiciled in the United Kingdom. Nothing could be more prejudicial to Australia than to diminish the security felt by capitalists who desire to invest their money there. One element in the security which at present exists is that there is the possibility of an ultimate appeal to the Queen in Council . . ." Cited in Ewart, *Kingdom of Canada*, p. 232. In 1909 J.M. Clark stated that the right of appeal "is also regarded as an important security and safeguard by British foreign investors." "The Judicial Committee of the Privy Council," *CLT*, 29 (1909), pp. 352-53.

The high cost of appeals, which played into the hands of the wealthy and thus buttressed the position of the economically strong, was a frequent criticism of the Privy Council. See Editorial, "Procedure before the Judicial Committee," *CLT*, 25 (1905), pp. 29-30; W.S. Deacon, "Gordon v Horne: Canadians and the Privy Council," *CLT*, 30 (1910), p. 877; Deacon, "Canadians and the Privy Council," *CLT*, 31 (1911), p. 128, and "Canadians and the Privy Council," *CLT*, 31 (1911), p. 10; C.E. Kaulbach, *Can. H. of C. Debates*, February 26, 1880, p. 241; "Labor's Views on Dominion-Provincial Relations," *Canadian Congress Journal*, 17 (February, 1938), p. 15; Pierson, *Canada and the Privy Council*, pp. 41-42, 70.

Sir Allen Aylesworth, a former Liberal minister of justice (1906-11), admitted in 1914 that the wealthy had an advantage in appeals due to their high cost, but that was "after all, but one of the advantages which the possession of wealth carries with it in every walk of life." "Address of Sir Allen Aylesworth, 7th Annual Meeting of the Ontario Bar Association," *CLT*, 34 (1914), p. 144.

59. Mallory, "The Courts and the Sovereignty of the Canadian Parliament," p. 169.

60. "Labor's Views on Dominion-Provincial Relations," p. 10.

61. Presidential address, *PCBA*, 6 (1921), p. 110.

62. Presidential address, *ibid.*, 12 (1927), pp. 112-113.

63. *Ibid.*, 24 (1939), pp. 204-05. In their report the previous year the committee referred to the disallowance of Alberta legislation as a "reversion to sound thought. Disallowance in some cases is just as important as enactment." The report continued to warn, however, that "quite apart from certain notorious Acts, much of this year's product reveals an inspiration which is wholly alien to our usual habits of thought . . . . The Committee believes that it is the general view of the profession that unless we can govern ourselves according to settled and generally recognized principles of right and wrong, we are headed either for anarchy or despotism . . . it can find no place in any civilized system of law for several Acts passed at the last Session of the Legislature of Alberta . . . these are only high water marks which stand above the general level and are more conspicuous on that account." The committee went on to castigate open-ended legislation in British Columbia and Saskatchewan that gave significant, vaguely defined authority to the Lieutenant-Governor-in-Council to make regulations for the carrying out of legislation. *Ibid.*, 23 (1938), pp. 191-93.

64. W.S. Johnson, "The Reign of Law Under an Expanding Bureaucracy," *CBR*, 22 (1944). Cheffins, *Constitutional Process in Canada*, chapter 3, contains a brief discussion of the factors behind this evolution in the procedures of government operation.

Cecil A. Wright stated in 1938: "we have to a great extent underestimated the importance of administrative tribunals and the place of modern legislation as regulating forces in modern society. Legislation has always been viewed with disfavour by the common law lawyer because of the traditional view of the common law broadening down from 'precedent to precedent,' and undoubtedly the general attitude of the profession today is not different from that of Lord Halsbury who is reputed to have said that 'the best Act you can have is a repealing Act.' One consequence of this is that our whole technique and approach to legislation is weak, and as a result antagonism between the legal profession and legislative and administrative bodies becomes more marked.

"We have, indeed, paid so much attention to past judicial policy, that courts and lawyers are frequently in danger of limiting present legislative policy by restrictive interpretations. The notion that a statute shall be deemed to have departed as little as possible from common law principles runs throughout many judicial decisions, yet, as a member of the House of Lords recently said, 'it is an unsafe guide in days of modern legislation, often or perhaps generally based on objects and policies alien to the common law." "Law and Law Schools," *PCBA*, 23 (1938), p. 115.

65. See G.L. Caplan, "The Failure of Canadian Socialism: The Ontario Experience," *Canadian Historical Review*, 44 (1963), for the extreme anti-socialist campaign waged by business in the closing years of the Second World War.

66. For American experience, see Benjamin R. Twiss, *Lawyers and the Constitution: How Laissez-Faire Came to the Supreme Court* (New York, 1962).

67. W.H. Hamilton, "The Path of Due Process of Law," *Ethics*, 48 (1938), p. 296, asserted that American courts were more resistant to laissez faire than other parts of the body politic. "It seems strange that so many jurists stood steadfast against the seductions of laissez-faire; history, political science, and economics can boast no such record . . . does the whole story, in irony, paradox, and com-

promise, derive from the innate conservatism of the law – a rock of ages which even the untamed strength of laissez-faire could move but could not blast."

68. Stanley, "Act or Pact?" pp. 112-13.

69. Given the strong criticism it subsequently received it is worthwhile to document the extent of its support in earlier years. See, for example, John T. Small, "Supreme Court and Privy Council Appeals," *CLT*, 29 (1909), pp. 51-52; Clark, "The Judicial Committee of the Privy Council"; "Address of Sir Allen Aylesworth," p. 139; "By the Way," *CLT*, 36 (1916), pp. 354-55, 662-63; W.E. Wilkinson, "Our London Letter," *CLT*, 41 (1921), p. 61, reporting Lord Cave; B[ram] T[hompson], "Editor's Note," *CLT*, 41 (1921), pp. 62-63; "Editorial," *CLT*, 41 (1921), pp. 83-86; Bram Thompson, "Editorial," *CLT*, 41 (1921), pp. 161-65; Edward Anderson, "Address to Manitoba Bar Association," *CLT*, 41 (1921), pp. 252-53; "Appeal to the Privy Council," *CLT*, 41 (1921), pp. 525-26; Pierson, *Canada and the Privy Council*, p. 39.

70. A.C. Galt, "Appeals to the Privy Council," *CLT*, 41 (1921), p. 172.

71. W. Nesbitt, "The Judicial Committee of the Privy Council," *CLT*, 29 (1909), p. 252.

72. Sir L.P. Duff, "The Privy Council," *CBR*, 3 (1925), pp. 278-79.

73. Sir Charles Fitzpatrick, "The Constitution of Canada," *CLT*, 34 (1914), p. 1031.

74. Galt, "Appeals to the Privy Council," pp. 168-69.

75. *PCBA*, 15 (1930), p. 37. Another writer stated that Viscount Haldane was "recognized as the greatest living authority on the interpretation of the British North America Act." W.E. Raney, "Another Question of Dominion Jurisdiction Emerges," *CBR*, 3 (1925), p. 617.

76. Nesbitt, "The Judicial Committee," p. 244.

77. Duff, "The Privy Council," p. 278. See also Nesbitt, "The Judicial Committee," pp. 243, 245-46; W.R. Riddell, "The Judicial Committee of the Privy Council," *CLT*, 30 (1910), pp. 305-06; W.H. Newlands, "Appeal to the Privy Council," *CBR*, 1 (1923), pp. 814-15.

78. Nesbitt, "The Judicial Committee," pp. 250-51; Riddell, "The Judicial Committee," p. 304. Ewart, *Kingdom of Canada*, p. 228, argued that if the Privy Council did try to produce uniformity of laws in the Empire appeals should be abolished, for each community required its own laws. In fact, however, he asserted that the Privy Council endeavoured to keep the various systems of laws distinct.

79. Nesbitt, "The Judicial Committee," pp. 250-51; Clark, "The Judicial Committee," pp. 349, 352-53; "By the Way," *CLT*, 37 (1917), pp. 624-25; "Address of Sir Allen Aylesworth," p. 140; Bram Thompson, "Editorial," *CLT*, 41 (1921), pp. 162-63; Howard Ferguson, *PCBA*, 15 (1930), p.37. The desire of the Macdonald Conservatives to retain appeals to the Privy Council when the Supreme Court Act of 1875 was under discussion was based "primarily on their concern for preserving Canada's links with the Empire." Russell, *Supreme Court*, p. 16.

80. Clark, "The Judicial Committee," p. 352; Galt, "Appeals to the Privy Council," p. 172.

81. Riddell, "The Judicial Committee," p. 304.

82. This argument was used by British officials in 1876 when the Liberal government attempted to cut off appeals to the Privy Council. See L.A. Cannon, "Some Data Relating to the Appeal to the Privy Council," *CBR*, 3 (1925), pp. 460-

62. In discussions on the Australian constitution in 1900 Chamberlain stated that "questions . . . which may sometimes involve a good deal of local feeling are the last that should be withdrawn from a tribunal of appeal with regard to which there could not be even a suspicion of prepossession." Cited in Ewart, *Kingdom of Canada*," p. 232. The British constitutional expert, A.B. Keith, asserted that the "true value of the appeal . . . lies in the power of the Judicial Committee to deal in perfect freedom from local or racial prejudice with issues deeply affecting the relations of the two nationalities in Canada, or of the provinces and the Federation, or of the provinces *inter se*." Cited in W.E. Raney, "Appeal to the Privy Council," *CBR*, 5 (1927), p. 608.

For the widespread Canadian support for this line of reasoning, see "Editorial Review," *CLT*, 27 (1907), pp. 403-04; Small, "Supreme Court and Privy Council Appeals," p. 51; Nesbitt, "The Judicial Committee," p. 249; Riddell, "The Judicial Committee," p. 304; Fitzpatrick, "The Constitution of Canada," p. 1031; "Appeal to the Privy Council," *CLT*, 41 (1921), p. 525, reporting Premier Taschereau of Quebec; James Aikins, "President's Address to Conference of Commissioners on Uniformity of Legislation," *PCBA*, 6 (1921), p. 286; Brossard, *La Cour Suprême*, p. 171.

83. "Presidential Address," *CBR*, 5 (1927), pp. 562-63.

84. Evan Gray made this point with vigour. "It is time the chief 'indoor sport' of constitutional lawyers in 'lambasting' the Privy Council and cavilling at decisions of that body was discontinued. The 'sport' never had any merit or excuse and it violates 'good form'–an essential element of all 'sport'. All this talk about distortion of the framework of Confederation and defeat of our national purposes by judicial authority is silly and puerile. If there is distortion, we Canadians all must take the responsibility for the distortion. If there is defeat of national purposes, let us do something worthy of our autonomy rather than continue to accept and complain of the defeat. Our constitution is what our forefathers made it and as we have applied it–not what British judges gave us. If we do not like the constitution as it is, we have always had leave to change it; let us change it–now–in an open, forthright and well-considered manner." " 'The O'Connor Report' on the British North America Act, 1867," *CBR*, 17 (1939), pp. 333-34.

85. The issue was posed but not answered by R. Cheffins: "It could be argued that the type of strong federal government envisaged by the political founders of the Canadian nation was impractical and not realizable in a country as large geographically and as culturally diverse as Canada. It could also be argued that the Judicial Committee was recognizing the realities of the social and political life of the nation in upholding the validity of provincial statutes. On the other hand it could be maintained that if the Privy Council had not ruled the way it did, then the provincial governments would never have assumed the importance which they did, and thus their position would not have to be continually sustained by judicial decisions." "The Supreme Court of Canada: The Quiet Court in an Unquiet Country," *Osgoode Hall Law Journal*, 4 (1966), p. 267.

Both Morton and Careless lay great stress on the contributions of the Judicial Committee to the strong position of the provinces in the 1920s. W.L. Morton, *The Kingdom of Canada* (Toronto, 1969), p. 444; Careless, *Canada*, p. 364. D.G. Creighton also emphasizes the causal role of the Judicial Committee in breaking down Macdonald's centralized federalism. "The Decline and Fall of the

Empire of the St. Lawrence," Canadian Historical Association, *Historical Papers, 1969*, p. 24. See also Scott, "The Development of Canadian Federalism," pp. 238-47; Goldenberg, "Social and Economic Problems in Canadian Federalism."
86. Kennedy, *Some Aspects of the Theories and Workings of Constitutional Law*, p. 100.
87. See N. McL. Rogers, "The Genesis of Provincial Rights," *Canadian Historical Review*, 14 (1933), for an incisive analysis of the weakness of the centralist basis of Confederation from the moment of its inception.
88. "The failure of the Dominion's economic policies, which formed such important elements in the new national interest, discouraged the growth of a strong, national sentiment; and local loyalties and interests began to reassert themselves." *Rowell-Sirois Report*, I, p. 54. See also E.R. Black and A.C. Cairns, "A Different Perspective on Canadian Federalism," *Canadian Public Administration*, 9 (1966), p. 29, and Cook, *Provincial Autonomy, Minority Rights and the Compact Theory*, chapter 3, especially p. 19.
89. Black and Cairns, "A Different Perspective," p. 29.
90. *Ibid.*, pp. 38-43.
91. Morrison, "Oliver Mowat," *passim*.
92. *Rowell-Sirois Report*, I, p. 55.
93. F.H. Underhill, *The Image of Confederation* (Toronto, 1964), p. 27.
94. Cited in A. Brady, "Quebec and Canadian Federalism," *CJEPS*, 25 (1959), pp. 260-61.
95. See the *Rowell-Sirois Report*, I, pp. 55-59, for a discussion. André Lapointe, "La jurisprudence constitutionnelle et le temps," is a suggestive impressionistic study to the effect that Privy Council decisions, 1880-84, constituted appropriate responses to the forces of regionalism developing at that time.
96. Gray, " 'The O'Connor Report,' " pp. 334-35.
97. "The Late Lord Watson," *CLT*, 23 (1903), p. 224.
98. For Mowat's position on the role of the provinces, his success with the Privy Council, and his favourable reception by the people of Ontario, see Lower, *Colony to Nation*, pp. 376-79. Creighton, *Canada's First Century*, p. 47, provides a critical assessment of Mowat's philosophy and conduct. G.W. Ross, *Getting into Parliament and After* (Toronto, 1913), pp. 187-88, states that "Sir Oliver Mowat's success in the courts of Canada, and particularly before the Privy Council, raised him greatly in the estimation of the whole people of Ontario. Were it not for these conflicts with the Dominion Government I doubt if Sir Oliver would have survived the general election of 1883." Morrison, "Oliver Mowat," provides the most detailed analysis of Mowat's strategy.
99. There is considerable academic support for the proposition that the federal system established in 1867 was too centralist for the underlying regional pluralism of Canadian society, and the related proposition that it was an act of creative judicial statesmanship for the Privy Council to adapt the constitution to pluralist realities. O.D. Skelton stated that the "provincial trend of court decisions paralleled or rather followed, with some time lag, the changes in Canada itself." *Special Committee on the British North America Act: 1935*, p. 27. "In all justice to the Judicial Committee," asserted Professor Brady, "they probably did no more than what the majority of Canadians in the earlier period desired. They gave judicial expression to the upsurge of provincialism, evident from the early eighties to the

decade after the First World War . . . " *Democracy in the Dominions* (2nd ed., Toronto, 1952), pp. 45-46. See also Brady, "Our Constitutional Tradition," p. 16. Michael Oliver states of the centralist intentions of the Fathers: "It must be concluded that they either seriously overestimated the range of shared assumptions between the two cultures, or badly underestimated the degree of unity on fundamentals which was necessary to run the centralized state they had tried to create." "Quebec and Canadian Democracy," *CJEPS*, 23 (1957), p. 504. Cheffins states that the "ineffectiveness" of the centralist features of the BNA Act "serves as a classic example of the futility of written positive law in the face of a social environment which refuses to accept the original statutory intention." *Constitutional Process in Canada*, pp. 37-38 (see also p. 132). G.P. Glazebrook states: "the Judicial Committee was a make-weight in scales that were otherwise uncertainly balanced. The committee did not create the provincial school of thought; and it is worthy of note that it was long after it had ceased to have jurisdiction that provincialism took on its most extreme form. Nevertheless the strong slant in the legal decisions . . . may be regarded as influential in the years in which the constitutional debate began." *A History of Canadian Political Thought* (Toronto, 1966), pp. 186-87. J.R. Mallory praised the political acumen of the Local Prohibition Case in 1896, but added that "No other judge since Lord Watson's time has attempted the judicial realignment needed by the times and comparable to that achieved by the Supreme Court of the United States after 1937." "The Courts and the Sovereignty of the Canadian Parliament," p. 177.

Even the leading Canadian constitutional expert, W.P.M. Kennedy, later to be so critical of the Privy Council, had strongly praised it in earlier writings. In 1930 he wrote: "I often wonder . . . with the inevitable divergencies in our national life due to race, religion, geography and such like, whether after all the way of the Privy Council up to 1929 has not been the better way. We might, apart from the Privy Council, have followed paths of greater juristic cohesion. We might have created a stronger legal nation; but it is problematical, had we done so, whether our legal cohesion would not have been compelled, if federation was to have survived, to give ground ultimately to those more compelling forces . . . and whether we should not have been forced ultimately, in the interest of continuing the union, to retrace our legal steps." Book review of E. Cameron, *The Canadian Constitution as Interpreted by the Judicial Committee, 1916-1929*, in *CBR*, 8 (1930), p. 708. Kennedy made the same point on several other occasions: see *Essays in Constitutional Law* (London, 1934), pp. 59-60, 101-02; *Some Aspects of the Theories and Workings of Constitutional Law*, pp. 93, 101-02.

See also J.A. Maxwell, "Aspects of Canadian Federalism," *Dalhousie Review*, 16 (1936-37), p. 277n; E. McWhinney, "Federalism, Constitutionalism, and Legal Change: Legal Implications of the 'Revolution' in Quebec," in Crépeau and Macpherson, *The Future of Canadian Federalism*, pp. 159-60; McWhinney, *Judicial Review*, pp. 25-26, 70-71; E. Forsey, "Concepts of Federalism: Some Canadian Aspects," in J.P. Meekison, ed., *Canadian Federalism: Myth or Reality* (Toronto, 1968), p. 349; Stanley, *A Short History of the Canadian Constitution*, p. 142.

100. P.E. Trudeau, *Federalism and the French Canadians* (Toronto, 1968), p. 198.

101. Cheffins, *Constitutional Process in Canada*, pp. 130-31, and W.R. Leder-

man, "Thoughts on Reform of the Supreme Court of Canada," *Alberta Law Review*, 8 (1970), p. 3, both point out the inappropriateness of a literal criticism of Privy Council decisions.

102. Clark, "The Judicial Committee," p. 348.

103. E.W., "Random Remarks Regarding the Judicial Committee," *CLT*, 36 (1916), pp. 370-71.

104. Bram Thompson, "Editorial," *CLT*, 41 (1921), p. 165.

105. "Editorial," *CLT*, 40 (1920), p. 261.

106. MacDonald, "Judicial Interpretation of the Canadian Constitution," pp. 282-83.

107. Jennings, "Constitutional Interpretation," p. 38.

108. Kennedy, *The Constitution of Canada*, p. 550. See also F.C. Cronkite, "The Social Legislation References," *CBR*, 15 (1937), p. 478.

109. Left-wing critics of the time disagree with this interpretation. See *The Canadian Forum* (March, 1937), p.4, and Dorothy Steeves in CBC, *The Canadian Constitution* (Toronto, 1938), pp. 97-98.

110. R. Cook, *Canada and the French Canadian Question* (Toronto, 1966), p. 53.

111. Creighton, *Canada's First Century*, pp. 213-14.

112. MacDonald, "The Privy Council and the Canadian Constitution," p. 1036.

113. MacDonald, "Judicial Interpretation of the Canadian Constitution," p. 281. MacDonald, "The Privy Council and the Canadian Constitution," pp. 1034-35, reiterates his earlier statement, and adds that we do not even have certainty (p. 1036). Laskin, " 'Peace, Order and Good Government' Re-examined," p. 1056, accused the Privy Council of laying down too many unnecessary dicta and generalities. McWhinney, *Judicial Review*, p. 54, suggests that the need for compromise in the committee may have produced obscurities in their decisions. Some earlier technical criticisms may be found in "Editorial Review," *CLT*, 6 (1886), p. 375, and A.H. Marsh, "The Privy Council as a Colonial Court of Appeal," *CLT*, 14 (1894), p. 92. See, by contrast, E.W., "Random Remarks Regarding the Judicial Committee," pp. 371-72, who praises the committee for its statesmanlike willingness to be inconsistent and to override legal quibbles. The caveat of H.A. Innis is also worthy of consideration: "But though interpretations of decisions of the Privy Council have been subjected to intensive study and complaints have been made about their inconsistency, inconsistencies have implied flexibility and have offset the dangers of rigidity characteristic of written constitutions." "Great Britain, the United States and Canada," in M.Q. Innis, ed., *Essays In Canadian Economic History* (Toronto, 1956), p. 404.

114. Ewart, *Kingdom of Canada*, pp. 226-28. Ewart repeated his opposition to this defence of the Privy Council on numerous occasions: *ibid.*, p. 20; *Kingdom Papers*, I, p. 88; "The Judicial Committee," *CLT*, 34 (1914), pp. 221, 230-31; "The Judicial Committee," *CLT*, 33 (1913), pp. 676-78; "Some Further Comments on Dominion-Provincial Relations," *PPCPSA*, 3 (1931), pp. 253-58.

115. *Can. H. of C. Debates*, February 26, 1880, pp. 253-55, and see Blake, cited in MacDonald, "The Privy Council and the Canadian Constitution," p. 1026. For Blake's later partial change of mind, see Russell, *Supreme Court*, p. 251, n173.

116. Raney, "Justice, Precedent and Ultimate Conjecture," p. 460; Thorson, *Can. H. of C. Debates*, April 5, 1937, pp. 2581-82; Scott, *Canada Today*, p. 77;

Tuck, "Canada and the Judicial Committee," pp. 71-73; Mallory, "The Five Faces of Federalism," p. 6.

117. A.H. Marsh, "The Privy Council as a Colonial Court of Appeal," *CLT*, 14 (1894), p. 94. See also Deacon, "Canadians and the Privy Council," pp. 126-27. This criticism was popular among the opponents of the New Deal decisions. Cahan, *Can. H. of C. Debates*, April 5, 1937, p. 2574, and Scott, "The Consequences of the Privy Council Decisions," pp. 493-94.

Jennings, "Constitutional Interpretation," is the best attempt to discuss the influence of Privy Council personnel on its judgements.

118. Jennings, "Constitutional Interpretation," pp. 1-2.

119. MacDonald, "The Canadian Constitution Seventy Years After," *CBR*, 15 (1937), pp. 426-27.

120. Tuck, "Canada and the Judicial Committee," p. 73 (see also pp. 55-56, 71-72). Versions of this point were made by various commentators. LaBrie, "Canadian Constitutional Interpretation and Legislative Review," p. 346; W.R. Lederman, "The Balanced Interpretation of the Federal Distribution of Legislative Powers in Canada," in Crépeau and Macpherson, *The Future of Canadian Federalism*, p. 111; Lederman, "Thoughts on the Reform of the Supreme Court of Canada," pp. 3-4.

121. McWhinney, *Judicial Review*, p. 72.

122. MacGuigan, "The Privy Council and the Supreme Court," pp. 425-26.

123. D.G. Creighton, speaking of the diversity of jurisdiction of the Privy Council, stated: "An expert knowledge of one of these legal systems might be regarded as a respectable accomplishment for an ordinary man. But the titans of the Judicial Committee, from long practice and profound study, have grown accustomed to the multifarious and exacting requirements of their office; and they apparently leap, with the agility of quick-change performers, from one legal metamorphosis to another . . . . To an outsider it might seem that there was at least the faint possibility of some bewilderment and confusion in these endlessly varied deliberations. The outsider might even be so far misled as to conceive of a noble judge who continued obstinately to peruse the Koran when he ought to have been consulting the *British North America Act*." "Federal Relations in Canada since 1914," in Chester Martin, ed., *Canada in Peace and War* (Toronto, 1941), pp. 32-33.

124. Ewart, "The Judicial Committee," p. 676. He also asserted that the Judicial Committee "suffers from a conviction of its own superiority – a conviction due (*a*) to the ruling character of the race to which its members belong, and (*b*) to the fact that, by sending our cases to it, we appear to acknowledge our incapacity."

125. *Ibid.*, p. 676.

126. "What gives its imposing respectability, its ponderous finality to a decision of the Privy Council is its unity. There may be considerable diversity of opinion, doubts, hesitations and dissents behind the curtain. But when the curtain goes up one judge delivers the opinion of the Court and it is law. It does not sprinkle like a garden hose; it hits like the hammer of Thor." A.T. Hunter, "A Proposal for Statutory Relief from the Privy Council Controversy," *CBR*, 4 (1926), p. 102. See McWhinney, *Judicial Review*, pp. 52-53, for a discussion of the practice and suggested explanations for its survival.

127. He continued: "Though the reports summarize the arguments of counsel, the emphasis given to the written opinion minimizes the case that the majority did

not accept. Finally, the opinion of the whole Board is given by one member. The substance is, no doubt, agreed to by the rest of the majority; but it is never certain that all the expressions would have been accepted by the majority if they had fully considered them. The type of opinion differs according to the judge who renders it. He comes to the conclusion desired by the majority and states the reasons acceptable to the majority; but anyone who has drafted a document knows that there are many ways of saying the same thing and that a draft often says more than is intended." Jennings, "Constitutional Interpretation," pp. 2-3.

128. Ewart, "The Judicial Committee," p. 676.

129. E.W., "Random Remarks Regarding the Judicial Committee," p. 370.

130. Browne, *The Judicial Committee and the British North America Act.*

131. The reference is to a tendency, not to ethnic unanimity. Frank Scott was correct in pointing out in 1947 that Quebec had "no single view" on the question of the retention of the Judicial Committee, and in noting that a minister of justice from Quebec, Télésphore Fournier, who introduced the bill to establish the Supreme Court in 1875, stated that he "wished to see the practice put an end to altogether," and that Ernest Lapointe held similar views. "Abolition of Appeals to the Privy Council: A Symposium," p. 571. Scott had earlier argued that minority rights had received better protection from the Supreme Court than from the Privy Council. "The Privy Council and Minority Rights," *Queen's Quarterly*, 37 (1930). It is also worthy of note that the elimination of appeals occurred under a French-Canadian Prime Minister. Pierson, *Canada and the Privy Council*, pp. 69-70, provides some evidence of French-Canadian opposition to appeals. The 1927 Labrador decision of the Privy Council turned some French Canadians against the system of appeals. See Brossard, *La Cour Suprême*, p. 189, and Dale C. Thomson, *Louis St. Laurent: Canadian* (Toronto, 1967), pp. 91, 208. Further, it is clear that there have been many English-Canadian supporters of the Privy Council right up to its final abolition. These observations do not, however, invalidate the statement about a tendency for opposed evaluations of the Judicial Committee to follow the French-English cleavage.

132. For French-Canadian support of the Privy Council's interpretation of the BNA Act and/or support for its continuation as a final appeal court, see L.P. Pigeon, "The Meaning of Provincial Autonomy," *CBR*, 29 (1951); Pigeon, "French Canada's attitude to the Canadian Constitution," in E. McWhinney, ed., *Canadian Jurisprudence* (Toronto, 1958); Jean Beetz, "Les attitudes changeantes du Québec à l'endroit de la constitution de 1867," pp. 117-18; *CLT*, 40 (1920), p. 315, reporting a speech by Mr. Horace J. Gagne of the Montreal Bar; "Appeal to the Privy Council," *CLT*, 41 (1921), p. 525, reporting a speech of Premier Taschereau of Quebec. Russell notes that in the nineteenth century French-Canadian support for the Judicial Committee, and opposition to the Supreme Court were primarily based on the belief that the composition, training, and background of the former was much to be preferred to that of the latter for interpretations of Quebec civil law. *Supreme Court*, chapter 1, *passim*. See also Brossard, *La Cour Suprême*, p. 125.

133. On this attitude of the abolitionists, see Jonas L. Juskaitis, "On Understanding the Supreme Court of Canada," *School of Law Review*, University of Toronto, 9 (1951), pp. 7-8; and Leonard H. Leigh, "The Supreme Court and the Constitution," *Ottawa Law Review*, 2 (1967-68), p. 323. Jacques Brossard, "The Supreme Court and the Constitution," in Ontario Advisory Committee on Con-

federation, *Quebec in the Canada of Tomorrow* (Toronto, n.d.), translated from *Le Devoir*, special supplement, June 30, 1967, stated: "It was, moreover, in opposing the centralizing aims of the federal government that the Judicial Committee signed its own death warrant; it was accused, not without reason, of having violated the centralizing spirit of the BNA Act of 1867."

134. Beetz, "Les attitudes changeantes," pp. 119-21. The divergent evaluations of the Judicial Committee and of a proposed independent Supreme Court are discussed by Peter Russell, "The Supreme Court's Interpretation of the Constitution since 1949," in Paul Fox, ed., *Politics: Canada* (2nd ed., Toronto, 1966), pp. 117-18. See also Russell, *Supreme Court*, pp. 31-32, 36-37. In addition to the ethnic-based opposition from French Canada there was also considerable provincial opposition to the unilateral nature of the federal action in abolishing appeals. P. Gérin-Lajoie, *Constitutional Amendment in Canada* (Toronto, 1950), pp. xvii-xviii. By 1949 French Canadians had become critical of the Privy Council's treatment of French civil law, but this "was counter-balanced by approval of its interpretation of the BNA Act." Russell, *Supreme Court*, p. 31.

135. Browne, *The Judicial Committee and the British North America Act.*

136. J.A. Corry, while doubtful of the final validity of Browne's thesis, gives the book a very favourable review in *Canadian Journal of Political Science*, 1 (1968), pp. 217-19. Critical reviews are provided by B. Laskin, *Canadian Public Administration*, 10 (1967), pp. 514-18, and E.R. Alexander, *UTLJ*, 17 (1967), pp. 371-77.

137. See the eminently sensible criticism by Corry, *ibid.*, pp. 218-19. Jennings's observation is also relevant. "The idea that judges spend days on end in reading all the decisions on any particular topic is one which is sometimes assumed by academic writers; it can, however, be designated as clearly false by anyone who has watched a court give judgement immediately at the end of an argument." "Constitutional Interpretation," p. 27.

138. W.R. Lederman, after noting the antithetical literal interpretations of the BNA Act by Browne and O'Connor, states that in his view "Browne and O'Connor simply cancel one another out. The truth is that the BNA Act was simply ambiguous or incomplete in many respects as originally drafted and the answers just were not in the Act as to how these ambiguities were to be resolved and the gaps filled." "Thoughts on the Reform of the Supreme Court of Canada," p. 2.

Note also the chronic "historical" controversy over the validity of the compact theory and between centralist and provincialist interpretations of the BNA Act and/ or the intentions of the Fathers. Glazebrook's comment is apt: "one has only to sample the speeches and writings of politicians, academics, and jurists to appreciate the wealth of interpretation of the intent and terms of the original union. It needs a conscious effort to realize that they are describing the same episode in Canadian history. Confederation, in fact, was what you thought it was – or often what it should have been. Which seems to suggest that particular interpretations and points of view were rationalized by tailored versions of the Constitution." *A History of Canadian Political Thought*, p. 264 (see also pp. 153, 258).

139. Philippe Ferland, "La Confédération à refaire," *Thémis*, 5 (1954), p. 105. Stanley, "Act or Pact?" p. 114, asserts that the pre-parliamentary history of the BNA Act appears to confirm the interpretation of the Judicial Committee rather than that of the critics.

The 1887 Interprovincial Conference, which advocated a much more decentralized federal system than prevailed under Macdonald's prime ministership, claimed that two decades of experience with the BNA Act have "disclosed grave omissions in the provisions of the Act, and has shown (when the language of the Act came to be judicially interpreted) that in many respects what was the common understanding and intention had not been expressed, and that important provisions in the Act are obscure as to their true intent and meaning." *Dominion, Provincial and Interprovincial Conferences from 1887 to 1926* (Ottawa, 1951), p. 20.

140. LaBrie, "Canadian Constitutional Interpretation," p. 310. K.N. Llewellyn's statement is also apt: "there is no quarrel to be had with judges *merely* because they disregard or twist Documentary language, or 'interpret' it to the despair of original intent, in the service of what those judges conceive to be the inherent nature of our institutions. To my mind, such action is their duty. To my mind, the judge who builds his decision to conform with his conception of what our institutions must be if we are to continue, roots in the deepest wisdom." "The Constitution as an Institution," *Columbia Law Review*, 23 (1934). p.33.

141. M.R. Cohen, *Reason and Law* (New York, 1961), p. 84.

142. G.H. Ross, "Interpreting the BNA Act," *CBR*, 7 (1929), p. 704. LaBrie, "Canadian Constitutional Interpretation," pp. 310, 318; *Rowell-Sirois Report*, I, p. 36.

143. *A.G. Ont.* v *A.G. Can.*, [1947], A.C. 127, at 154.

144. Robinson, "Lord Haldane and the British North America Act," p. 58. See also A.M. Bickel, "The Original Understanding and the Segregation Decision," *Harvard Law Review*, 69 (1955).

145. Various American writers have noted that the appeal to history in American constitutional interpretation has led to an abuse of history and does not in fact act as a control on the court. See, in particular, A.H. Kelly, "Clio and the Court: An Illicit Love Affair," in P.B. Kurland, ed., *The Supreme Court Review* (Chicago, 1965); J. TenBroek, "Admissibility and Use by the United States Supreme Court of Extrinsic Aids in Constitutional Construction," *California Law Review*, 26 (1937-38), pp. 448, 451; C.S.Hyneman, *The Supreme Court on Trial* (New York, 1964), pp. 207-08. Felix Frankfurter, "Reflections on Reading Statutes," in A.F. Westin, ed., *The Supreme Court: Views from Inside* (New York, 1961), pp. 75, 84-85, 88-92, argues the advantages in appealing to historical materials, although he also notes the difficult problems this entails. The difficulty in using historical material is also noted by W.O. Douglas, "Judges as Legislators," in Westin, *ibid.*, pp. 68-69. A.A. North, *The Supreme Court, Judicial Process and Judicial Politics* (New York, 1966), pp. 18-29, provides a neutral discussion. E. Bodenheimer, *Jurisprudence* (Cambridge, Mass., 1962), pp. 348-53, is a good discussion of whether courts should take the original meaning at the time of statutory creation, or the contemporaneous ones understood at the time of decision.

146. See MacDonald, "Constitutional Interpretation and Extrinsic Evidence," for a discussion.

147. *Edwards* v *A.G. Can.*, [1930], A.C. 124, at 137.

148. He added: "it seems to us fallacious, as well as reckless, for the author to suggest that seventy years after Confederation he can assist us by such contemporary records to say that those who framed the Confederation Act intended to do other than what they embodied in the words of the statute.

"Indeed the matter goes deeper than that; what they are seeking to discover who speak of the pre-confederation intention of the framers of confederation or of the constituent provinces has no real existence. The search is pursuit of a 'will-O-wisp'; when once you leave the natural light afforded by the text of the BNA Act, you are in a realm of unreality. . . .

"Neither should we continue the pretension of the author that by a miracle of understanding and foresight, the Canadian Fathers of Confederation provided in 1867 a constitution suitable to any future." Gray, " 'The O'Connor Report' on the British North America Act 1867," pp. 316-18, 334.

See also Stanley, "Act or Pact?" p. 112, for the morass of contradictions involved in attempting to determine the "intentions" of the Fathers. "The one sure guide as to what the Fathers really agreed to agree upon, was the language of their resolutions, or better still, the language of the British North America Act itself. And in construing this Act in the way they have, the judges probably arrived at a more accurate interpretation than have the multitude of critics who have so emphatically disagreed with them."

149. MacDonald, "Judicial Interpretation of the Canadian Constitution," pp. 280-81. His approach agreed with K.N. Llewellyn's assertion that with an ancient statute "the sound quest does not run primarily in terms of historical intent. It runs in terms of what the words can be made to bear, in making sense in the new light of what was originally unforeseen." *The Common Law Tradition* (Boston, 1960), p. 374. See also W. Friedman, *Law and Social Change in Contemporary Britain* (London, 1951), pp. 252, 254-55.

150. Mallory, "The Courts and the Sovereignty of the Canadian Parliament," p. 173.

151. W.E. Rumble attributes the same achievement to the American legal realists. *American Legal Realism* (Ithaca, 1968), pp. 232-33.

152. H.V. Jaffa, "The Case for a Stronger National Government," in R.A. Goldwin, ed., *A Nation of States* (Chicago, 1968), p. 121.

153. Browne suggests that the "constituent statute argument equates 'liberal' with 'federal' (and so 'literal' with 'provincial')." *The Judicial Committee and the British North America Act*, p. 31. This is not entirely true. As indicated in this essay there was also a critique of the Privy Council that was both "literal" and "federal."

154. The weak reasoning is similar to that noted by Smiley in "national interest" justifications for conditional grants. D.V. Smiley, *Conditional Grants and Canadian Federalism* (Toronto, 1963), pp. 48-52.

155. B.N. Cardozo, *The Nature of the Judicial Process* (New Haven, 1960), pp. 174-75.

156. Lapointe also notes the incompatibility of the two, and argues that the Privy Council conducted itself in accordance with the constitutional rather than the fundamentalist approach. "La jurisprudence constitutionnelle et le temps," pp. 27-28.

"The manner of framing the question," writes Llewellyn, "is psychologically of huge importance. 'Is this within the powers granted by the Document?' throws the baseline of inquiry back a century and a half, constricts the vision to the static word, turns discussion into the channels of logomachy. It invites, and too often produces, artificial limitation of attention to the non-essential, the accidental: to wit, what language happens to stand in the Document, or in some hoary – or beardless–text of its 'interpretation' . . . .

"Contrast the effect of framing the question thus: 'Is this within the leeway of change which our going governmental scheme affords? And even if not, does the nature of the case require the leeway to be widened to include it?' The baseline then becomes so much of the past only *as is still alive*, and the immediate future comes to bear as well. The tone and tendency of the very question is dynamic. The 'nature of the case' invites attention to explicit policy. While that continuity with the past which, if not a duty, is wisdom quite as well as a necessity, is carefully preserved – only that the past concerned is that embodied not in an ancient Text, but in a living Government." "The Constitution as an Institution," pp. 32-33.

157. Russell, *Supreme Court*, p.35.

158. F.H. Underhill, "O Canada," *The Canadian Forum*, 11 (June, 1931), p. 332, cited in Horn, "League for Social Reconstruction," p. 433.

159. Ferland, "La Confédération à refaire," pp. 106-07; Beetz, "Les attitudes changeantes du Québec à l'endroit de la constitution de 1867," p. 120.

160. Corry, "Commentaries," in Crépeau and Macpherson, *The Future of Canadian Federalism*, p. 38.

161. McWhinney, *Judicial Review*, p. 69.

162. Tuck, "Canada and the Judicial Committee," p. 75.

163. J.R. Mallory recently contrasted the capacity of the Supreme Court of the United States to " 'follow the election returns' " with the Privy Council, which "was so deficient in both sense and sensibility that the allocation of power in the constitution, by the end of the 1930's, had achieved a remarkable incongruity between the resources, capacities, and responsibilities of the federal and provincial governments." "The Five Faces of Federalism," p. 7. See also MacDonald, "The Privy Council and the Canadian Constitution," pp. 1032-33, 1035, 1027; MacDonald, "The Constitution in a Changing World," pp. 43-44; MacDonald, "Judicial Interpretation of the Canadian Constitution," p. 278; Tuck, "Canada and the Judicial Committee," p. 34; B. Laskin, "Reflections on the Canadian Constitution after the First Century," in Meekison, *Canadian Federalism*, p. 139.

164. A.B. Keith, "Privy Council Decisions: A Comment from Great Britain," *CBR*, 15 (1937), p. 435.

165. Rumble, *American Legal Realism*, pp. 220-21, 227, 232.

166. J.A. Corry, "Decisions of the Judicial Committee, 1930-9," *CJEPS*, 5 (1939), pp. 511-12. See also Rumble, *American Legal Realism*, p. 231, on the difficulty of defining relevant criteria for judicial decisions. Herbert Wechsler, "Toward Neutral Principles of Constitutional Law," *Harvard Law Review*, 73 (1959), is an important attempt to define a judicial process that is "genuinely principled, resting with respect to every step . . . in reaching judgement on analysis and reasons quite transcending the immediate result . . . on grounds of adequate neutrality and generality." He is hostile to criteria concerned with immediate results that turn the court into a "naked power organ" rather than a court of law. He describes the resultant *ad hoc* evaluation as the "deepest problem of our [American] constitutionalism"(pp. 15, 12).

167. A related question is whether or not Canadian federalism would have had a less turbulent history if the task of judicial interpretation had been undertaken by the Supreme Court. McWhinney, *Judicial Review*, pp. 73-74, provides evidence on both sides of the question, although personally doubtful that the Supreme Court would have acted differently. Glazebrook, *A History of Canadian Political Thought*, p. 258, finds no proof that the Supreme Court would have done oth-

erwise than the Judicial Committee. MacGuigan argues that, from the evidence, it is impossible to decide whether or not the Supreme Court approved of the decisions of the Judicial Committee. "The Privy Council and the Supreme Court: A Jurisprudential Analysis," p. 421. R.F. McWilliams, "The Privy Council and the Constitution," p. 579, also doubts that the Supreme Court would have differed in its interpretation from the Privy Council. Russell, *Supreme Court*, pp. 255-56, n5, notes the difficulty in arguing that the Supreme Court was more pro-dominion than the Privy Council. On the other hand, supporters of the Supreme Court, who note that it and the Judicial Committee usually agreed, have been cautioned not to ignore the fact that the Supreme Court had to take the previous decisions of the committee as the major premise in its thinking. MacDonald, "The Canadian Constitution Seventy Years After," p. 426. Scott argues that an independent Supreme Court would have produced decisions much more favourable to the federal government. *Canada Today*, p. 77; "Development of Canadian Federalism," p. 246.

168. A point strongly made by W.E. Raney sixty years ago. "Justice, Precedent and Ultimate Conjecture," p. 461.

169. Innis, "Great Britain, the United States and Canada," p. 404. Sir Allen Aylesworth told the Ontario Bar Association that "It is . . . no disparagement to Canadian lawyers or to Canadian judges to say that the men, or some of the men at any rate, who constitute the Judicial Bench in England, and some of the men who sit at the Council Board as members of the Judicial Committee are better read lawyers, are stronger lawyers than any men we have, either at the Bar or upon the Bench, in Canada, and in these circumstances it is a matter of actual daily practical advantage to the people of this country that they should have still the right to take to that Court their complicated cases as between citizen and citizen for final adjudication." Address of Sir Allen Aylesworth," p. 143.

Bram Thompson stated: "The reader of the Law Reports is constantly confronted with cases which the Privy Council decisions prove to have been decided in our local Courts upon the grossest misconception of even elementary principles. Indeed, some of our Courts seem to delight in rendering judgements which are, to say the least of them, utterly perverse." "Editorial," *CLT*, 41 (1921), p. 164. Russell notes that the early weakness of the Supreme Court inhibited moves to abolish appeals. *Supreme Court*, p. 24.

Electoral Politics: Introduction

1. For a seminal discussion of unintended, dysfunctional consequences of social action, see Robert K. Merton, *On Theoretical Sociology* (New York, 1967), chapter 3.

2. In particular, see the article by J.A.A. Lovink, "On Analysing the Impact of the Electoral System on the Party System in Canada," *Canadian Journal of Political Science*, 3, 4 (December, 1970), pp. 497-516, and Cairns's reply, pp. 517-21. Other important contributions to this literature include: Richard Johnston and Janet Ballantyne, "Geography and the Electoral System," *Canadian Journal of Political Science*, 10, 4 (December, 1977), pp. 857-66; William P. Irvine, *Does Canada Need a New Electoral System?* (Kingston, Ontario, 1979); John C. Courtney, "Reflections on Reforming the Canadian Electoral System," *Canadian Public Administration*, 23 (1980), pp. 427-57.

3. In addition to the debate noted above, readers may find the critique of the concept of "province-building," which Cairns and Edwin R. Black did so much to draw to our attention, by R.A. Young, Philippe Faucher, and André Blais instructive of the role that contrasting methodological assumptions can play in the substantive interpretation of Canadian politics. See Black and Cairns, "A Different Perspective on Canadian Federalism," *Canadian Public Administration*, 9, 1 (March, 1966), pp. 27-44; and Young, Faucher, and Blais, "The Concept of Province-Building: A Critique," *Canadian Journal of Political Science*, 17, 4 (December, 1984).

Background to the Elections of 1979 and 1980

1. Official figures.

2. Counting 1896 and 1925 as Liberal victories. In 1896 the Liberals received thirty more seats, but 1.2 percentage points fewer votes, than the Conservatives and formed the government. In 1925 the Liberals remained in office with Progressive support, although they received fewer seats and fewer votes than the Conservatives.

3. Counting 1957 and 1979 as Conservative victories, although in each case the new minority Conservative government was based on less voter support than the Liberal government it replaced.

4. And for a short period in 1926.

5. Donald Smiley, "Intergovernmental Relations in Canada: Where Does the Taxpayer Come In?" paper presented to the Annual Conference of the Institute of Public Administration of Canada, Winnipeg, August, 1979, mimeo, p. 4.

6. In choosing a centralist variant of federalism, they were also responding to their own interpretation of the contribution of American constitutional arrangements to the American Civil War, which was the backdrop to their discussions. They concluded that too loose a federation, with residuary powers given to the states, strengthened centrifugal forces, led to doctrines of states' rights, and in extreme cases could lead to the carnage of civil war. To avoid the repetition of such a disaster, concessions to regional diversity were kept to a minimum.

7. George Grant, *Lament for a Nation: The Defeat of Canadian Nationalism* (Toronto, 1965), p. 71.

8. See Eugene Forsey, *Freedom and Order* (Toronto, 1974), pt. 1, esp. pp. 21-49.

9. Alexander Brady, "Canada and the Model of Westminister," in William B. Hamilton, ed., *The Transfer of Institutions* (Durham, N.C., 1964), pp. 67-68.

10. "With Canadian experience of nearly a century, sectional representation and nomination by the central government seem irreconcilable in principle. . . . Macdonald and other leaders . . . granted the forms demanded by sectional sentiments and fears, but they made sure that these forms should not endanger the political structure." Robert A. MacKay, *The Unreformed Senate of Canada*, rev. ed. (Toronto, 1963), p. 43.

11. James R. Mallory, "Responsive and Responsible Government," *Proceedings and Transactions of the Royal Society of Canada*, vol. 12, 4th series (1974), p. 209.

12. Thomas A. Hockin, "Flexible and Structured Parliamentarism: From 1848

to Contemporary Party Government," *Journal of Canadian Studies*, 14, 2 (Summer, 1979), p. 14.

13. David K. Foot, "Political Cycles, Economic Cycles, and the Trend in Public Employment in Canada," in Meyer W. Bucovetsky, ed., *Studies in Public Employment and Compensation in Canada*, Institute for Research on Public Policy Series on Public Sector Employment in Canada, vol. 2 (Montreal, 1979), pp. 68-71, 79.

14. Gérard Veilleux, "Intergovernmental Canada – Government by Conference? – A Fiscal and Economic Perspective," paper presented to the Annual Conference of the Institute of Public Administration of Canada, Winnipeg, August, 1979, mimeo, p. 5.

15. Government of Canada, *Royal Commission on Financial Management and Accountability: Final Report* (Hull, 1979), p. 21.

16. Ralph Heintzman, "The Educational Contract," *Journal of Canadian Studies*, 14, 2 (Summer, 1979), p. 2.

17. John Stewart, "Strengthening the Commons," *Journal of Canadian Studies*, 14, 2 (Summer, 1979), p. 39.

18. Robert L. Stanfield, "The Present State of the Legislative Process in Canada: Myths and Realities," in William A.W. Neilson and James C. MacPherson, eds., *The Legislative Process in Canada: The Need for Reform* (Toronto, 1978), p. 47.

19. For a good analysis, see Donald V. Smiley, *Constitutional Adaptation and Canadian Federalism since 1945*, Documents of the Royal Commission on Bilingualism and Biculturalism, no. 4 (Ottawa, 1970).

20. Task Force on Canadian Unity, *A Future Together: Observations and Recommendations* (Ottawa, 1979), p. 16.

21. Smiley, "Intergovernmental Relations."

22. Task Force on Canadian Unity, *Future Together*, chapter 2.

23. Task Force on Canadian Unity, *A Time to Speak: The Views of the Public* (Ottawa, 1979), p. viii.

24. See Edward McWhinney, *Quebec and the Constitution, 1960-1978* (Toronto, 1979), for a useful corrective to the pessimism of many English-Canadian writers on the "crisis."

25. William Johnson, "Canada's Fate Looks Bleak," *Globe and Mail*, May 22, 1979.

26. Ronald L. Watts, "Survival or Disintegration," in Richard Simeon, ed., *Must Canada Fail?* (Montreal and London, 1977), p. 52.

27. For the most recent and best analysis available, see William P. Irvine, *Does Canada Need a New Electoral System?* Queen's Studies on the Future of the Canadian Communities (Kingston, 1979).

28. Robert Burns, *One Citizen, One Vote: Green Paper on the Reform of the Electoral System* (Quebec, 1979), pp. 16, 25, 28, 33.

Electoral System and Party System

1. E.E. Schattschneider, *Party Government* (New York, 1942), pp. 62, 70; S.M. Lipset, "Party Systems and the Representation of Social Groups," *European Journal of Sociology*, I (1960), pp. 61-63, 80; M. Duverger, *Political Parties* (London, 1965), Book II; M. Duverger, "The Influence of the Electoral System on Political Life," *International Social Science Bulletin*, 3 (Summer, 1951); V.O. Key, *Public Opinion and American Democracy* (New York, 1961), chapter 5. See also

A. DeGrazia, "General Theory of Apportionment," *Law and Contemporary Problems*, XVII (1952), and D.A. Rustow, "Some Observations on Proportional Representation," *Journal of Politics*, XII (1950). F.A. Hermens, *Democracy or Anarchy?* (Notre Dame, 1941), and Enid Lakeman and J.D. Lambert, *Voting in Democracies* (London, 1955), discuss proportional representation from opposed viewpoints.

2. "We English-speaking peoples," stated Sir Richard Cartwright, "have made a sort of fetish of our present system, and appear to think that if you will only cut up a country or a province into equal divisions and give every man, wise or igno-rant, rich or poor, the right to vote, you have devised a machine which will give you automatically a perfect representation. This is a huge mistake." *Reminiscences* (Toronto, 1912), p. 314. See also F.H. Underhill, "Canadian Liberal Democracy in 1955," in G.V. Ferguson and F.H. Underhill, *Press and Party in Canada* (Toronto, 1955), pp. 41-43.

3. D.V. Smiley, "The Two-Party System and One-Party Dominance in the Liberal Democratic State," *Canadian Journal of Economics and Political Science*, 24 (1958), pp. 316-17, discusses the effects of the electoral system on major and minor parties. Schattschneider, *Party Government*, pp. 74-75, and Pendleton Her-ring, *The Politics of Democracy* (New York, 1940), pp. 182-83, note that the most important third parties in the United States have been sectional.

4. There is an unavoidable problem of circular reasoning here. There is an impor-tant difference between saying the electoral system favours parties that *are* sectional and saying the electoral system encourages parties to *be* sectional.

5. If 1958 is excluded as a deviant case the contrast is even more glaring, 727 Liberals from Quebec confronted 85 Conservatives, a ratio of 8.6 to 1, in contrast to the ratio of 2.1 to 1 that existed at the level of the voter.

6. A. Brady, *Canada* (London, 1932), pp. 13-14; A. Siegfried, *The Race Question in Canada* (Toronto, 1966), p. 114.

7. McLeod is undoubtedly correct in his suggestion that national unity would be served if Canadians were "divided *across* ethnic barriers on lines of support for competing policies," but he fails to note the barrier the electoral system has placed, at least historically, in the way of this objective. J.T. McLeod, "Party Structure and Party Reform," in A. Rotstein, ed., *The Prospect of Change* (Toronto, 1965), pp. 18-19.

8. H. McD. Clokie, *Canadian Government and Politics* (Toronto, 1944), pp. 81-83; McLeod, "Party Structure and Party Reform," pp. 4-5, 9, 14; Brady, *Canada* pp. 102-03; A. Brady, *Democracy in the Dominions* (Toronto, 2nd ed., 1952), pp. 110-12; R.M. Dawson, *The Government of Canada* (Toronto, 4th ed., 1963), rev. by N. Ward, pp. 469-70; J.A. Corry and J.E. Hodgetts, *Democratic Gov-ernment and Politics* (Toronto, 3rd ed., 1963), chapters VIII-IX; J.M. Beck and D.J. Dooley, "Party Images in Canada," *Queen's Quarterly*, 67 (1960), p. 433; F.H. Underhill, *Canadian Political Parties* (Ottawa, 1957), pp. 4-5. For a critical discussion of brokerage politics, see John Porter, *The Vertical Mosaic* (Toronto, 1965), pp. 373-77.

9. The confusion over what the parties actually do is of long standing. Siegfried observed that Canadian statesmen "seem to fear great movements of opinion, and they devote themselves to weakening such movements. . . . Let a question of race or religion be raised, and . . . the elections will become struggles of political prin-

ciple, sincere and passionate. Now this is exactly what is feared by the prudent and far-sighted men who have been given the responsibility of maintaining the national equilibrium." Less frequently quoted is the directly contrary statement that "The appeal to racial exclusiveness combined with religious bigotry is the first and last cartridge of the politicians of the Dominion. Before thinking of any other reason, or after all other reasons have been exhausted, they come to or return to this." Siegfried, *Race Question*, pp. 113, 130. A similar contradiction is implicit in Robert Alford's statement: "Although the major parties are not distinctly Left and Right in their policies and appeals, they have, by that very token been an *integrating* force in Canadian society, since they *emphasize* regional, religious, and ethnic representation and compromises rather than either universalistic or class representation." *Party and Society* (Chicago, 1963), p. 260; emphasis added.

10. Pierre Elliott Trudeau observes that French-Canadian Liberals have encouraged their potential supporters to use "their voting bloc as an instrument of racial defence, or of personal gain. Their only slogans have been racial slogans." "Some Obstacles to Democracy in Quebec," *Canadian Journal of Economics and Political Science*, 24, 3 (August, 1958), reprinted in Mason Wade, ed., *Canadian Dualism* (Toronto, 1960), p. 256.

11. Roger Graham, *Arthur Meighen: And Fortune Fled* (Toronto, 1963), p. 340. See also Graham, "Arthur Meighen and the Conservative Party in Quebec: The Election of 1925," *Canadian Historical Review*, 36 (1955), for an analysis of this election in Quebec. For appeals to racial passions in 1921 and 1925, see Graham, *Meighen: And Fortune Fled*, pp. 140-43, 340-43, and Blair Neatby, *Mackenzie King 1924-1932: The Lonely Heights* (Toronto, 1963), p. 73.

12. The impact of the conscription issue on party strategy and voter choice in Quebec is discussed in N. Ward, ed., *A Party Politician: The Memoirs of Chubby Power* (Toronto, 1966). Power suggests that with the exceptions of 1926, 1930, and 1935, it was an issue in every election from 1911 to 1940 inclusive.

13. John Meisel, *The Canadian General Election of 1957* (Toronto, 1962), pp. 167-68.

14. This induced *Le Devoir* to observe "sombrely that the composition of the new Cabinet reduced Quebec 'to the status of a second-class, nearly a third-class province.' Neither the Conservative nor the Liberal parties, it argued, can rule without the support of at least twenty-five French Canadians in the House. 'And it is in the interest of the French-language group to be strongly represented in every government, whatever may be its party name; for every time that group has lacked an influential representation, French Canadians have been subjected to grave injustices.' " J.R. Mallory, "The Election and the Constitution," *Queen's Quarterly*, 64 (1957), p. 481.

15. D.H. Wrong, "Parties and Voting in Canada," *Political Science Quarterly*, 73 (1958), p. 403.

16. J.M. Beck, "Quebec and the Canadian Elections of 1958," *Parliamentary Affairs*, 12 (1958-59), pp. 95-96. Siegfried, *Race Question*, pp. 163-64, 207-08, provides examples of the importance of French-English cleavages on election results and on party appeals at the turn of the century. As late as 1962, in some parts of Quebec, the Liberals tried to "link Diefenbaker with the historic 'Tory enemies' of French Canada. The names Borden, Meighen, Bennett, and Drew are still spat out as epithets by Liberal orators on the hustings." P. Regenstreif, "The

Liberal Party of Canada: A Political Analysis" (Ph.D. thesis, Cornell University, 1963), p. 477.

17. By the 1963 election the politics of sectionalism once more reduced the Conservatives to a token effort in Quebec, "largely directed to holding the few seats they had. The Prime Minister himself did little more than show the flag." John Saywell, ed., *Canadian Annual Review for 1963* (Toronto, 1964), p. 23. In the 1965 campaign the major parties exchanged sectional insults, with the Liberals charging that the Conservatives did not have and would not gain meaningful representation in Quebec, to which the Conservatives retorted that the Liberals would lack representation elsewhere. John Saywell, ed., *Canadian Annual Review for 1965* (Toronto, 1966), p. 85.

18. John Meisel, "The Stalled Omnibus: Canadian Parties in the 1960s," *Social Research*, 30 (1963), pp. 383-84.

19. Leslie Lipson, "Party Systems in the United Kingdom and the Older Commonwealth: Causes, Resemblances, and Variations," *Political Studies*, 7 (1959), pp. 27-28. See Ward, *A Party Politician*, pp. 389, 392, for Power's recognition of the importance of Quebec to the Liberals.

20. N. Ward, "The National Political Scene," in Wade, ed., *Canadian Dualism*, pp. 266, 272.

21. Sir Richard Cartwright argued in his *Reminiscences*, p. 352, that because the provinces differ in wealth and interests, "the temptation to the poorer provinces to sell themselves to the party in office is always very great and is certain to be traded on by practical politicians on both sides."

Graham, *Meighen: And Fortune Fled*, pp. 299, 303, describes the pressures on Meighen to devise an attractive western policy, as otherwise his party "has not the ghost of a chance on the prairies in an election." In contrast to King's assiduous courting of the Prairie provinces, waffling on the tariff and promises of special western policies, Meighen decided to preach the tariff to the unconverted. He was rewarded with ten seats and King with twenty in 1925.

Liberal courting of British Columbia in 1925 by reducing rates on flour and grain going to Pacific ports for export is noted in Walter R. Sharp, "The Canadian Elections of 1925," *American Political Science Review*, 20 (1926), p. 111, n3. Lionel H. Laing, "The Pattern of Canadian Politics: The Elections of 1945," *American Political Science Review*, 40 (1946), provides a sectional interpretation of the 1945 election in terms of results and to a lesser extent of strategy.

22. H.A. Scarrow, "Distinguishing between Political Parties – The Case of Canada," *Midwest Journal of Political Science*, 9 (1965), p. 72. He also notes (pp. 75-76n) the tendency of a candidate to appeal for support "on the ground that only his party has a chance of winning office, and that consequently the voters of the district or region had better jump on the winning bandwagon if they want to be represented in the cabinet. Diefenbaker made wide use of this appeal in Quebec in 1958." Paul Hellyer appealed to prairie voters for Liberal support in the 1965 federal election to "elect more members to the Government side to make sure the views of this area are considered." *Winnipeg Free Press*, October 29, 1965.

23. The CCF seems to have been an exception. See Walter D. Young, "The National CCF: Political Party and Political Movement" (Ph.D. thesis, University of Toronto, 1965), for an analysis of the special role played by the central office, in effect by David Lewis, for long periods in the formation of policy and strategy.

24. The fact is that influence in caucus and party is conditioned by seniority. N. Ward, *The Canadian House of Commons: Representation* (Toronto, 2nd ed. 1963), pp. 140-43, is relevant here with its implication that the spokesmen for the sectional strongholds of the party will enjoy a pre-eminent position compared to the more fluctuating representation where the party is weak.

25. Scarrow, "Distinguishing between Political Parties," p. 69. See also John R. Williams, *The Conservative Party of Canada: 1920-1949* (Durham, N.C., 1956), pp. 14-15, and Ward, "The National Political Scene," pp. 268-70, for related comments.

26. See the interesting analysis of the 1935 election by Escott Reid, which asserted that the difference in ethnic composition of the Liberal and Conservative parliamentary parties would incline the Liberals to isolationism and the Conservatives to a more imperialistic policy. "The Canadian Election of 1935 and After," *American Political Science Review*, 30 (1936), pp. 117-18.

27. See Regenstreif, "Liberal Party," pp. 472-77, and Alford, *Party and Society*, p. 258, for party policy differences and party images related to French-English relations.

28. Other factors not considered here also influence party policy and attitudes. Meisel has cogently argued that the Liberals entered the 1957 federal election with a national approach remarkably insensitive to regional needs, an approach born of long and intimate contact with a centralist-oriented civil service and a lack of feedback from backbenchers in the Commons. By contrast, the Conservatives, who entered the election as an Ontario party in terms of existing parliamentary representation, proved remarkably sensitive to the needs of regions and groups neglected by the Liberals. John Meisel, "The Formulation of Liberal and Conservative Programmes in the 1957 Canadian General Election," *Canadian Journal of Economics and Political Science*, 26 (1960).

29. In the mid-fifties Ward made the general point that all opposition parties had "little experience in dealing with French Canadians as trusted colleagues in caucus," with a resultant development of traditions reflecting that fact. "The National Political Scene," p. 267.

30. Williams, *Conservative Party*, pp. 197-200.

31. *Ibid.*, pp. 197-98.

32. Ward, "The National Political Scene," pp. 269-70.

33. The history of the CCF reveals that the sectional backgrounds of party MPs did not orient the party in the direction of its western supporters. In fact, the party rapidly moved away from its agrarian stronghold and became, from the viewpoint of the national leaders, and especially David Lewis, the most important person in the determination of party policy, a party with an urban, industrial, working-class, and central Canada orientation. Young, "The National CCF," pp. 127-28, 131, 132, 139-40, 148-49, 159-60, 166, 200-01, 204, 249-50, 310.

34. "Of course," he continued, "times and circumstances do arise where profound personal convictions conflict with party success or personal ambition, and where one must make decisions that one knows to be unpalatable to the voters." Ward, *A Party Politician*, p. 318.

35. J. Schumpeter, *Capitalism, Socialism and Democracy* (New York, 3rd ed., 1962), p. 285.

36. Neatby, *King: The Lonely Heights*, pp. 66-67. See also pp. 222-24.

37. E.P. Dean provides several striking examples in "How Canada Has Voted: 1867-1945," *Canadian Historical Review*, 30 (1949). Duverger, who argued that "Parliamentary strength is always much more important than real strength in the country," provides a British illustration of the way in which this perceptual bias operates: "The fact that the Labour party had obtained only 48.7% of the poll in 1945 was completely obliterated by the fact that it controlled 390 votes in the Commons; public opinion itself considered Labour as having a strong majority." *Political Parties*, p. 400.

38. The provisions of Sections 51 and 51A of the BNA Act allocating parliamentary seats to provinces are important contributing factors in facilitating provincial or sectional interpretations of election results. As a byproduct the system precludes the possibility of electoral boundaries crossing provincial boundaries and makes the province a natural and easy unit for interpreting election results. In addition, of course, it transforms struggles over representation into struggles over provincial rights. I am indebted to Professor Walter Young for drawing these factors to my attention.

39. J.E. Hodgetts, "Regional Interests and Policy in a Federal Structure," *Canadian Journal of Economics and Political Science*, 32 (1966), p. 10.

40. W.L. Morton, *The Kingdom of Canada* (Toronto, 1963), p. 450; R. Cook *et al.*, *Canada: A Modern Study* (Toronto, 1963), p. 254; Neatby, *King: The Lonely Heights*, p. 74; and Underhill, "Canadian Liberal Democracy in 1955," p. 40.

41. F.H. Underhill, *The Image of Confederation* (Toronto, 1964), p. 54.

42. McLeod, "Party Structure and Party Reform," p. 10. He adds that this is not "peculiar to Quebec."

43. P. Regenstreif, "The Canadian General Election of 1958," *Western Political Quarterly*, 13 (1960), pp. 362-63. See also Wrong, "Parties and Voting in Canada," pp. 403-04.

44. H.G. Thorburn, *Politics in New Brunswick* (Toronto, 1961), p. 176. New Brunswick, Thorburn argues, "has been on the winning side whenever this could be divined with any accuracy before the election" (p. 183); see also p. 49.

45. The sections have been defined as Maritimes/Atlantic, Quebec, Ontario, Prairies, and British Columbia.

46. In 1925 and 1957 the Liberals and Conservatives respectively have been identified as winners for the purpose of the above calculation.

47. Schattschneider, *Party Government*, p. 111. This point is made by Clokie, *Canadian Government and Politics*, pp. 87-89, in a discussion implying that class cleavages are more real than sectional cleavages.

48. Porter, *Vertical Mosaic*, pp. 373-77; F.H. Underhill, *In Search of Canadian Liberalism* (Toronto, 1960), p. 167.

49. Porter, *Vertical Mosaic*, pp. 373-74.

50. Alford, *Party and Society*, p. 339; Porter, *Vertical Mosaic*, pp. 368-69; V.O. Key, *Public Opinion and American Democracy*, p. 109; Key, *Politics, Parties, and Pressure Groups* (New York, 2nd ed., 1947), p. 152.

51. Duverger, *Political Parties*, p. 383.

52. S.M. Lipset, *Political Man* (New York, 1963), p. 13. The extensive literature on cross-pressures is relevant here with its emphasis that multiple-group membership and identification have "the effect of reducing the emotion in political choices." *Ibid.*

53. Underhill, *Image of Confederation*, pp. 53-54.

54. For example, in recent articles Leon Epstein has specifically downgraded its importance: Epstein, "A Comparative Study of Canadian Parties," *American Political Science Review*, 58 (1964), pp. 48, 57-58. McLeod, in an extensive catalogue of factors relevant to explaining the party system, does not discuss the electoral system, except for incidental mention of its contribution to single-party dominance. McLeod, "Party Structure and Party Reform," p. 9. The views of Lipson and Meisel are discussed in the following paragraphs.

Smiley is an exception in according some significance to the electoral system. He notes that the system favours sectionally based minor parties, and that it was "strategic" in destroying the Canadian two-party system between 1935 and 1953. "The Two-Party System and One-Party Dominance," pp. 316-17.

55. Lipson, "Party Systems in the United Kingdom and the Older Commonwealth," pp. 20-21.

56. He supports his argument by noting that both the two-party system and its successor multi-party system existed within the same institutional framework. Meisel, "The Stalled Omnibus," p. 370.

57. W.S. Livingston, *Federalism and Constitutional Change* (Oxford, 1956), pp. 7-9.

58. Alford, *Party and Society*, pp. 42-49, discusses various factors sustaining sectionalism.

59. Scarrow, "Distinguishing between Political Parties," and John Meisel, "Recent Changes in Canadian Parties," in Hugh G. Thorburn, ed., *Party Politics in Canada* (Scarborough, 2nd ed., 1967).

60. Lipset, "Party Systems and the Representation of Social Groups," pp. 76-77; Duverger, *Political Parties*, pp. 382-84.

Federal System and Intergovernmental Dimension

1. W.S. Livingston, *Federalism and Constitutional Change* (Oxford, 1956), p. 2.

2. Samuel H. Beer, "Political Overload and Federalism," *Polity*, x (1977), p. 8; cf. Beer's Presidential Address to the American Political Science Association, "Federalism, Nationalism, and Democracy in America," *American Political Science Review*, 72 (1978).

3. *Canadian Public Administration*, 22, 2 (Summer, 1979), pp. 175-76.

4. *Ibid.*, p. 195.

5. For example, see Donald V. Smiley, *The Federal Condition in Canada* (Toronto, 1987), especially pp. 6-9, 89-91; Herman Bakvis and William Chandler, eds., *Federalism and the Role of the State* (Toronto, 1987); and Philip Resnick, "State and Civil Society: The Limits of a Royal Commission," *Canadian Journal of Political Science*, 20, 2 (June, 1987), pp. 379-401.

The Governments and Societies of Canadian Federalism

1. W.S. Livingston, *Federalism and Constitutional Change* (Oxford, 1956), p. 4.

2. The title of a famous 1939 article by Harold J. Laski, reprinted in A.N. Christensen and E.M. Kirkpatrick, eds., *The People, Politics, and the Politician* (New York, 1941).

3. J.A. Corry, "Constitutional Trends and Federalism," in A.R.M. Lower *et al.*, *Evolving Canadian Federalism* (Durham, N.C., 1958), p. 97.

4. *Ibid.*, p. 108.

5. John Porter, *The Vertical Mosaic* (Toronto, 1965), p. 380.

6. My intellectual debt to Prefessors E.R.Black, Richard Simeon, D.V. Smiley, and others will be readily evident in the following pages, and is gratefully acknowledged. The new text by T.A. Hockin, *Government in Canada* (Toronto, 1976), emphasizes "the dynamic of government in Canada" (p. xi) and thus overlaps considerably with the argument presented below.

7. D.V. Smiley, *Canada in Question: Federalism in the Seventies* (2nd ed.; Toronto, 1976); pp. 10-11, and chapter 2.

8. See Luce Patenaude, *Le Labrador à l'heure de la contestation* (Montréal, 1972), and Jacques Brossard *et al.*, *Le Territoire Québécois* (Montréal, 1970), pp. 17-19, for materials and analysis from a Quebec perspective on the Labrador dispute.

9. For an excellent technical description of boundary changes, see Norman L. Nicholson, *The Boundaries of Canada, its Provinces and Territories,* Canada, Department of Mines and Technical Surveys, Geographical Branch, Memoir no. 2 (Ottawa, 1964).

10. February 12, 1972, cited in Edgar Gallant, "Maritime Cooperation and Integration – A Progress Report," in O.J. Firestone, ed., *Regional Economic Development* (Ottawa, 1974), p. 167.

11. This is the combined total of 349,063 wage-earners, full-time and other, excluding B.C., but including Yukon and the Northwest Territories, for general government services, Statistics Canada, *Provincial Government Employment October-December 1976* (Ottawa, 1977), p. 6; 136,463 salary-earners and wage-earners, full-time and other, for provincial government enterprises, *ibid.*, p. 28; and 33,197 employees of the B.C. government, excluding B.C. Ferries, *Public Service Commission Annual Report* (Victoria, 1977), p. 23, for a total of 518,723.

12. Statistics Canada, *Federal Government Employment July-September 1976* (Ottawa, 1977), p. 11.

13. Based on unadjusted employment figures of 9,688,000 for September, 1976. *Canadian Statistical Review* (February, 1977), p. 49.

14. Statistics Canada, *Local Government Employment July-September 1976* (Ottawa, 1977), p. 5. "If we add to the list of civil servants . . . [at all three levels] those employed in a vast array of nondepartmental agencies, boards, commissions, enterprises, and teachers and hospital employees, we would find that at least one in every five in the labour force in the country is on a public payroll." J.E. Hodgetts and O.P. Dwivedi, *Provincial Governments as Employers* (Montreal and London, 1974), p. 2.

15. Roy P. Fairfield, ed., *The Federalist Papers* (2nd ed.; Garden City, N.Y., 1966), p. 2.

16. For a relevant case study, see A. Paul Pross, "Input versus Withinput: Pressure Group Demands and Administrative Survival," in A. Paul Pross, ed., *Pressure Group Behaviour in Canadian Politics* (Toronto, 1975).

17. "A classic case [of the survival capacity of public organizations] is the Halifax Disaster Relief Commission, established to handle claims arising from the Halifax explosion of 1917. In late 1975, the federal government introduced a bill to repeal the act respecting the Commission and to transfer authority for continuation of pensions and allowances to the Canadian Pension Commission. So long-lived was the commission that the bill winding it up had to make pension provisions for

employees of the Commission itself." Donald Gow, "Rebuilding Canada's Bureaucracy," edited and revised by Edwin R. Black and Michael J. Prince (Kingston, 1976), mimeo, p. 40.

18. *Ibid.*

19. André Bernard, "The Quebec Perspective on Canada: The Last Quarter Century–Language Strife," a paper prepared for the University of Saskatchewan Conference on Political Change in Canada, March 17, 1977, p. 1. This leadership role is a response to the social and political fact that "No power in the world can prevent Francophone Quebecers from perceiving themselves as a society and as a nation, original and distinct from the Canadian whole." Léon Dion, *Québec: The Unfinished Revolution* (Montreal and London, 1976), p. 45.

20. Smiley, *Canada in Question*, p. 108.

21. Corry, "Constitutional Trends and Federalism," p. 101.

22. Claude Morin, *Quebec versus Ottawa: The Struggle for Self-government 1960-1972* (Toronto, 1976), p. 95.

23. *Ibid.*, chapter 13.

24. Dion, *Québec: The Unfinished Revolution*, p. 86.

25. For an extremely helpful general discussion of institutionalization, see Samuel P. Huntington, "Political Development and Political Decay," in Norman J. Vig and Rodney P. Stiefbold, eds., *Politics in Advanced Nations* (Englewood Cliffs, N.J., 1974). "Institutionalization is the process by which organizations and procedures acquire value and stability. The level of institutionalization of any political system can be defined by the adaptability, complexity, autonomy, and coherence of its organizations and procedures" (p. 115). In comparative terms, the Canadian political system is highly institutionalized.

26. Richard Simeon, "The 'Overload Thesis' and Canadian Government," *Canadian Public Policy*, 2 (1976), p. 550, italics in original. Similar statements abound in the literature. "For today's citizens," states Dion, "as for their fathers, the State is still a distant 'they,' alien and almost inimical . . ." (*Québec: The Unfinished Revolution*, p. 87). Smiley speculates that "elites are somewhat unresponsive to popular attitudes and that the citizenry for whatever reasons has a considerable tolerance for this unresponsiveness" (*Canada in Question*, p. 201). J.R. Mallory observes that "the mass of citizenry is perhaps as far away from the real decisions of government as they were two hundred years ago, and the cabinet system provides strong institutional barriers to the development of more democratic ways of doing things" ("Responsive and Responsible Government," *Transactions of the Royal Society of Canada*, Fourth Series, XII [1974], p. 208). A recent volume on pressure groups documents instances in which government agencies withstood "considerable input pressure from the external environment, and that they may significantly influence that environment, if not dominate it" (A. Paul Pross, "Pressure Groups: Adaptive Instruments of Political Communication," in Pross, ed., *Pressure Group Behaviour in Canadian Politics*, p. 21). J.E. Anderson suggests "that in Canada the relations between civil servants and pressure groups are usually dominated by civil servants" ("Pressure Groups and the Canadian Bureaucracy," in W.D.K. Kernaghan, ed., *Bureaucracy in Canadian Government* [2nd ed.; Toronto, 1973], p. 99).

27. Morin, *Quebec versus Ottawa*, p. 43.

28. Dion, *Québec: The Unfinished Revolution*, p. 138.

29. John Meisel, "Citizen Demands and Government Response," *Canadian Public Policy,* 2 (1976), p. 568.

30. Simeon, "The 'Overload Thesis' and Canadian Government," p. 546.

31. Bernard. "Quebec Perspective on Canada," p. 1.

32. Dion, *Québec: The Unfinished Revolution,* p. 156.

33. *Ibid.,* pp. 124, 169-70.

34. *Ibid.,* p. 156.

35. Morin, *Quebec versus Ottawa,* p. 130.

36. "I am deeply concerned that, on the evidence of the two-year examination carried out by the Audit Office, Parliament – and indeed the Government – has lost or is close to losing effective control of the public purse." *Conspectus of the Report of the Auditor General of Canada to the House of Commons* (Ottawa, 1976), p. 3.

37. Ontario Economic Council, *The Process of Public Decision-Making* (Toronto, 1977), p. 48.

38. Ontario Economic Council. *The Ontario Economy to 1987* (Toronto, 1977), p. 38.

39. Geoffrey Young. "Federal-Provincial Grants and Equalization," in Ontario Economic Council, *Intergovernmental Relations* (Toronto, 1977), pp. 43-44.

40. Donald R. Huggett. "Tax Base Harmonization," in Ontario Economic Council, *Intergovernmental Relations,* p. 56.

41. The appropriately cautious statement of Paul Pross should be kept in mind as a salutary check on some of the more speculative suggestions in the following paragraphs: "we know only enough to suggest that federalism is both an important influence on pressure group behaviour and that group manipulation of intergovernmental relations may have a significant effect on the policy process." "Pressure Groups: Adaptive Instruments of Political Communication," p. 23.

42. J.R. Mallory, *Social Credit and the Federal Power in Canada* (Toronto, 1967), pp. 32, 37.

43. P.E. Trudeau, *Federalism and the French Canadians* (Toronto, 1968), p. 138.

44. Pross, "Pressure Groups: Adaptive Instruments of Political Communication," pp. 22-23, and David Kwavnick, "Interest Group Demands and the Federal Political System: Two Canadian Case Studies," esp. pp. 71-72, both from Pross, ed., *Pressure Group Behaviour in Canadian Politics.*

45. Kwavnick, "Interest Group Demands," p. 81.

46. *Ibid.,* p. 82.

47. M.W. Bucovetsky, "The Mining Industry and the Great Tax Reform Debate," in Pross, ed., *Pressure Group Behaviour in Canadian Politics,* p. 106.

48. *Ibid.,* pp. 108-09.

49. Roy C. Macridis, "'Interest Groups in Comparative Analysis," *The Journal of Politics,* 23 (1961), p. 38. He speculates that "this parallelism between the political system and the interest configuration is true everywhere." Compare Kwavnick's hypothesis: "the distribution of power between the central and provincial governments influences the structure, cohesion and even the existence of interest groups; that is, that the strength and cohesion of interest groups will tend to mirror the strength, in their particular area of concern, of the government to which they enjoy access. Interest groups which are provincially based and which enjoy access to the provincial governments will be strong compared with nation-

ally-based groups enjoying access to the national government when the provincial governments enjoy a stronger position than the national government in the areas of concern to those interest groups, and vice versa," and, "In short, the pressure goes where the power is – and takes its organization with it." ("Interest Group Demands." pp. 72, 77.) See, in general, David Truman, *The Governmental Process: Political Interests and Public Opinion* (2nd ed.; New York, 1971).

50. Helen Jones Dawson, "National Pressure Groups and the Federal Government," in Pross, ed., *Pressure Group Behaviour in Canadian Politics,* pp. 30-35.

51. *Ibid.,* p. 31. In summary, Professor Dawson states: "Clearly Canadian federalism has had, and continues to have, a formidable impact upon the organization and behaviour of the pressure groups. It has complicated and confused their tasks while increasing their expenses and policy formulation problems" (p. 35).

52. The next few pages are heavily dependent on Smiley, *Canada in Question,* chapter 4, and Edwin R. Black, "Federal Strains within a Canadian Party," in Hugh G. Thorburn, ed., *Party Politics in Canada* (2nd ed.; Scarborough, 1967). Black summarizes his interpretation with the statement: "Both the structure and the internal operation of a major party resemble that of the Canadian system of government. The sovereignty of provincial party units is as real and extensive as that of the provinces with respect to Ottawa" (p. 139).

53. Carl. J. Friedrich, *Limited Government: A Comparison* (Englewood Cliffs, N.J., 1974), p. 55.

54. See Black, "Federal Strains within a Canadian Party," for an instructive case study of the impact of federalism on federal-provincial party relationships.

55. Smiley, *Canada in Question,* pp. 108-09.

56. *Ibid.,* p. 109-10.

57. *Ibid.,* p. 110.

58. See Reginald Whitaker, "The Liberal Party and the Canadian State: A Report on Research and a Speculation" (January, 1977), mimeo, esp. p. 37.

59. Kwavnick, "Interest Group Demands," p. 71. Twenty years ago Corry identified the development of national associations and mammoth nation-wide corporations "compelled to think in nation-wide . . . terms," as crucial to the centralization of power in Ottawa. "Constitutional Trends and Federalism," pp. 109, 111, 114.

60. Pross, "Pressure Groups: Adaptive Instruments of Political Communication," pp. 6-9.

61. See J.E. Hodgetts, "Regional Interests and Policy in a Federal Structure," *Canadian Journal of Economics and Political Science,* 32 (1966), pp. 13-14, on the creation of regions for policy purposes by governments and the attempts to generate regional demands from these artificially created administrative units.

62. See my "The Electoral System and the Party System in Canada, 1921-1965," *Canadian Journal of Political Science,* 1 (1968), pp. 55-80, for the contribution of the electoral system to the regionalization of the party system.

63. John Meisel, "Recent Changes in Canadian Parties," in Thorburn, ed., *Party Politics in Canada,* p. 34.

64. See William E. Connolly, *The Terms of Political Discourse* (Lexington, Mass., 1974), for a stimulating discussion of political language highly relevant for the following few pages.

65. Edwin R. Black, *Divided Loyalties: Canadian Concepts of Federalism* (Mon-

treal and London, 1975), p. 3.

66. This is particularly evident in Trudeau who, although committed to federalism, is basically an advocate of liberal individualism and a ferocious opponent of any move in the direction of basing political systems on nationalist criteria of ethnicity. Black, *Divided Loyalties,* pp. 209-10; Smiley, *Canada in Question,* p. 175.

67. The group or community claims of the provinces are for external consumption. Within their own political spheres, provincial politicians speak of the rights of individual British Columbians, Newfoundlanders, etc.

68. Cited in Donald V. Smiley, *The Canadian Political Nationality* (Toronto, 1967), p. 80.

69. See Black's discussion in *Divided Loyalties,* chapter 7, of the tortured and confused two-nations controversy of the late sixties.

70. Although resort to the past has lost relevance as a debating technique, the BNA Act remains as an uncertain arbiter of conflicting claims for policy-making authority. In circumstances of political competition, now as in the past, each government tends to attribute amplified meaning to its constitutional assignments of statutory authority and restrictive definitions to the explicitly worded lawmaking authority of the other level of government. See Smiley's fascinating discussion of Quebec-Ottawa differences in interpreting provincial jurisdiction over education (*Canada in Question,* pp. 30-34).

The contemporary federal strategy of linguistic manipulation, for which there are provincial counterparts, is described by Claude Morin as follows: "Confronting a Quebec government that was sensitive about its constitutional prerogative – more often the case with the Union Nationale – Ottawa made sure to avoid the impression of a frontal assault on provincial sectors. 'Training' was the word used rather than 'education,' 'problems of urban growth' replaced 'municipal affairs,' the 'fight against unemployment' replaced 'social development,' 'community development' was the new expression for 'culture.' Ottawa could speak freely on any subject providing the terms it used did not ring suspiciously of those areas which Quebec, atavistically or otherwise, had come to regard as being within its own jurisdiction" (*Quebec versus Ottawa,* pp. 78-79).

71. Richard Simeon, "The Federal-Provincial Decision Making Process," in Ontario Economic Council, *Intergovernmental Relations,* p. 26. See also John Meisel, "Cleavages, Parties, and Values in Canada," paper presented to the International Political Science Association, ixth World Congress, Montreal, 1973, pp. 3, 6-8 (mimeo), on the significant role of federal and provincial governments as the key protagonists for the expression of the three major political cleavages in Canada – ethnic, regional, and economic/regional.

72. J.E. Hodgetts, *The Canadian Public Service: A Physiology of Government 1867-1970* (Toronto, 1974), p. 42.

73. Norton E. Long, "Power and Administration," *Public Administration Review*, 9 (1949), p. 261.

74. Morin, *Quebec versus Ottawa,* p. 161.

75. Dion, *Québec: The Unfinished Revolution,* pp. 102-03.

76. Cited in W.A. Matheson, *The Prime Minister and the Cabinet* (Toronto, 1976), p. 150, italics in original. "No strong man in the emotionally satisfying sense has ever ruled this country – none will if it is to survive," stated Lester Pear-

son. "Attempting to reconcile what appears to be the irreconcilable will continue to be the task of Prime Ministers and in this task Prime Ministers tend to look uninspiring" (*ibid.,* p. 29).

77. Donald V. Smiley, "The Structural Problem of Canadian Federalism," *Canadian Public Administration,* 14 (1971), p. 332.

78. See Simeon, "The Federal-Provincial Decision Making Process," pp. 31-32, for a good brief discussion.

79. "Political scientists attempt to explain political phenomena. They view politics as a dependent variable, and they naturally look for the explanations of politics in other social processes and institutions. This tendency was reinforced by the Marxian and Freudian intellectual atmosphere of the 1930s and 1940s. Political scientists were themselves concerned with the social, psychological, and economic roots of political behaviour. Consequently, social change, personality change, and economic change were, in their view, more fundamental than political change. If one could understand and explain the former, one could easily account for the latter." Samuel P. Huntington,"The Change to Change," in Roy C. Macridis and Bernard E. Brown, eds., *Comparative Politics: Notes and Readings* (4th ed.; Georgetown, 1972), p. 408.

80. See A.P. d'Entrèves, *The Notion of the State* (Oxford, 1967), pp. 33-34, 62-63, on the weakness of the concept of the state in the English-speaking world and on the hostility of political scientists to its employment.

81. Jean Blondel, *Comparing Political Systems* (New York, 1972), p. 111.

The Other Crisis of Canadian Federalism

This paper was originally published as Inaugural Lecture No. 2, November, 1977, by the University of Edinburgh, Centre of Canadian Studies.

1. Canadian Tax Foundation, *The National Finances 1976-7* (Toronto, 1977), p. 16. Total government revenue, excluding transfers, was 39.3 per cent of gross national product in 1975. *Ibid.,* p. 20.

2. "Cleavages, Parties, and Values in Canada," paper presented to the International Political Science Association (Montreal, 1973), mimeo, pp. 3, 6.

3. Originally published in 1939, and reprinted in A.N. Christensen and E.M. Kirkpatrick, eds., *The People, Politics, and the Politician* (New York, 1941).

4. Quoted in L.R. Pratt, "The State and Province-Building: Alberta's Development Strategy, 1971-1976," Occasional Paper 5, Department of Political Science, University of Alberta, mimeo, p. 26.

5. *Ibid.,* p. 23.

6. *Ibid.,* pp. 21-22.

7. Donald V. Smiley, "The Federal Dimension of Canadian Economic Nationalism" (June, 1973), mimeo, p. 18. The transformation of the role of government in Quebec is also manifest in the international arena, evidenced by a proliferation of Quebec bureaus abroad and by a highly developed participation in various international organizations, especially those that pertain to the Francophone communities of Africa. See Louis Sabourin, "Quebec's International Competence," *International Perspectives* (March/April, 1977). See also Claude Morin, *Quebec versus Ottawa* (Toronto, 1976), chapters 6 and 7.

8. Cited in Donald V. Smiley, *The Canadian Political Nationality* (Toronto, 1967), pp. 62-63.

9. Harry Eckstein, "Planning: the National Health Service," in Richard Rose, ed., *Policy-Making in Britain* (London, 1969), p. 233.

10. Roger Opie, "The Making of Economic Policy," in Hugh Thomas, ed., *Crisis in the Civil Service* (London, 1968), p. 72.

11. Eckstein, "National Health Service," p. 233.

12. J.K. Galbraith, *The Affluent Society* (London, 1958), esp. chapter 18.

13. F.A. Hayek, *Law, Legislation and Liberty*, Vol. 2, *The Mirage of Social Justice* (London, 1976), p. 68.

14. Harry G. Johnson, "The Relevance of *The Wealth of Nations* to Contemporary Economic Policy," *Scottish Journal of Political Economy*, XXIII (June, 1976), p. 171.

15. Cited in F.A. Hayek, *The Constitution of Liberty* (London,1960), pp. 445-46n.

16. See Richard Simeon, "The 'Overload Thesis' and Canadian Government," *Canadian Public Policy*, 2 (1976), p. 546; and John Meisel, "Citizen Demands and Government Response," *Canadian Public Policy*, 2 (1976), p. 568.

17. In the words of a former federal cabinet minister, Paul Hellyer, "We all know, needless to say, the universal law of bureaucracy: the civil servants multiply arithmetically, while the rules multiply geometrically, but the results do not multiply at all." Cited in David M. Cameron, "Urban Policy," in G.B. Doern and V. Seymour Wilson, eds., *Issues in Canadian Public Policy* (Toronto, 1974), p. 246.

18. Richard Simeon, "Current Constitutional Issues," pp. 19-20, and Richard Simeon, "The Federal-Provincial Decision Making Process," pp. 28, 35, both in Ontario Economic Council, *Intergovernmental Relations* (Toronto, 1977).

19. Edwin R. Black, *Divided Loyalties: Canadian Concepts of Federalism* (Montreal and London, 1975), p. 227.

20. "I am deeply concerned that, on the evidence of the two-year examination carried out by the Audit Office, Parliament – and indeed the Government – has lost or is close to losing effective control of the public purse." *Conspectus of the Report of the Auditor General of Canada to the House of Commons* (Ottawa, 1976), p. 3.

21. In the succinct words of Adam Smith, referring to an earlier era: "It is the system of government, the situation in which they are placed, that I mean to censure; not the character of those who have acted in it. They acted as their situation naturally directed, and they who have clamoured the loudest against them would, probably, have not acted better themselves." Cited in Alan Peacock, "The Credibility of Liberal Economics," Seventh Wincott Memorial Lecture, Institute of Economic Affairs (London, 1977), p. 13n.

22. See W.R. Lederman, "Some Forms and Limitations of Co-operative Federalism," *Canadian Bar Review*, 45 (1967), p. 410, on the continuing significance of the legal distribution of powers for the intergovernmental bargaining power of the federal and provincial governments.

23. A.V. Dicey, *Introduction to the Study of the Law of the Constitution*, 10th ed. (London, 1968), pp. 175-80.

24. See Morin, *Quebec versus Ottawa*, pp. 78-79, and Donald V. Smiley, *Canada in Question*, 2nd ed. (Toronto, 1976), pp. 30-33, for Ottawa's efforts to find a language of justification for a strong federal role in education.

25. Cited in Donald V. Smiley, "Rationalism or Reason: Alternative Approaches

to Constitutional Review in Canada," paper presented to the Priorities for Canada Conference of the Progressive Conservative Party of Canada (October, 1969), mimeo, p. 7.

26. Cameron, "Urban Policy," p. 233. In a classic case of special pleading the task force asserted that "it is illogical, if not inconceivable, that the Government of Canada could have ministers dealing with fisheries, forestry, veteran affairs, and other matters which involve a minority of the population, but none to deal on a full-time basis with the urban problems which involve more than 70 per cent of the population, not to mention housing which involves virtually everyone." *Ibid.*, p. 233.

27. Anthony G.S. Careless, *Initiative and Response: The Adaptation of Canadian Federalism to Regional Economic Development* (Montreal and London, 1977), p. 128.

28. *Ibid.*, p. 169.

29. *Ibid.*, p. 212.

30. *Ibid.*, pp. 216-17.

31. J.R. Mallory, *Social Credit and the Federal Power in Canada* (Toronto, 1954), pp. 53-56, and chapter 3.

32. See Morin, *Quebec versus Ottawa*, chapter 5; Robert S. Best, "Youth Policy," in Doern and Wilson, *Issues in Canadian Public Policy*, p. 143; Careless, *Initiative and Response*, pp. 3, 6; and Richard Simeon, "Regionalism and Canadian Political Institutions," in J. Peter Meekison, ed. *Canadian Federalism: Myth or Reality*, 3rd ed. (Toronto, 1977), p. 303.

33. Careless, *Initiative and Response*, p. 177.

34. For the contrary assertion that federalism, or devolution, increases incentives for citizens to participate in the political process and by the resultant greater understanding of government produces a "recognition of its limitations," see Peacock, "Credibility of Liberal Economics," p. 27. See also p. 13.

35. Donald V. Smiley, "Federal-Provincial Conflict in Canada," in Meekison, *Canadian Federalism*, p. 16.

36. Peter Aucoin, "Federal Health Care Policy," pp. 62-63, and G.R. Weller, "Health Care and Medicare Policy in Ontario," pp. 98-99, 96, 108, both in Doern and Wilson, *Issues in Canadian Public Policy*.

37. M.W. Bucovetsky, "The Mining Industry and the Great Tax Reform Debate," in Paul Pross, ed., *Pressure Group Behaviour in Canadian Politics* (Toronto, 1975), pp. 98, 100-01.

38. Richard Schultz, "Interest Groups and Intergovernmental Negotiations: Caught in the Vise of Federalism," in Meekison, *Canadian Federalism*.

39. J.S. Dupré *et. al.*, *Federalism and Policy Development: The Case of Adult Occupational Training in Ontario* (Toronto, 1973), p. 109.

40. See *ibid.*, and Careless, *Initiative and Response*, for relevant case studies.

41. The Rt. Hon. Patrick Gordon Walker notes the tremendous resistance of ministers in the same cabinet to policy co-ordination, because of its tremendous drain on the time and energy of men with departmental responsibilities. "Beyond a certain point – the more you plan, the less you do.

"Ministers conceive a deep distaste for embarking upon projects that will entail more and longer meetings with their colleagues. This means that even Socialist Ministers are selective about the sectors of the national life that they can attempt to plan." "On Being a Cabinet Minister," in Rose, ed., *Policy-Making in Britain*, pp. 123-24. The resistance is obviously greater when, as in Canada, policy co-ordination requires the agreement of politicians in another government, perhaps thousands of miles away.

42. "For an Independent Quebec," in Meekison, *Canadian Federalism*, p. 491.

43. "The Governments and Societies of Canadian Federalism," *Canadian Journal of Political Science*, 10 (December, 1977), p. 724.

44. In the words of Claude Morin when he was Quebec's Deputy Minister of Federal-Provincial Affairs: "Formerly Quebec went to Ottawa, waving some arti-cle of the Constitution, and said, 'This article forbids you to do what you are about to carry out.' To which Ottawa retorted, 'You are quite right, but would you mind if, for the time being, we went ahead anyway?' And Quebec submitted . . . Now that's all over. Quebec's motto is: We're through fooling around! It seems ridiculous to me to invoke the Constitution. It is like invoking St. Thomas." Cited in Smiley, *The Canadian Political Nationality*, p. 80. See also Alan C. Cairns, "The Living Canadian Constitution," in Meekison, *Canadian Federalism*.

45. W.A. Mackintosh, *The Economic Background of Dominion-Provincial Rela-tions*, ed. J.H. Dales (Toronto, 1964), "Introduction," p. 2.

Constitutional and Political Change

1. For a brilliant exploration of this theme, see Sheldon S. Wolin, "Max Weber: Legitimation, Method, and the Politics of Theory," in William E. Connolly, ed., *Legitimacy and the State* (New York, 1984), pp. 63-87.

2. Alan C. Cairns, "Political Science in Canada: Some Observations and Reflec-tions," *Transactions of the Royal Society of Canada*, Fourth Series, xviii (1980), p. 270.

3. Alan C. Cairns, "The Canadian Constitutional Experiment," *Dalhousie Law Journal*, 9, 1 (November, 1984), p. 88.

4. *Ibid.*, p. 103.

5. *Ibid.*, p. 114.

6. In Keith Banting and Richard Simeon, eds., *And No One Cheered* (Toronto, 1983), p. 31.

7. *Ibid.*, p. 28.

8. *Ibid.*, p. 55.

Politics of Constitutional Conservatism

1. Several paragraphs and phrases in this article are taken from an earlier article by the author in "The Magazine" section of the *Vancouver Province*, April 18, 1982.

2. See Alan Cairns, "Constitution-Making, Government Self-Interest, and the Problem of Legitimacy in Canada," in Allan Kornberg and Harold Clarke, eds., *Political Support in Canada: The Crisis Years* (Durham, N.C., 1983).

3. G. Bruce Doern, "Spending Priorities: The Liberal View," in G. Bruce Doern, ed., *How Ottawa Spends Your Tax Dollars: Federal Priorities 1981* (Toronto, 1981), pp. 1, 9.

4. Canada, Task Force on Canadian Unity, *A Future Together: Observations and Recommendations* (Ottawa, 1979), p. 48.

5. Section 91(1) gave the federal Parliament exclusive legislative authority over

"the amendment from time to time of the Constitution of Canada, except as regards matters coming within the classes of subjects by this Act assigned exclusively to the Legislatures of the provinces, or as regards rights or privileges by this or any other Constitutional Act granted or secured to the Legislature or the Government of a province . . ." and other matters not germane to this particular federal-provincial controversy.

6. The federal position was explained by Marc Lalonde, Minister of State for federal-provincial relations, when he placed the bill in the context of "the decision that will have to be taken by the people of Quebec in the course of the coming months as to whether they want Quebec to continue to be a part of Canada or not." He continued: "Some of the changes would be of concern to the provincial governments, especially those relating to the House of the Federation and the Supreme Court. Obviously, agreement on them, as well as on other provisions, would be desirable. However, to be realistic, it is most unlikely that agreement is going to be given to these or to any proposals by all provincial governments. Premier Lévesque and his government have never concealed their objective. It is not to improve the Constitution of Canada so that Quebec can be more comfortable within it; it is not to make Canada a more effective union or a place where French Canadians will be more content; it is to get Quebec out of Confederation. They are not likely to agree on constitutional changes for which a major objective is to keep Quebec a part of Canada. So what are we to do? Are we to be paralysed? Are we to say that federal jurisdiction under Section 91(1) cannot be exercised if *any* province disagrees – even if it is a matter clearly within federal jurisdiction? The federal government is not prepared to accept such a proposition. . . . Parliament must be able to act, in the national interest, in areas where it legally can – with agreement of the provinces if at all possible, but without being the helpless prisoner of a province if agreement is impossible. To fail to act, in the face of a national crisis, could be irresponsible." *Statement by the Honourable Marc Lalonde . . . to the Joint Parliamentary Committee on the Constitution*, August 15, 1978, pp. 1, 4.

7. Except, of course, for a possible unilateral secession by Quebec after some acceptable democratic process of consultation with the Quebec people.

8. Michael Valpy described the meeting at which the Accord was released "as one of the funny curiosities of Canadian history – like the Canadian Army's 1920s battle plan to attack America." From "A Somewhat Mediocre Bunch," *Vancouver Sun*, April 20, 1981, p. A4.

9. *Globe and Mail*, May 7, 1981. See Ronald J. Zukowsky, *Struggle over the Constitution* (Kingston, 1981), p. 110, for the main differences between the Accord and the earlier proposal discussed at the September, 1980, First Ministers' Conference, which in turn was based on the Alberta amending formula.

10. Ian Mulgrew, "Moratorium on patriation urged before top court ruling," *Globe and Mail*, August 15, 1981. See also the report of Robert Sheppard who, after stating that some provinces had tried to toughen up the opting-out provision, continued: "Provincial sources say that Premier René Lévesque, bullish from a smashing electoral win in Quebec earlier in the week, insisted on redrafting many of the provisions that had been agreed to informally by provincial representatives in Winnipeg a few weeks ago." *Globe and Mail*, April 17, 1981.

11. See Edward McWhinney, *Canada and the Constitution, 1979-1982*

(Toronto, 1982), pp. 101, 119, for an acerbic critique of the Gang of Eight.

12. See Zukowsky, *Struggle*, pp. 71-86, for a good discussion of the committee.

13. For the details, see Sheilagh M. Dunn, *The Year in Review 1981: Intergovernmental Relations in Canada* (Kingston, 1982), pp. 27-28, 31-32.

14. *Minutes of Proceedings and Evidence of the Special Joint Committee of the Senate and of the House of Commons on the Constitution of Canada*, No. 52, February 3, 1981, p. 91.

15. On the other hand, although the court lacked a veto, it was not, apparently, entirely without influence and persuasive powers. During the September, 1980, First Ministers' Conference, a columnist for *The Toronto Star* asserted that any enlargement of the court was unlikely. "Part of the reason for this is the quiet but efficient lobbying of the present members of the court, who feel that expansion is neither necessary nor desirable." Andrew Szende, "Conference Notebook," *Toronto Star*, September 12, 1980. That same month, while the Trudeau government was pondering its course of action, Chief Justice Laskin gave two interviews with the *Financial Post*, which constituted a defence of the existing court. *Financial Post*, September 20, 1980, and September 27, 1980. See also *Financial Post*, March 21, 1981, p. 9, for an editorial, "Don't fiddle with the Supreme Court," commenting on a vigorous defence of the Supreme Court by the Chief Justice before the Empire Club in Toronto.

16. Although an unsuccessful attempt was made at the last minute by Conservative senators to retain an absolute Senate veto. In November, 1980, a subcommittee of the Standing Senate Committee on Legal and Constitutional Affairs issued a *Report on Certain Aspects of the Canadian Constitution* (Ottawa, 1980) which, among other proposals, recommended the replacement of the Senate's absolute veto by a six-months suspensive veto. Correspondence from Senator Maurice Lamontagne and former Senator Eugene Forsey makes it clear that the suspensive veto was intended to apply to the Senate's role in constitutional amendments.

17. Edward McWhinney has suggested that several weaknesses in the Constitution Act were due to oversight, haste, and confusion, partly reflecting the perils of the "telex diplomacy" of the period between the November, 1981, First Ministers' Conference and the final debate in Parliament. McWhinney, *Canada and the Constitution*, pp. 106, 109.

18. See, however, the prescient comment of the Kirby memorandum, "Report to Cabinet on Constitutional Discussions, Summer 1980, and the Outlook for the First Ministers' Conference and Beyond," August 30, 1980, p. 51, that the court "might very well . . . make a pronouncement, not necessary for the decision, that the patriation process was in violation of established conventions and therefore in one sense was 'unconstitutional' even though legally valid."

19. McWhinney, *Canada and the Constitution*, p. 118.

20. There was some business input into the Special Joint Committee, but negligible participation from labour interests. Zukowsky, *Struggle*, pp. 73-76.

21. Subsequently published as Jean Chrétien, *Securing the Canadian Economic Union in the Constitution* (Ottawa, 1980).

22. Dunn, *Year in Review*, pp. 214-15. See also *Vancouver Sun*, November 29, 1980, p. A6, for an analysis of the discrepancy between the positions of Lyon and the Manitoba public on the Charter.

23. *Vancouver Sun*, September 16, 1980, p. B14.
24. See *Vancouver Sun*, October 28, 1980, p. A9, for Barrett's opposition to the bulk of the Social Credit government's constitutional position.
25. See the Kirby memorandum, "Report to Cabinet on Constitutional Discussions," for an excellent example of political intelligence.
26. *Globe and Mail*, January 8, 1982, p. 8.
27. Zukowsky, *Struggle*, p. 37.
28. See *ibid*., pp. 53-55, for a discussion. Premier Blakeney's assessment was that "the basic problem . . . was an inability on the part of Mr. Trudeau and Mr. Lévesque to agree on some things. That was an aftermath of the referendum that had not yet disappeared. Mr. Lévesque, as it developed, had not yet reached the conclusion that his best interests and those of the PQ lay with getting a settlement." Joan Sutton, *Toronto Star*, September 25, 1980, p. A10.
29. John Gray, *Globe and Mail*, September, 29, 1981, p. D4.
30. Dunn, *Year in Review*, p. 23.
31. "Constitution: Quick reaction from regions," *Financial Post*, October 3, 1981, p. 7.
32. McWhinney, *Canada and the Constitution*, p. 102.

Canadian Constitutional Experiment

This was the third in the 1983 Dorothy J. Killam Lecture Series, "Law on the Eve of 1984," presented at Dalhousie Law School on November 24, 1983. The author warmly thanks Cynthia and Doug Williams for their many helpful suggestions to improve the successive versions of this lecture.

1. Donald Smiley, "The Structural Problem of Canadian Federalism," *Canadian Public Administration* 14 (Fall, 1971).
2. *Vancouver Sun*, March 7, 1981.
3. Albert O. Hirschman, *Shifting Involvements: Private Interest and Public Action* (Princeton, N.J., 1982).
4. In the final round of hectic bargaining the federal government threw out the tantalizing possibility that a national referendum might be employed to break the intergovernmental deadlock. Also, the federal amending formula in the unilaterism package contained a referendum option. Further, if intergovernmental agreement was not possible on an amending formula, and if several conditions were met, the electorate would be given the choice by referendum to determine whether a federal government formula, or a competing formula supported by seven provinces with 80 per cent of the population, should govern future amendments.

Selected Bibliography

Books

Prelude to Imperialism: British Reactions to Central African Society, 1840-1890. London: Routledge and Kegan Paul, Ltd., 1965.

Alan C. Cairns, S.H. Jamieson, and K. Lysyk. *A Survey of the Contemporary Indians of Canada: Economic, Political and Educational Needs and Policies*, ed. H.B. Hawthorn. A Report submitted to the Department of Indian Affairs and Northern Development. Ottawa: Queen's Printer, 1966, Vol. 1.

—— and Philip G. Wigley, eds. *Radical Political Thought in Canada and the United Kingdom Compared and Contrasted: Seminar Papers No. 4, 1977-78.* Edinburgh: University of Edinburgh, Centre of Canadian Studies, 1978.

—— and Cynthia Williams, eds. *Constitutionalism, Citizenship and Society*, Vol. 33, prepared for the Royal Commission on the Economic Union and Development Prospects for Canada. Toronto: University of Toronto Press, 1986.

—— and Cynthia Williams, eds. *The Politics of Gender, Ethnicity and Language in Canada*, Vol. 34, prepared for the Royal Commission on the Economic Union and Development Prospects for Canada. Toronto: University of Toronto Press, 1986.

Articles

Alan C. Cairns and Edwin R. Black. "A Different Perspective on Canadian Federalism," *Canadian Public Administration*, IX, 1 (March, 1966), 27-44.

"The Electoral System and the Party System in Canada, 1921-1965," *Canadian Journal of Political Science*, I, 1 (March, 1968), 55-80.

"The Living Canadian Constitution," *Queen's Quarterly*, LXXVII, 4 (Winter, 1970), 1-16.

"A Reply to J.A.A. Lovink, 'On Analysing the Impact of the Electoral System on the Party System in Canada,' " *Canadian Journal of Political Science*, III, 4 (December, 1970), 517-21.

"The Judicial Committee and Its Critics," *Canadian Journal of Political Science*, IV, 3 (September, 1971), 301-45.

"The Study of the Provinces: A Review Article," *B.C. Studies*, No. 14 (Summer, 1972), 73-82.

"Comment," *B.C. Studies*, No. 16 (Winter 1972-73), 81-82.

"Alternative Styles in the Study of Canadian Politics," *Canadian Journal of Political Science*, VII, 1 (March, 1974), 102-28.

"National Influences on the Study of Politics," *Queen's Quarterly*, LXXXI, 3 (Autumn, 1974), 333-47.

"Political Science in Canada and the Americanization Issue," *Canadian Journal of Political Science*, VII, 2 (June, 1975), 192-234.

"The Governments and Societies of Canadian Federalism," *Canadian Journal of Political Science*, X, 4 (December, 1977), 695-725.

"The Other Crisis of Canadian Federalism," Inaugural Address, Centre of Canadian Studies, Edinburgh, November, 1977, 1-24; reprinted in *Canadian Public Administration*, 22, 2 (Summer, 1979), 175-95.

"Recent Federalist Constitutional Proposals: A Review Essay," *Canadian Public Policy* (Summer, 1979), 348-65.

"From Interstate to Intrastate Federalism in Canada?" *Bulletin of Canadian Studies*, II, 2, 13-34; reprinted as Institute Discussion Paper No. 5, Institute of Intergovernmental Relations, Queen's University, 1979.

"The Electoral System, the Party System and the Canadian Constitutional Crisis," *Etudes Canadiennes* (numero Special 1979), 85-97.

"The Constitutional, Legal, and Historical Background," in Howard Penniman, ed., *Canada at the Polls, 1979 and 1980: A Study of the General Elections* (Washington, D.C.: American Enterprise Institute, 1981), 1-23.

"Political Science in Canada," in A.G. McKay, ed., *Transactions of the Royal Society of Canada*, 4th Series, Vol. 18 (1980), 262-71.

"Research on the Institutions of Canadian Federalism," in *Proceedings of the Workshop on 'The Challenge of Research on the Canadian Communities'* (Ottawa: Social Sciences and Humanities Research Council of Canada, 1980), 77-91.

"Commentaries: An Overview of the Trudeau Constitutional Proposals," *Alberta Law Review*, XIX, 3 (1981), 401-07.

"Constitution-Making, Government Self-Interest and the Problem of Legitimacy in Canada," in Allan Kornberg and Harold Clarke, eds., *Political Support in Canada: The Crisis Years* (Durham, N.C.: Duke University Press, 1983), 380-448.

"The Politics of Constitutional Conservatism," in Keith Banting and Richard Simeon, eds., *And No One Cheered: Federalism, Democracy and the Constitution Act* (Toronto: Methuen, 1983), 28-58.

"The Canadian Constitutional Experiment," *Dalhousie Law Journal*, 9, 1 (November, 1984), 87-114.

"The Politics of Constitutional Renewal in Canada," in Keith Banting and Richard Simeon, eds., *Redesigning the State: The Politics of Constitutional Change in Industrial Nations* (Toronto: University of Toronto Press, 1985), 95-145.

—— and Dan Wong. "Socialism, Federalism and the B.C. Party Systems 1933-1983," in Hugh Thorburn, ed., *Party Politics in Canada*, 5th Edition (Scarborough: Prentice-Hall, 1985), 283-302.

"The University and Society: Historical and Sociological Reflections," in William A. Neilson and Chad Gaffield, eds., *Universities in Crisis: A Medieval Institution in the 21st Century* (Montreal: Institute of Research on Public Policy, 1986), 251-68.

"The Embedded State: State-Society Relations in Canada," in Keith Banting, ed., *State and Society: Canada in Comparative Perspective*, Vol. 31, prepared for the Royal Commission on the Economic Union and Development Prospects for Canada (Toronto: University of Toronto Press, 1986), 53-86.

"Comment on Fred Vaughan, 'Critics of the Judicial Committee: The New Orthodoxy and an Alternative Explanation,'" *Canadian Journal of Political Science*, XIX, 3 (September, 1986), 521-29.

—— and Douglas E. Williams, "Writings in Political Science," in William New, ed., *The Literary History of Canada*, 3rd Edition (Toronto: University of Toronto Press, 1988).